100 YEARS
of AVIATION

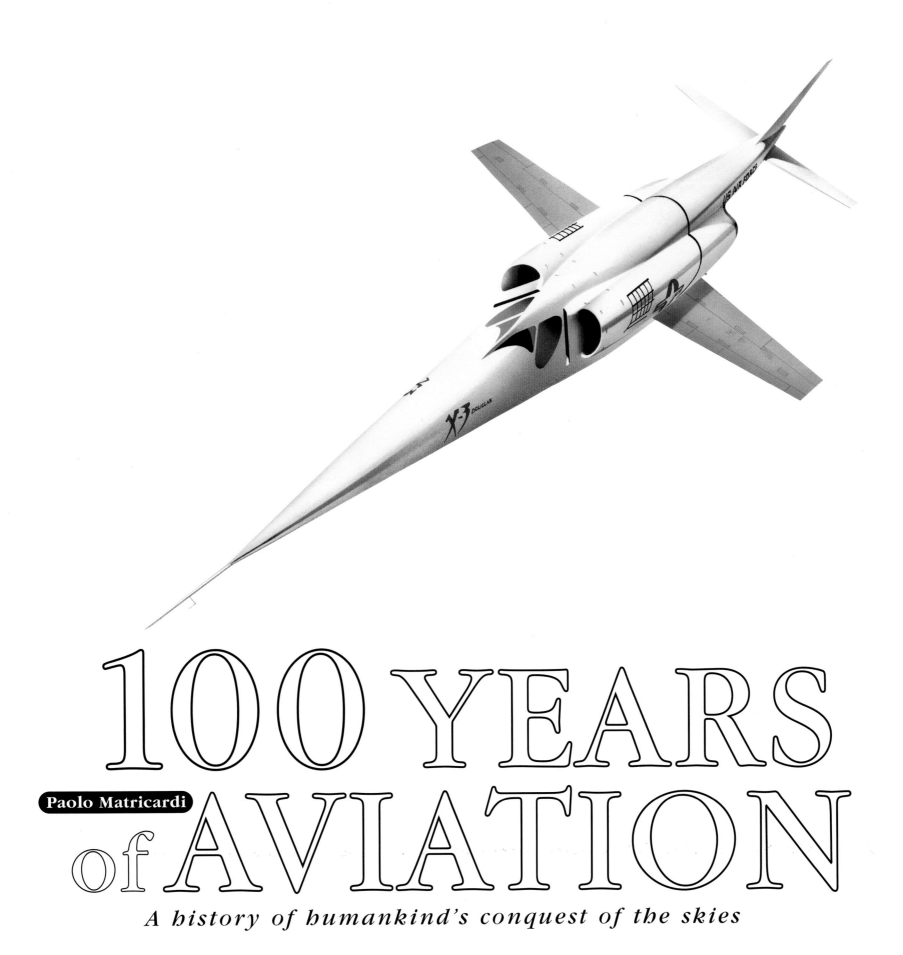

100 YEARS of AVIATION

Paolo Matricardi

A history of humankind's conquest of the skies

BARNES & NOBLE BOOKS

NEW YORK

Art Director: Giorgio Seppi

Text coordination: Tatjana Pauli

Editing and layout: Ervin srl, Roma

Photographs: Archivio Mondadori, Ervin, Benvenuti, NASA

Illustrations: Vincenzo Cosentino, Amedeo Gigli, Nicola Arolse, Marco Giardina, Studio Kromos

Translation: Jeff Jennings

Typesetting: Michael Shaw

This edition published by Barnes & Noble, Inc. by arrangement with Mondadori

2004 Barnes & Noble Books

M 10 9 8 7 6 5 4 3 2 1

ISBN 0-7607-6103-5

Printed and bound in Spain by Artes Gráficas Toledo, SA

CONTENTS

INTRODUCTION

One hundred years. The first century in the life of the airplane. A century marked by epic adventures, amazing progress, and compelling heroes – both men and machines. As time goes on and air travel becomes an ever more integral vehicle of global communication, we all feel in some way part of that history. Yet despite the almost incredible advances in technology and safety in recent decades, powered flight still seems to us unbelievable somehow, unnatural even – and perhaps for this reason, utterly thrilling. Whether reclining comfortably on a passenger jet taking us from one side of the world to the other, or simply stopping to contemplate the genealogy that links a rickety old biplane to a supersonic fighter jet, we will always remain in awe of the fact that these machines actually fly.

But reliving the exploits of the pioneers of "heavier-than-air" craft, or re-

constructing the great military campaigns that featured airplanes as protagonists are not merely idle ways of savoring that awe. By stepping back and ex-
amining the history of the 20th century through the lens of aviation, we see
the profound degree to which it has conditioned every aspect of our age, as
well as the possibilities it poses for our future.

It all began just 100 years ago on the foggy morning of December 17,
1903, in a field on the American east coast, when a fragile handbuilt flying
machine left the ground for a few seconds, thereby finally making humankind's
age-old dream of flight a reality, and transporting its creators, Orville and
Wilbur Wright, directly to the pantheon of history's great contributors.

Taking that unforgettable day as its departure point, this book recounts
the first century of powered flight in a chronology highlighted by the airplanes
that have left such deep and lasting signs, both good and bad, on our era.

The dream of flight

A dream as ancient as humankind, a dream made real on a foggy morning just one brief century ago. It is indeed hard to believe that the modern aircraft that fight our battles, deliver our mail, and ferry us around the globe are all direct descendents of that first fragile machine, offspring of a continual, inexorable evolution. The one hundred years of aviation history are inseparable from the history of the 20th century. Airplanes have marked our progress, conditioned the outcomes of our wars, led us to new scientific discoveries, and taken us into space. And just as they have shaped our past, they will also help define our future.

THE PATH SKYWARD

Above, the balloon in which Pilâtre de Rozier and D'Arlandes made the first manned ascent in history, November 21, 1783

Left,
Aerial Steam Carriage,
William Samuel Henson,
1842

Monoplane, Victor Tatin, 1879

It would be oversimplifying to think of that morning of December 17, 1903, when Orville and Wilbur Wright launched their 'Flyer I' as the departure point for the definitive conquest of the skies. For it was also an arrival point, the culmination of many centuries of designs and dreams, of bold attempts and noble failures. After the first, legendary investigations of Leonardo da Vinci (1452-1519) into the scientific principles of flight, the next real step was taken by the discoverers of the aerostat, or 'lighter-than-air' craft. On November 21, 1783, François Pilâtre de Rozier and François d'Arlandes climbed into wicker balcony attached to a balloon filled with heated air, untied the mooring ropes, and flew for five and a half miles over Paris in history's first manned flight. The true *inventors* of the 'lighter-than-air' craft, the Montgolfier brothers, had successfully demonstrated the hot-air balloon six months earlier at Versailles, but had opted to avoid the risk of flying themselves, sending up a terrified sheep, goose, and rooster in their stead. However, despite the enthusiasm generated by the aerostat, now the height of fashion, it wasn't until the next century that the many unresolved problems of mechanical flight were addressed again in a scientific way. An essential contribution was made by the Englishman, George Cayley, who has the distinction of having discovered the basic principles of flight

– that is, the relation between weight, lift, drag, and thrust, illustrated in his treatise *On Aerial Navigation* of 1809-10. His research had an enormous impact. Improvisation was no longer necessary, now that there was a scientific basis, a fixed equation that codified the relation between the four fundamental forces that governed a flying machine. But, while the problems of lift, weight and drag could be resolved relatively simply, the fourth force, thrust, remained an obstacle. At the time, the only available form of mechanical propulsion was the steam engine, but its size and weight were obviously not suited to flight. William Samuel Henson, among others, tried anyway: in 1842 he made drawings for an 'Aerial Steam Carriage' which, while being the first propeller-driven fixed-wing aircraft ever designed, was never built. The Frenchmen Alphonse Pénaud and Victor Tatin did much to further our understanding of aerodynamics. Another Frenchman, Felix Du Temple, put a tractor propeller on a monoplane in 1874, and in 1881 the Russian Alexander Mozhaiski attempted a similar enterprise. On the one hand, these experiments demonstrate that mechanical flight would be impossible without a valid form of propulsion, while on the other they stimulated the research into aerodynamics that would eventually result in an

efficient and maneuverable wing. Pioneers in this field were the German Otto Lilienthal – the first man to fly in a glider –, the Australian Lawrence Hargrave, the Scotsman Percy Sinclair Pilcher, and the French-born American, Octave Chanute. This latter's work on oscillating glider wings led to the moveable wing flap, which is what makes it possible to regulate direction and altitude. Two other important landmark events took place prior to the Wright brothers' success. In France, Clément Ader built two steam-powered aircraft, the Éole and the Avion III, the first of which rose approximately four inches from the ground on October 9, 1890. In America, Samuel Pierpont Langley tried to launch his 'Aerodrome' from a bridge over the Potomac in October 1903. Though unsuccessful, the 'Aerodrome' secured a place in history as the first flying machine with a combustion engine.

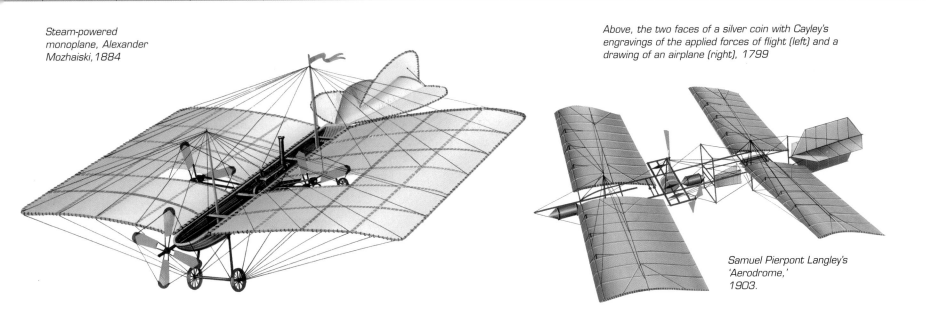

Steam-powered monoplane, Alexander Mozhaiski, 1884

Above, the two faces of a silver coin with Cayley's engravings of the applied forces of flight (left) and a drawing of an airplane (right), 1799

Samuel Pierpont Langley's 'Aerodrome,' 1903.

Wilbur Wright takes off from a tall pylon at Auvours, September 21, 1908

Opposite page, the 'June Bug,' designed by Glenn Hammond Curtiss

1903

INFANCY

THE FLIGHT AT KITTY HAWK, DEPARTURE POINT

FOR THE FUTURE OF THE AIRPLANE, BUT ALSO

THE CULMINATION OF CENTURIES OF DESIGNS AND

DREAMS, BOLD ATTEMPTS AND NOBLE FAILURES.

1911

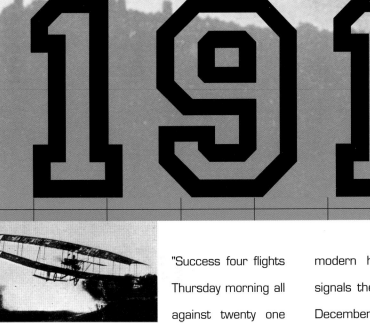

"Success four flights Thursday morning all against twenty one mile wind started from level with engine power alone average speed through air thirty one miles longest 57 seconds inform Press home Christmas."

A handful of words, a concise telegram. This is the first official testimony of an event destined to mark a major turning point in modern history, for this laconic message signals the birth of the airplane. The date is December 17, 1903; the place, Kitty Hawk, North Carolina; the addressee, Milton Wright, the sender's father. Odd phrasing and inaccuracy aside (the longest flight in fact lasted 59 seconds), the implications that these simple words would have are immeasurable.

Let us remember that day in the detail it deserves, a hundred years later, by reading the formal announcement made by Orville and Wilbur Wright to the Associated Press on January 5, 1904.

"On the morning of December 17th, between the hours of 10:30 o'clock and noon, four flights were made, two by Orville Wright and two by Wilbur Wright. The starts were all made from a point on the level sand about 200 feet west of our camp, which is located a quarter of a mile north of the Kill Devil sand hill, in

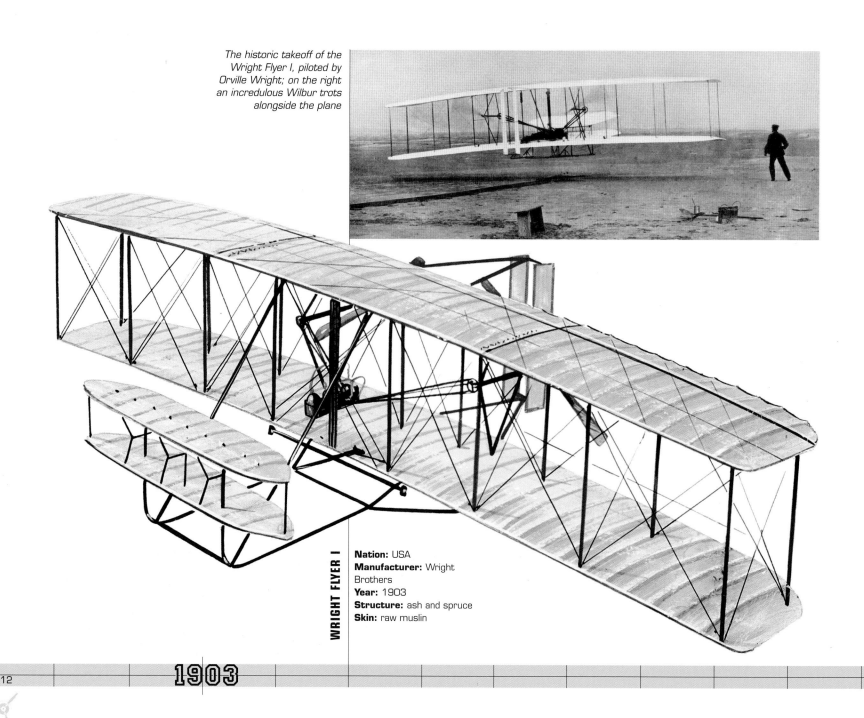

The historic takeoff of the Wright Flyer I, piloted by Orville Wright; on the right an incredulous Wilbur trots alongside the plane

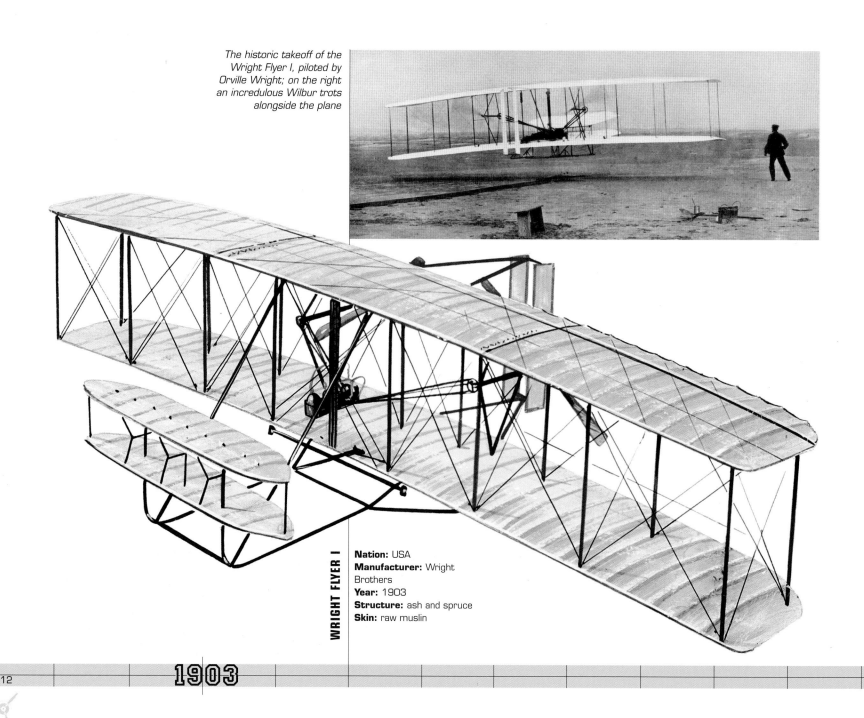

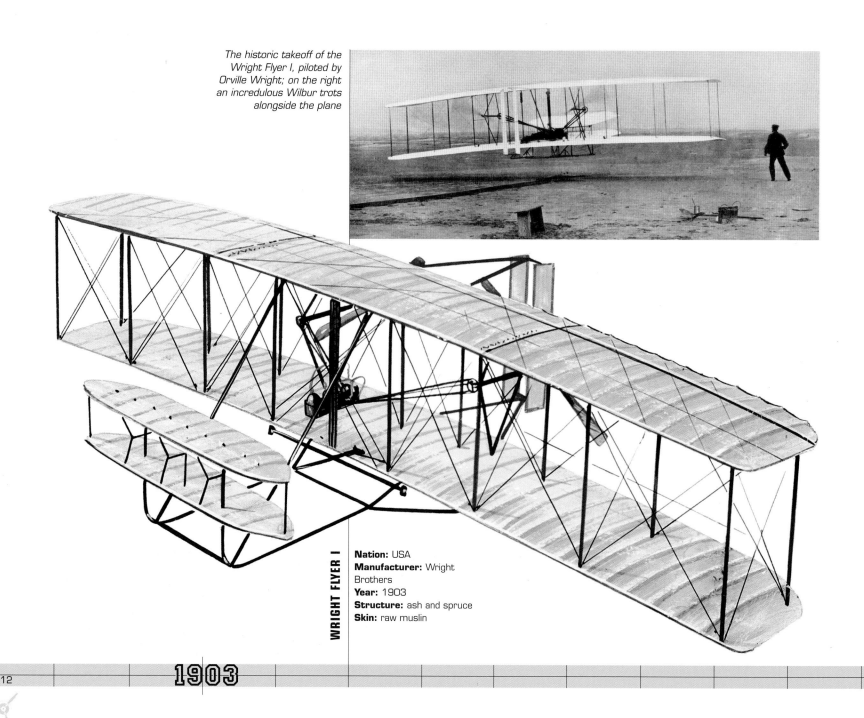

WRIGHT FLYER I

Nation: USA
Manufacturer: Wright Brothers
Year: 1903
Structure: ash and spruce
Skin: raw muslin

1903

1903-1911

Dare County, North Carolina. The wind at the time of the flights had a velocity of 2 miles an hour at ten o'clock, and 24 miles an hour at noon, as recorded by the anemometer [...] thirty feet from the ground. Ground measurements, made with a hand anemometer at a height of four feet from the ground, showed a velocity of about 22 miles when the first flight was made, and 20 1/2 miles at the time of the last one. The flights were directly against the wind. Each time the machine started from the level ground by its own power alone with no assistance from gravity, or any other source whatever. After a run of about 40 feet along a monorail track, which held the machine eight inches from the ground, it rose from the track and under the direction of the operator, climbed upward on

The Wright brothers, partners in the first human flight in a 'heavier-than-air', engine-powered machine.

Nation: France
Manufacturer: Alberto Santos-Dumont
Year: 1906
Structure: bamboo and pine
Skin: cotton

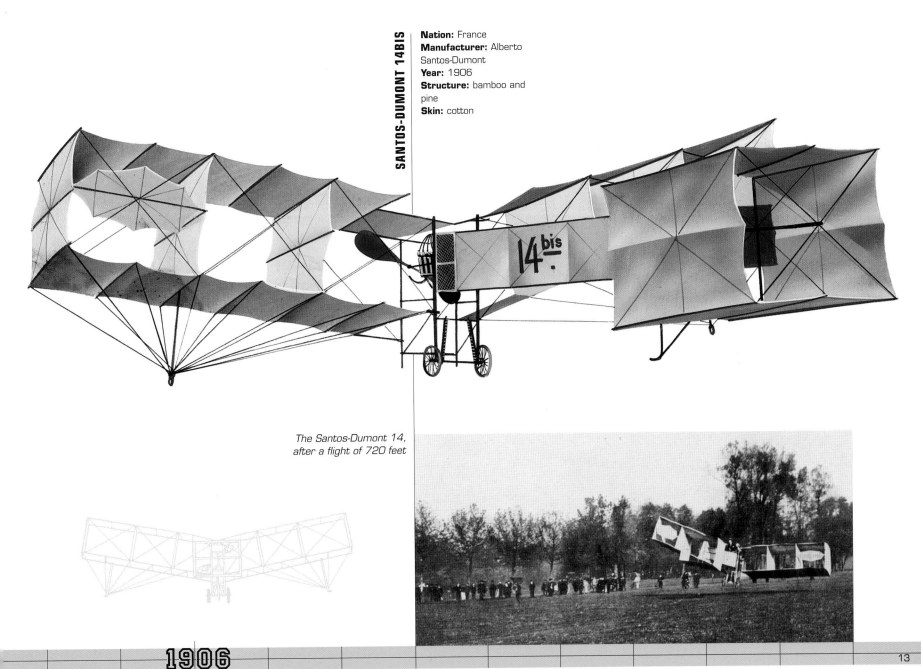

The Santos-Dumont 14, after a flight of 720 feet

1906

an inclined course until eight or ten feet from the ground was reached, after the course was kept as near horizontal as the wind gusts and the limited skill of the operator would permit. Into the teeth of a December gale the 'Flyer' made its way forward with a speed of ten miles an hour over the ground and 30-35 miles an hour air. It had previously been decided that for reasons of personal safety these first trials would be made as close to

the ground as possible. The height chosen was scarcely sufficient for maneuvering in so gusty a wind and with no previous acquaintance with the conduct of the machine and its controlling mechanisms. Consequently the first flight was short. The succeeding flights rapidly increased in length and at the fourth trial a flight of fifty-nine seconds was made, in which time the machine flew a little more than a half a mile through the air, and a distance of

852 feet over the ground."

The deadpan flatness of this account is complemented by a rather more emotive one, which perfectly captures the atmosphere and the tension of that morning. It is a photograph, taken at 10:35 by one John T. Daniels, staff member at the US Coast Guard's Kill Devil Lifesaving Station, who witnessed the event along with four others. Against a backdrop of winter fog, the image

VOISIN FARMAN BIPLANE

Nation: France
Manufacturer: Voisin Frères
Year: 1907
Structure: ash and steel tubing
Skin: cotton

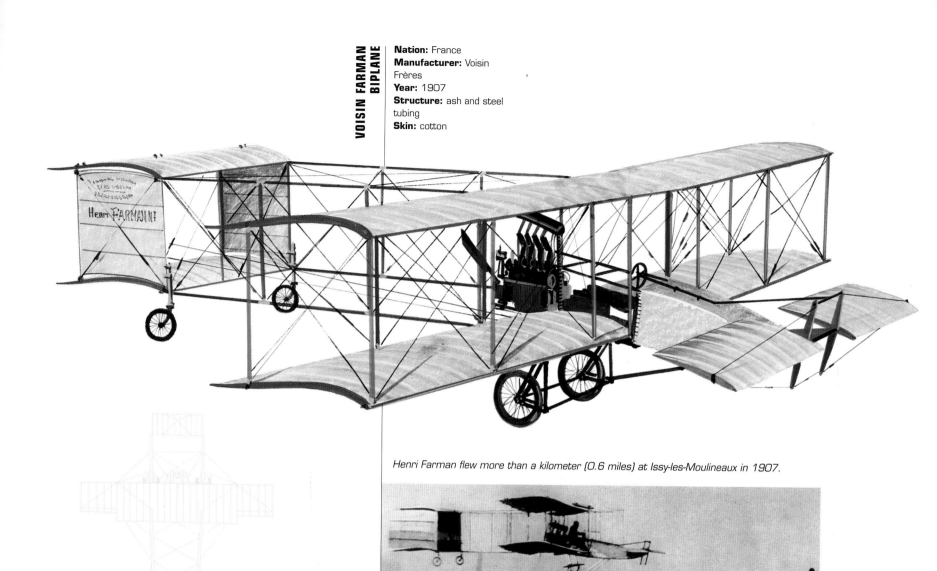

Henri Farman flew more than a kilometer (0.6 miles) at Issy-les-Moulineaux in 1907.

1907

unites the two great protagonists of that day, man and machine: the Flyer I at the moment it leaves the end of a long wooden monorail, propellers churning, listing slightly to the left; Orville Wright, lying face-down between the wings; Wilbur Wright, who leans toward the plane like a proud yet nervous father teaching his child to ride a bicycle. In Orville's words: "The first flight lasted only twelve seconds, a flight very modest compared with that of birds,

but it was, nevertheless, the first in the history of the world in which a machine carrying a man had raised itself by its own power into the air in free flight, had sailed forward on a level course without reduction of speed, and had finally landed without being wrecked." But neither the photo nor the press release refer to the moment of panic just after the fourth flight which put an abrupt end to the enthusiasm: a violent gust of wind overturned the

Flyer as it rested on the sand, snapping several structural elements, damaging the engine and drive train, and injuring Daniels. "Any hope of making other flights that year vanished," was Orville's desolate comment.

AMERICA

Orville and Wilbur Wright were intensely involved in the 'aeronautical fever' of the closing years of the 19th century, and were great-

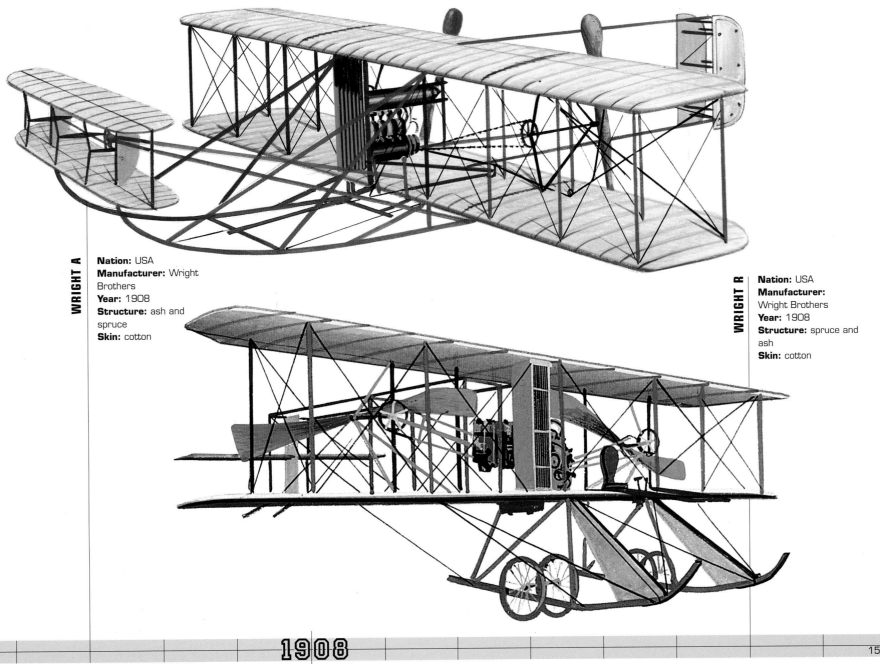

WRIGHT A

Nation: USA
Manufacturer: Wright Brothers
Year: 1908
Structure: ash and spruce
Skin: cotton

WRIGHT R

Nation: USA
Manufacturer: Wright Brothers
Year: 1908
Structure: spruce and ash
Skin: cotton

1908

ly influenced by their contemporaries, particularly Otto Lilienthal and Octave Chanute. After completing construction of the first glider at their Dayton, Ohio bicycle factory in 1899, they moved to North Carolina, having determined that the wind conditions at Kitty Hawk were ideal for their purposes. To give an idea of the rigor and tenacity of their research, consider the fact that in 1901 the Wright brothers designed and built the world's first wind tunnel for testing the intensity and direction of the forces acting upon the wing. The following year, with three successful gliders to their credit, Orville and Wilbur decided they were ready to try building a mechanically-propelled flying machine. The configuration of the Flyer I was simple: a biplane with a wooden structure covered in cotton, anterior vertical stabilizers, a 12-horsepower gasoline engine that drove two giant counter-rotating propellers by a chain-and-sprocket transmission, and a hip cradle that allowed the movement of the pilot's body to control the wings and rudder. The industry of the time wasn't able to satisfy the brothers' needs with regard to the motor, but they didn't lose heart: in just six weeks, with the help of mechanic Charles Taylor, they built their own.

The success of December 17, incredibly enough, was not immediately recognized. The skepticism that had followed the failure of

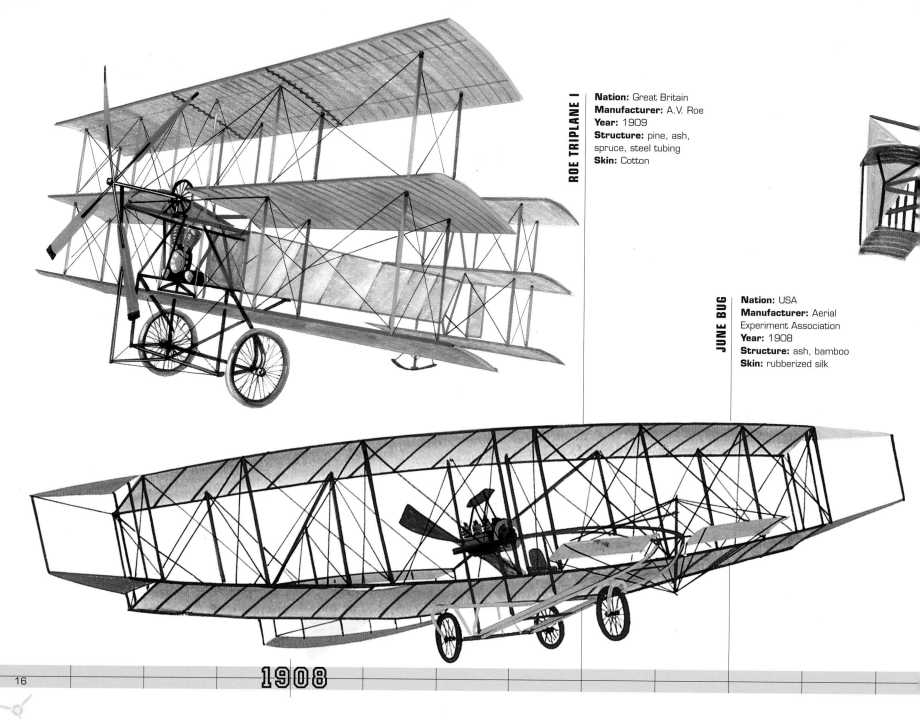

Nation: Great Britain
Manufacturer: A.V. Roe
Year: 1909
Structure: pine, ash, spruce, steel tubing
Skin: Cotton

Nation: USA
Manufacturer: Aerial Experiment Association
Year: 1908
Structure: ash, bamboo
Skin: rubberized silk

1908

Langley's 'Aerodrome' had grown, and grew worse when, in May of 1904, the Wrights invited the press to Hoffman Prairie to witness the new and improved Flyer II. When the engine contracted a case of stage fright and refused to perform, negative comments, rather than the plane, flew that day. The brothers wisely withdrew from the official spotlight and continued their research in silence, to excellent result: on October 16, 1905, the Flyer III stayed aloft for 39 minutes, circling a field 30 times for a total distance of nearly 25 miles. The world's first practical airplane had been built and flown, yet official myopia continued to reign. The Department of Defense refused the Wrights' offer to supply their plane, and the brothers had to wait another three years before their next chance to make the world understood the importance of their achievement.

EUROPE

This momentary blindness allowed the Europeans, particularly the French, to make up for lost time. In 1901 Ferdinand Ferber picked up where Lilienthal had left off and three years later demonstrated a stable and maneuverable glider. Ferber's work drew the impassioned attention of many, among whom the future protagonists of French aviation: Louis Blériot, Gabriel Voisin, Robert Esnault-Pelterie

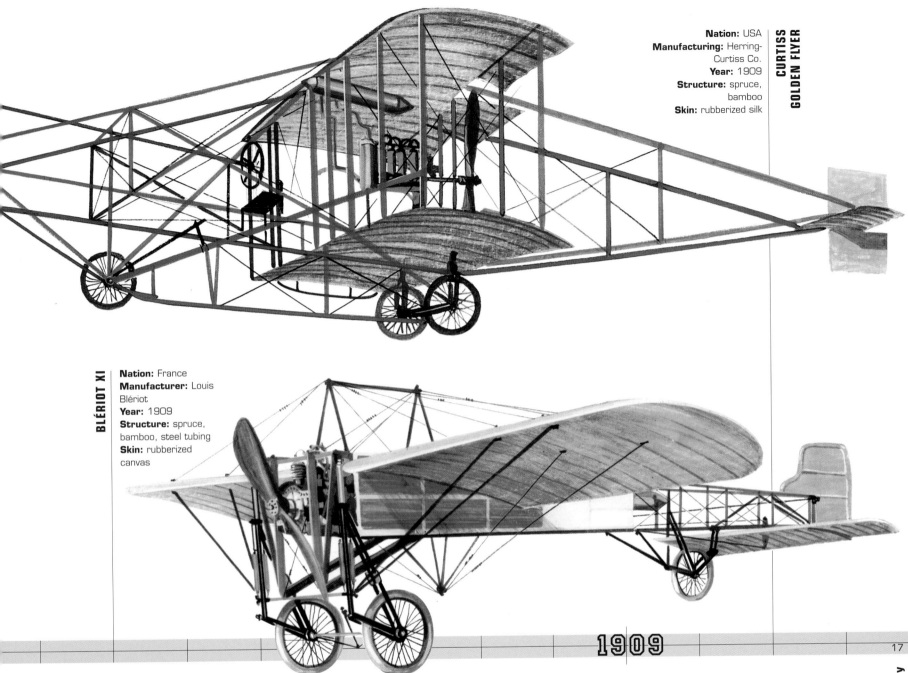

Nation: USA
Manufacturing: Herring-
Curtiss Co.
Year: 1909
Structure: spruce,
bamboo
Skin: rubberized silk

BLÉRIOT XI

Nation: France
Manufacturer: Louis
Blériot
Year: 1909
Structure: spruce,
bamboo, steel tubing
Skin: rubberized
canvas

1909

17

Infancy

and the American Ernest Archdeacon. The latter, founder of the Aéro-Club, created an incentive by sponsoring a series of prizes, including a trophy for the pilot of the first French airplane to fly for at least 25 meters, and 1,500 francs for the first to break 100 meters. The prizes were highly sought after, but two years had to pass before the first one was awarded. The winner was the Brazilian Alberto Santos-Dumont, who moved to Paris in

1898 and had been impressing his aeronautical colleagues with his dirigible flights. On September 13, 1906, his first airplane – the '14 bis' – covered 7 meters at Bagatelle before an enthusiastic crowd. On October 23 he managed 60 meters, and on November 12 he earned his 1,500-franc prize by flying 200 meters, remaining aloft for 21 seconds. Though a humble achievement compared to that of the Wright brothers three years

earlier, Santos-Dumont can be credited for having galvanized public opinion and stimulated his fellow aviators to redouble their efforts. In fact, a species of 'flying fever' spread through Europe like an epidemic, and on November 9, 1907, Henri Farman conquered a major threshold, remaining in flight for more than one minute.

In Germany the era of the airplane was inaugurated in June of 1908 by the Danish Ja-

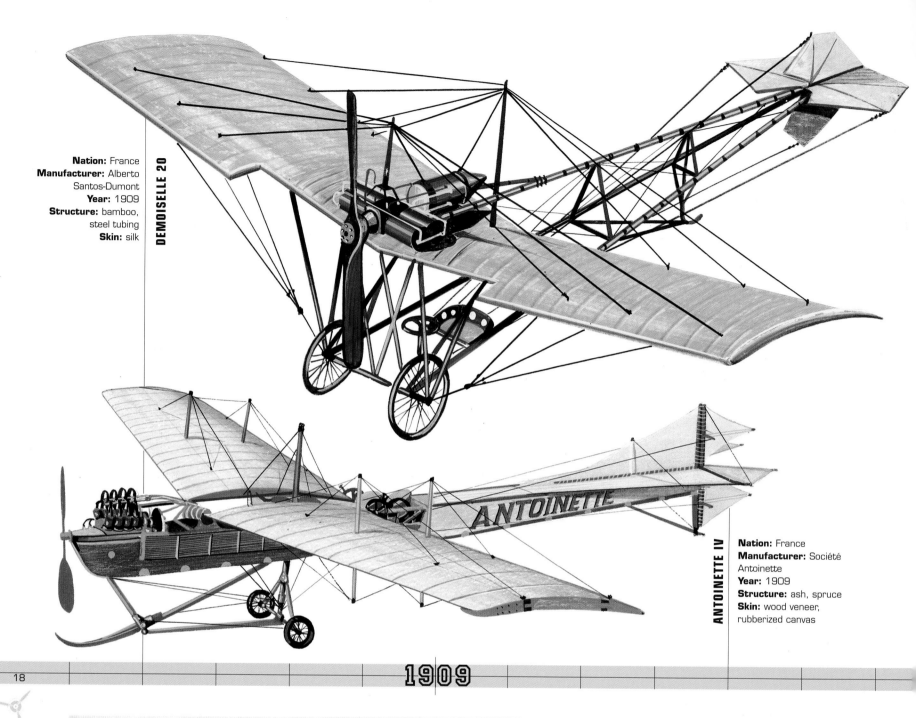

Nation: France
Manufacturer: Alberto Santos-Dumont
Year: 1909
Structure: bamboo, steel tubing
Skin: silk

DEMOISELLE 20

ANTOINETTE IV

Nation: France
Manufacturer: Société Antoinette
Year: 1909
Structure: ash, spruce
Skin: wood veneer, rubberized canvas

1909

1909-1911

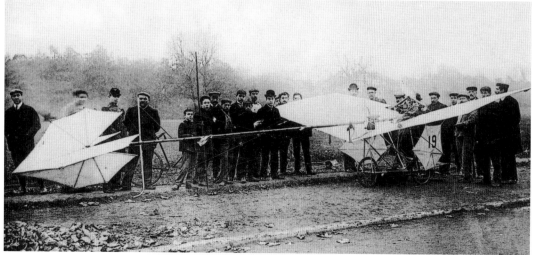

cob Christian Hansen Hellehammer and his namesake, the Hellehammer IV. In Great Britain the landmark date was July 23, 1909, when Alliot Verdon Roe successfully flew his Triplane. But the key moment for international aviation was in 1908, when American and European aeronautical culture came together for the first time. Orville and Wilbur Wright, hav-

The first Demoiselle, built by Alberto Santos-Dumont in 1907.

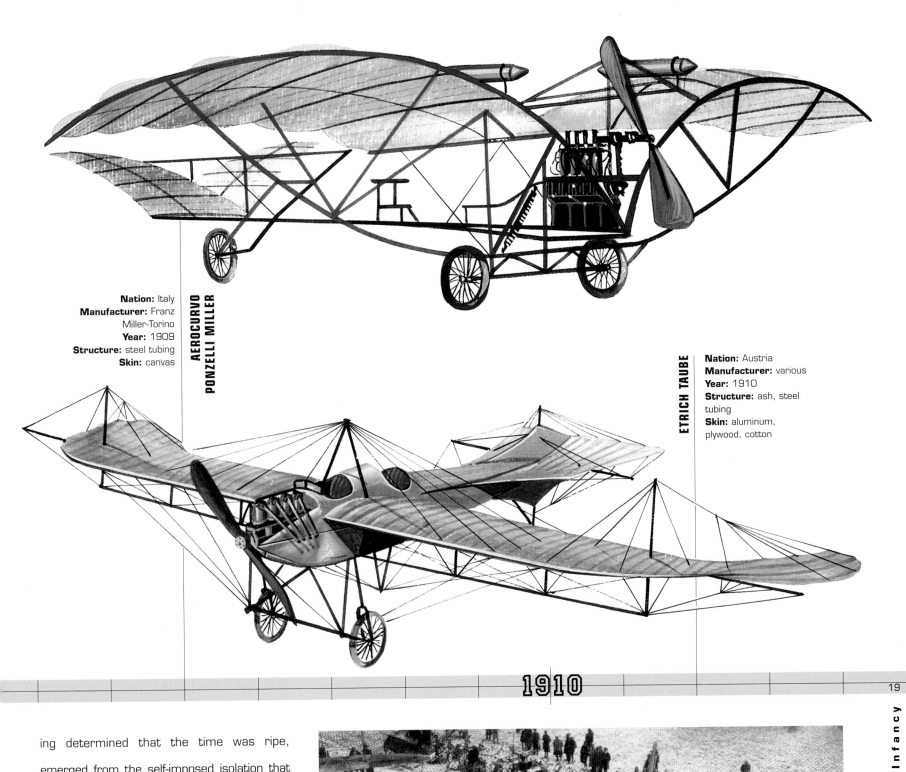

Nation: Italy
Manufacturer: Franz Miller-Torino
Year: 1909
Structure: steel tubing
Skin: canvas

AEROCURVO PONZELLI MILLER

Nation: Austria
Manufacturer: various
Year: 1910
Structure: ash, steel tubing
Skin: aluminum, plywood, cotton

ETRICH TAUBE

ing determined that the time was ripe, emerged from the self-imposed isolation that had shielded them from public scrutiny since 1904. Orville set out on the daunting task of winning over the American government and military authorities, while Wilbur relocated to Europe with their latest creation, the Wright A. From August to December, Wilbur captivated

A captured Etrich Taube is displayed along with other war trophies to the Parisian public.

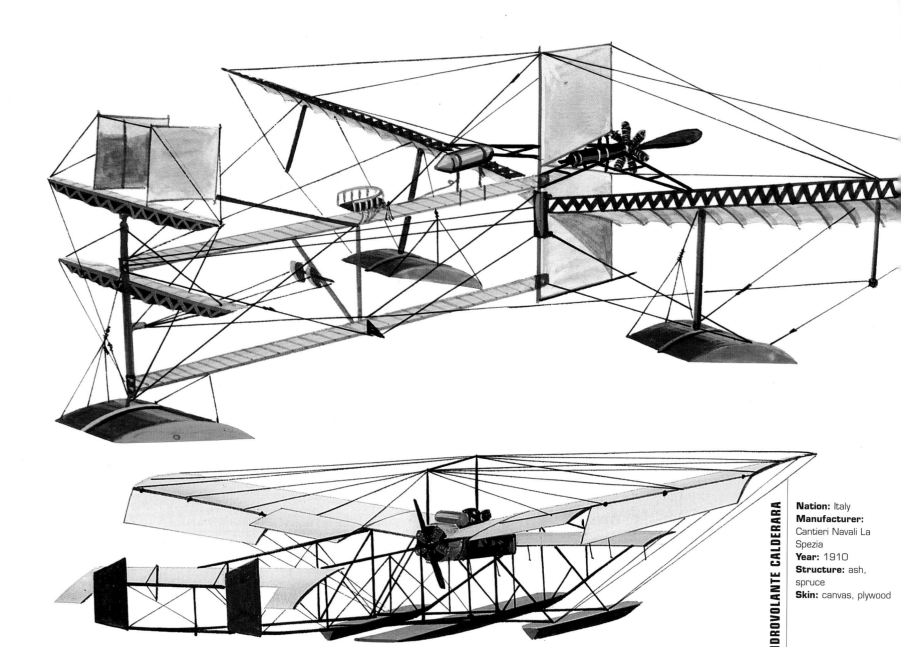

Nation: Italy
Manufacturer: Cantieri Navali La Spezia
Year: 1910
Structure: ash, spruce
Skin: canvas, plywood

IDROVOLANTE CALDERARA

20

1903-1911

European aviation enthusiasts with his flying exhibitions at Le Mans. The resulting exchange of ideas and experiences further accelerated the evolution of the 'heavier-than-air' * craft. In France, flight records were broken by Henri Farman, Léon Delagrange and Louis Blériot, while in Britain the banner of progress was carried by Samuel F. Cody and Alliot Verdon Roe. Back in the States, the Aerial Experiment Association, a group of

THE BIRTH OF THE HYDROPLANE

The French engineer Henri Fabre has the distinction of having significantly expanded the boundaries of what an airplane can do. On March 28, 1910, at the port of La Mède in Marseilles, an airplane took off not from land but from water, flew, and came to rest without incident on its plywood pontoons. The Hydravion and Fabre himself were an unlikely pair of heroes: an awkward and fragile monoplane, and a pilot who had never flown before. Nevertheless, on that fateful morning Henri Fabre overcame the odds and took his place in aviation history.

The Austrian Wilhelm Kress had been experimenting with hydroplanes since the beginning of the century, and in 1905-06 Voisin, Blériot and Archdeacon all made attempts. But it was Fabre's success that led the American Glenn Curtiss to adapt his Golden Flyer for water take-off with the installation of a large central pontoon and two lateral stabilizers in the place of the customary wheels. On January 26, 1911, Curtiss made his first successful hydroplane flight over San Diego Harbor. On February 17, he caught the attention of the US Navy by landing on the deck of the battleship *Pennsylvania*, at anchor off the California coast. The Navy promptly commissioned him to design and build what would become the Curtiss Hydro A.1, and with that, naval aviation was born. Meanwhile, Europe was by no means out of the running. Italy, which had entered the field a bit late, quickly recognized the great military potential of the hydroplane. The shipyard at the port city of La Spezia had already been building a plane of this type, designed by Mario Calderara, since 1910. Other projects followed, the most noteworthy being the Crocco and Ricaldoni hydroplane of 1912.

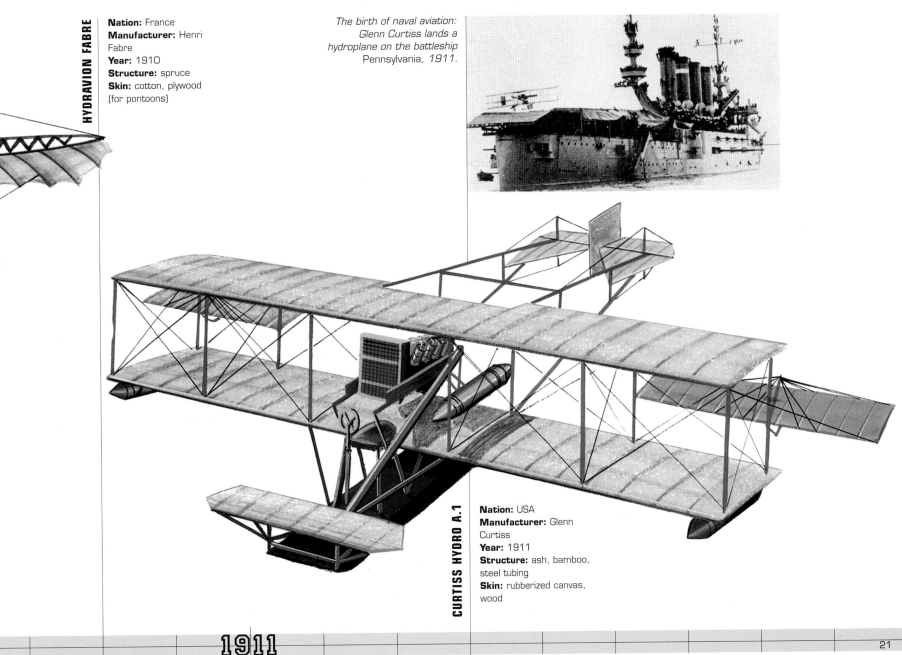

Nation: France
Manufacturer: Henri Fabre
Year: 1910
Structure: spruce
Skin: cotton, plywood (for pontoons)

The birth of naval aviation: Glenn Curtiss lands a hydroplane on the battleship Pennsylvania, 1911.

Nation: USA
Manufacturer: Glenn Curtiss
Year: 1911
Structure: ash, bamboo, steel tubing
Skin: rubberized canvas, wood

1911

Canadians and Americans founded in 1907 by Alexander Graham Bell, contributed to the cause with Glenn Curtiss's June Bug and John McCurdy's Silver Dart.

The airplane was now ready to demonstrate its enormous potential to the world. Two events, both in 1909, signaled the first confident steps of the infant science of aviation: the crossing of the English Channel by Louis Blériot in his Type XI monoplane on July 25,

and the Reims Air Meet of August 22-29. This latter was the first of the sporting competitions that for the next two decades would provide a powerful impetus to the evolution of aeronautical technology.

Of the major European nations, Italy remained somewhat behind. In July of 1908, Voisin and Archdeacon flew their French-built planes for an astonished audience in Turin, but it wasn't until January 13 of the following

year that the first Italian aircraft, a triplane built by Aristide Faccioli, flew for 30 or so feet. Other early efforts include the Aerocurvo Ponzelli-Miller, a plane built to participate at the 1909 International Air Show in Brescia but which failed to take off (it flew a year later at Turin after several modifications, but even then without great success). The Asteria company and Gianni Caproni also made important early contributions.

1914-1918

1914

WAR IN THE SKIES

A NEW ROLE FOR THE AIRPLANE

FROM THE FIRST ITALIAN MISSIONS OVER LIBYA

TO THE BATTLE FOR AIR SUPREMACY

DURING WORLD WAR ONE

1918

"We are presently well aware of the importance of commanding the sea. Very soon, command of the air will prove no less important." With the echoes of the seminal Reims Air Meet of 1909 still ringing in Europe's ears, an Italian officer, Major Giulio Douhet, was the first to intuit the vast military potential of the airplane and the strategic role it would play in future conflicts. Though it wasn't until 1921 that Douhet committed these prophetic words to print in a treatise entitled, not surprisingly, *Command of the Air*, their practical applications did not wait so long. The first occasion was the war in Libya, during which Italian planes conducted the first wartime air operations in history: on October 23, 1911 Captain Carlo Piazza flew a reconnaissance mission in a Blériot XI monoplane; on November 1 Lieutenant Giulio Gavotti released four small bombs from an Etrich Taube monoplane over Ain Zara and Tadjoura, the world's first bombing raid. The explosions caused more panic than damage, and were negligible compared to the deluges of fire and death that would terrorize Europe in the coming years. But it was enough to secure a new role for the airplane, suddenly no longer an intriguing gadget for winning altitude and distance prizes, but a

Nation: France
Manufacturer: Société Anonyme des Aéroplanes Morane-Saulnier
Type: fighter
Year: 1914
Crew: 1 person

Roland Garros invented a 'deflection plate' which allowed fighter pilots to fire machine guns through the propeller without damaging it.

1913

1914-1918

THE ROTARY ENGINE

The invention of the rotary engine changed the world of aviation forever. The brothers Louis and Laurent Seguin had begun working on such an device in France in 1908, applying a principle introduced in 1887 by the Australian Lawrence Hargrave. By 1909 their Parisian factory, the Société des Moteurs Gnome, was producing the first of what would become a long series of ever more powerful engines that dominated airplane manufacture throughout World War I. The main architectural innovation of the rotary engine lay in the mobility of the cylinders: only the crankshaft was bolted down, while the crankcase and radially-arranged cylinders rotated freely around it, thereby driving the propeller. The result was an air-cooled propulsion unit, compact and light, with a particularly favorable weight-to-power ratio ideal for machines that had to be, above all else, lightweight and fast. Moreover, its elevated torque and consequent gyroscopic effect gave the airplane exceptional agility. The rotary engine inevitably became the preferred means of propulsion for fighter planes and, given the times, demand from all over Europe was soon soaring. The Germans, despite having developed several excellent inline engines over the years, turned to the rotary, the most famous of which was the Oberursel, more or less an exact copy of a French engine made by Le Rhône, a company that merged with Gnome in 1919. Over the course of their development, these engines grew in power from 50 to nearly 200 horsepower by war's end. The most widely used configuration had nine cylinders.

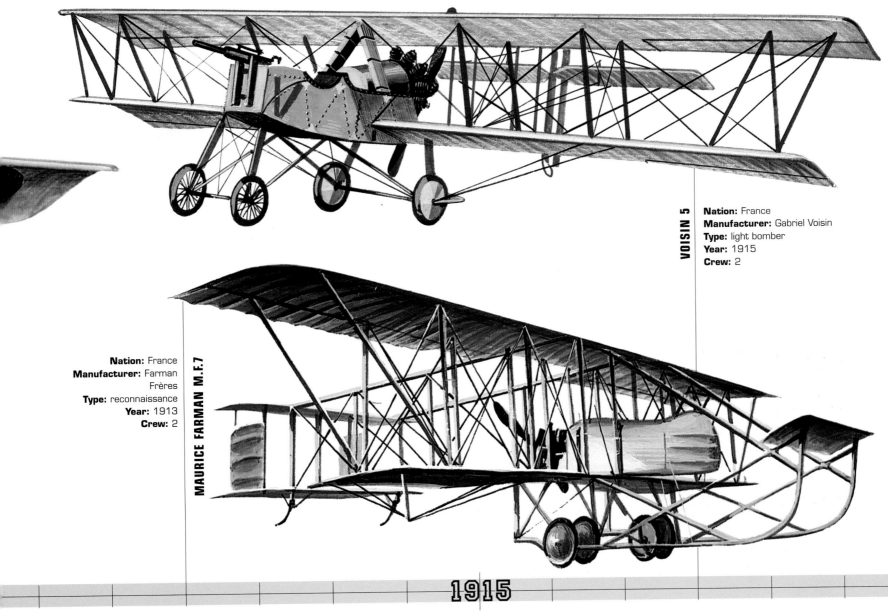

VOISIN 5

Nation: France
Manufacturer: Gabriel Voisin
Type: light bomber
Year: 1915
Crew: 2

Nation: France
Manufacturer: Farman Frères
Type: reconnaissance
Year: 1913
Crew: 2

MAURICE FARMAN M.F.7

1915

War in the skies

lethal weapon capable of revolutionizing military tactics and recasting the role of traditional armies. With the advent of World War I, the optimistic enthusiasm of aviation's first decade was cancelled, replaced by a new and brutal scenario in which the airplane played both hero and villain.

THE BIRTH OF MILITARY AVIATION

The effects of this shift in the role of the airplane were felt by all the nations involved in the long and bloody conflict of World War I. In the United States, Glenn Curtiss conducted the first experiments using the airplane as a means of bombardment (June 1, 1910), paving the way for Italy's bombing raids in Libya. In 1911 Curtiss perfected the difficult art of taking off and landing on the deck of a ship. France was the first European country to constitute an air force: since 1910 the armed forces had been commissioning warplanes and had trained some 60 pilots; in 1911, the French began arming its reconnaissance planes. Italy's first Air Battalion was formed in Turin on July 1, 1912, supported by a technical crew whose task it was to develop and test new aviation technologies. Among the first projects was the construction in that same year of 10 dirigibles, 150 airplanes, and the concomitant training of the pilots who would

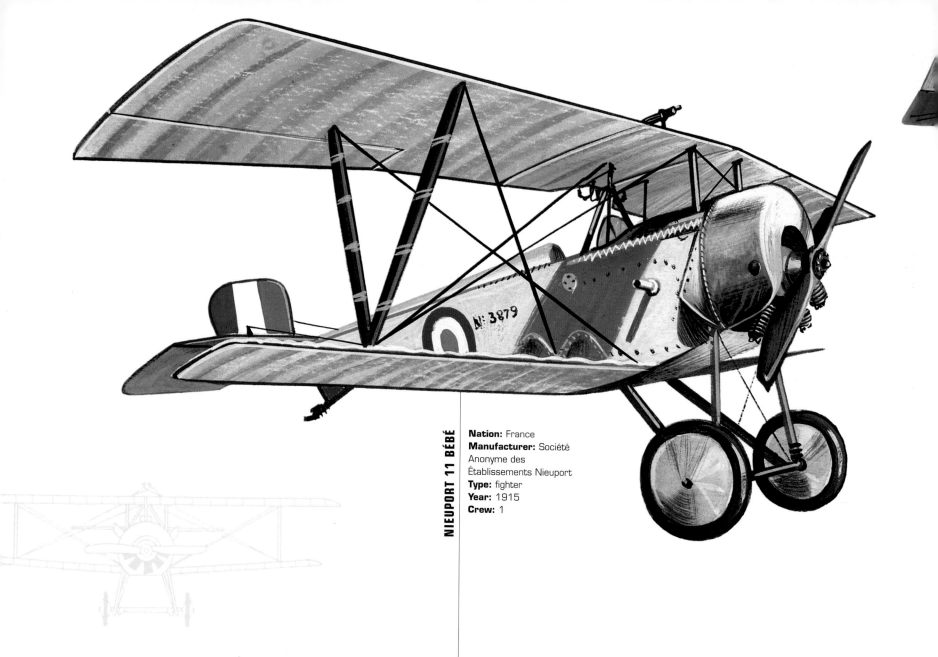

Nation: France
Manufacturer: Société Anonyme des Établissements Nieuport
Type: fighter
Year: 1915
Crew: 1

Nº 3879

1915

fly them. The entire team was commanded by Vittorio Cordero di Montezemolo, with Giulio Douhet as his vice-commander. In Great Britain, the Army founded its Royal Flying Corps on April 13, 1912, and soon thereafter the Navy constituted the Royal Naval Air Service. Germany introduced an air division into its army, while additional planes were enlisted by

The French pilot Guynemer checks the engine of his Nieuport 11 Bébé.

Nation: Russia
Manufacturer : R.B.V.Z.
Type: bomber
Year: 1915
Crew: 4-7

Nation: Germany
Manufaturer: Fokker
Flugzeug-Werke GmbH
Type: fighter
Year: 1915
Crew: 1

CAMOUFLAGE AND INSIGNIA

With the outbreak of WWI, it became evident that the airplane had to be rendered less visible, both on land and in the sky. Up to this point, no one had really given much thought to an airplane's appearance, but now every nation had to face the problem of camouflage, oftentimes coming up with quite original solutions. The colors tended toward dark greens and browns for the top surfaces, light beiges and blues for the bottom. It was also necessary to be able to distinguish friend from foe, so each nation developed its own system of identification codes and insignia. The Allies used three concentric circles, their colors varying from country to country, while the Germans chose a white square framing a black cross, symbol of the Teutonic Knights. An important discovery was the optical effect created by stripes of two or more colors, which served to 'dissolve' the plane's silhouette, a camouflage technique favored mostly by the French and the Germans. This evolved into even more sophisticated patterns of interlocking polygons of four or more different colors which were effective on both the top and bottom surfaces.

the central command. In czarist Russia, the great engineer Igor Sikorsky introduced 'Le Gigante' in 1913, the world's largest plane to date and precursor to the multi-engine strategic bombers of the future.

As history has all too often proved, war turned out to be a great stimulus for technological progress. The evolution was rapid and relentless. The workshops of the first airplane manufacturers soon gave way to enormous

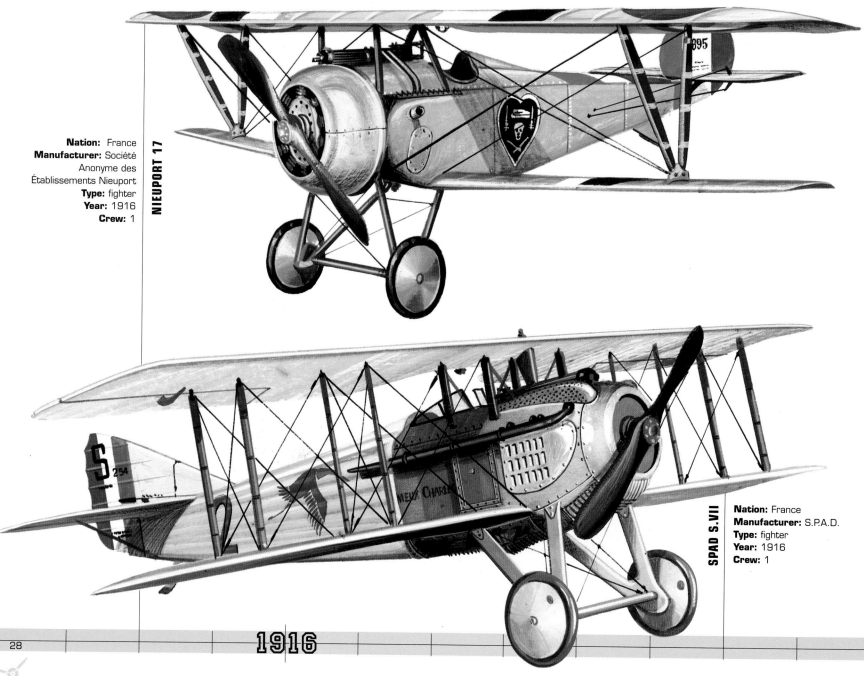

Nation: France
Manufacturer: Société Anonyme des Établissements Nieuport
Type: fighter
Year: 1916
Crew: 1

NIEUPORT 17

Nation: France
Manufacturer: S.P.A.D.
Type: fighter
Year: 1916
Crew: 1

SPAD S.VII

1916

1914-1918

factories that operated on Henry Ford's revolutionary example. Engine manufacturers established separate divisions entirely dedicated to the aviation industry: the French with their Hispano-Suiza and the innovative Gnome rotary engine, among the most widely used; the Germans with their Mercedez-Benz inlines; the English Rolls-Royce V-12s; the American

Charles Nungesser aboard his Nieuport 17, one of the finest combat planes of its day.

Liberty. As horsepower increased, design evolved, such that by war's end airplane engines were four times more powerful and half as heavy. This meant that the traditional wood structures and canvas skins could be replaced by metal structures and wooden, even metal skins. Another key development was the monoplane, though the single-wing aircraft did not completely replace the biplane until several decades later.

HANDLEY PAGE O/100

Nation: Great Britian
Manufacturer: Handley Page Ltd.
Type: heavy bomber
Year: 1916
Crew: 4

*A rack of bombs
ready for loading
onto a Handley Page.*

FIGHTERS AND BOMBERS

Equally rapid advances were made in the area of armaments, likewise stimulated by the needs of the battlefield and by the course of the war itself. While the earliest warplanes were mainly used for monitoring enemy troop movements and artillery positions, defending themselves with rifles or by dropping steel ball-bearings on the enemy's wings to perforate the fabric, the appearance of the machine gun in 1914 transformed what were basically reconnaissance planes into true fighting machines. Initially the guns were placed either on pivoting mounts accessible to the navigator or affixed to the upper wing. Then, with the application in 1915 of the first synchronizers, which made it possible to fire directly through the spinning propeller, the guns were mounted on the prow. The planes themselves, which had become lighter, faster and more agile over time, were now also better armed, and allowed both the flying and the fighting to be done by a single man. The fighter plane had been born.

The bomber underwent a similar evolution, in which the overall improvements in aviation performance extended to the efficiency and quantity of the ordnance it carried. The ball bearings and small anti-personnel bombs of the early bombers were replaced by far more

Nation: Great Britian
Manufacturer: Sopwith Aviation Company
Type: fighter
Year: 1917
Crew: 1

Nation: Great Britian
Manufacturer: Sopwith Aviation Company
Type: fighter
Year: 1917
Crew: 1

1917

A Sopwith Camel of the RAF 209th Squadron. A plane of this type may have shot down von Richthofen, a.k.a the 'Red Baron' in 1918.

deadly fragmentation, high-explosive and incendiary bombs, which ranged in weight from 200 to 2,000 pounds. Indeed, by 1918 the British Handley Page V/1500, precursor of the gigantic bombers of World War II, was lumbering off the runway with two bombs weighing 3,000 pounds *each* and dropping them on the enemy with devastating effect.

If the fighter plane emerged from the conflict as the quintessential aerial weapon the bomber distinguished itself above all as a strategic tool. Every nation involved was fully aware of this, and spared no effort in developing ever larger, more powerful and more specialized machines. Great Britain produced

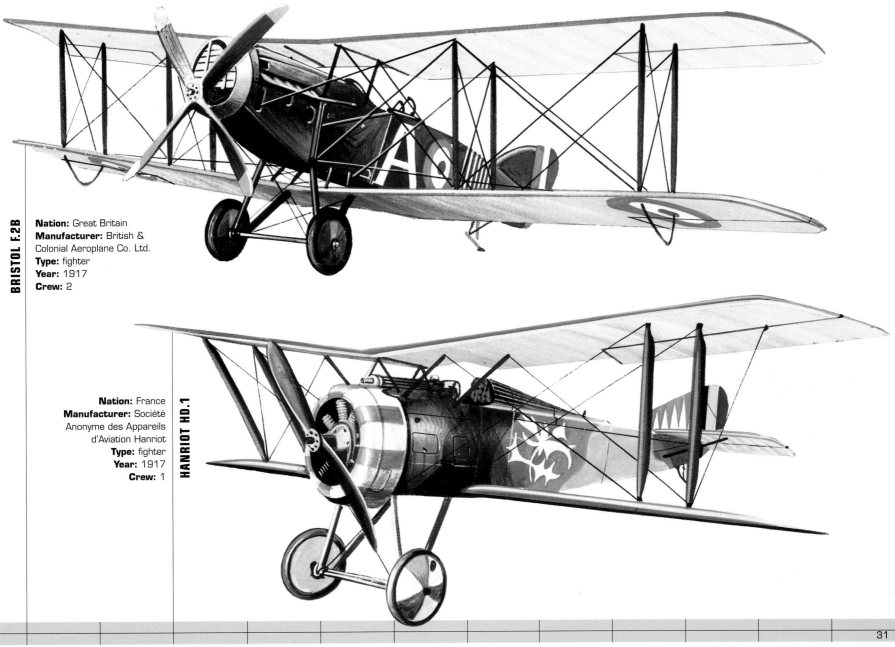

Nation: Great Britain
Manufacturer: British &
Colonial Aeroplane Co. Ltd.
Type: fighter
Year: 1917
Crew: 2

Nation: France
Manufacturer: Société
Anonyme des Appareils
d'Aviation Hanriot
Type: fighter
Year: 1917
Crew: 1

a series of Handley Page twin-engine and four-engine bombers; Germany countered with its Gotha and Friedrichshafen twin-engines and colossal Zeppelin Staaken four-engines; Italy, whose fighter planes were not among the best, was nonetheless an important player thanks to the excellent heavy bombers built by Caproni.

THE BATTLE FOR AIR SUPREMACY

For the first time in human history, air supremacy rather than traditional ground armies determined victory and defeat in battle. The role of the fighter plane proved to be key in this regard. After a period of relative equilibrium, the appearance in the summer of 1915 of the Fokker E.III monoplane tipped the scales dramatically in favor of the Germans. This plane, in addition to being fast and agile, was the first to be equipped with synchronized machine guns, and the relatively slow and vulnerable Allied reconnaissance planes were no match for it. "The Fokker Scourge" ruled the skies over Europe from August 1, 1915 until March 1916, when a new French fighter, the Nieuport 17, joined in the Battle of Verdun and tipped the scales back toward something resembling a fair fight. The Allies seized the moment and eventually gained air superiority with the deployment of newer, better planes like the Spad S.VII, at the time the highest

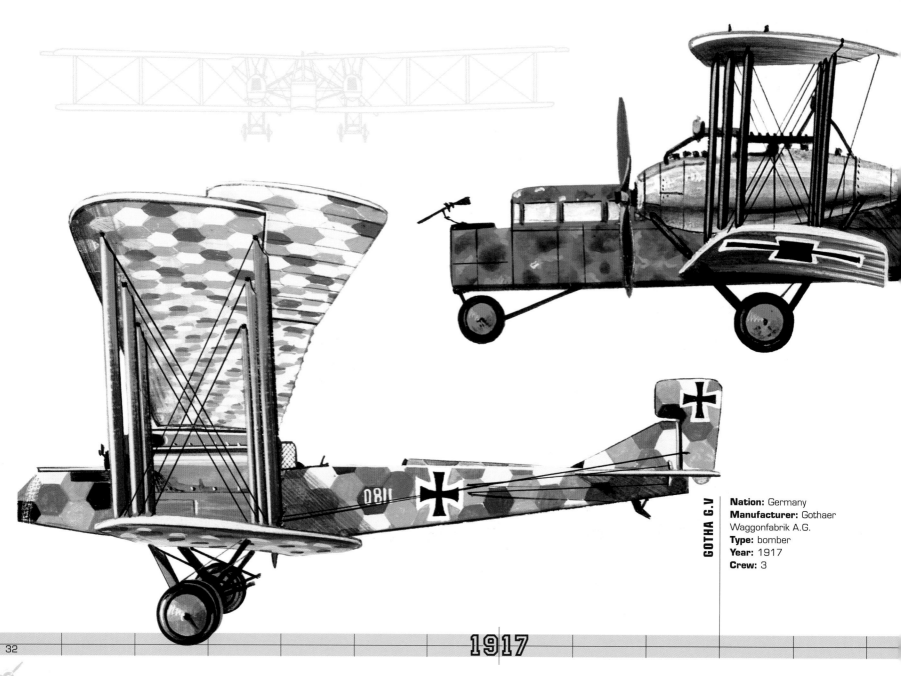

GOTHA G.V

Nation: Germany
Manufacturer: Gothaer Waggonfabrik A.G.
Type: bomber
Year: 1917
Crew: 3

1917

expression of aeronautical technology to date. But the battle was hardly over. The German response was quick and decisive, taking the form of a series of new fighters (the Albatros D.I, D.II and D.III; the Halberstadt D.II and D.III) which hit the front lines in autumn 1916. These planes, along with an efficient reorganization of all its armed forces, gave the advantage back to Germany. The Allies had to wait until the spring of 1917 to recover

from this devastating counterblow, which they did by introducing the French Spad S.XIII, the British RAF S.E.5, the Bristol Fighter, the Sopwith Triplane and the legendary Sopwith Camel.

From this moment onward air supremacy remained in Allied hands, not so much for the quality of their machines (the Germans were building superb airplanes such as the Fokker D.VII and D.VIII, the Roland D.VI and the Pfalz

D.XII) as for the quantity. In the spring/summer of 1918, an estimated 2,390 German planes were pitted against no fewer than 10,000 Allied aircraft. Independently of what was transpiring on the ground, this fact alone ensured that the end of WWI and its inevitable outcome were now only a matter of time.

THE GREAT ACES

The air war was a stage that spotlighted

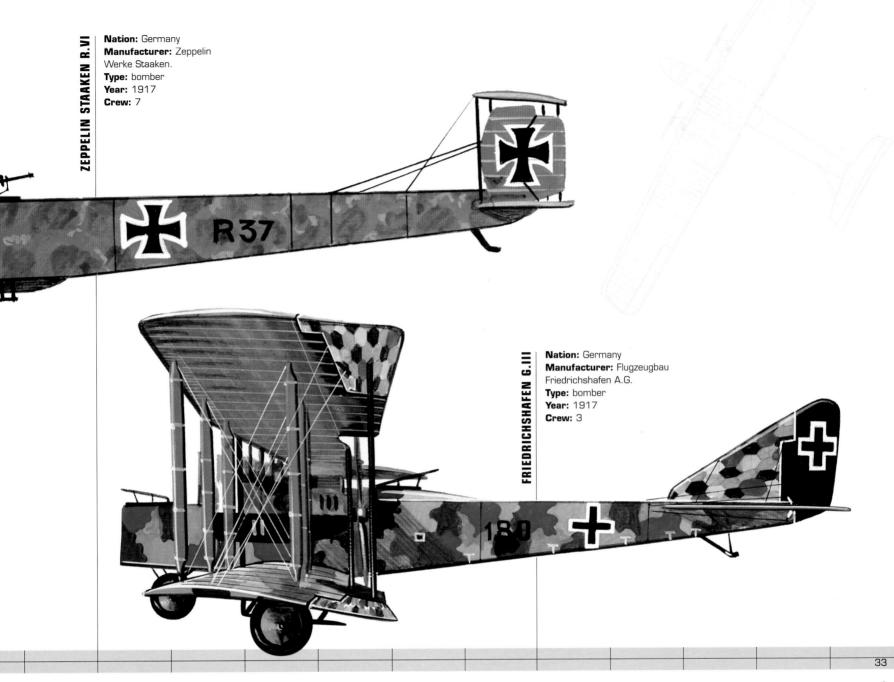

ZEPPELIN STAAKEN R.VI

Nation: Germany
Manufacturer: Zeppelin
Werke Staaken.
Type: bomber
Year: 1917
Crew: 7

R37

FRIEDRICHSHAFEN G.III

Nation: Germany
Manufacturer: Flugzeugbau
Friedrichshafen A.G.
Type: bomber
Year: 1917
Crew: 3

180

not only the planes, but the men who flew them – the 'flying aces.' The figure of the ace was invented for propagandistic reasons by the Germans, but quickly caught on elsewhere. The hunger for heroes is, after all, insatiable, and no one was more suited to capturing the public imagination than the men who battled in the fiery heavens, piloting miraculous machines that had not even existed barely a decade earlier. Each country estab-

SQUADRON INSIGNIA

Throughout the war pilots regularly broke the rigorous rules of camouflage by 'personalizing' their airplanes. Squadron insignia had always been used for reasons of identification, along with geometric camouflage patterns. But these soon evolved into outright pictorial decorations using extravagantly colorful motifs that extended along the entire fuselage, chosen according to the personal tastes of the aces themselves. Counterproductive though it may seem, the practice served to elevate morale and even worked as a psychological eterrent: a conspicuously exuberant enemy is, in the end, more intimidating than a cautious one, for he creates through this exuberance an air of invincibility. The most extreme case was that of von Richthofen and his 'Flying Circus,' whose planes were painted in bold, aggressive colors and plastered with squadron insignia in order to assert the squadron's *esprit de corps* and its sense of absolute superiority.

81st Fighter Squadron, Italy

German Fighter Squadron Jasta 18

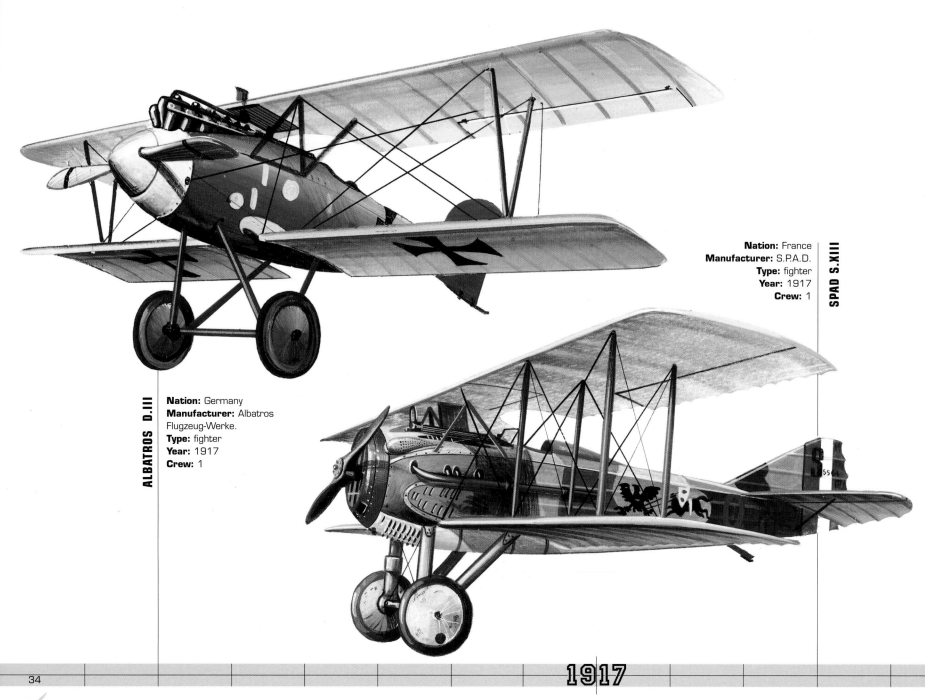

1917

lished strict criteria for attributing combat victories to individual pilots, and every kill was recorded in carefully maintained ledgers in the spirit of a contest, where victory was determined by points rather than which side one was on. In the end, the trophy went to the German ace Manfred von Richthofen (80 kills), followed by René Paul Fonck (France, 75), Edward Mannock (Great Britain, 73), Godwin Brumowski (Austria, 40), Willy Coppens de

Houthulst (Belgium, 37), Francesco Baracca (Italy, 34), Eddie Rickenbacker (USA, 26) and Alexander Kazakov (Russia, 17). In most cases the fame of these pilots was directly linked to the planes they flew. Though von Richthofen fought with a number of different planes, he will forever be associated with his red Fokker triplane, just as the legend of Willy Coppens de Houthulst is inseparable from his Hanriot, and Francesco Baracca's from his Spad.

PEACE AND PROGRESS

At the outbreak of war in August 1914 the airplane was still very much in its gestational phase. By the cessation of hostilities in November 1918, it had become a mature and dependable means of transport, thanks to the industrial and technological advances fueled by military needs. A typical fighter at that time had a 220-horsepower engine, a speed of 130 miles per hour, and an altitude

Nation: Germany
Manufacturer: Fokker
Flugzeug-Werke GmbH
Type: fighter
Year: 1917
Crew: 1

FOKKER DR.I

War in the skies

THE RED BARON

Of all the legends of aviation, there is one in particular that seems immortal: Manfred von Richthofen, better known as the Red Baron, supreme German fighter ace, with a record 80 combat kills. The story of his exploits was consecrated as myth on April 21, 1918, when his Fokker Dr.I triplane crashed in the Somme valley near Sailly-le-Sec after engaging a patrol of English Sopwith Camels commanded by Captain Arthur Roy Brown, a Canadian. Von Richthofen was only 26, but his fame was already immense. A handsome man of noble lineage, cruel in battle but always respectful of his conquered adversary, he quickly became a hero for ally and enemy alike. He was the incarnation of the ancient ideal of the chivalrous warrior, universally feared and admired – and imitated. Between 1916 and 1918, young German pilots under the spell of the his charisma clamored to join his famous 'Flying Circus' squadron (*Jagdgeschwader 1*), which was fighting on the French front. But another factor that certainly contributed to the myth of the Red Baron is the still unsolved mystery of his death. For decades historians and aviation aficionados have argued as to whether he was killed in an aerial dogfight by a bullet from Captain Brown's Sopwith, or by a rifle shot fired from the ground by an Australian sergeant, Cedric Popkin. Documentary evidence, eyewitness accounts, and careful reconstructions all point to one conclusion: that both scenarios are equally plausible, and that the debate will not be resolved any time soon.

Nation: Great Britain
Manufacturer: Vickers Ltd.
Type: heavy bomber
Year: 1918
Crew: 3

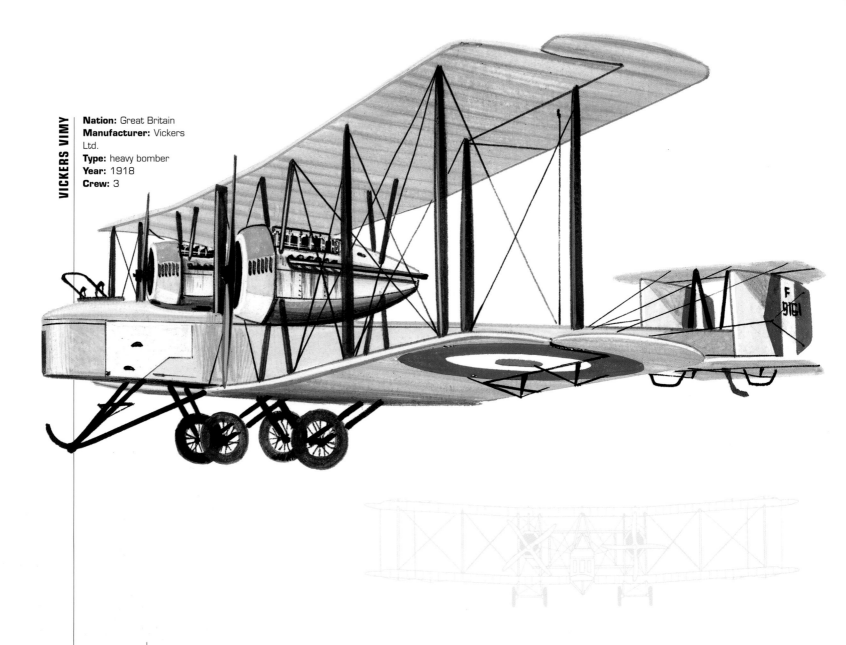

1918

ACROSS THE ATLANTIC

It was an English bomber that inaugurated the era of transoceanic flight. The twin-engine Vickers Vimy, developed too late to participate in the war, was the protagonist of the first ocean crossing. In June 1919 Captain John Alcock and Lieutenant Arthur Whitten Brown boarded their heavily modified Vimy and flew non-stop from St. John's, Newfoundland to Clifden, Ireland, a journey of 1,985 miles. The risks they ran during this heroic flight – fog, ice, wind – served to demonstrate to any remaining naysayers that the airplane had definitively reached maturity. Five months later another 'first' was captured, this time by two intrepid Australian brothers, Ross and Keith Smith. Also flying in a Vimy, they flew from from Hounslow, England to Darwin, Australia, covering the 11,130 miles in just under 136 hours.

The Vickers Vimy flown by Alcock and Brown in the first transatlantic flight. The crossing was successful, the landing somewhat less so.

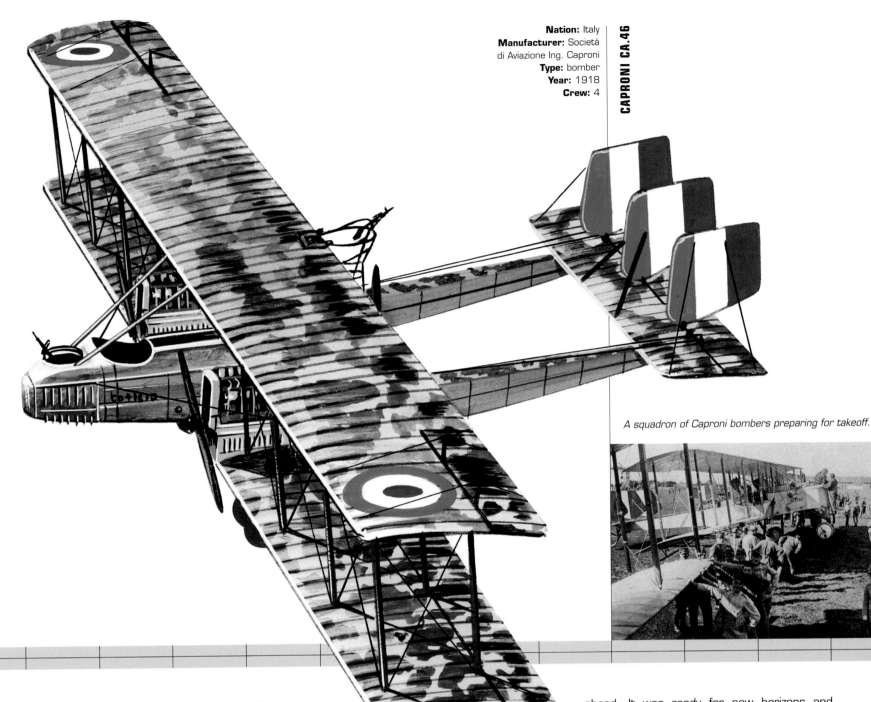

Nation: Italy
Manufacturer: Società
di Aviazione Ing. Caproni
Type: bomber
Year: 1918
Crew: 4

CAPRONI CA.46

A squadron of Caproni bombers preparing for takeoff.

ceiling of 18,000 feet, an astonishing improvement in performance with respect to that of just four years prior. At the same time, the industrial apparatus had taken enormous steps forward in terms of sheer production capacity: at war's start there were approximately 400 planes at the front; whereas on the day of the armistice there were nearly 13,000. In fact, the production of aircraft between 1914 and 1918 numbered

177,000 units, fully 18 times more than all the flying machines of every type produced worldwide between 1903 and 1914.

The die for future growth had been cast, and despite the reduced demand brought about by the end of the war, there was no stopping aviation from pressing

ahead. It was ready for new horizons and new adventures, and the path it took was that of civil transport. The world's first passenger airline had been born on January 1, 1914, when an enterprising manufacturer from St. Louis christened the Benoist XIV, a small hydroplane. The war put what would be merely a temporary halt to the development of one the century's great industries: commercial air travel.

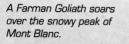

A Farman Goliath soars over the snowy peak of Mont Blanc.

Opposite page: a Breguet 14 T, 1919

F-ADDT

1919

1919-1941

COMMERCIAL AVIATION IS BORN

THE CIVIL AIR TRANSPORT INDUSTRY

INAUGURATED THE AIRPLANE'S GOLDEN AGE

A PERIOD OF GREAT EXPANSION

THAT MADE THE WORLD A SMALLER PLACE.

1941

A distance of 120 miles in 2 hours 18 minutes. These apparently innocuous figures represent the distance and flight time of the first regular commercial passenger service offered in Europe. On February 5, 1919 the Deutsche Luft Reederei company opened daily service between Berlin and Weimar with an AEG J.II biplane left over from the war and modified to accommodate two passengers. Founded in December of 1917, DLR had been running cargo flights and transporting mail and newspapers through the final years of the war. Then, sensing the great potential of this new means of transport, it decided to brave the unexplored territory of passenger travel. The initial results were less than exhilarating: in the first month of operation only 19 people had the courage to climb aboard that fragile flying machine of wood and canvas to make a voyage that would have been easier and cheaper to do by train. But the idea had been planted, and in a Europe still reeling from the devastation of war, the image of hope and progress represented by the airplane was too captivating to resist.

FRANCE

France's pride in its aeronautical achievements necessitated an immediate reaction to German

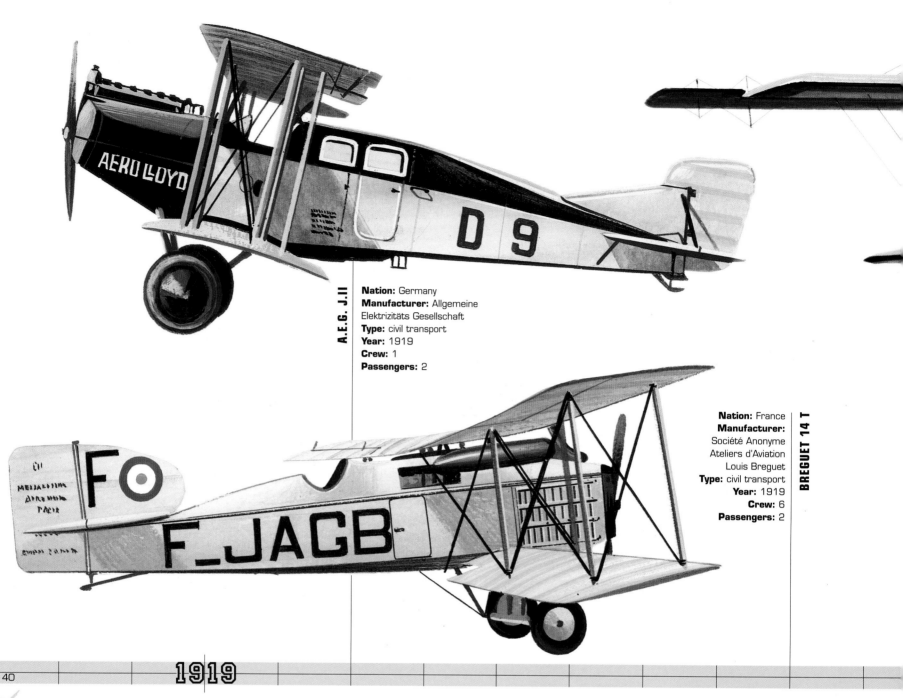

Nation: Germany
Manufacturer: Allgemeine Elektrizitäts Gesellschaft
Type: civil transport
Year: 1919
Crew: 1
Passengers: 2

A.E.G. J.II

Nation: France
Manufacturer: Société Anonyme Ateliers d'Aviation Louis Breguet
Type: civil transport
Year: 1919
Crew: 6
Passengers: 2

BREGUET 14 T

1919-1941

primacy in commercial air travel. On March 22, 1919, Lucien Bossotrout climbed aboard a modified twin-engine Farman F.60 Goliath bomber and inaugurated the first regular service between Paris and Brussels. The flight lasted 2 hours and 50 minutes; the ticket cost 365 francs. A couple of months later, Farman, heretofore a manufacturer, founded its own air transport company, Lignes Aériennes Farman, the second such enterprise in Europe.

Farman's initiative, however, had been preceded by numerous isolated, 'unofficial' attempts to explore the possibilities and potential of commercial air travel. One small but ambitious company from Toulouse, Lignes Aériennes Latécoère, had already made the first flight to Barcelona on December 24, 1918, and planned to extend service to Africa and South America. Indeed, on February 25, 1919 the company's Breguet 14 took a handful of pas-

sengers to Alicante, and on March 20 made it all the way to Rabat, Morocco. In the meantime, Farman had picked up the pace and was flying the prestigious Paris-London route, with intentions to expand into northern Europe and Africa, thereby upping the stakes and fueling the spirit of competition. The Compagnie des Messageries Aériennes, or CMA, debuted as France's second official airline on May 1, with daily service from Paris to Lille, and by Sep-

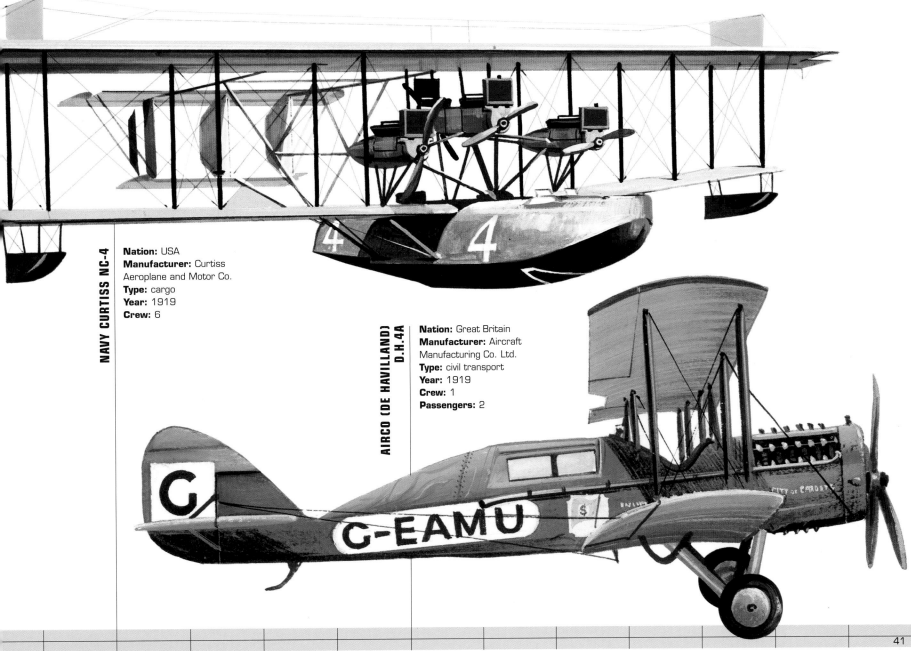

Nation: USA
Manufacturer: Curtiss Aeroplane and Motor Co.
Type: cargo
Year: 1919
Crew: 6

Nation: Great Britain
Manufacturer: Aircraft Manufacturing Co. Ltd.
Type: civil transport
Year: 1919
Crew: 1
Passengers: 2

tember CMA was serving Brussels and London as well. A third airline opened its doors for business in July of 1919, the Compagnie des Transports Aéronautiques du Sud-Ouest, with flights from Bordeaux to Biarritz, San Sebastian and Bilbao. Others would follow suit that same year: the Compagnie Générale Transaérienne Française, the Compagnie des Grands Express

In the spring of 1919 a Curtiss NC-4 flew from The Netherlands to Lisbon in 25 hours.

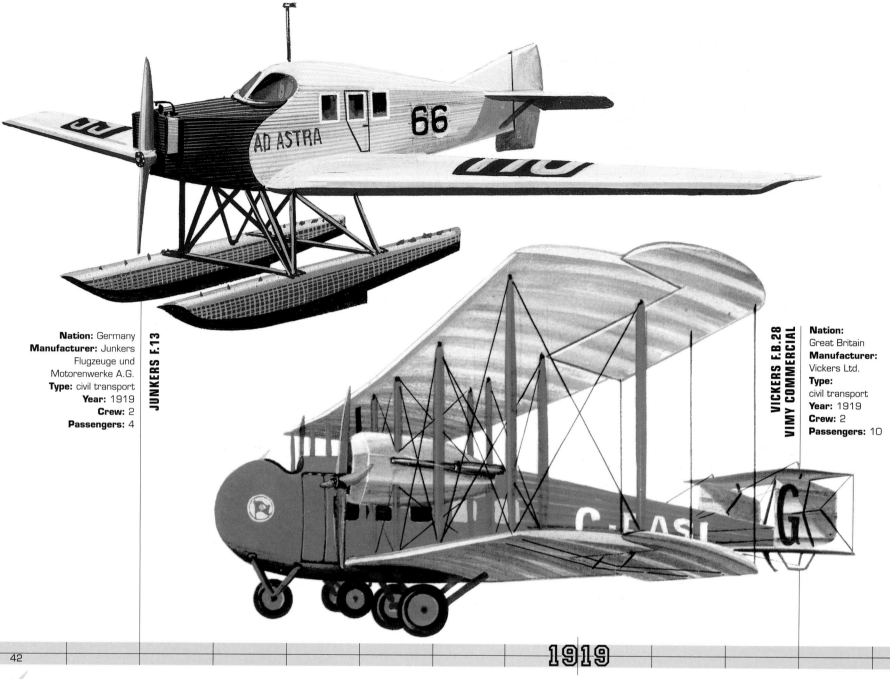

Nation: Germany
Manufacturer: Junkers Flugzeuge und Motorenwerke A.G.
Type: civil transport
Year: 1919
Crew: 2
Passengers: 4

JUNKERS F.13

Nation: Great Britain
Manufacturer: Vickers Ltd.
Type: civil transport
Year: 1919
Crew: 2
Passengers: 10

VICKERS F.B.28 VIMY COMMERCIAL

1919

Aériens, Aéro Transport Ernoul and Aéro Transport.

This fervor testifies not only to the drive and vision of individual entrepreneurs, but to the foresight of the French government, which recognized the importance of commercial air transport for the country's economy and stature. In addition to aiding private initiatives

A Junkers F.13 serving the route between Teheran, Iran and Baku, Azerbaijan.

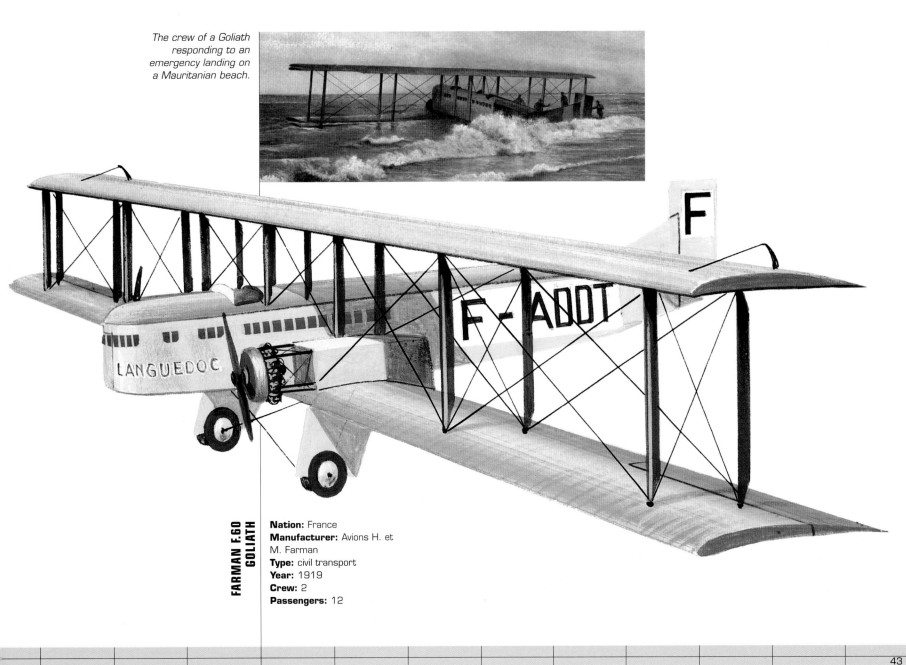

The crew of a Goliath responding to an emergency landing on a Mauritanian beach.

FARMAN F.60 GOLIATH

Nation: France
Manufacturer: Avions H. et M. Farman
Type: civil transport
Year: 1919
Crew: 2
Passengers: 12

with legislation and subsidies, in January 1920 the government instituted a ministry of aeronautics and air transport, with separate departments assigned to specific aviation concerns such as standardized cartography, technical services, and air traffic regulations. This ministry also established the national meteorological network. The airlines took full advantage of the state's acknowledgment of their efforts, and used the financing to expand

yet further. Over the course of 1920, some 2,400 commercial flights took place. New routes were inaugurated, newer ones were planned, with an especially keen eye toward Eastern Europe. One company whose activities exemplify this period of expansion was the Compagnie Franco-Roumaine de Navigation Aérienne (CFRNA). On September 20, 1920 it opened the route to Strasbourg, on October 7, Prague. Warsaw was added to the intinerary

on April 12, 1921, then Budapest in May 1922. The route from Paris to Constantinople, opened on October 15, 1922, incorporated stops in Strasbourg, Innsbruck, Vienna, Budapest, Belgrade and Bucharest. On the southern front, Lignes Aériennes Latécoère (which had become the Compagnie Générale d'Enterprises Aéronautiques, or CGEA, in April 1921) continued to expand toward Africa. This market had grown enormously, with many

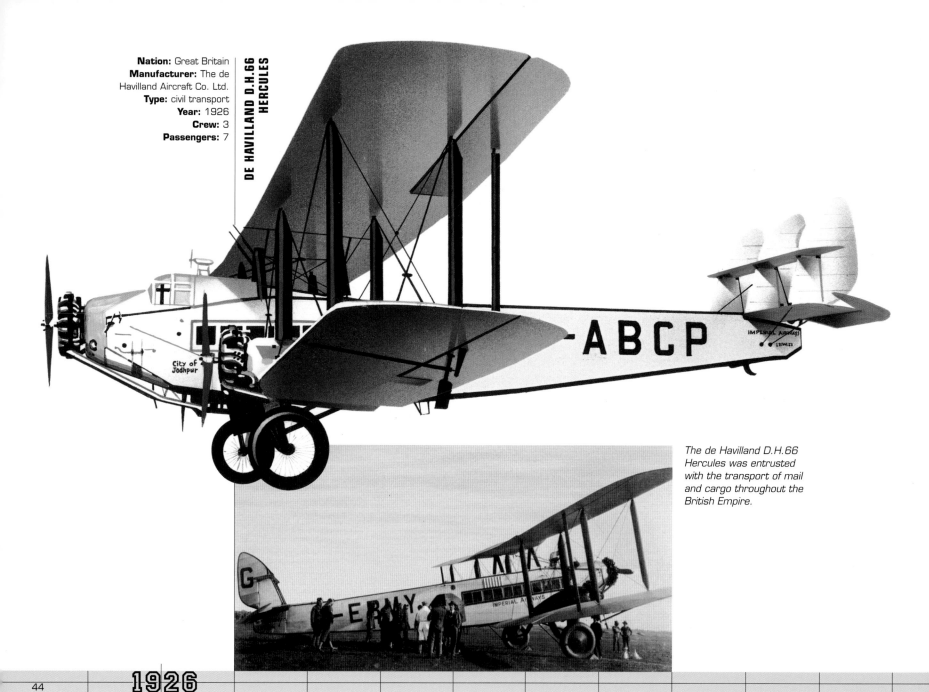

Nation: Great Britain
Manufacturer: The de Havilland Aircraft Co. Ltd.
Type: civil transport
Year: 1926
Crew: 3
Passengers: 7

DE HAVILLAND D.H.66 HERCULES

The de Havilland D.H.66 Hercules was entrusted with the transport of mail and cargo throughout the British Empire.

1926

operators competing for the same routes. As such, the first mergers were born. In 1921 the Compagnie des Grands Express Aériens absorbed the Compagnie Générale Transaérienne Française. Then, in January 1923 CGEA merged with the Compagnie des Messageries Aériennes to create the first colossus of commercial air transport, known as Air Union. The effects of this expansion are perhaps best measured in purely numerical terms: in 1920,

a total of 942 passengers were served by all of the nascent French airlines; five years later, that number had grown to 20,000. By 1932, French airliners flew a total of 5,800,000 miles, with 420,000 tons of cargo capacity and seats for 310,000 passengers.

The year 1933 marked a major turning point in French air transport. Competition from other European countries had become ferocious. So, with the aim of maximizing the

nation's ingenuity and potential, the French government negotiated the unification of four of the larger airlines into a single, centrally administered giant. Air France was created on August 30, 1933 from the merger of Air Orient, Air Union, CIDNA, SGTA and Aéropostale. The newborn company commanded a worldwide network of nearly 24,000 miles and a fleet of 259 airplanes. The impetus that the merger gave to technological and industrial

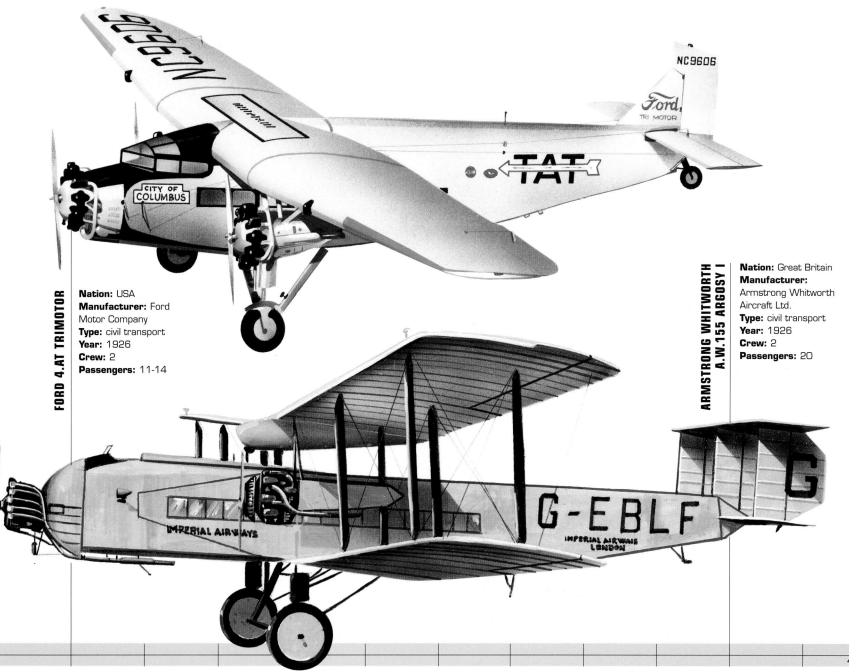

Nation: USA
Manufacturer: Ford
Motor Company
Type: civil transport
Year: 1926
Crew: 2
Passengers: 11-14

Nation: Great Britain
Manufacturer:
Armstrong Whitworth
Aircraft Ltd.
Type: civil transport
Year: 1926
Crew: 2
Passengers: 20

'LIGHTER-THAN-AIR' CRAFT

During the infancy of commercial transport, the airplane was no match for its older sibling and rival, the 'lighter-than-air' craft. As early as October 1909 a German, Count Ferdinand von Zeppelin, inventor of the structured dirigible, had founded the first aerial transport company in the world, DELAG. And it did some big business for its day: between March 1912 and November 1913 the majestic Zeppelin airships made 881 flights, carrying 19,100 passengers over a total of nearly 65,000 miles. Service resumed after the war, at which point Britain had begun planning an ambitious program of dirigible service within the Commonwealth. In the meantime Germany had built the gigantic *Graf Zeppelin* (see photo) and in 1928 opened the transatlantic route to the United States. But the hydrogen airship's destiny was not a happy one. Of the many dirigible accidents that occurred over the years, the worst was the explosion of the *Graf Hindenburg* at Lakehurst, NJ on May 6, 1937, causing an abrupt end to the age of the dirigible.

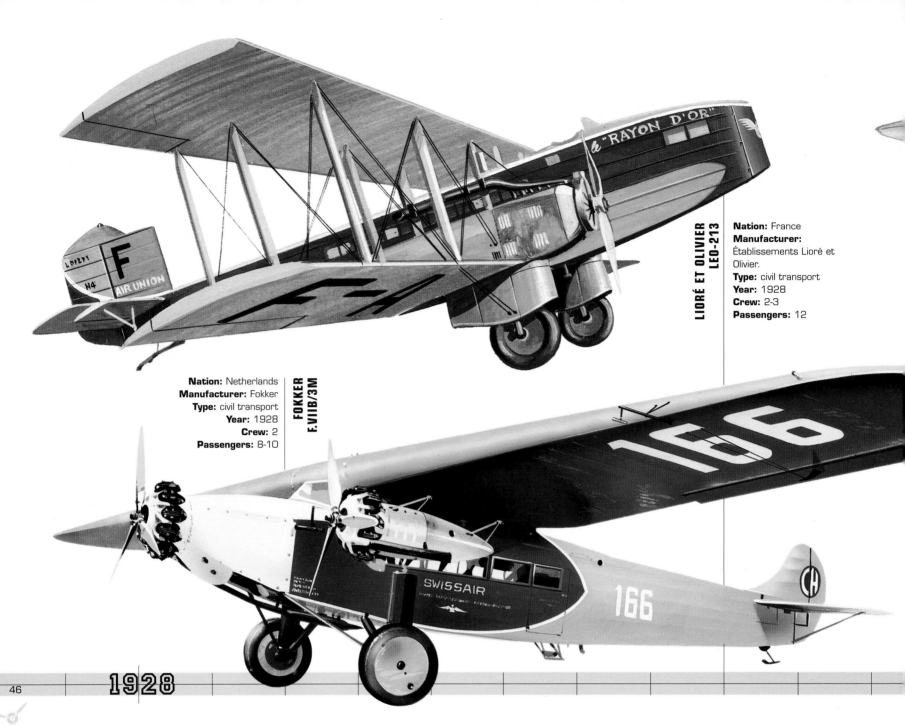

LIORÉ ET OLIVIER LEO-213

Nation: France
Manufacturer: Établissements Lioré et Olivier.
Type: civil transport
Year: 1928
Crew: 2-3
Passengers: 12

FOKKER F.VIIB/3M

Nation: Netherlands
Manufacturer: Fokker
Type: civil transport
Year: 1928
Crew: 2
Passengers: 8-10

progress was nearly as powerful as if the country had been at war, and led France to the avant-garde of world aviation. Airplanes improved in dependability and performance, new thresholds were continually being conquered: in 1934 Air France was offering regular service to South America in

The Southern Cross, a Fokker F.VII/3m trimotor, famous for its trans-Pacific flight from San Francisco to Brisbane, Australia.

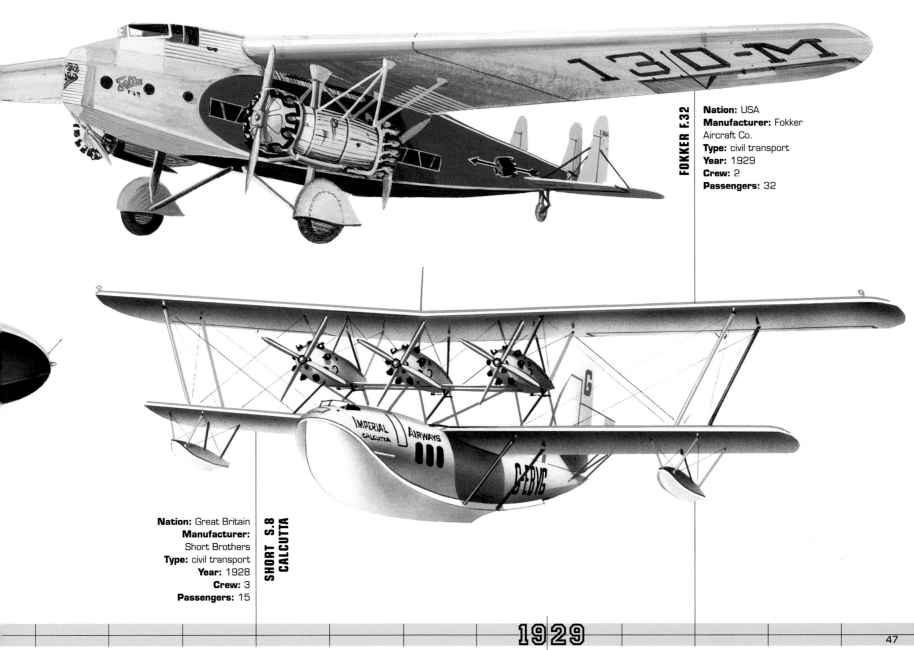

FOKKER F.32

Nation: USA
Manufacturer: Fokker
Aircraft Co.
Type: civil transport
Year: 1929
Crew: 2
Passengers: 32

Nation: Great Britain
Manufacturer:
Short Brothers
Type: civil transport
Year: 1928
Crew: 3
Passengers: 15

SHORT S.8 CALCUTTA

1929

its Couzinet Arc-en-ciel trimotor; two years later the Dakar route was opened. In 1937 it began exploring the North American market, and the next year routes had been opened to China and Hong Kong. Again, the story is best told by numbers: in 1939 Air France was serving 100,000 passengers annually, nearly double the 55,000 who flew in 1930 with the four major French airlines, Air Union, Farman CIDNA and Aéropostale.

GERMANY

During the early years of commercial aviation France's most aggressive rivals were the Germans. The historic flight by the world's first passenger airline, Deutsche Luft Reederei, was hardly a one-time achievement. The Berlin-Weimar route was followed by links between Berlin, Frankfurt and Hamburg. By 1919 the entire German territory had been amply covered by the commercial air transport network.

New companies joined DLR, such as Lloyd Luftverkehr Sablatnig, Saechsische Luft Reederei, Bayerischer Luft Lloyd and Albatros. At the time Germany could confidently claim absolute primacy in the comprehensiveness of its national network – this in defiance, however, of the Treaty of Versailles, which rigorously forbade the country from building large, long-range aircraft. A key event took place in 1924, when a number of small airlines merged to

Nation: Great Britain
Manufacturer: Handley Page Ltd.
Type: civil transport
Year: 1930
Crew: 2
Passengers: 24

G-A

G-AAGX

G-AAXF

The Handley Page H.P.42 W Helena was in service until 1941, after which its fuselage was used as an office by an affectionate RAF squadron.

1930

1919-1941

form two larger consortia, Junkers Luftverkehr and Deutsche Aero Lloyd. The cumulative network extended over most of Europe, thanks in part to collaborative accords with the major airlines of other countries. An example of similar international cooperation dates back three years earlier, with Aero Lloyd's participation in the founding of Deruluft (Deutsche Russische Luftwerkehrs), Russia's first commercial airline. But the decisive year was

1926, when Junkers and Aero Lloyd merged to form Deutsche Lufthansa, the biggest and busiest and most ambitious airline in Europe and symbol of Germany's supremacy in the field. The first Lufthansa flight took place on April 6, and within a few months the new company had extended its network yet further, and was unrivalled in regularity and efficiency. Its fleet in 1927 consisted in 120 of the most advanced and prestigious aircraft on the

market. Demand for newer, faster and more capacious machines was constant, and this drove German industry to surpass itself, with companies like Junkers and Dornier building extraordinarily fine aircraft. By the early 1930s Lufthansa led the European field in number of passengers. In fact, that single company carried an estimated 110,000 passengers in 1930, as compared to the 14,000 served by all of the other smaller companies combined,

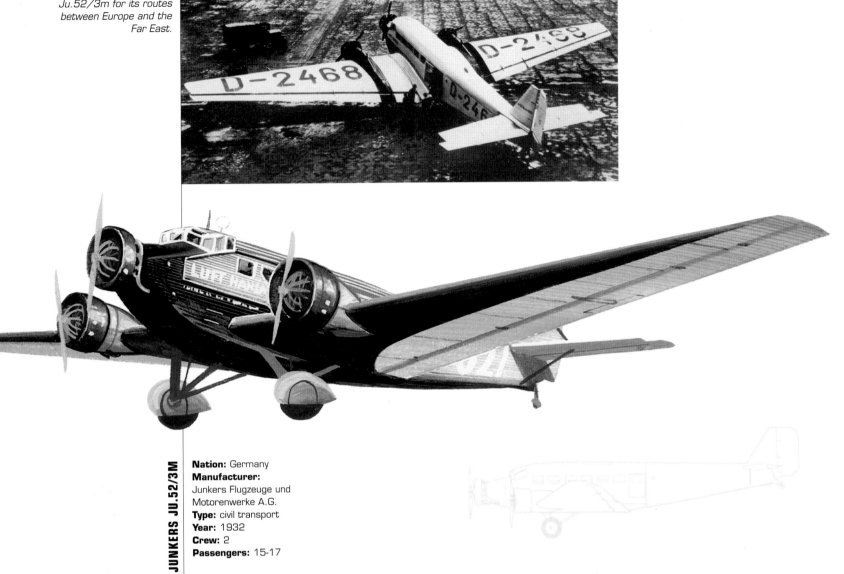

The Deutsche Lufthansa airline used the Junkers Ju.52/3m for its routes between Europe and the Far East.

JUNKERS JU.52/3M

Nation: Germany
Manufacturer:
Junkers Flugzeuge und Motorenwerke A.G.
Type: civil transport
Year: 1932
Crew: 2
Passengers: 15-17

then grouped under the consortium Deutsche Verkehrsflug. On September 28, 1934, just eight years after its creation, Lufthansa flew its 1,000,000th passenger. At that point, it had established affiliations with twelve other companies, with whom it operated a comprehensive web of international routes.

The greatest expansion took place, however in the years immediately preceding World War II. The new aircraft being built in Germany during the 1930s were only apparently commercial in function – in truth they were the smiling mask of what would become the Luftwaffe, Nazi Germany's air force. In 1932 the Junkers Ju.52/3m trimotor, future workhorse of the German military, and two years later the Heinkel He.70 appeared, the fastest commercial liner of its time. In 1935-36 the Junkers Ju.86 and the Heinkel He.111 made their debut posing as civil transport planes, only to become two of the most notorious bombers of World War II. And then in 1938 Lufthansa introduced an even more advanced machine, the four-engine Focke Wulf Fw.200, known as the Condor, terror of the Allied convoys. During the precious few years that these planes performed peacetime functions, they undoubtedly contributed to the progress of civil aviation, and made Lufthansa the number one airline in Europe.

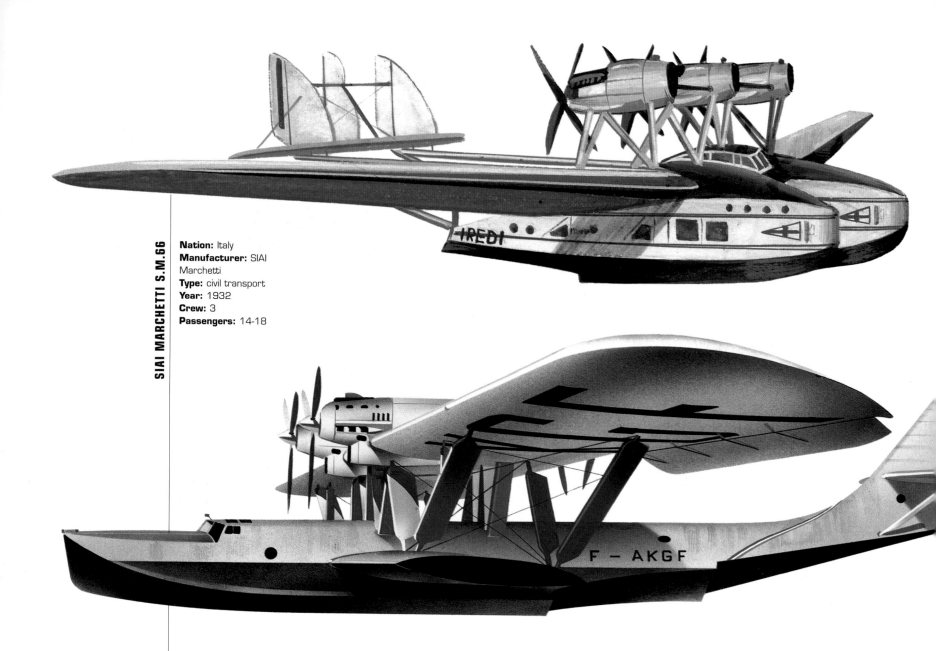

Nation: Italy
Manufacturer: SIAI Marchetti
Type: civil transport
Year: 1932
Crew: 3
Passengers: 14-18

1932

GREAT BRITAIN

The third great European industrial power, Great Britain, lagged behind in the civil aviation field. Contrary to those of France and Germany, the British government demonstrated utter disinterest in the first commercial airlines, this within an overall attitude among the population

The huge four-engine Latécoère 300 hydroplane was designed for delivering mail to and from South America.

A Curtiss Condor dwarfs a Gee Bee stunt plane.

Nation: France
Manufacturer: Forges et Ateliers de Construction Latécoère
Type: cargo
Year: 1932
Crew: 4
Load: 2,200 lbs (1,000 kg)

Nation: USA
Manufacturer: Curtiss Aeroplane and Motor Co.
Type: civil transport
Year: 1933
Crew: 2
Passengers: 15

1933

at large of indifference toward the airplane itself as a means of transport and communication. It wasn't until April 1919 that the state formally authorized civil aviation. The first company to attempt to provide regular commercial service was the great A.V. Roe & Co. On May 10, 1919 a three-seater Avro biplane opened the triangular route linking Alexander Park, Southport, and Blackpool, a circuit of about 55 miles. The experiment was a failure: service was suspended after just four months and 194 flights. In the meantime another small company had emerged, Aircraft Transport and Travel (ATT), which has the distinction of having inaugurated the first international passenger service in history on August 25, 1919, from London to Paris. The route was served by converted de Havilland D.H.4 bombers; the flight between the Hendon and Le Bourget airfields took two and a half hours. Despite the success of the route and the company's reputation for punctuality and safety, ATT became the first victim of official indifference when, on December 15, 1920, mounting financial difficulties resulted in its closing. The state did not intervene. During its brief presence on the civil aviation scene, ATT was the only real competition of Handley Page Transport, an offshoot of the established manufacturing giant. Using modified heavy bombers of the O/400 class,

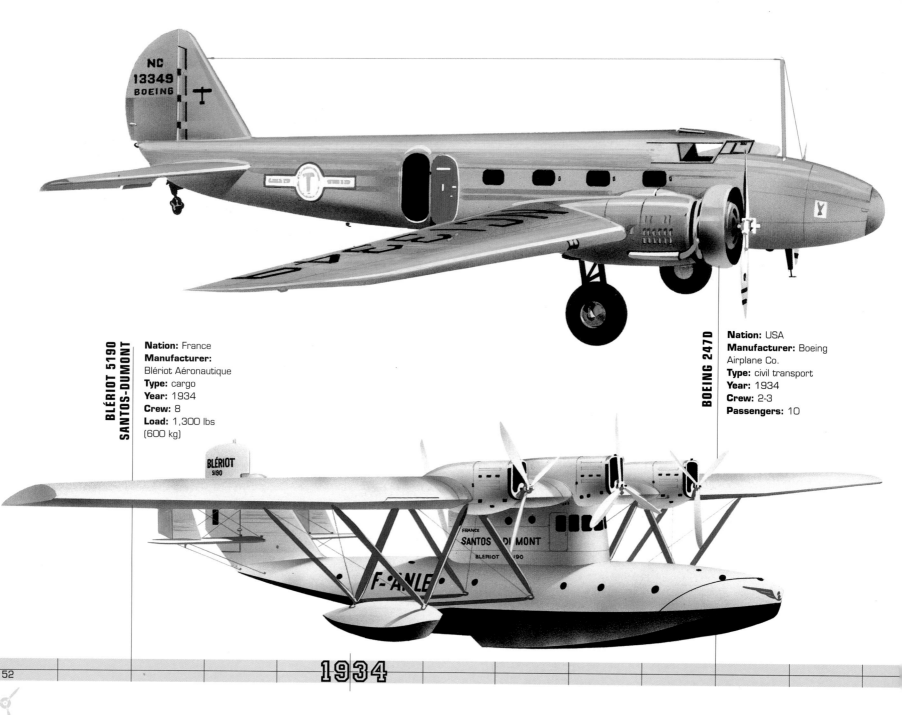

Nation: France
Manufacturer:
Blériot Aéronautique
Type: cargo
Year: 1934
Crew: 8
Load: 1,300 lbs
(600 kg)

Nation: USA
Manufacturer: Boeing
Airplane Co.
Type: civil transport
Year: 1934
Crew: 2-3
Passengers: 10

1934

Handley Page opened its own service to Paris the week following ATT's historic initiative (September 2, 1919). But it was no contest, for Handley Page, apart from the superiority of its planes, also had immense economic resources. And it didn't spare those resources when it came to improving its transport division: in 1920, Handley Page built for itself the first true English passenger plane, the WB twin-engine. The quality of this aircraft, and the

fact that it was specifically designed for civilian passengers, unlike the converted bombers of past practice, secured Handley Page's hold on the market. But not even these kinds of successes registered with the authorities, who remained deaf to requests for political and economic support. This unfortunate situation, which severely penalized many of the smaller British airlines by making them vulnerable to increasing international competition, went on

to create more victims. The British Aerial Transport Company, or BAT, founded in 1917 and as such one of the nation's first airlines, was unable to sustain its ambitious service linking London, Birmingham and Amsterdam. Bankruptcy also claimed the Supermarine Aviation Company, North Sea Aerial and General Transport, and the Air Post of Banks. The stalemate was finally resolved in 1921, thanks to the foresight and determination of

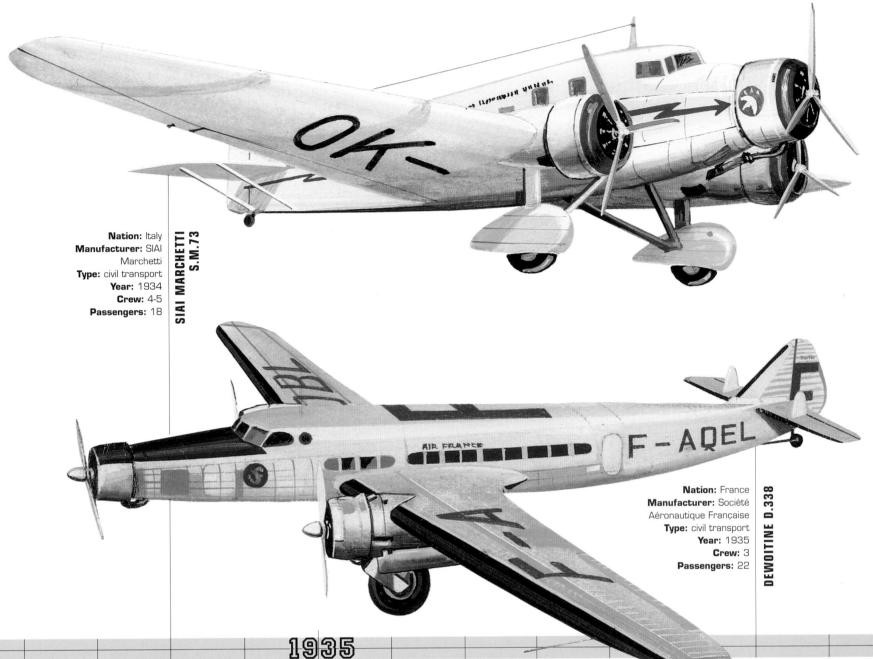

Nation: Italy
Manufacturer: SIAI Marchetti
Type: civil transport
Year: 1934
Crew: 4-5
Passengers: 18

SIAI MARCHETTI S.M.73

Nation: France
Manufacturer: Société Aéronautique Française
Type: civil transport
Year: 1935
Crew: 3
Passengers: 22

DEWOITINE D.338

1935

Handley Page and Instone Air Lines (founded May 1920). On February 28, the two companies agreed to suspend all service to France as a sign of protest. What better way to stir the government from its torpor than to undermine national prestige by handing France, the historic rival, a monopoly on all Channel flights? The reaction was immediate. Public opinion

The first Dewoitine D.33, nicknamed 'Le Trait d'Union,' was destroyed in a forced landing in 1931.

Commercial aviation is born

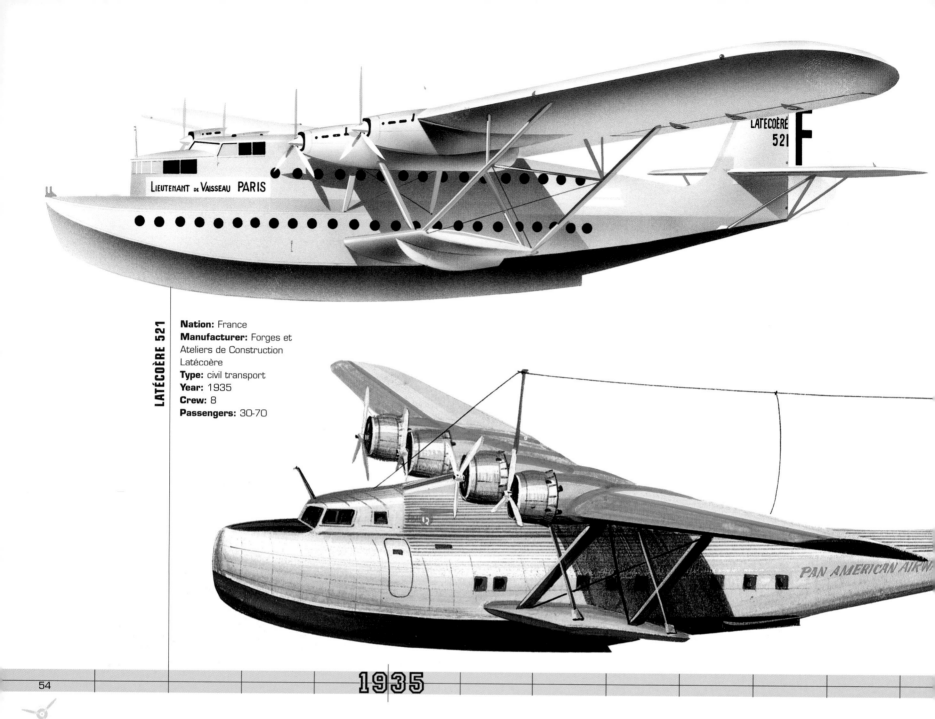

Nation: France
Manufacturer: Forges et Ateliers de Construction Latécoère
Type: civil transport
Year: 1935
Crew: 8
Passengers: 30-70

LATÉCOÈRE 521

1935

rallied behind the protesters, and press and Parliament assaulted the government. In the end, it was decided that each airline would receive a subsidy of £25,000. Though not a princely sum even for those times, it did represent the first official acknowledgment of the importance of civil aviation. As a result, the engine of British enterprise and initiative got the jumpstart it needed, and new airlines began sprouting up everywhere: Daimler Airways in

1922, British Marine Air Navigation in 1923, along with many others. The market settled into a convivial cohabitation. Handley Page concentrated on the prestigious London-Paris route, Instone focused on Brussels, Daimler on Amsterdam, and British Marine on the more pedestrian English and French coastal routes. The critical year would be 1923. The government realized that without a long-term plan and appropriate budget,

British aviation would not survive the competition. And so it was that on December 3, following the example of the French and German governments, the four principal British airlines signed a preliminary accord for an eventual merger. A subsidy of £1 million over ten years was the least of the resulting advantages: the fleet would become enormous, the territory covered would become comprehensive, and the new airline would enjoy access

SIAI MARCHETTI S.M.74

Nation: Italy
Manufacturer: SIAI Marchetti
Type: civil transport
Year: 1935
Crew: 4
Passengers: 27

Only three SIAI Marchetti S.M.74s were ever built.

MARTIN M.130 CHINA CLIPPER

Nation: USA
Manufacturer: Glenn L. Martin Co.
Type: civil transport
Year: 1935
Crew: 5
Passengers: 48

to the national industrial network. The merger took place officially on March 31, 1924, and Imperial Airways was born. The doors opened for business the following day. Growth was slow but steady. Imperial first asserted itself in Europe, then began expanding aggressively toward Africa, Central Asia and the Far East. By the 1930s, whatever holes that were left in this vast web were occupied by small private interests: Hillman Airways in 1932, Spartan

Air Lines in 1933, and in 1935 United Airways and British Continental, all of which then joined together in that same year to form British Airways. When Scottish Airways was founded in 1937 from a merger of Highland Airways and Northern & Scottish Airways, British commercial aviation had finally reached its full maturity and no longer had any reason to envy the European competition.

THE UNITED STATES

On the other side of the Atlantic, aviation was undergoing quite another kind of evolution. While Europe was applying its accumulated experience to the development of commercial transport, the Americans were using their enormous industrial capacity to build up an efficient air force. Their dependency on the French and British aeronautical industries for planes, technology and spare parts during

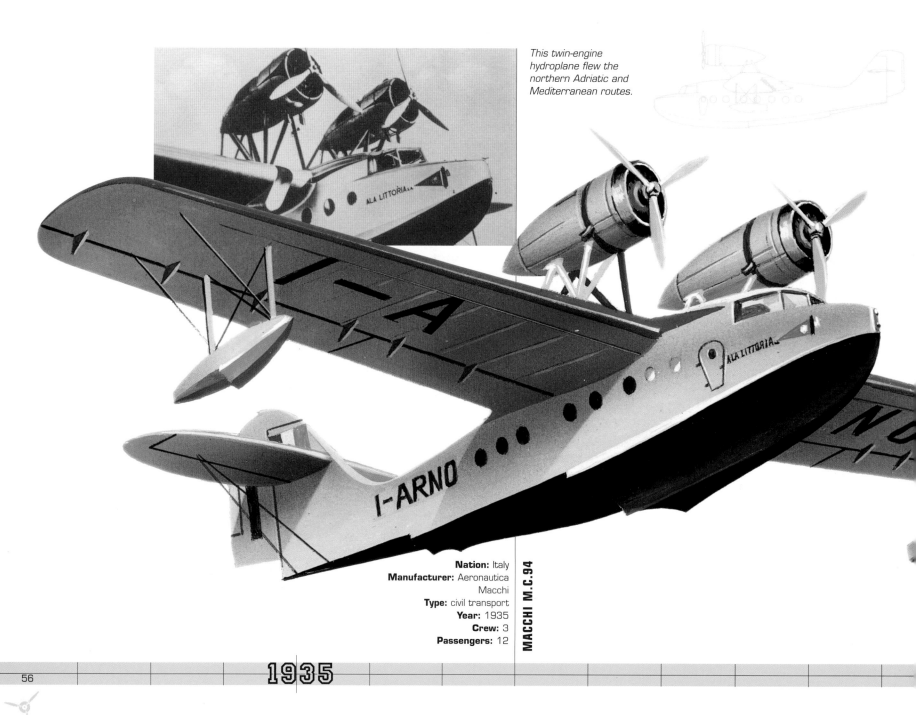

This twin-engine hydroplane flew the northern Adriatic and Mediterranean routes.

I-ARNO

Nation: Italy
Manufacturer: Aeronautica Macchi
Type: civil transport
Year: 1935
Crew: 3
Passengers: 12

MACCHI M.C.94

1935

World War I had not gone down well, and they weren't about to let that happen again. So, the civilian sector was put on the back burner, despite the fact that commercial aviation had been invented there as early as 1914, when the Benoist XIV hydroplane was used for the short-lived service between St. Petersburg and Tampa. The early years of American civil transport were dedicated exclusively to mail and cargo. In 1917 the

AIR MAIL

Postal transport was the first civil role played by the airplane. In the pioneering years the notion of ferrying passengers on machines that were not yet completely safe and trustworthy was simply too risky. The first experiments took place on August 10, 1910, in Blackpool, England. On February 18, 1911, the Frenchman Henri Piquet carried a small quantity of letters and printed matter for a distance of five miles, making the first air mail run in history. In the same year, for a period of three weeks corresponding to the festivities surrounding the coronation of George V, regular air-mail flights were made from London to Windsor. The short-term project was a resounding success: in just three weeks 25,000 letters and 90,000 postcards were successfully delivered. But it was in the United States that the concept of air mail really took off, acquiring a legendary status on a par with that of the Pony Express, with daring pilots and incredible machines battling against time and inclement weather, all in the name of dependable service. The crowning moment of the early days came in 1920: with Omaha finally connected to Sacramento, the dream of a coast-to-coast route from New York to San Francisco had become a reality. The flight was an arduous test of endurance, determination and planning. Going west it took 34 hours and 20 minutes, going east 29 hours and 15 minutes, and new planes had to be provided six times during the journey: at Cleveland, Chicago, Omaha, Cheyenne, Salt Lake City, and Reno.

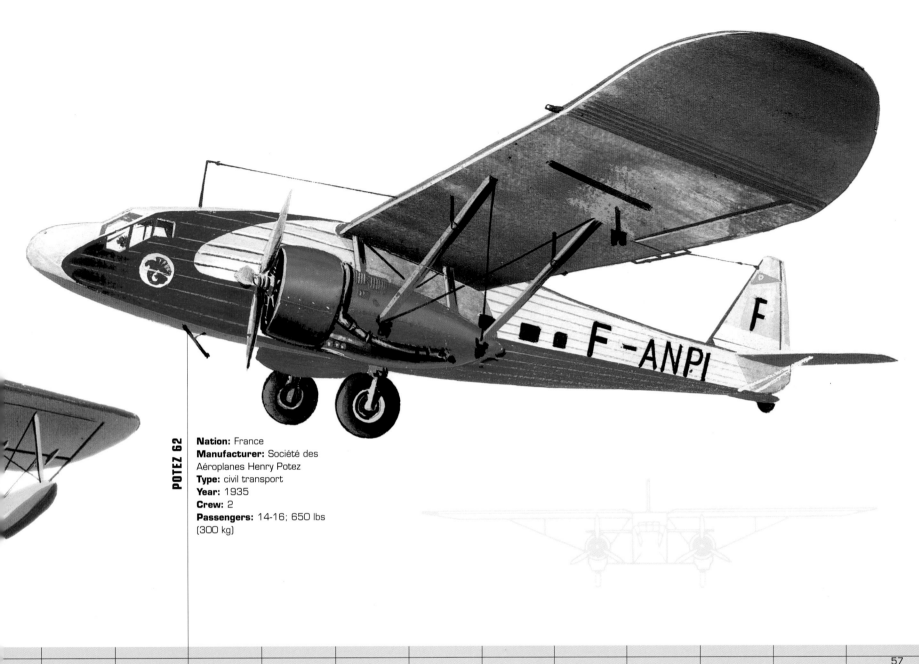

POTEZ 62

Nation: France
Manufacturer: Société des Aéroplanes Henry Potez
Type: civil transport
Year: 1935
Crew: 2
Passengers: 14-16; 650 lbs (300 kg)

government began sponsoring the development of the sector, and after numerous difficulties in finding the right aircraft for the job, the first postal route connecting New York to Washington D.C. was opened on May 15, 1918, using old Curtiss JN-4H military training planes. By August of that year new machines had been designed specifically for that purpose, and in 1919 the national postal fleet numbered about 120 aircraft, thanks in large part to the

acquisition of a hundred or so British de Havilland D.H.4 biplanes left over from the war. The postal network expanded quickly through the year 1920. Chicago was reached on May 15, and the New York-San Francisco route was established on September 8, 1920. The project grew until 1927, when the government decided to privatize, with Boeing Air Transport taking the Chicago-San Francisco route and National Air Transport taking Chicago-New

York. Up to that point, the federal postal service had flown 10 million miles and delivered 6.5 million tons of mail. Numbers aside, the success of the postal service marked a definitive shift in the official attitude toward civil aviation and provided the commercial and industrial incentive that would soon make America the world leader in aerial transport. Numerous companies were created at that time, opening up new subsidiary postal and passenger

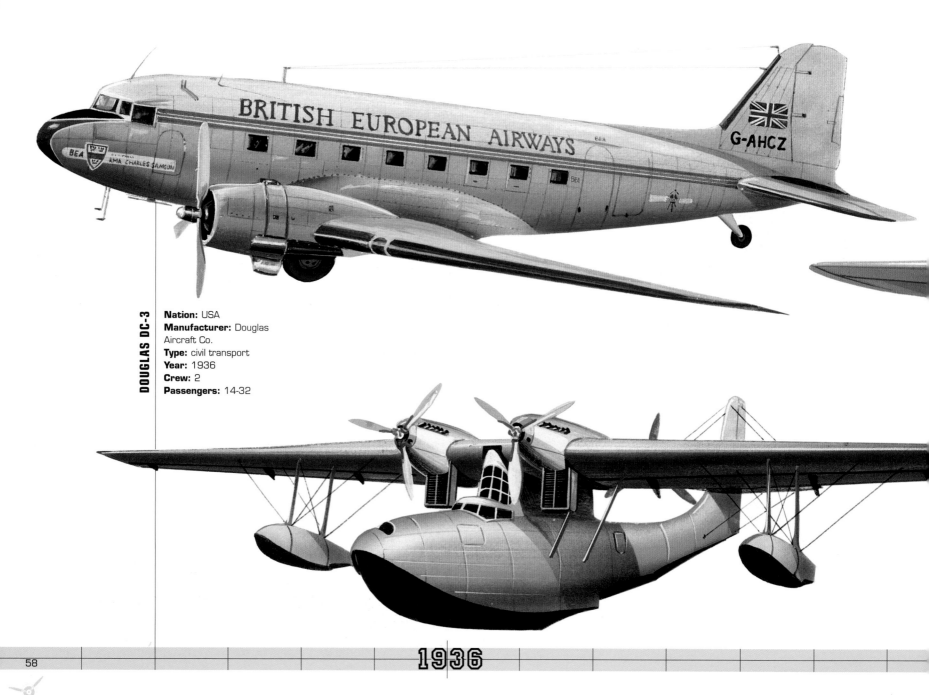

Nation: USA
Manufacturer: Douglas Aircraft Co.
Type: civil transport
Year: 1936
Crew: 2
Passengers: 14-32

1936

routes. Among the busiest were Colonial Air Transport, National Air Transport, Ford Motor and Western Air Express, the latter of which took its place in the record books by opening the first regular passenger service between Los Angeles and Salt Lake City by way of Las Vegas on May 23, 1926.

The real impetus for the massive development to come, however, was Charles Lindbergh's 1927 historic transatlantic solo flight.

The public was seized anew with 'airplane fever,' and more importantly, key industrialists and policy-makers were finally convinced that the airplane was a safe and dependable means of transport and was ready for commercial exploitation. It was in this climate of optimism that the first great American airline was born, Transcontinental Air Transport (TAT), an initiative financed by such important shareholders as the Wright Brothers, Curtiss and

the Pennsylvania Railroad. The man of the moment, Charles Lindbergh, was named director of technical operations. From that moment on, the story of American air transport is a veritable leap-frog contest characterized by newer and smarter enterprises, technological advances and corporate mergers, culminating in the 1930s with the creation of what history would remember as the 'Big Five': American Airlines, formed from the merger of fifteen

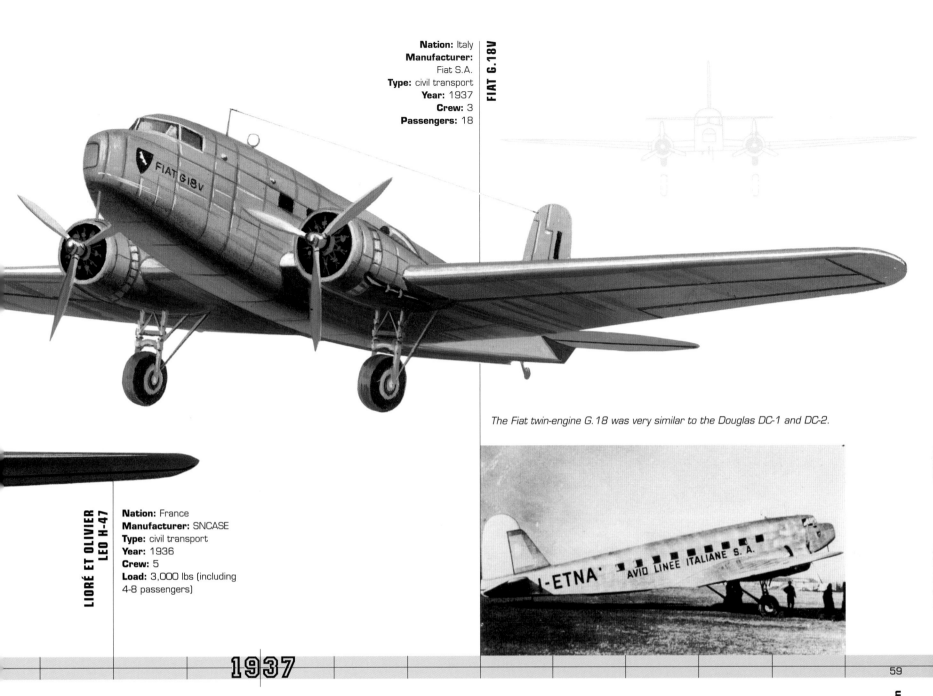

Nation: Italy
Manufacturer:
Fiat S.A.
Type: civil transport
Year: 1937
Crew: 3
Passengers: 18

FIAT G.18V

The Fiat twin-engine G.18 was very similar to the Douglas DC-1 and DC-2.

LIORÉ ET OLIVIER
LEO H-47

Nation: France
Manufacturer: SNCASE
Type: civil transport
Year: 1936
Crew: 5
Load: 3,000 lbs (including
4-8 passengers)

1937

59

Commercial aviation is born

companies; United Airlines, a conglomerate of six airlines; Eastern Air Lines and Transcontinental & Western Air (TWA), each made up of two smaller airlines; and last but not least, Pan American Airways, which would quickly become the single largest airline in the world. In the shadow of these giants many smaller companies proliferated, by 1930 already numbering more than 40, with an overall fleet of 500+ aircraft and a territorial coverage of nearly

35,000 miles. This furious expansion soon brought the United States to a position of unchallenged domination in the field. With more than 160,000 passengers served in 1929 alone – a 160% increase over the 60,000 of the year before – the US had outperformed Germany, number one in Europe, by nearly 50,000 passengers. Needless to say, technology and industry grew at an equal pace with the air transport market. From its secondary

status in the period immediately following the Great War, the aeronautical industry gradually became a driving force of the American economy. The products introduced by Boeing, Douglas, Lockheed and Sikorsky became known the world over, and the resulting prosperity corresponded directly with that of America as a whole. To this day we still fly on the descendents of the Boeing 247 of 1933, the first modern passenger liner, and the Douglas DC-1,

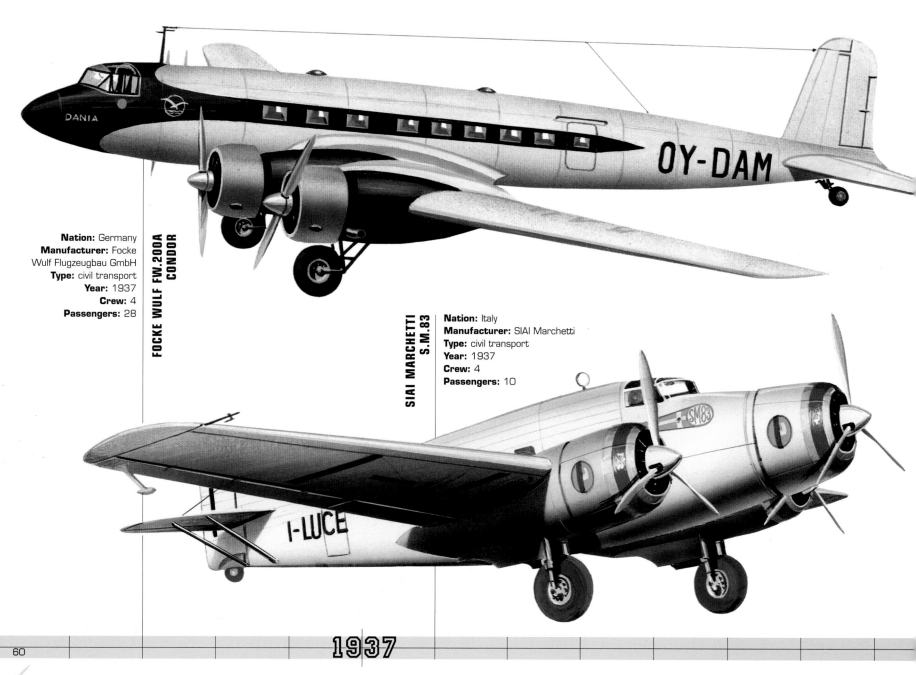

Nation: Germany
Manufacturer: Focke Wulf Flugzeugbau GmbH
Type: civil transport
Year: 1937
Crew: 4
Passengers: 28

FOCKE WULF FW.200A CONDOR

DANIA

OY-DAM

SIAI MARCHETTI S.M.83

Nation: Italy
Manufacturer: SIAI Marchetti
Type: civil transport
Year: 1937
Crew: 4
Passengers: 10

I-LUCE

1937

progenitor of the DC-3, the most famous transport plane in the history of aviation.

ITALY AND THE REST OF EUROPE

Italy was the last of the major European powers to develop commercial aviation. Though the first airlines were founded in 1923 (AEI and SISA) and 1925 (SANA, Transadriatica), the first regular commercial flights didn't get underway until 1926, when the country could

finally be said to have recovered from the political and economic crisis that followed World War I. Nonetheless, Italy can lay claim to being the first nation in Europe to have officially recognized postal transport as a valid investment for the future. Occasional service between Civitavecchia and Sardinia had been running since spring 1918, then on November 25 of that year a regular route connecting Venice, Trieste, Pola and Fiume was inaugurated. Italy's postal

service went international on March 2, 1919, when Caproni aircraft began transporting mail every three days between Padua and Vienna. Unlike the situation elsewhere, the success of the postal service did not serve to encourage the next logical step of passenger transport. In January 1920 there were only three operative postal routes in Italy: Rome-Pisa-Milan, Turin-Milan-Venice and Genoa-Pisa. The frontrunners in the European commercial aviation race,

Nation: Great Britain
Manufacturer: Short Brothers Ltd.
Type: civil transport
Year: 1939
Crew: 4
Passengers: 40

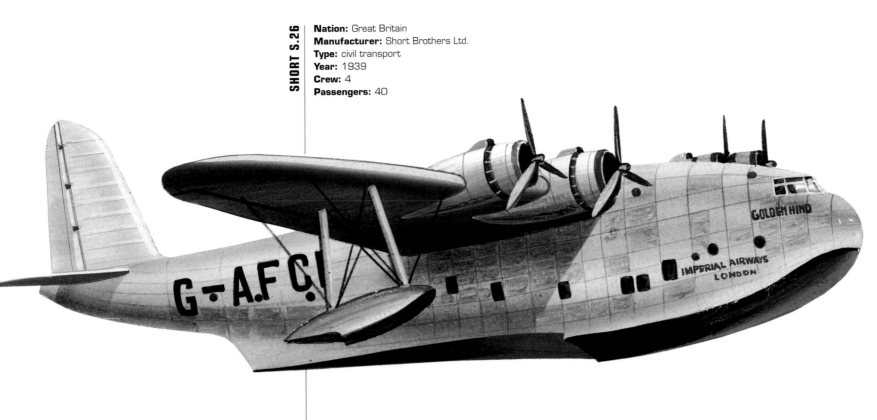

The first of the large C-series hydroplanes built by Short Brothers.

1939

France and Germany, seemed distant dots on the horizon. Then in 1926 Italy awoke with a jolt from its slumber. On February 1, Transadriatic opened the Rome-Venice route; on April 1, SISA inaugurated service between Turin, Venice and Trieste; six days later SANA began flying the Genoa-Rome-Naples route; and on August 1, Aero Espresso made the bold leap from Brindisi to Constantinople. With the entrance into the market in 1927 of the

Società Aerea Mediteranea (SAM) and in 1928 of Avio Linee Italiane (ALI), Italy had become a major player. By 1930 these six companies operated a network that extended from Rhodes to Tripoli to Berlin, and the number of passengers transported stood at 40,000, earning Italy a third-place finish behind Germany and France, and ahead of Great Britain.

The second half of the 1930s was Italy's

golden age of aviation. The success of Italian pilots in international competitions of the period was only one of the factors that drove civil aviation to new heights. Most important was an industrial base which had become efficient and forward-looking. Manufacturers were working at full tilt designing and building highly competitive new aircraft for both the military and civilian sectors. Expansion was inevitable and inexorable. On August 28,

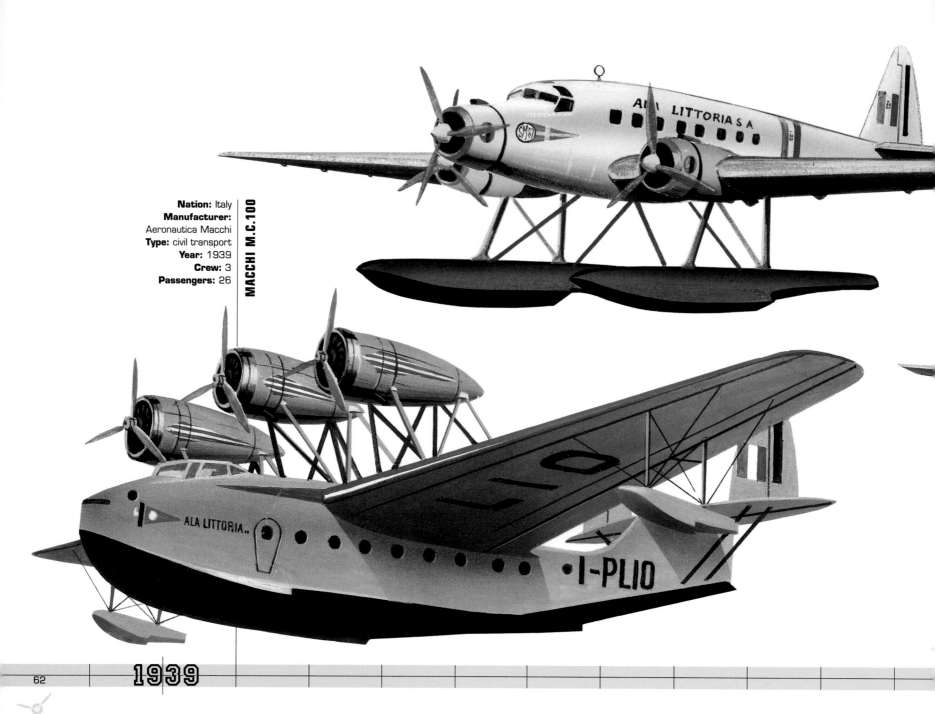

Nation: Italy
Manufacturer: Aeronautica Macchi
Type: civil transport
Year: 1939
Crew: 3
Passengers: 26

MACCHI M.C.100

1939

1934 the national airline Ala Littoria was formed from the merger of SISA, Aero Espresso, SANA and SAM (this last having absorbed Transadriatica in 1931), leaving ALI the only remaining independent airline. Advantaged by the economic and political support of the state, Ala Littoria was an immediate success and was thus able to tighten up its network of routes to the colonies, providing more flights to more destinations, as well as extend its European routes. On April 1, 1935 Budapest was reached, on July 29 Paris. Flights to Cadiz were added on December 7, 1936; Prague and Bucharest followed in May and October 1937. But the culmination of Italy's expansion came in 1939, when a subsidiary of Ala Littoria created specifically to serve South America, the Linee Aeree Transcontinentali Italiane (LATI), began offering regular service between Rome and Rio de Janeiro, making LATI the first airline to open up the skies of the southern Atlantic. Using SIAI Marchetti S.M.83 trimotors, LATI made weekly flights until a new war put an end to the enterprise in December 1941, just three months after having added service to Buenos Aires.

Of the other European nations that played a role in the evolution of civil air transport, the Netherlands is foremost, thanks to the activities of the great aircraft designer, Anthony

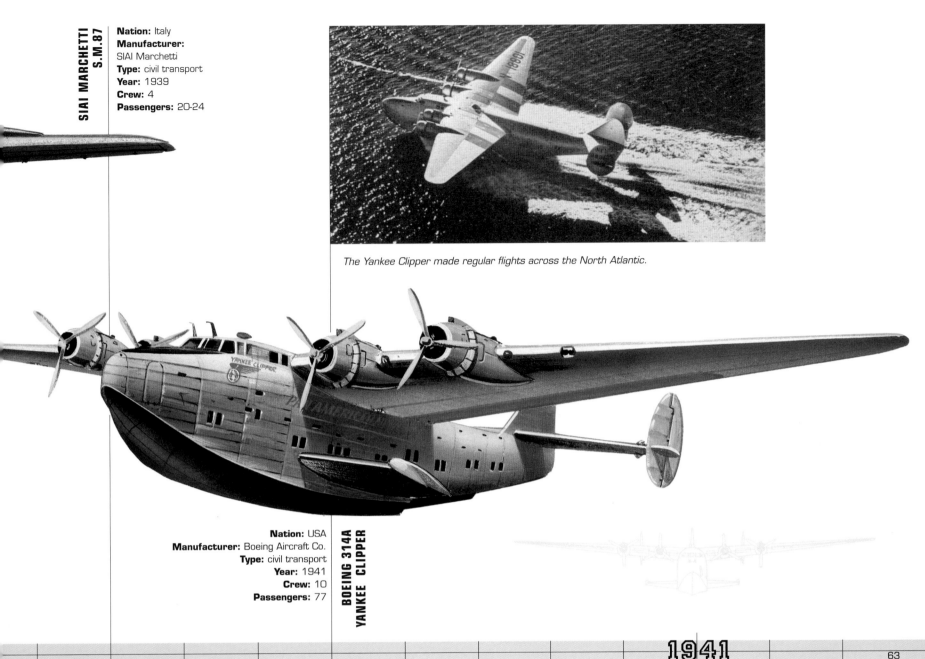

SIAI MARCHETTI S.M.87

Nation: Italy
Manufacturer: SIAI Marchetti
Type: civil transport
Year: 1939
Crew: 4
Passengers: 20-24

The Yankee Clipper made regular flights across the North Atlantic.

Nation: USA
Manufacturer: Boeing Aircraft Co.
Type: civil transport
Year: 1941
Crew: 10
Passengers: 77

BOEING 314A YANKEE CLIPPER

1941

Fokker. Renowned for the fighters he designed for the Germans during the World War I, he returned to his native land at war's end to build a factory dedicated to the production of commercial airplanes. The prototype of all his transport planes was the F.II, the model that would help transform a small airline known as KLM (Koninklijke Luchtvaart Maatschapij, or Royal Dutch Airlines) into a world leader. Founded on October 7, 1919, KLM began offering regular passenger service between Amsterdam and Croydon, England in a Fokker F.II on September 30, 1920. This marked the beginning of a unique relationship that would last for many years, until 1934 to be exact, when KLM's founder Albert Plesman rejected Anthony Fokker's most ambitious aircraft design to date – the F.XXXVI – in favor of the American twin-engine Douglas DC-2. Nevertheless, the names of Fokker and KLM will remain forever linked in the history books as the first exclusive collaboration between airline and manufacturer, whereby the latter built not 'generic' planes for the wider market, but custom aircraft that responded to the specific needs of KLM. The fame of Dutch planes, such as the Fokker F.VII series, and of the national airline soon transcended the borders of the tiny country and made itself felt throughout Europe and the rest of the world.

The Travel Air Mystery Ship won the 1929 National Air Races by breaking the 200-mph mark.

Opposite page: the Savoia S.13 bis, 1919

TEXACO Nº13

1913

THE QUEST FOR SPEED

THE EARLY AERONAUTICAL COMPETITIONS

BROUGHT EUROPE AND THE U.S. TOGETHER

IN A TECHNOLOGICAL RACE

TO BUILD A FASTER, BETTER AIRPLANE.

1935

Today, few of us are surprised by the performance of modern airplanes, accustomed as we are to considering even a supersonic jet a normal feature of the world around us. Flying from one hemisphere to another in a machine traveling six miles above the Earth at 600 miles per hour has become such a part of lives as to leave us almost indifferent. And as for the most advanced military aircraft, we are more likely to be astounded by their astronomical costs than by the fact that they are genuine miracles of modern technology, probably because their technology is so incredibly sophisticated that we cannot wrap our minds around it. So we just take it for granted. A hundred years ago, however, the idea of flying faster than an automobile or a train, of pushing this newborn means of transport to its limits in thrilling sportsmanly competitions fascinated both the pioneers of aviation and the public alike. Every foot in altitude, every yard in distance, every mile per hour faster signified victory, success, the conquest of a new threshold. It would be impossible to overestimate the importance of the spirit that guided these competitions for the evolution of the modern airplane.

The first great aviation fair in history,

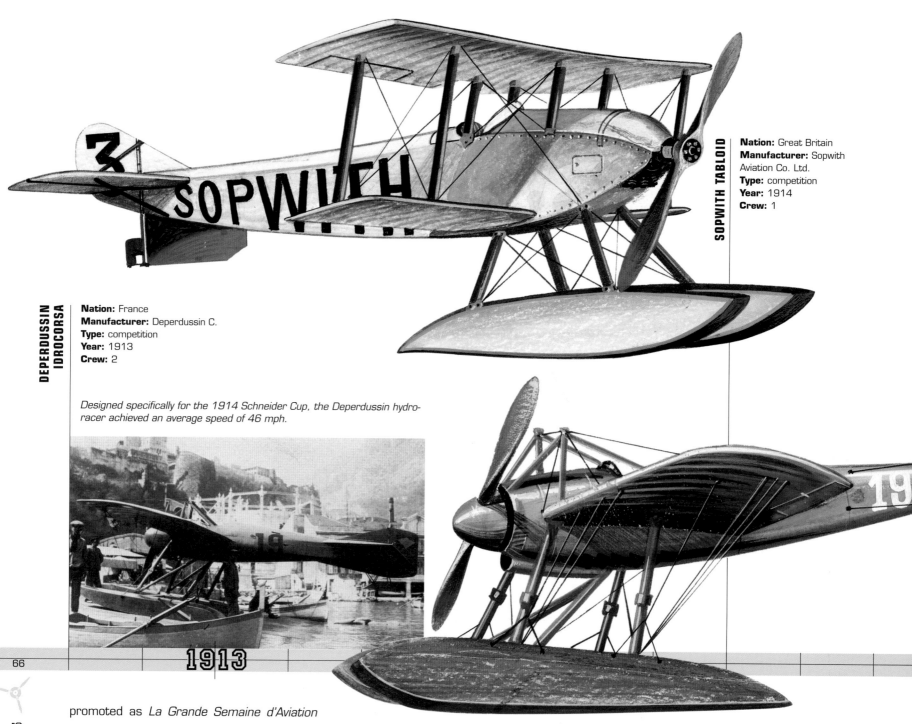

Nation: Great Britain
Manufacturer: Sopwith
Aviation Co. Ltd.
Type: competition
Year: 1914
Crew: 1

Nation: France
Manufacturer: Deperdussin C.
Type: competition
Year: 1913
Crew: 2

Designed specifically for the 1914 Schneider Cup, the Deperdussin hydro-racer achieved an average speed of 46 mph.

1913

promoted as *La Grande Semaine d'Aviation de la Champagne*, was held in the environs of Reims, France, August 22-29, 1909. Organized by wine producers of the outlying Champagne region, it was not just an air meet, it was an affirmation of the importance of the airplane and all it represented. The cream of European society attended: generals, princes, ambassadors, industrialists and politicians abounded, and the atmosphere

was charged with the electric enthusiasm that had been generated by Louis Blériot's crossing of the English Channel just one month before. Until the Reims Air Meet, the name by which the event came to be known, the breaking of flight records had been a solitary enterprise, with individuals in different parts of the world attempting to fly higher, faster, longer. Reims was the first time that

the pioneers of aviation gathered with their rickety flying machines to challenge each other on the same ground. The Gordon Bennett Trophy, a much sought-after speed/distance prize named for the American publishing magnate who sponsored it, was awarded to Glenn Curtiss and his Golden Flyer on August 28. The day before, Henri Farman had won the Grand Prix for having covered 120 miles

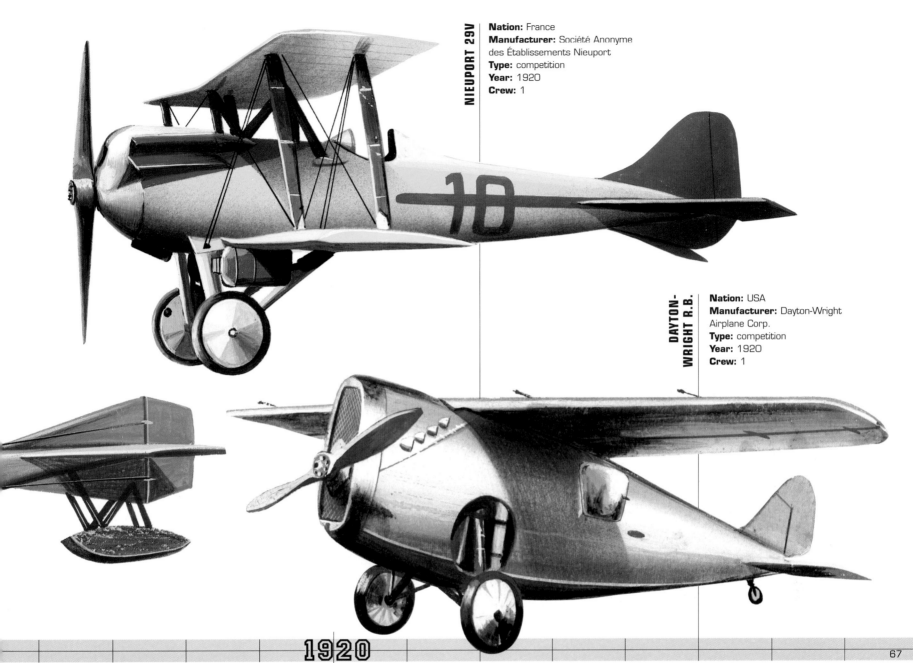

NIEUPORT 29V

Nation: France
Manufacturer: Société Anonyme des Établissements Nieuport
Type: competition
Year: 1920
Crew: 1

DAYTON-WRIGHT R.B.

Nation: USA
Manufacturer: Dayton-Wright Airplane Corp.
Type: competition
Year: 1920
Crew: 1

1920

THE GORDON BENNETT TROPHY

History's first air speed race, the Gordon Bennett Trophy captivated the world during aviation's pioneer years. Five annual races were held prior to the Great War, from 1909 to 1913; the last race took place on September 28, 1920 at Étampes, outside Paris. The Étampes race was a particularly boisterous swansong for the Bennett Trophy, in that the British and American teams were ferociously determined to prevent France, which had won the 1912 and 1913 races, from winning the coveted trophy for the third time. The most fearsome adversary was an American plane, the Dayton-Wright R.B., a fast monoplane designed with Orville Wright's collaboration specifically for the Bennett event. The R.B. was very advanced for its day, with a closed cockpit, retractable landing gear, and even rudimentary wing flaps. But it was unlucky: a damaged guide wire forced the pilot to withdraw from the race. Lively discussion ensued, and there was even talk of sabotage. In the end, the winner was the Frenchman Sadi Lecointe in his Nieuport 29V, which covered the 200-mile circuit in 1 hour, 6 minutes and 17 seconds, with a fastest lap of 173.5 miles per hour. Indeed, the winner's podium was entirely French: Bernard de Romanet placed second with a Spad 20 bis, and Georges Kirsch placed third in another Nieuport 29V.

The Nieuport of Sadi Lecointe, winner of the Gordon Bennett Trophy, 1920.

The quest for speed

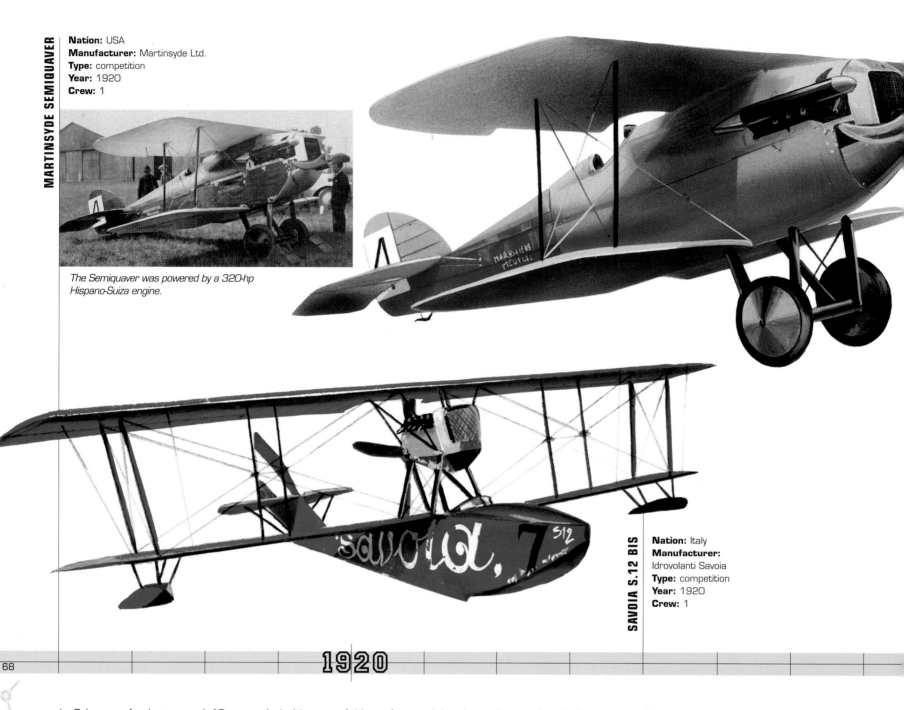

MARTINSYDE SEMIQUAVER

Nation: USA
Manufacturer: Martinsyde Ltd.
Type: competition
Year: 1920
Crew: 1

The Semiquaver was powered by a 320-hp Hispano-Suiza engine.

SAVOIA S.12 BIS

Nation: Italy
Manufacturer: Idrovolanti Savoia
Type: competition
Year: 1920
Crew: 1

in 3 hours, 4 minutes and 46 seconds in his Farman III biplane. Other important records were set that week by the Blériot XII, which managed to acheive what was then the incredible speed of 48 miles per hour, and by the Antoinette VII, which climbed to the unprecedented altitude of 505 feet, earning for its pilot Hubert Latham the impressive sum of 10,000 francs.

The enthusiasm and collegial exchange of ideas fostered by these international air meets were put on hold for the duration of World War I, but returned full force immediately afterward. The airplane had evolved by leaps and bounds during the conflict: its structure was more solid and its materials more resilient, its engines were more powerful and its aerodynamics more finely tuned. Dependability and maneuverability had improved a hundredfold. And so it was that speed became once again the predominant concern, and air meets were the perfect forum for testing and demonstrating it. The competitions involved pilots, manufacturers, businessmen, sponsors, technicians and aficionados, and very often also captured the interest of governments and the military establishment, who were fully aware that faster stunt planes today meant better warplanes tomorrow. The popularity of the phenomenon

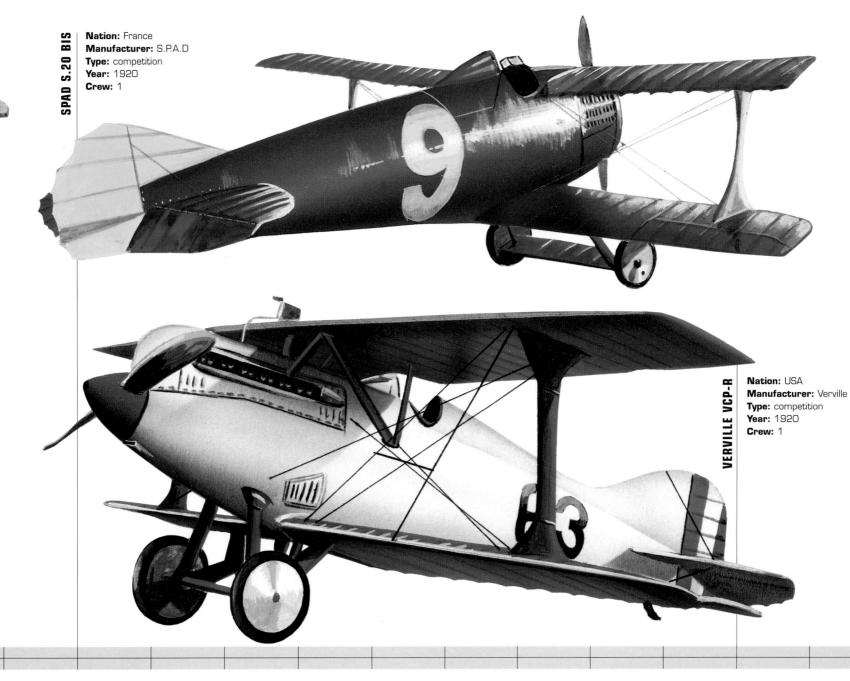

Nation: France
Manufacturer: S.P.A.D
Type: competition
Year: 1920
Crew: 1

Nation: USA
Manufacturer: Verville
Type: competition
Year: 1920
Crew: 1

grew with equal intensity on both sides of the Atlantic until the 1930s. Meets, fairs and races were held more or less everywhere, but certain of them assumed particular importance from the outset. In Europe, the most prestigious was the Schneider Cup, which represented both the pinnacle and the end of the great European air challenges. In the States the legendary National Air Races overshadowed all others, drawing thousands

THE AERIAL DERBY AND THE BEAUMONT CUP

The British passion for air meets was no less than France's. The first important speed race of the post-war years was the 4th annual Aerial Derby, held on June 21 1919 at Hendon, where the competitors had to fly a circuit around London. The trophy at stake, instituted and sponsored by the *Daily Mail* newspaper, had been won the first three years in a row (1912-14) by French planes. This time, however, it was Britain's turn, as it would be for the next four years of the race. Among the many interesting new airplanes competing, the Martinsyde Semiquaver was a standout. When it averaged 155 mph in the 1920 Derby race, its comical name became synonymous with speed in the public imagination. The rivalry between Great Britain and France was perpetuated in two meets of another important race, the Beaumont Cup, sponsored by the American-born industrialist Louis D. Beaumont in 1924 and 1925. The circuit was about 200 miles long, but there was a very specific clause attached: in order to claim the tantalizing prize of 100,000 francs, the pilot did not simply have to be the fastest, but had to maintain an average speed of at least 180 miles per hour. It was one of Gustave Delage's 'thoroughbreds of the sky' designed for Nieuport that rose to the challenge, leaving its adversaries in the dust. Piloted by Sadi Lecointe, the Nieuport-Delage 42 won both Beaumont Cup races, amply satisfying the strict conditions: in 1924 it averaged 198.4 mph; in 1925, it dropped to 196.5 mph.

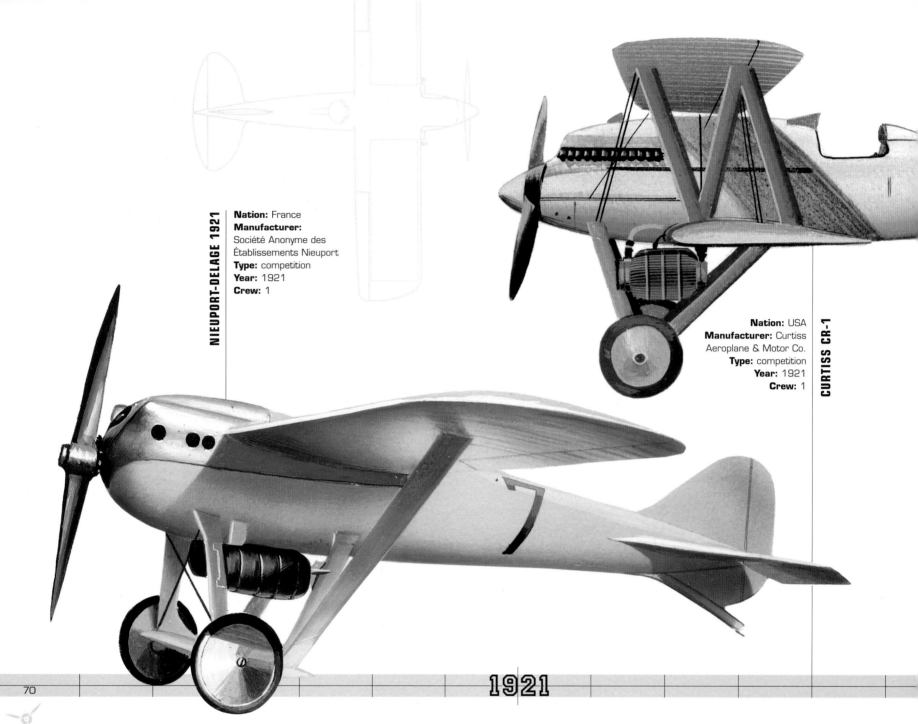

Nation: France
Manufacturer: Société Anonyme des Établissements Nieuport
Type: competition
Year: 1921
Crew: 1

Nation: USA
Manufacturer: Curtiss Aeroplane & Motor Co.
Type: competition
Year: 1921
Crew: 1

1921

of spectators and maintaining its popularity until the eve of World War II.

THE SCHNEIDER CUP

The Schneider Cup was the Olympics of hydroplane racing, with pilots exalting the nations they represented. Winning the Cup (contested 12 times between 1913 and 1931) boosted national pride. On December 5, 1912 the French industrialist, Jacques

THE DEUTSCH DE LA MUERTHE CUP

French planes, in particular those developed by Nieuport through the genius of its designer Gustave Delage, monopolized the five successive annual races that bore the name of an important figure in the history of aviation, the industrialist Henry Deutsch de la Meurthe. This fabulously wealthy airplane aficionado had instituted in 1912 a prize for the fastest plane to run a 125-mile circuit around the city of Paris. The first race (May 1, 1912) was won by a Nieuport piloted by Emmanuel Hellen, with an average speed of 78.6 mph. The second (October 27, 1913) went to Eugène Gilbert and his Deperdussin, average speed 102.2 mph. The competition was suspended during World War I, returning in September of 1919 for the third contest, which was taken by Sadi Lecointe in his Nieuport 29V, the winning speed now up to 166.4 mph. With de la Muerthe's death in 1920, the Cup as it had been was no longer, but it was replaced in 1921 by another race held in his honor. This time the distance was increased to 185 miles and the race was easily won by the new Nieuport-Delange monoplane piloted by Georges Kirsch (176.7 mph). In 1922 the victor was the same 29V that had just won the latest Bennet Trophy, flown by Fernand Lasne at an average speed of 181.2 mph. An Italian plane entered these last two races: the Fiat R.700 biplane, designed for the occasion by Celestino Rosatelli and outfitted with one of the most powerful engines of the time, the 700-horsepower Fiat A-14. Unfortunately, mechanical problems compelled the pilot Francesco Brak Papa to withdraw from the races.

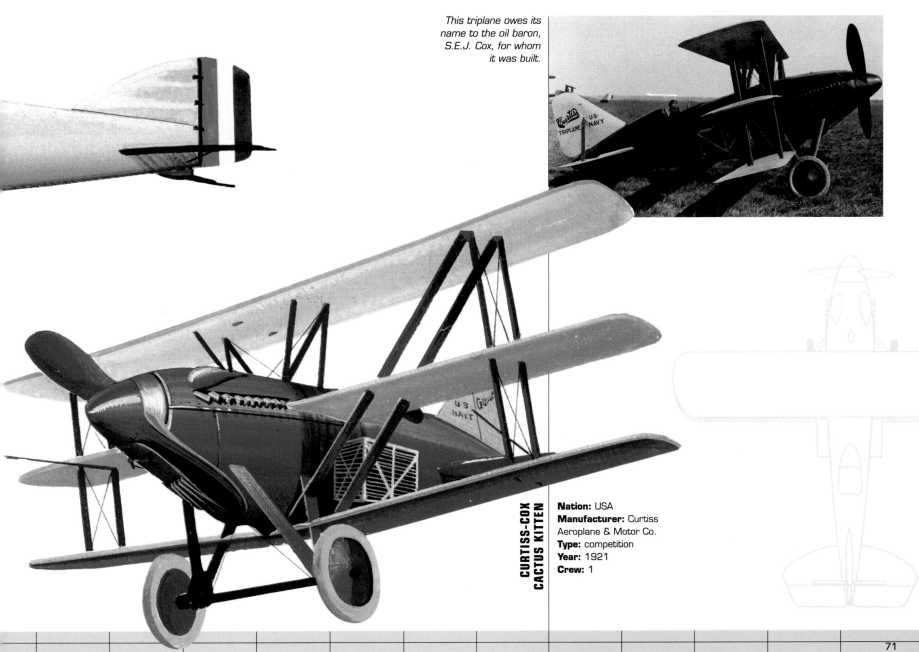

CURTISS-COX CACTUS KITTEN

Nation: USA
Manufacturer: Curtiss Aeroplane & Motor Co.
Type: competition
Year: 1921
Crew: 1

Schneider, announced the *Coupe d'Aviation Maritime* – the Schneider Cup. Any nation winning the trophy three times in five years also won 25,000 francs (ca. $75,000 in today's US dollars). Schneider hoped to encourage development of the hydroplane and its commercial use, an aim forgotten in the glamour of the competition itself.

The elaborate rules reflected the hydroplane's unique characteristics. Contes-

tants had to achieve the greatest speed on a 175-air mile circuit, taxi on water for 500 yards, and twice per race touch down at fixed points. In 1921 the rules changed to reflect recent improvements in aircraft performance: 175 miles became 250; 500 yards became 5,000 yards; planes also had to float at anchor for six consecutive hours – seaworthiness test. Aviation teams ('aero clubs') could enter three planes each, with

three in reserve.

The two pre-war Schneider Cup competitions were held in Monaco. On April 16, 1913 Maurice Prévost and his Deperdussin Racer won with a median speed of 46 mph – the only French victory. Prévost's speed was not extraordinary, but the rules were designed to award overall performance. In 1914 the British Sopwith Tabloid biplane – essentially a Camel with pontoons – won,

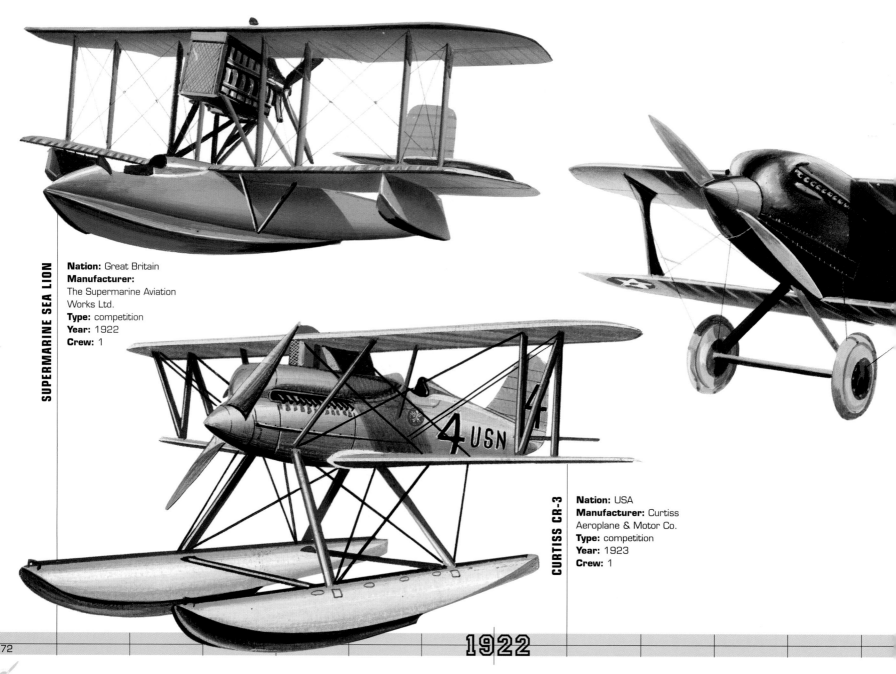

Nation: Great Britain
Manufacturer:
The Supermarine Aviation
Works Ltd.
Type: competition
Year: 1922
Crew: 1

Nation: USA
Manufacturer: Curtiss
Aeroplane & Motor Co.
Type: competition
Year: 1923
Crew: 1

1922

with Howard Pixton nearly doubling Prévost's average speed with a thoroughly respectable 87.3 mph. In the third event (delayed by WWI until 1919) increased significantly, Italy joined France and Britain, and dominated the competition for the next three years.

The 1919 race was annulled because of fog and procedural irregularities, but Guido Jannello in a Savoia S.13 bis finished the circuit, with an average speed of 131 mph.

The fourth competition, held in Venice on September 21, 1920, was won by Luigi Bologna, who averaged 106.6 mph in a Savoia S.12 bis. In August 1921, in Venice, Giovanni De Briganti piloted a Macchi M.7 to victory with a speed of 118.6 mph. The sixth competition, held on August 12, 1922 in Naples, looked promising for Italy until Henri Biard in his Supermarine Sea Lion II (the only British entry) stopped the chronometers at

an unbeatable 146.6 mph.

The Schneider Cup now reverberated across the Atlantic. The United States, ending its focus on its own competitions, decided to challenge Europe. In the next three competitions, the Americans made every effort to win and reestablish their aeronautical superiority, co-opted by Europe during WWI. They won with their first attempt: on September 28, 1923 on the Isle of Wight, David Ritten-

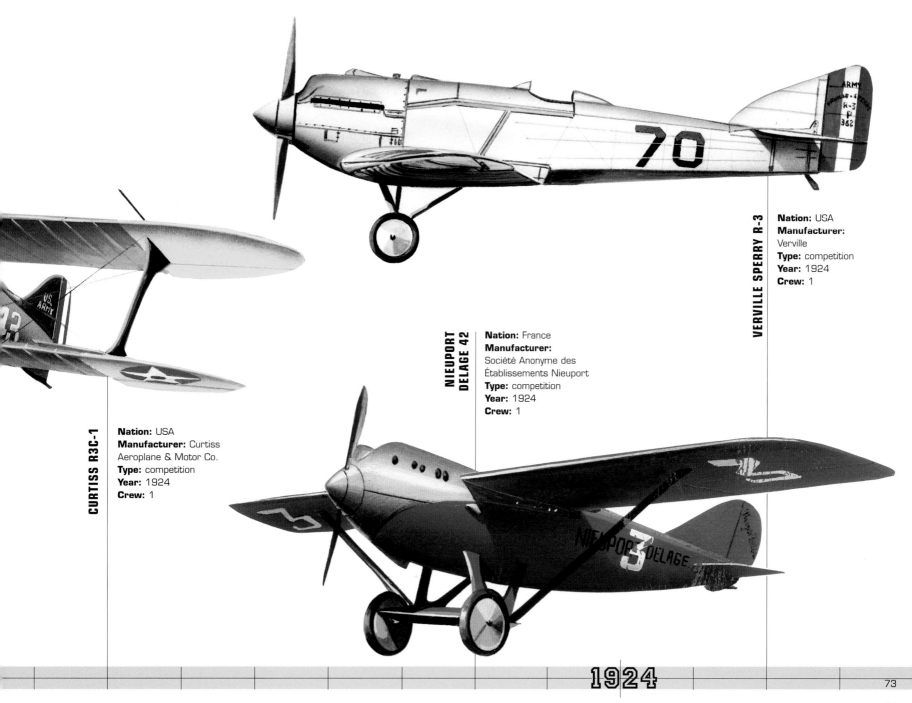

Nation: USA
Manufacturer: Curtiss
Aeroplane & Motor Co.
Type: competition
Year: 1924
Crew: 1

Nation: France
Manufacturer:
Société Anonyme des
Établissements Nieuport
Type: competition
Year: 1924
Crew: 1

Nation: USA
Manufacturer:
Verville
Type: competition
Year: 1924
Crew: 1

1924

house, flying Navy Curtiss CR-3 hydroplane (a variant of the Pulitzer Cup champion in the U.S.) defeated the British with an average speed of 178.3 mph. There was no 1924 competition because the British and Italian experienced technical problems, but in 1925 the Americans again won, this time with a Curtiss R3C-2 piloted by James Doolittle. But

The Verville-Sperry R-3 won the Pulitzer Trophy in 1924.

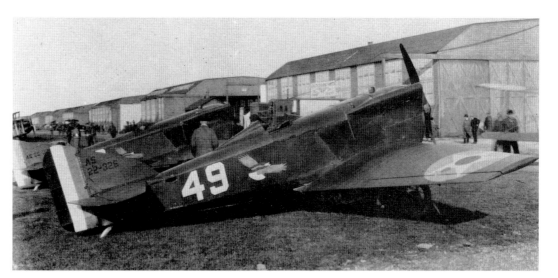

Nation: USA
Manufacturer: Travel Air
Type: competition
Year: 1929
Crew: 1

R614K

31

MACCHI M.39

Nation: Italy
Manufacturer:
Aeronautica Macchi
Type: competition
Year: 1926
Crew: 1

5

1926

the Americans were denied a third victory. On November 13, 1926, at Hampton Roads, Virginia, Marco De Bernardi in an Italian Macchi M.39 recorded an astonishing average speed of 243.1 miles per hour, roundly defeating the Americans on their home ground.

The Macchi M.39 won the 1926 Schneider Cup. Three planes of this type competed that year, piloted by De Bernardi, Ferrarin, and Bacula. The competition was held in Norfolk, VA, November 11-13.

Nation: Great Britain
Manufacturer: The Supermarine Aviation Works Ltd.
Type: competition
Year: 1931
Crew: 1

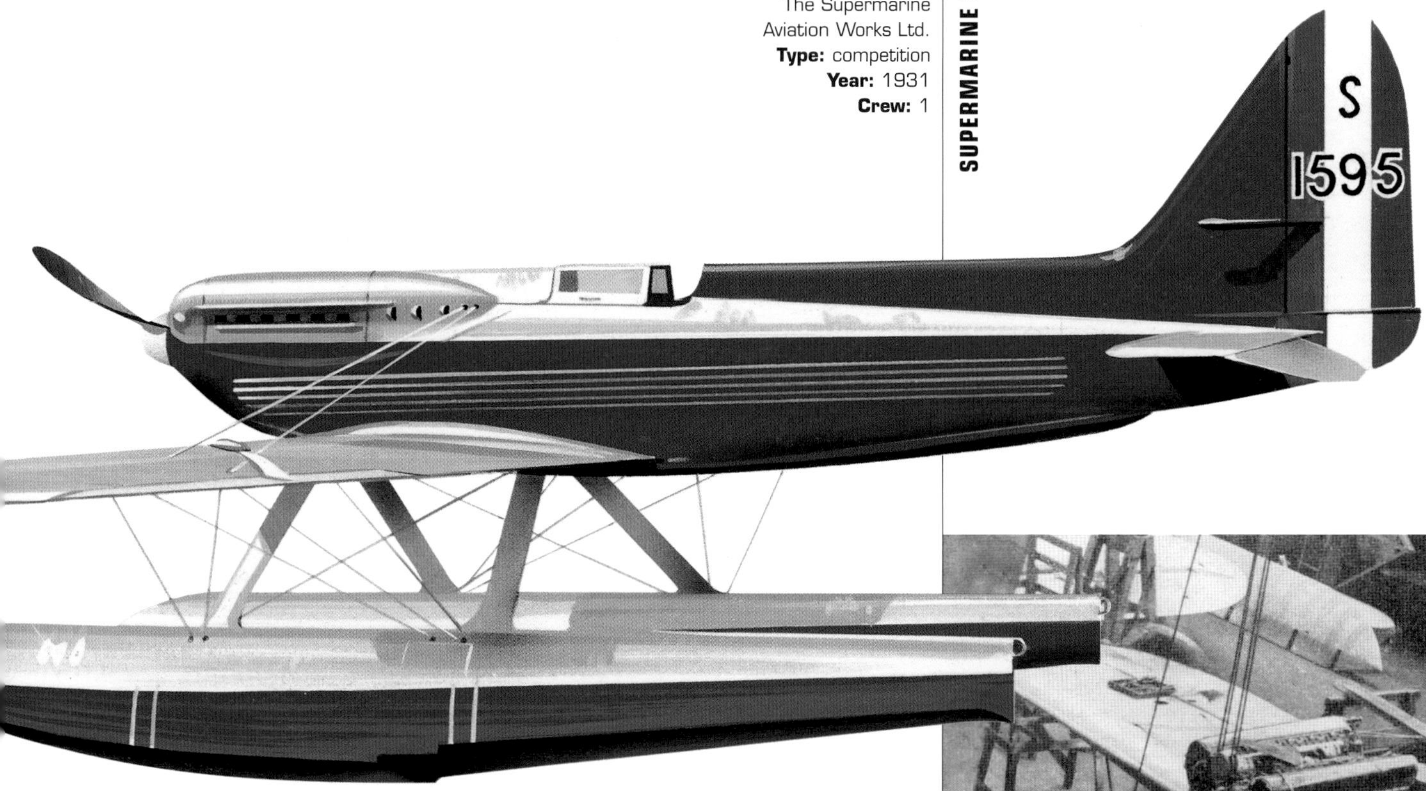

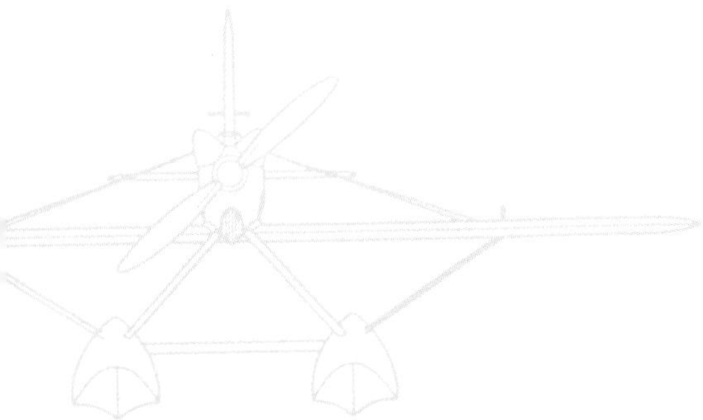

The engine of the Supermarine S.6B, winner of the 1931 Schneider Cup, was a 2,350-horsepower Rolls-Royce V-12 inline.

1931

The quest for speed

Whether because of damaged national pride or real economic problems, America withdrew from further competitions. Only Italy and Britain entered the next two competitions (1927, 1929). The British took revenge on the Italians, dominant early in the decade, by winning in September 1927, when S.N. Webster flew a Supermarine S.5 to victory in Venice (283.3 mph), and in 1929, when H.R.D Waghorn clocked 330.6 mph in his

Supermarine S.6 at Cowes. The 1931 Cup (the last) was something of a fiasco. John Boothman set a new world record of 342.1 mph in his Supermarine S.6B to 'win.' However, he flew alone against the clock; the French and Italian teams couldn't get their planes ready in time. In 1924, the chivalrous Americans postponed the event when the British and Italian teams were behind schedule; the British did not reciprocate in 1931.

Despite no further Schneider Cup competitions, the hydroplane continued to evolve, particularly in Italy. In 1933, on April 10, Francesco Agello set a new world record of 392.5 mph in the last, best and certainly most aesthetically beautiful of the great hydro-racers, the superb Macchi-Castoldi M.C.72. Six months later Agello broke his own record with a speed of 444.7 mph, which to this day remains unmatched.

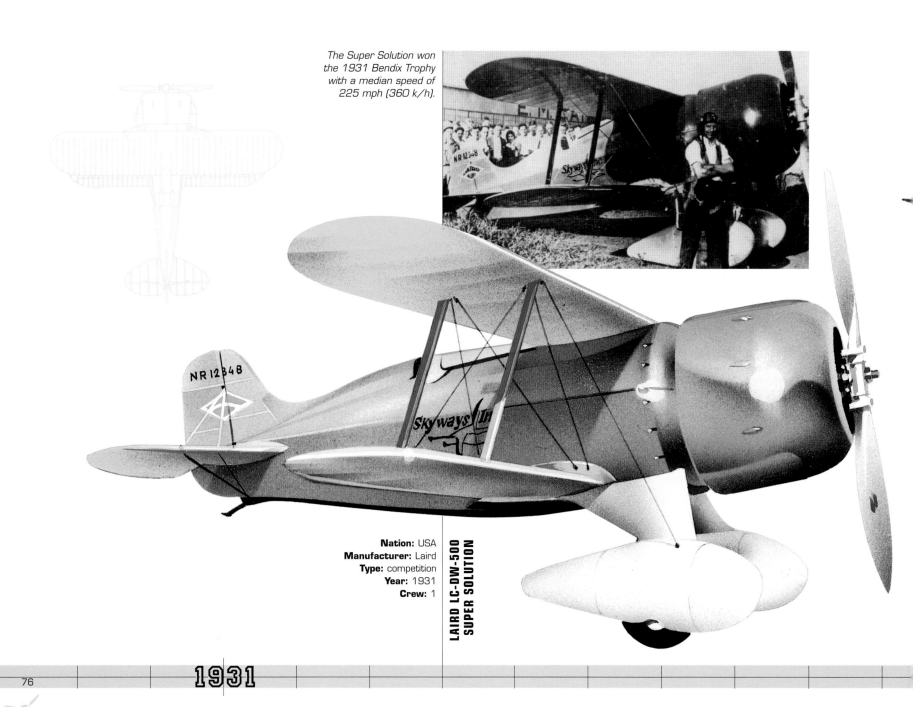

The Super Solution won the 1931 Bendix Trophy with a median speed of 225 mph (360 k/h).

Nation: USA
Manufacturer: Laird
Type: competition
Year: 1931
Crew: 1

LAIRD LC-DW-500 SUPER SOLUTION

1931

THE GREAT AMERICAN AIR MEETS

The Curtiss hydro-racer, winner of the Schneider Cup in 1923 and 1924, was among the brightest stars of a generation of competition aircraft that proliferated and prospered in the 1920s in America. Of the myriad air meets staged all over the United States in those years, a few matched the prestige of their European counterparts.

Perhaps the most stimulating from the pilots' and designers' viewpoint was the Pulitzer Trophy. Instituted in 1919 by the publishing brothers Ralph, Joseph Jr., and Herbert Pulitzer as a cross-country distance competition, it was absorbed into the larger context of the National Air Races in 1920 and transformed into a closed-course speed race. This enjoyed enormous popularity until 1925, after which interest began to wane.

If the Pulitzer Trophy was for a time more highly sought after than others, it was perhaps because there were US Navy and Army planes and pilots among the official entries. The planes were almost invariably the 'thoroughbreds of the sky' built for the military by Glenn H. Curtiss. In the 1921 race, military pilots claimed first and second place with the CR-1 and the Curtiss-Cox Cactus Kitten. The next year various Curtiss planes took the top four slots. In 1923 the Navy R2C-1 took first

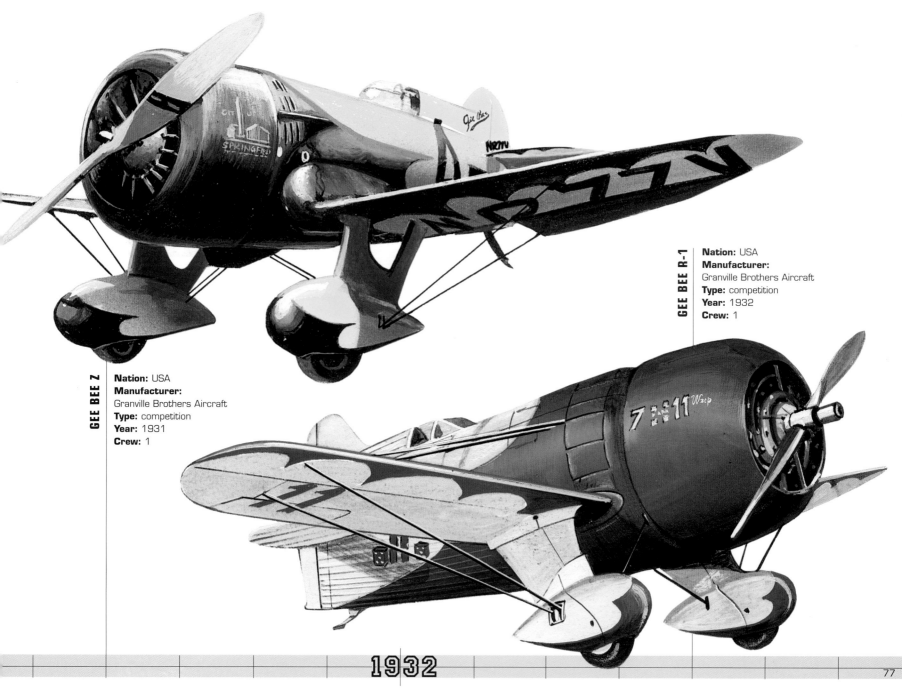

Nation: USA
Manufacturer:
Granville Brothers Aircraft
Type: competition
Year: 1932
Crew: 1

Nation: USA
Manufacturer:
Granville Brothers Aircraft
Type: competition
Year: 1931
Crew: 1

1932

GREAT BRITISH ENGINES

The Napier Lion, developed in the final months of WWI, was one of the most important British contributions to aviation of its day. Designed by A.J. Rowledge, it was a liquid-cooled inline, with twelve cylinders on three blocks – a format known as a 'W-block' – that generated 450 hp. The numerous versions produced over the years by Napier continued to increase in output until reaching 1,320 hp/3,600 rpm. The version that powered the Supermarine Sea Lion II, winner of the 1922 Schneider Cup, had a nominal output of 450 hp and a maximum of 531, with a turbocharger that made it the most powerful engine in the world at the time. Among the other great British engines was the Rolls-Royce V-12, designed in 1929 for the Supermarine hydro-racer that won the Cup two years later, thanks to the 2,350 hp/3,200 rpm performance of its superlative engine.

and second, and 1925 Curtiss repeated its feat of 1922 by taking the top four places with three different planes (1924 was a 'failure' insofar as Curtiss managed only the second and third places). When the military officially withdrew from all sporting competitions in 1925, the Air Races lost much of their importance until 1929, when the spark was reignited by the victory of the Travel Air Mystery Ship over Curtiss's latest Army fighter, the Hawk P-3A.

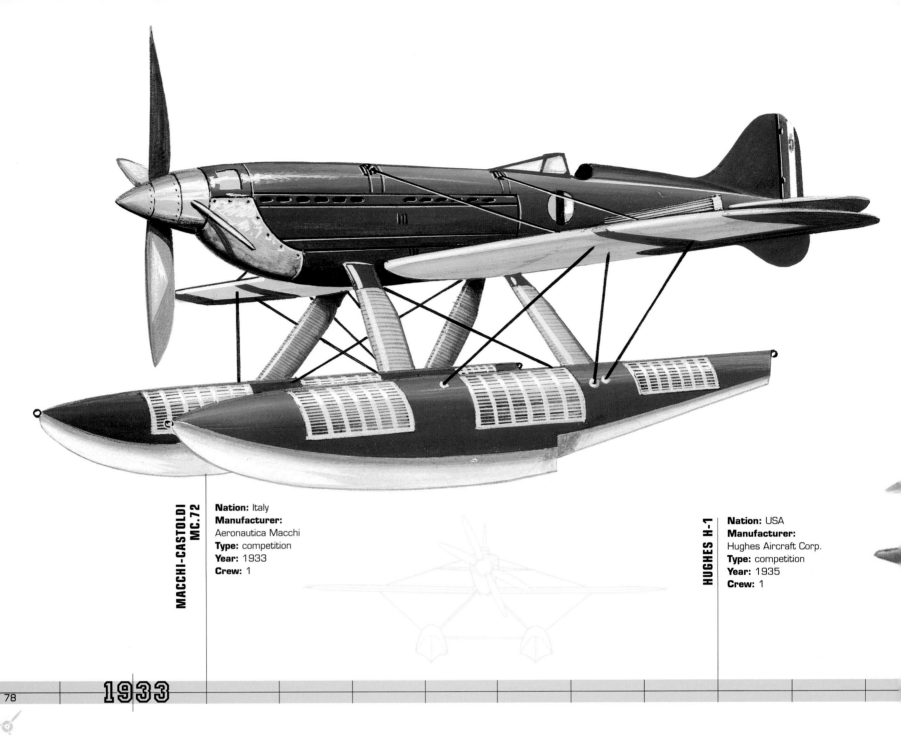

Nation: Italy
Manufacturer:
Aeronautica Macchi
Type: competition
Year: 1933
Crew: 1

Nation: USA
Manufacturer:
Hughes Aircraft Corp.
Type: competition
Year: 1935
Crew: 1

1933

1913-1935

In 1930 it was decided to institute another closed-course race that would match the charisma of the now defunct Pulitzer. And so the Thompson Trophy was born, which would be held annually until 1939, then resumed for a brief period after WW II. The radial engine was the distinguishing feature of the planes of this era. In fact, a radial had powered the Mystery Ship in its stunning and unexpected victory in the 1929 National Air Races event.

THE LARGEST ENGINE OF ITS TIME

The 24-cylinder Fiat A.S.6 engine, a veritable monster in terms of both power output and dimensions, gave Italy the world speed record for a hydroplane. Set on October 23, 1934 by Francesco Agello, piloting a Macchi-Castoldi M.C.72 at 444.7 miles per hour, the record remains, incredibly, unbeaten to this day. The A.S.6 is essentially the coupling of two V-12, liquid-cooled Fiat A.S.5 engines with the consequent double drive shaft, which made it possible to attach two propellers rather than one. The fact that the propellers were counter-rotating maximized the enormous output (3,000 hp, 3,300 rpm) as well as equalizing each other's powerful torque, rendering the plane extremely stable in flight. However, unlike British industry, which had taken the Rolls-Royce R and developed it into the immortal family of Merlin engines during World War II, Italian industry inexplicably did not take the Fiat A.S.6 any further. Despite having built the most powerful airplane engine in the world, in subsequent years Italy would completely lose track of the important advantages it had acquired during the Schneider Cup competition years. This oversight heavily penalized aeronautical development in Italy, with particularly crippling consequences during World War II. The problem was overcome, though far too late, only when the Germans began supplying Italy with its superb Daimler Benz inline engines.

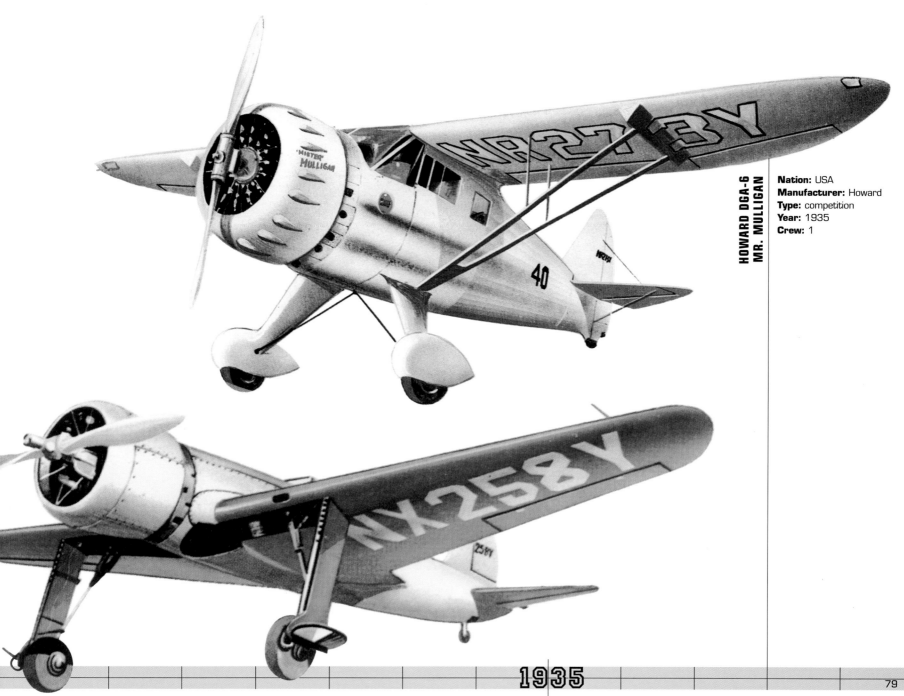

Nation: USA
Manufacturer: Howard
Type: competition
Year: 1935
Crew: 1

HOWARD DGA-6
MR. MULLIGAN

This powerful new engine type would be used by all the great protagonists of the Thompson Trophy: from Matt Laird's 'Solution' and 'Super Solution' to the Wedell-Williams racers; from the Laird-Turner L-RT Meteor (winner of the '38 and '39 trophies) to the tough little Gee Bee monoplanes that would become the most famous of all the American competition racers. A radial engine was responsible for the world speed record of 354 mph set in 1935 by the Hughes H-1, the same plane that two years later, in January 1937, set the long-distance speed record by flying from Los Angeles to Newark in 7 hours and 28 minutes: 2,504 miles at a median speed of 335.2 mph.

The Thompson Trophy Race wasn't the only game in town, however. From 1931 to 1939 another important competition, the Bendix Trophy, challenged it for headlines. Instituted by Vincent Bendix, president of the homonymous aeronautics company, it was a cross-country race from Burbank, California to Cleveland, Ohio, a distance of nearly 2,100 miles. Flying a closed-course pylon race was one thing, but crossing a continent demanded both speed and endurance. The competition served to inspire technological improvements in that regard which would prove useful in WW II. And in fact, a military fighter, the Seversky Sev-S2, won the last three Bendix Trophy races.

The arrival of the Blériot
XI at Northfall Meadow,
England.

Opposite page: The
Blériot XI's Anzani
engine and propeller.

1921

1921-1934

CONNECTING THE CONTINENTS

THE ERA OF TRANSOCEANIC CROSSINGS

LED TO THE DISCOVERY OF NEW ROUTES

WHICH PROVIDED THE BASIS

FOR TODAY'S COMPLEX AIR TRAFFIC NETWORK.

1934

"At the risk of smashing everything, I cut the ignition at 65 feet. Now it was up to chance. The landing gear took it rather badly, the propeller was damaged, but so what? *I had crossed the Channel!*" Surely there is no better way to capture the tension and excitement of that historic enterprise than to cite these words of its protagonist, Louis Blériot, the first man to fly across the English Channel. The great French pioneer had left Les Baraques, near Calais, at 4:41 AM on Sunday, July 25, 1909 and touched down at 5:17 in Northfall Meadow, Dover, where today there stands a monument commemorating that nearly disastrous landing. But the 24.1 miles in between had been even worse. The distance to be covered stretched the theoretical range of the tiny 25-hp Anzani engine, which tended to sputter at the end of every piston stroke, covering the pilot in a thick film of grease and grime. The risk of failure was great. "For ten long minutes I kept on, lost in that vast area," wrote Blériot, "seeing nothing on the horizon. Then the wind and the mist caught me, and I had to fight it with my hands, my eyes. Where the devil was I?" Finally the silhouette of the English coast appeared through the fog, and the nightmare quickly turned to joy. "England's isolation has

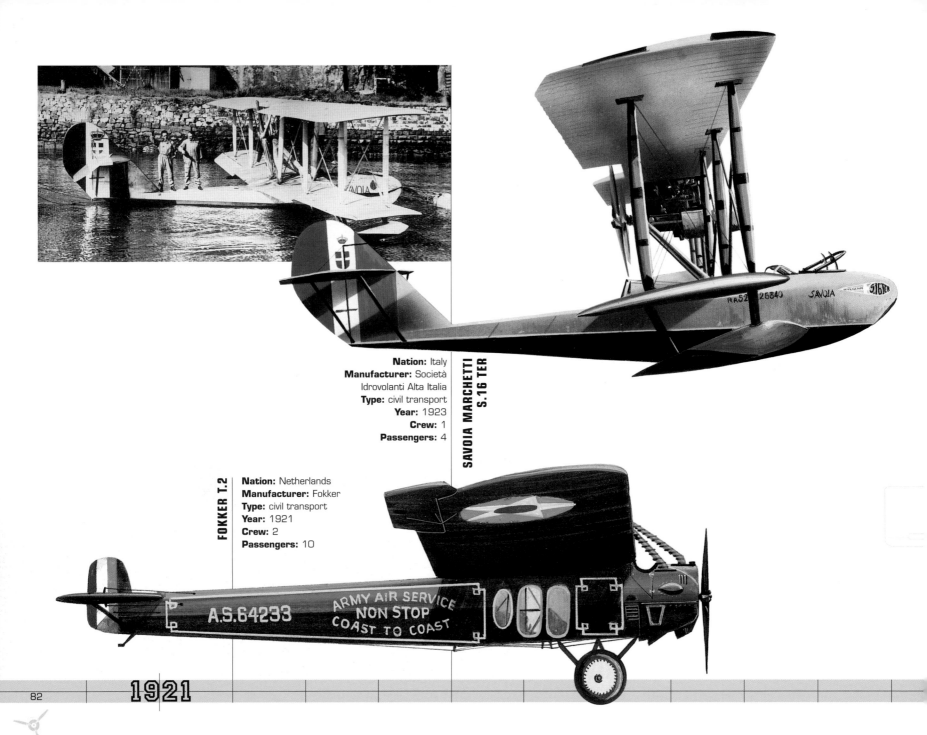

Nation: Italy
Manufacturer: Società Idrovolanti Alta Italia
Type: civil transport
Year: 1923
Crew: 1
Passengers: 4

SAVOIA MARCHETTI S.16 TER

FOKKER T.2

Nation: Netherlands
Manufacturer: Fokker
Type: civil transport
Year: 1921
Crew: 2
Passengers: 10

A.S.64233 ARMY AIR SERVICE NON STOP COAST TO COAST

1921

ended once and for all," announced a British newspaper the next day. And it was true. Blériot's flight had demonstrated for the first time that the airplane was capable of closing distances, crossing obstacles, and uniting nations. And thus a new challenge had been posed, one even more suggestive than the traditional one of speed, a challenge that would lead to the development of commercial aviation and transcontinental flight.

TAMING THE NORTH ATLANTIC

With the airplane having achieved maturity in the crucible of war, crossing the Atlantic Ocean was next great challenge. The idea had long fascinated aviators, but the airplane hadn't been ready for it. Now, in 1919, it was no longer inconceivable that man might conquer that enormous distance and its menacing meteorological conditions, at the time a notion no less daunting than that of reaching the moon

in the 1960s. It meant plunging into the unknown, challenging the forces of nature armed with nothing more than a machine and personal courage. Understandably, then, the men who dared to make the crossing were revered as heroes. The first were the Englishmen John Alcock and Arthur Whitten Brown who, on June 14-15, 1919 completed the first nonstop North Atlantic crossing. Their account of those 15 hours and 57 minutes reads like a

DORNIER DO.J WAL

Nation: Germany
Manufacturer: C.M.A.S.A.
Type: civil transport
Year: 1923
Crew: 2
Passengers: 8-14

The Do.J Wal touches down in New York Harbor after crossing the North Atlantic by way of Iceland and Greenland.

1923

thriller: they got lost several times in the thick fog, and the Vickers Vimy plane was so weighed down with ice that it barely managed to remain above the waves churned up by an unexpected storm. Six times during the flight, Brown had to overcome his mobility problems caused by war injuries to climb out of the cockpit to liberate the wings and air intakes from the ice that threatened to drag the plane into the sea. On two occasions, Alcock wrote what

he was certain were his last entries in the flight log, "so that they might be of use to other pilots."

Alcock and Brown had chosen the shortest possible easterly route, from Newfoundland, Canada to the westernmost tip of Northern Ireland, a total of 1,895 uninterrupted miles. Just one month earlier, the Atlantic had technically been crossed, but not without stops. On May 6, 1919, three Curtiss hy-

droplanes (Navy Curtiss NC-1, NC-3 and NC-4) took off from New York City for Trepassey Bay, Newfoundland with the intention of then covering the 1,406 miles to Horta, in the Azores. Two of the planes were forced to withdraw, but the third, the NC-4 piloted by Albert Read, made it to Horta. After rest and repairs, Read flew to Portugal on May 20, and then on to Plymouth, England, arriving on May 31. Another great feat consolidated the success of

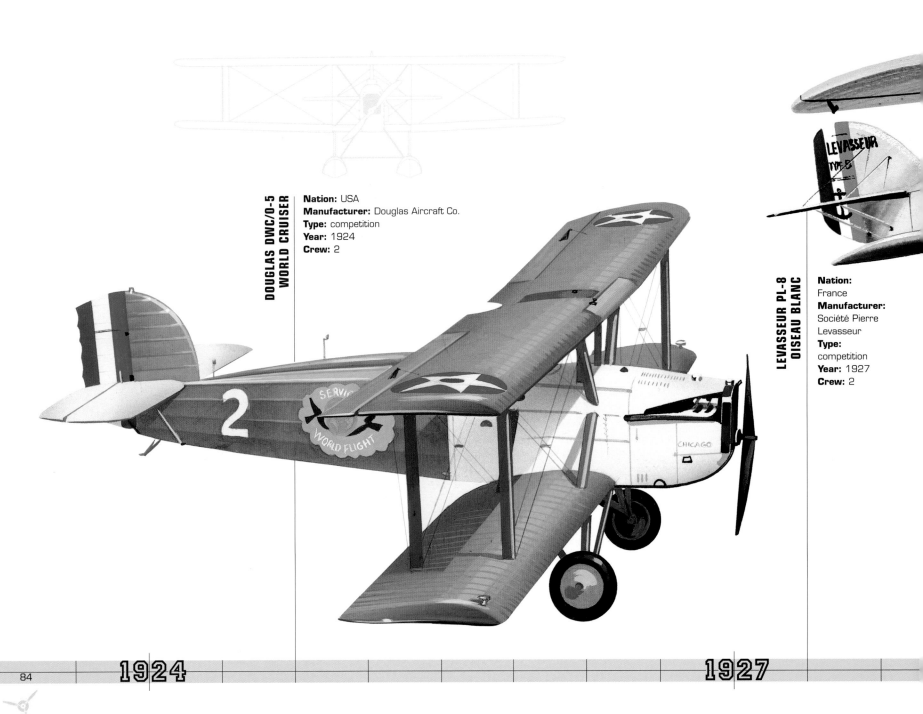

DOUGLAS DWC/O-5 WORLD CRUISER

Nation: USA
Manufacturer: Douglas Aircraft Co.
Type: competition
Year: 1924
Crew: 2

LEVASSEUR PL-8 OISEAU BLANC

Nation: France
Manufacturer: Société Pierre Levasseur
Type: competition
Year: 1927
Crew: 2

1924

1927

these ventures: the British dirigible R.34's two-way Atlantic crossing in July of the same year. At 1:42 AM on July 2, 1919 the gigantic airship lifted off at East Fortune, Scotland with 30 men aboard. Despite serious meteorological difficulties, the R.34 reached Mineola, New York four days later. The return flight departed at 3:54 AM on the 10th, and arrived at Pulham, Norfolk on July 13, having clocked 80 hours of flight time.

THE GREAT 'RAIDS' OF THE 1920S

In 1924 the United States organized a spectacular round-the-world 'raid,' the term used for long-distance flights of several planes in formation. Four Douglas World Cruisers were chosen for the enterprise, each named for an American city: Seattle, Boston, Chicago and New Orleans. The four US Navy biplanes took off from Seattle on April 6 and two of them – the Chicago and the New Orleans – touched down in that

same city on September 28, having successfully circumnavigated the globe by way of Japan, India, Persia, France and England. The total distance of 28,000 miles was covered in an elapsed time of 175 days, of which 371 hours of flight time at an average speed of 75 mph.

Meanwhile, the southern Atlantic Ocean, separating Africa from South America, had yet to be conquered. The southern crossing was first attempted in 1922 by a Portuguese

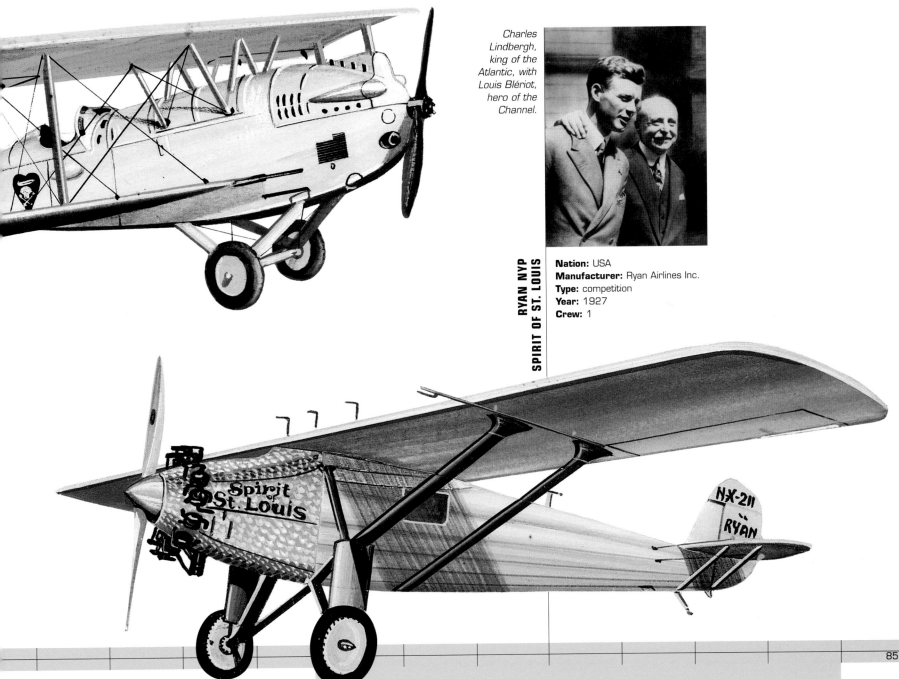

Charles Lindbergh, king of the Atlantic, with Louis Blériot, hero of the Channel.

Nation: USA
Manufacturer: Ryan Airlines Inc.
Type: competition
Year: 1927
Crew: 1

team, Sacadura Cabral and Gago Coutinho, who departed from Lisbon on March 30 in a Fairey III hydroplane and made it to Rio de Janeiro – with several stops along the way – on June 17. Numerous similar ventures were undertaken in the years that followed, but the first non-stop crossing of the South Atlantic wasn't made until 1928. The SIAI Marchetti S.M.64 was an exceptional plane, designed and built for the express purpose of breaking

A TRAGEDY OBSCURED BY LINDBERGH'S VICTORY

Charles Nungesser and François Coli are two names perhaps not as renowned as that of Charles Lindbergh, but which testify equally powerfully to the passion and enthusiasm that characterized the era of the transatlantic crossing. Unfortunately their attempt, which preceded Lindbergh's by just twelve days, ended in tragedy. Nungesser, third among France's great flying aces of WWI with 45 combat victories, had set as his goal the first non-stop transatlantic flight in a westerly direction, from Europe to North America. To this end he had carefully modified a plane originally used for military reconnaissance, the Levasseur PL-8 biplane, powered by a hardy Lorraine-Dietrich 450-horsepower engine. Baptized *Oiseau Blanc*, or 'White Bird' for its white sheathing interrupted only by the pilot's personal insignia and the French national colors, the plane took off from Le Bourget on May 8, 1927 at 5:21 AM with more than 1,000 gallons of fuel and navigator Coli aboard. Right from the outset, the adventure was fraught with bad omens: during take-off Nungesser had to jettison the landing gear because the plane was too heavy to lift off. The over-water leg of the trip went relatively well, but just as Nungesser and Coli sighted the Newfoundland coast the *Oiseau Blanc* was caught in a sudden and violent blizzard, and crashed into the sea.

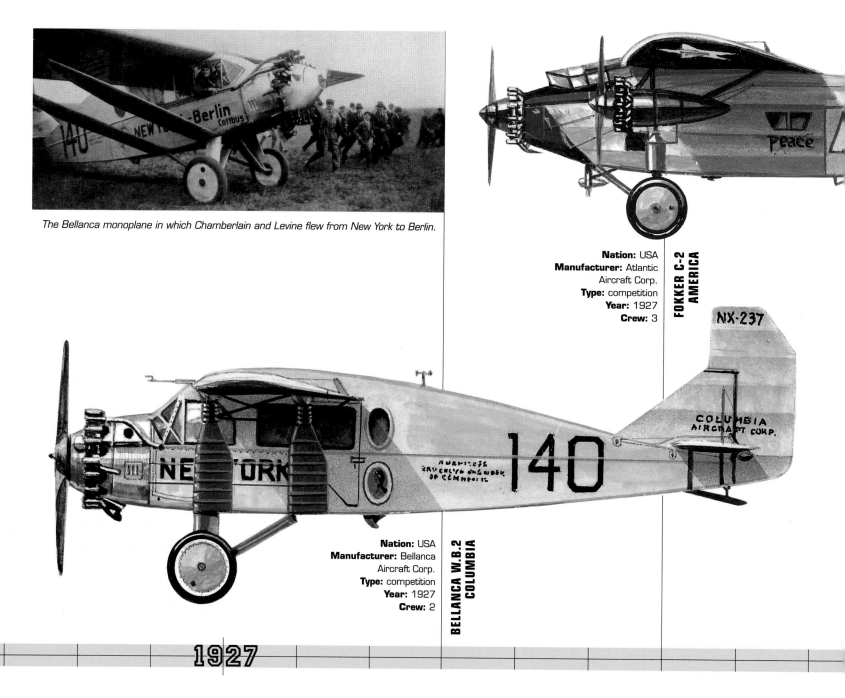

The Bellanca monoplane in which Chamberlain and Levine flew from New York to Berlin.

Nation: USA
Manufacturer: Atlantic Aircraft Corp.
Type: competition
Year: 1927
Crew: 3

FOKKER C-2 AMERICA

Nation: USA
Manufacturer: Bellanca Aircraft Corp.
Type: competition
Year: 1927
Crew: 2

BELLANCA W.B.2 COLUMBIA

1927

distance and endurance records. And this is precisely what it did on July 3, 1928, when Arturo Ferrarin and Carlo Del Prete climbed aboard at Montecelio, near Rome, and landed five days later at Port Natal, Brazil, having traveled 4,492.5 miles to shatter the world distance record. The record was challenged a year later by two French-built Breguet XIXs, but without success. The first, flown by the Spaniards Jiménez and Iglesias and baptized

Jesús del Gran Poder, flew from Seville to Bahia, Argentina for a distance of 4,087.5 miles – more than 400 miles less than the Italian team. The second, piloted by Challe and Borges, a Frenchman and a Uruguayan, also chose to depart from Seville but crashed two days later near Pernanbuco, Brazil.

MacReady and Kelly made the first non-stop flight across the North American continent, from New York to San Diego. Note the parachutes, which had become mandatory in 1924.

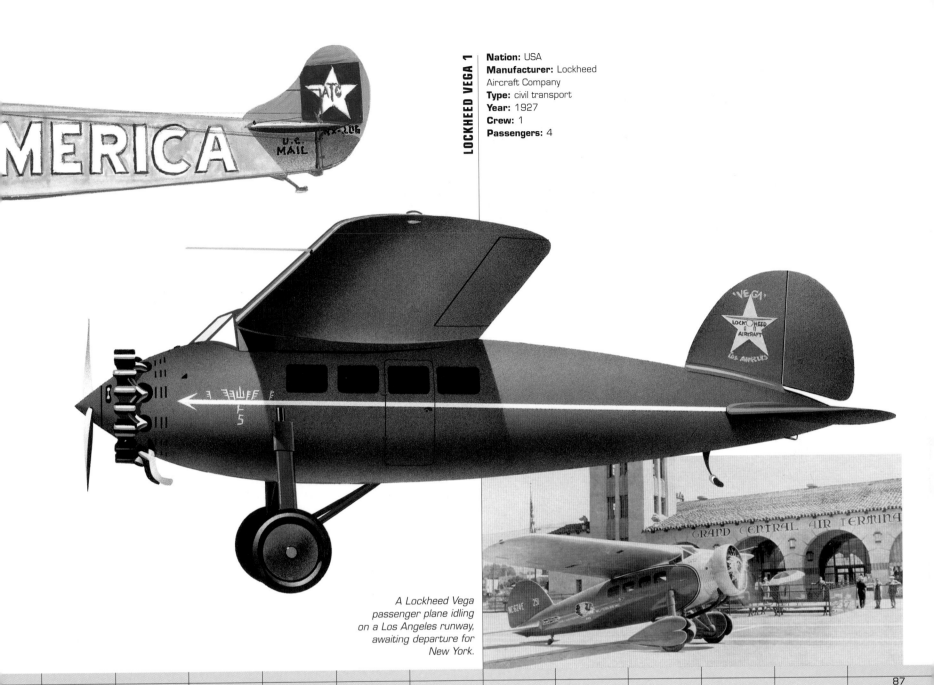

LOCKHEED VEGA 1

Nation: USA
Manufacturer: Lockheed Aircraft Company
Type: civil transport
Year: 1927
Crew: 1
Passengers: 4

A Lockheed Vega passenger plane idling on a Los Angeles runway, awaiting departure for New York.

87

Connecting the continents

The Italians had both a knack and a taste for extravagant cross-country raids. On February 11, 1920 two single-engine S.V.A.9s flown by Arturo Ferrarin and Guido Masiero, accompanied by mechanics Gino Cappannini and Roberto Maretto, left Rome for Tokyo, which they reached nearly 11,500 miles and four months later. Five years later Francesco De Pinedo and his hydro-biplane Savoia Marchetti S.16 ter proposed to make the same flight and then return by way of Australia. Leaving Sesto Calende on April 20, 1925, he and his mechanic Ernesto Campanelli flew to Tokyo, then to Melbourne, then to Rome, where they arrived on November 7. The figures: 360 air hours, 67 stops, and 34,400 miles, making it the longest flight in history to date.

The growth of commercial aviation and the concomitant need for new routes led to the exploration of Africa, with which Europe had important trade relations. The first to pave the way were the French, who by 1919 had already crossed the entirety of western Africa. The first Sahara crossing, from Paris to Dakar, was made between January and March 1920 by Vuillemin and Chalus, piloting a Breguet 16 Bn-2. The British opened the southern route when Alan Cobham flew a de Havilland 50J biplane from London to Capetown and back between November 16, 1925 and March 13,

Nation: Italy
Manufacturer: SIAI Marchetti
Type: competition
Year: 1928
Crew: 2-3

The S.M.64 of Ferrarin and Del Prete at Montecelio being readied to cross the South Atlantic to Brazil.

Nation: France
Manufacturer: Société Anonyme des Ateliers d'Aviation Louis Breguet
Type: competition
Year: 1929
Crew: 2

1928

1926. That same year the Frenchmen Dagnaux and Dufert flew from Paris to Tananarive (Antananarivo), Madagascar in a Breguet XIX. The aforementioned Cobham flew the last great African adventure between November1927 and May 1928, following all 22,500 miles of the continent's perimeter.

THE ATLANTIC CROSSINGS OF THE 1930S

The conquest of the tempestuous North Atlantic, however, was not by any means complete. Alcock and Brown's historic flight was bested in 1927 by Charles Lindbergh and his Ryan NYP *Spirit of St. Louis.* The story is well-known: on May 20 the small monoplane, loaded past capacity with fuel, took off from Roosevelt Field, New York, at 7:52 AM and landed at Paris's Le Bourget airport 33 hours, 30 minutes and 28 seconds later, having flown 3,544 miles at an average speed of 117.5 miles per hour. Lindbergh was greeted by a huge crowd in France, and once back in America he was celebrated as a national hero. Apart from the fact that he had flown between two viable metropolitan airports rather than between two points of felicitously proximate rocky coast, there was something about the fact that Lindbergh had flown solo that captivated the public. A few days later the Atlantic was challenged again, this time by a Bellanca W.B.2 Columbia flown by

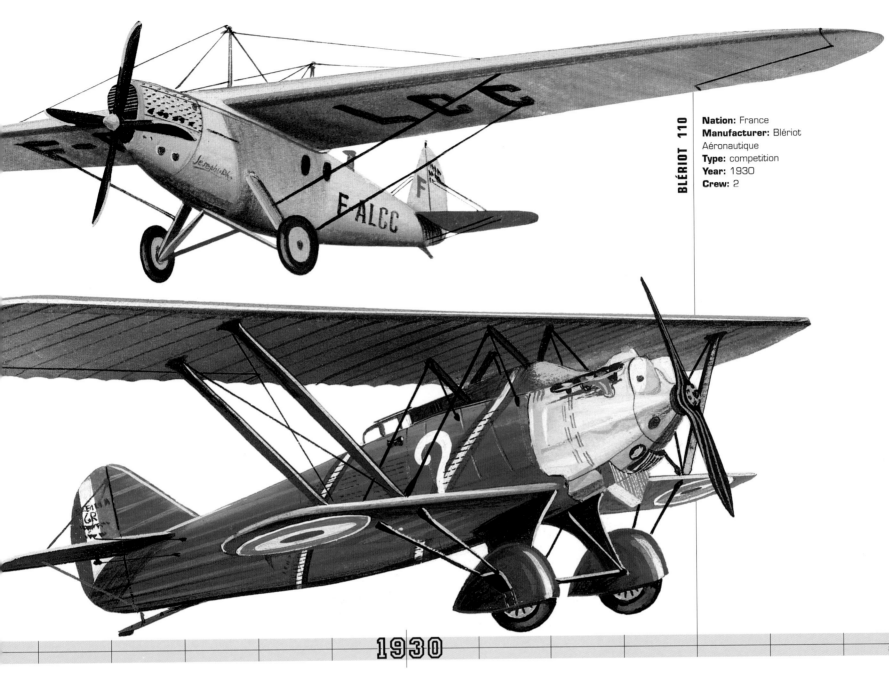

BLÉRIOT 110

Nation: France
Manufacturer: Blériot Aéronautique
Type: competition
Year: 1930
Crew: 2

1930

Clarence Chamberlin and Charles Levine. Their flight from Roosevelt Field to Berlin was almost 400 miles longer than Lindbergh's, but didn't receive nearly as much attention. Commander Richard Byrd made an attempt that same month in a Fokker C-2 America, but he was forced to make a sea landing at Vers-sur-Mer in Normandy, just a few miles from Paris. The Germans were next to try the Atlantic. When Hermann Kohl, Gunther von Huenefeld and James

Fitzmaurice left Dublin for Greenly Island, Greenland on April 12, 1928, their small single-engine Junkers W.33 Bremen became the first plane to cross the ocean in a westerly direction, notoriously more difficult than the reverse. The westerly crossing was attempted again between September 1-4, 1930 by a Breguet XIX

Maurice Bellonte and Dieudonné Costes crossed the Atlantic non-stop from Paris to New York aboard a Breguet XIX 'Question Mark.'

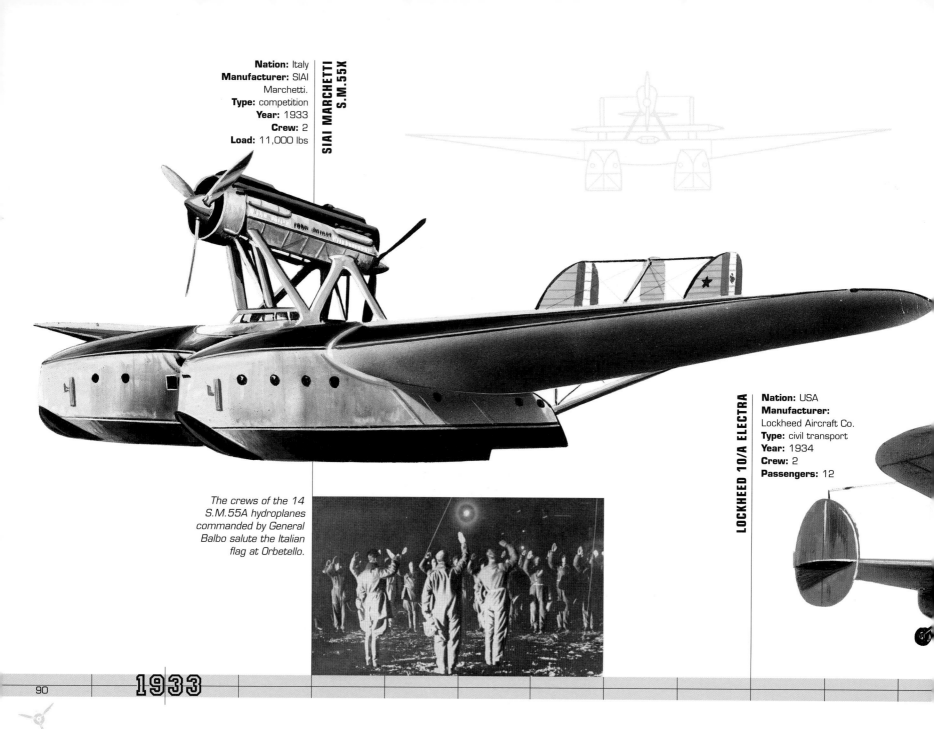

Nation: Italy
Manufacturer: SIAI Marchetti.
Type: competition
Year: 1933
Crew: 2
Load: 11,000 lbs

SIAI MARCHETTI S.M.55X

The crews of the 14 S.M.55A hydroplanes commanded by General Balbo salute the Italian flag at Orbetello.

Nation: USA
Manufacturer: Lockheed Aircraft Co.
Type: civil transport
Year: 1934
Crew: 2
Passengers: 12

LOCKHEED 10/A ELECTRA

90

1933

1921-1934

CHAMPIONS OF ENDURANCE

Long-distance flying went through a phase of particular intensity during the 1930s. The rivalry between manufacturers, pilots and nations was as ferocious as it was fascinating, and the planes themselves became capable of increasingly greater feats of endurance and speed. One such plane was the British de Havilland D.H.88 Comet, a streamlined twin-engine built for the England-Australia Race of 1933. The Comet not only won the race, but outdid itself shortly thereafter by flying a round-trip 26,500-mile raid from England to Australia to New Zealand and back in an amazing 10 days, 21 hours and 22 minutes (it's noteworthy that similar distances often took months for other planes to cover). Another challenger was the French Blériot 110, which seemed to break a major speed/distance record every Year: in 1931 Lucien Bossoutrot and Maurice Rossi flew a 110 to beat the record held by the Italian S.M.64, covering 5,515 miles in 75 hours 23 minutes; in 1932 that same record was set anew at 6,626 miles in 76 hours 34 minutes; in 1933, Rossi and his 110, flying this time with Paul Codos, shattered all non-stop speed/distance records by traveling 5,690 miles in just 55 hours and 30 minutes.

The Soviet aviation industry began coming into its own at this period, its pride and joy being the gigantic Tupolev ANT 25, which in 1934 set the world record for distance in a closed course (7,775 miles in 75 hours 2 minutes). On June 20, 1937 the Tupolev made the first non-stop flight from Moscow to Washington, DC (5,330 miles in 63 hours 25 minutes), and a month later it took the world record for a non-stop flight, departing from Moscow and going all the way to San Jacinto, California (6,340 miles in 62 hours 17 minutes).

Super TR *Point d'Interrogation* ('Question Mark') piloted by Maurice Bellonte and Dieudonné Costes, this time from Paris to New York and then to Dallas for a total of 5,250 miles. But the finale of this adventurous chapter in the history of flight was reached in 1933 by the spectacular 'mass crossing' made by 25 Italian S.M.55X hydroplanes commanded by General Italo Balbo. The fleet left Orbetello, reached New York, then turned around and flew back to

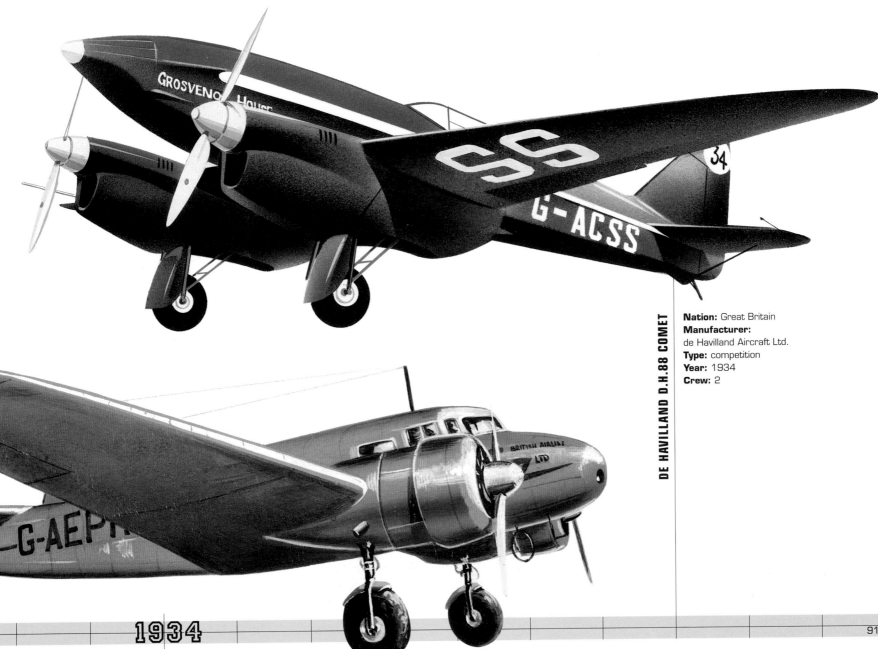

Nation: Great Britain
Manufacturer:
de Havilland Aircraft Ltd.
Type: competition
Year: 1934
Crew: 2

1934

Rome, for an overall journey of 12,400 miles. Three years earlier Balbo had pulled off a similar feat by leading 14 S.M 55As from Orbetello to Rio de Janeiro.

The mania for inventing ever more ambitious variations on the crossing theme continued, particularly with round-the-world flights. Among the most famous of these is the 50,300-mile circumnavigation — more than twice the actual circumference of the Earth —

by the Australian pilot Charles Kingford Smith. Leaving San Francisco on May 31, 1928 in a trimotor Fokker F.VIIb-3m Southern Cross, he crossed the Pacific in three legs, reached Australia, then literally hopped the entire globe until returning more than two years later, on July 4, 1930. In June 1931, Wiley Post and Harold Getty flew 15,600 miles in 107 hours and 2 minutes in a Lockheed Vega nicknamed 'Winnie Mae.' These kinds of adventures, clearly of in-

terest to the growing commercial airline industry, continued through the late 1930s. Amelia Earhart was the period's most famous figure. In May 1932 she had been the first woman to make a solo crossing of the Atlantic. Her attempt in 1937 to circumnavigate the globe in a twin-engine Lockheed Model 10 Electra, however, ended in tragedy when on July 2 she and her plane 'disappeared' over the Pacific Ocean in circumstances that have never been explained.

A formation of Douglas SBD Dauntless dive-bombers, armed with underwing and fuselage bombs.

Opposite page: Boeing B-29 Superfortresses releasing their devastating loads.

1937

THE NEW WAR

THE AIRPLANE IS THE MAIN PROTAGONIST

OF WW II AND CONSEQUENTLY

AIR SUPREMACY BECOMES THE CENTRAL

TENET OF MILITARY DOCTRINE

1945

A Japanese round-the-world raid made between August 26 and October 20, 1939, not by a commercial or sporting plane but by a bomber, symbolically closed aviation's 'golden age.' The sleek twin-engine Mitsubishi G3M2 was one of the most advanced machines Japan had yet developed. A dozen or so G3M2s were adapted for commercial use; one of them, baptized *Nippon* and identified as J-BACI, was further modified for the circumnavigation. Sponsored by the *Mainichi Shimbun* newspaper, the bomber and its crew of six left Tokyo and then covered 33,000 miles in just 194 hours of flight time, a brilliant demonstration of both efficiency and grit. But it was also more: it was a demonstration of power, an explicit and alarming signal as to what Japan was preparing to do, and what Japan was capable of doing. Coincidentally, just five days after the Mitsubishi bomber took off from Tokyo, Germany invaded Poland and World War II was officially underway.

Japan spent two more years building up its offensive capacity before joining the fray, shaking the world with the power and scale of its air forces. The war was now being fought on two sides of the globe, encompassing vast distances, and as such the air-

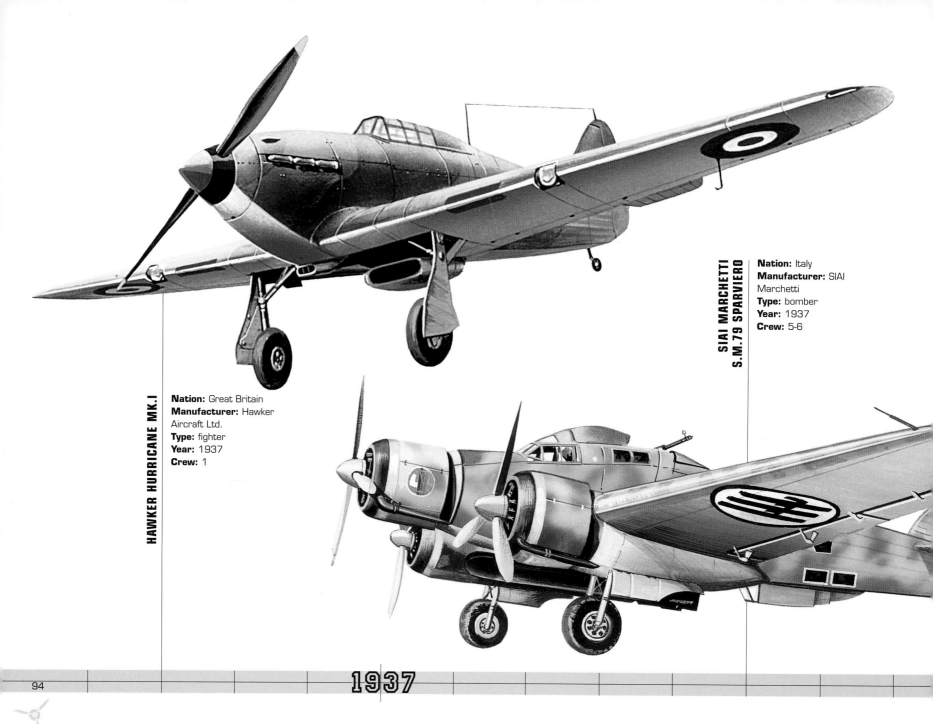

HAWKER HURRICANE MK.I

Nation: Great Britain
Manufacturer: Hawker Aircraft Ltd.
Type: fighter
Year: 1937
Crew: 1

SIAI MARCHETTI S.M.79 SPARVIERO

Nation: Italy
Manufacturer: SIAI Marchetti
Type: bomber
Year: 1937
Crew: 5-6

1937

1937-1945

plane once again was the central protagonist. Never before in the history of warfare had air superiority been such a determining factor. Just as the Italian Giulio Douhet and the American William Mitchell had foreseen back in the 1920s, the airplane became the foundation of military strategy, and air superiority became the central criterion of survival for all of the many nations involved, the single factor capable of tipping the scales toward victory or defeat.

An S.M.79 Sparviero, known as the Gobbo Maledetto, meaning 'cursed hunchback.'

THE REARMING OF GERMANY

Germany's defeat in the First World War halted the nation's great expansion of military avia-

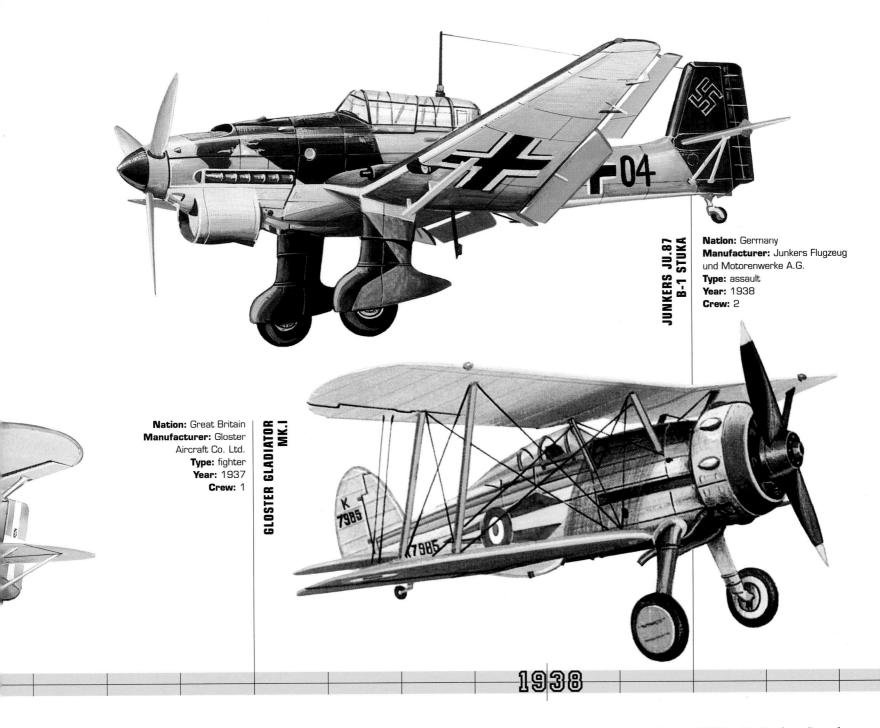

JUNKERS JU.87 B-1 STUKA

Nation: Germany
Manufacturer: Junkers Flugzeug und Motorenwerke A.G.
Type: assault
Year: 1938
Crew: 2

GLOSTER GLADIATOR MK.I

Nation: Great Britain
Manufacturer: Gloster Aircraft Co. Ltd.
Type: fighter
Year: 1937
Crew: 1

1938

tion. The Treaty of Versailles imposed severe conditions: Germany required to surrender all its remaining 20,000 aircraft and 27,000 plane engines, its armed forces were forbidden to possess any type of aircraft, and industry was forbidden to build any type of military equipment. Those who believed that these rigorous conditions would quell the threat of a new military build-up were quite mistaken. Right after key treaty provisions expired in 1926, Germany

began building a war machine that was to soon menace the world. This time, Germany masked military ambitions behind the veil of commercial aviation. Deutsche Lufthansa quickly became Europe's most enterprising airline. Its growth served to stimulate the nation's industries, to encourage development of efficient organizational structures, and to train an entire generation of pilots and technicians. Hitler's ascent to power in 1933 accelerated the process, cul-

minating in March 1935 with the founding of the Luftwaffe, the Third Reich's new air force.

The Spanish Civil War, which Germany used as a testing ground for its burgeoning war machine, was a preamble to the far larger conflict that was about to explode. In September 1939, when Hitler invaded Poland, the Luftwaffe was the world's most powerful air force; it had 4,840 warplanes, of which 1,750 were bombers and 1,200 fighters, all the most advanced of their

FIAT C.R.42 FALCO

Nation: Italy
Manufacturer: Fiat S.A.
Type: fighter
Year: 1939
Crew: 1

1939

day. Moreover, the German military-industrial complex was already capable of producing 1,000 new planes per month. Using this immense power to conduct his famous *blitzkrieg*, or 'lightning war,' Hitler overran Poland, then Denmark, Norway, Belgium, the Netherlands, and finally France. Names like Junkers, Messerschmitt, Dornier and Heinkel came to be spoken as though they were mythological monsters, as cruel as they were invincible.

The exhilaration of these early victories, however, was short-lived. In the summer of 1940 German expansion in Europe came to an abrupt halt on the shores of the English Channel. The Battle of Britain, the first large-scale air battle of WWII, became the Luftwaffe's first defeat, and underscored a critical shortcoming of German air power. Though tactically peerless, the Luftwaffe was never able to develop an effective long-range bomber, and this heavily con-

strained Hitler's plans for expansion. Nonetheless, the Third Reich compensated for the deficiency with the sheer quantity of its aircraft, ingeniously adapting existing types to different battle conditions and requirements. German industry responded in full to the Führer's needs, churning out extraordinary numbers of warplanes right up until the moment when the country finally crumbled beneath the bombs of Allied planes. In 1940 an already impressive 10,800

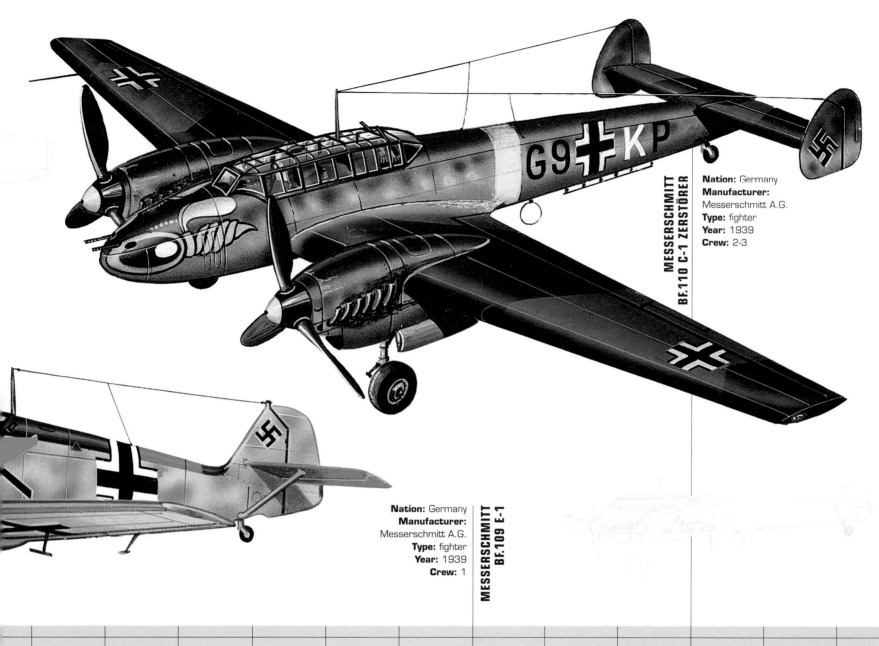

Nation: Germany
Manufacturer:
Messerschmitt A.G.
Type: fighter
Year: 1939
Crew: 2-3

Nation: Germany
Manufacturer:
Messerschmitt A.G.
Type: fighter
Year: 1939
Crew: 1

THE IMMORTAL ROLLS-ROYCE MERLIN

A derivation of an engine developed in the late 1930s for the Schneider Cup, more than 150,000 Merlins were built during the war years. The Merlin powered all of the most prestigious British planes of WWII, from the Hurricane to the Spitfire, from the Lancaster bomber to the twin-engine Mosquito. It was a 12-cylinder V-block type, liquid-cooled with a supercharger. Output ranged from 990 horsepower in the early prototypes to nearly 2,000 hp in the final versions.

warplanes were built; by 1944 that number had reached 39,800, with another 8,000 in the first five months of 1945. One side-effect of this colossal effort proved to be the most important turning point for the future of both military and commercial aviation: in late 1944, Germany became the first nation to build and successfully operate a jet-powered airplane, the Messerschmitt Me.262. Not long afterward, the Arado Ar.234 bomber and the Heinkel He.162 in-

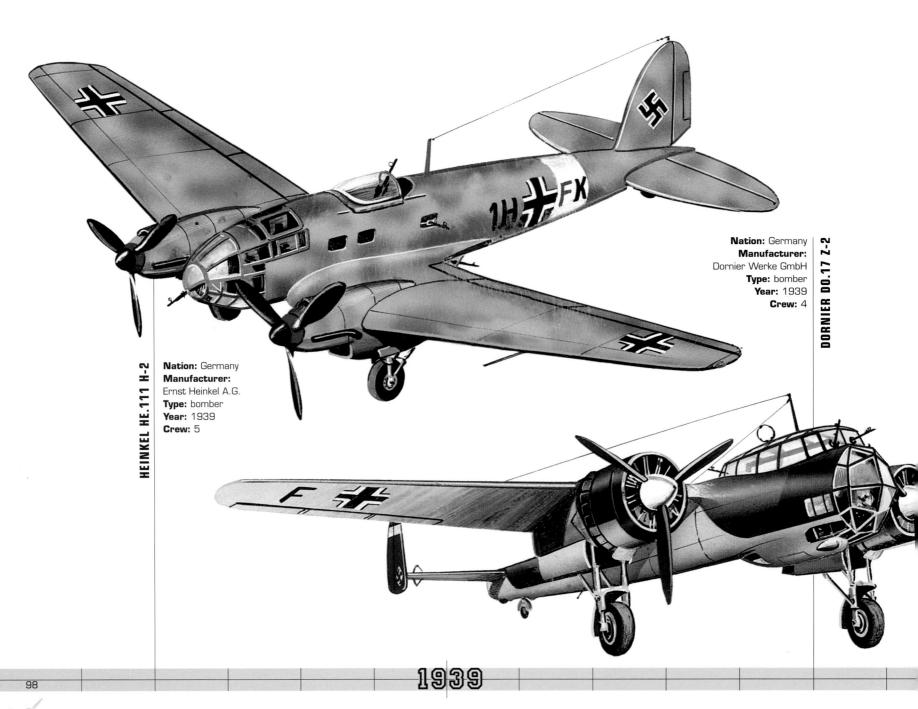

HEINKEL HE.111 H-2

Nation: Germany
Manufacturer: Ernst Heinkel A.G.
Type: bomber
Year: 1939
Crew: 5

DORNIER DO.17 Z-2

Nation: Germany
Manufacturer: Dornier Werke GmbH
Type: bomber
Year: 1939
Crew: 4

1939

terceptor, both jet-propelled, were helping the dying nation to make its last stand.

THE FALL OF FRANCE

France was the German *blitzkrieg*'s most important victim. The country that had contributed so much to the birth of the airplane, and had emerged from World War I as a great

The Dornier Do.17 Z was nicknamed the 'Flying Pencil' for its slender and elongated fuselage.

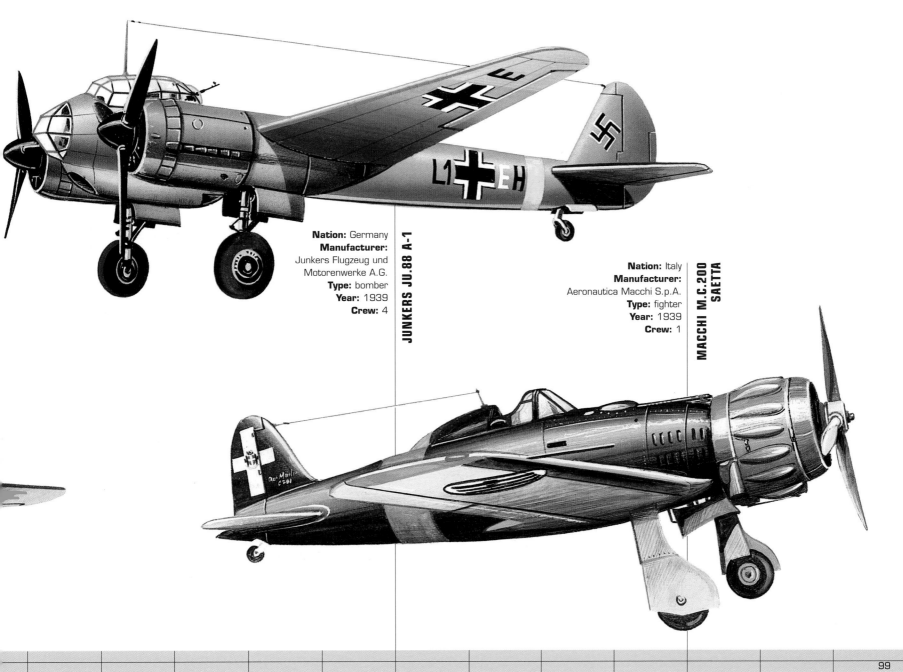

Nation: Germany
Manufacturer: Junkers Flugzeug und Motorenwerke A.G.
Type: bomber
Year: 1939
Crew: 4

JUNKERS JU.88 A-1

Nation: Italy
Manufacturer: Aeronautica Macchi S.p.A.
Type: fighter
Year: 1939
Crew: 1

MACCHI M.C.200 SAETTA

aeronautical powers had let itself be caught completely unprepared for the new war. Throughout the Twenties and much of the Thirties, France had dedicated all its formidable resources and ingenuity to civil aviation, all but ignoring the military. Only in 1936, with the founding of the Armée de l'Air, did French industry begin addressing military needs. The master plan was to nationalize and restructure the majority of private aircraft and engine man-

ufacturers and then build up the newborn air force, all according to a precise schedule. But the plan was never implemented; it was simply too elaborate. As a result, the French aeronautical industry continued to work in a disorganized fashion, unable to coordinate its efforts to satisfy the government's urgent need to rearm. A few good warplanes were designed and built, like the Morane Saulnier M.S.406 and the Dewoitine D.520 fighters,

but the prototyping phase of even the best planes was endless, and only a very small percentage of the aircraft being developed ever made it to production. The consequences of the grave delay were seen during the ten months that France managed to hold off the Germans, from September 1939 to June 1940. France entered the conflict with just 1,400 operative airplanes, two thirds of which were utterly obsolete. When Hitler invaded the

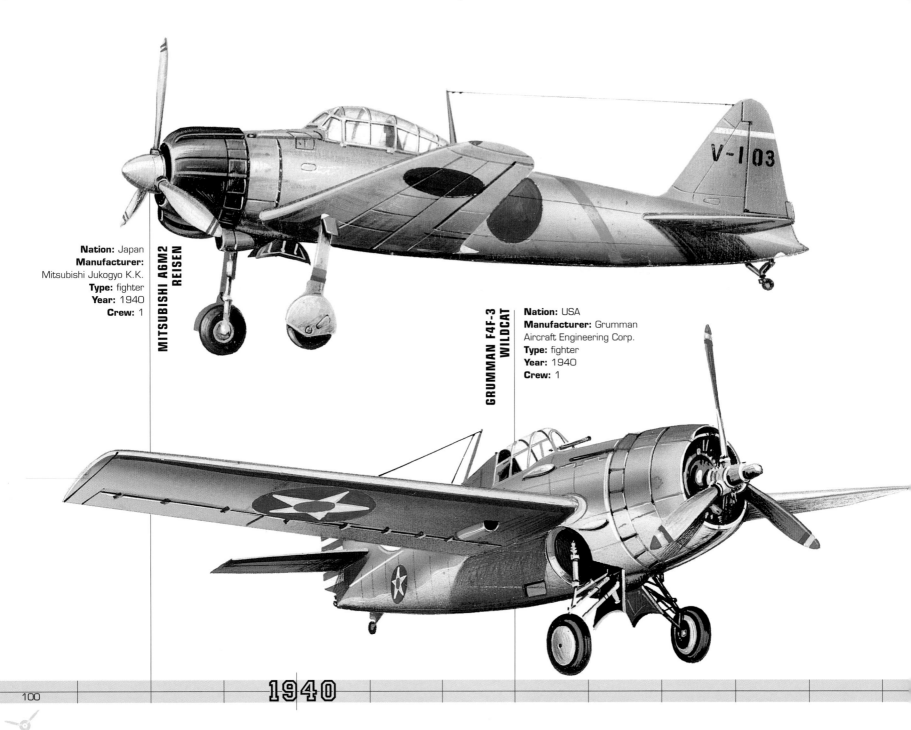

Nation: Japan
Manufacturer: Mitsubishi Jukogyo K.K.
Type: fighter
Year: 1940
Crew: 1

MITSUBISHI A6M2 REISEN

Nation: USA
Manufacturer: Grumman Aircraft Engineering Corp.
Type: fighter
Year: 1940
Crew: 1

GRUMMAN F4F-3 WILDCAT

1940

Netherlands, Belgium and Luxembourg on May 10, 1940, the situation had changed somewhat (1,501 modern planes available, 784 of which were fighters), thanks in large part to the acquisition of foreign planes, mostly American. But it was too little, and too late. For the next four years, French pilots would take to the sky in the knowledge that their inferior numbers and inferior planes were of virtually no use against the Reich.

THE BRITISH RESPONSE

It was no accident that British air forces were the first to resist Germany's devastating power: they were far and away the best prepared. The Royal Air Force, created on April 1, 1918 through unification of the Royal Flying Corps and the Royal Naval Air Service, had emerged from World War I as a major world air power. At war's end Britain had 22,000 aircraft, 3,300 of which were mod-

ern front-line bombers and fighters that had played a decisive role in the Allied victory. However, in 1919 the military budget was drastically cut: fewer planes were built, progress slowed, and industrial capacity shrank. The situation so worsened over the next decade that in 1933 the RAF had only a paltry 850 planes. The disturbing political developments on the Continent fueled a reaction, however, and by September 3, 1939

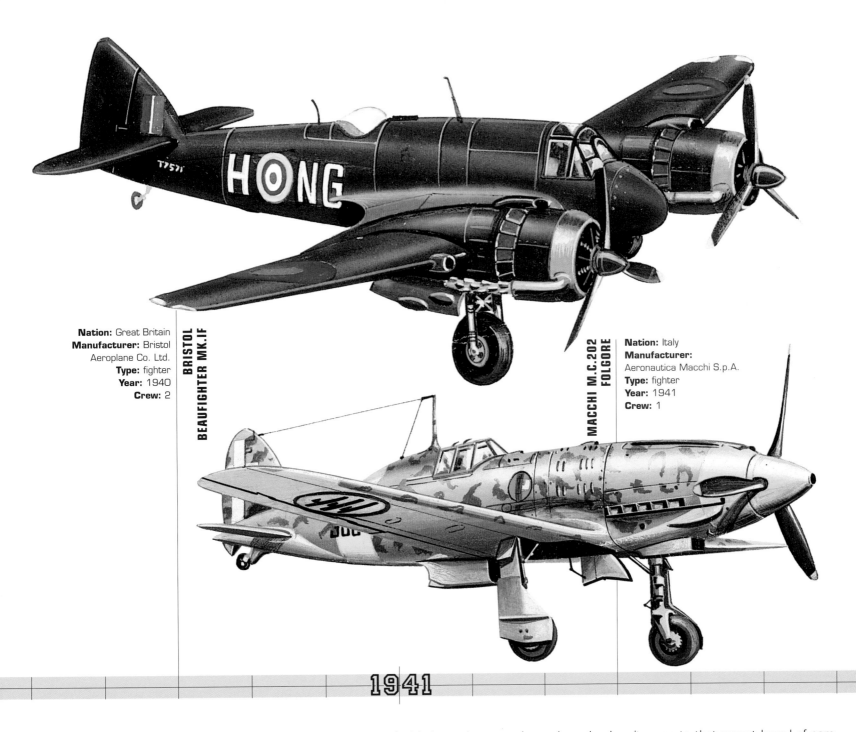

Nation: Great Britain
Manufacturer: Bristol Aeroplane Co. Ltd.
Type: fighter
Year: 1940
Crew: 2

BRISTOL BEAUFIGHTER MK.IF

MACCHI M.C.202 FOLGORE

Nation: Italy
Manufacturer: Aeronautica Macchi S.p.A.
Type: fighter
Year: 1941
Crew: 1

1941

(the day Great Britain declared war against Germany), the Royal Air Force had 9,343 planes, of which 3,550 were advanced fighters and bombers. Britain naval aviation forces, the Fleet Air Arm, had been expanding as well, though more slowly. The majority of its aircraft were hydroplanes bought from the United States. During World War II the British were able to keep step with German warplane production, mobilizing the entire na-

tional aeronautical industry in a massive and well-organized effort. In 1938 Britain produced 400 new planes; in 1939 the number leapt to 7,000, reaching 29,220 in 1944. By 1945 the RAF had 50,000 planes in service, 8,395 of them top-notch combat aircraft, while the Fleet Air Arm had 11,500, of which 1,300 were used in battle.

The quality of these planes never failed to match the demands made on them, especial-

ly when it came to that purest breed of combat plane, the fighter. In 1937 the British had introduced the first truly modern monoplane, the Hurricane, followed a year later by the Supermarine Spitfire, which in the coming conflict would prove to be one of the finest fighters of its time. These in fact were the planes of 'The Few,' as Churchill famously dubbed the pilots who successfully defended England from the Luftwaffe during the Battle of Britain. For

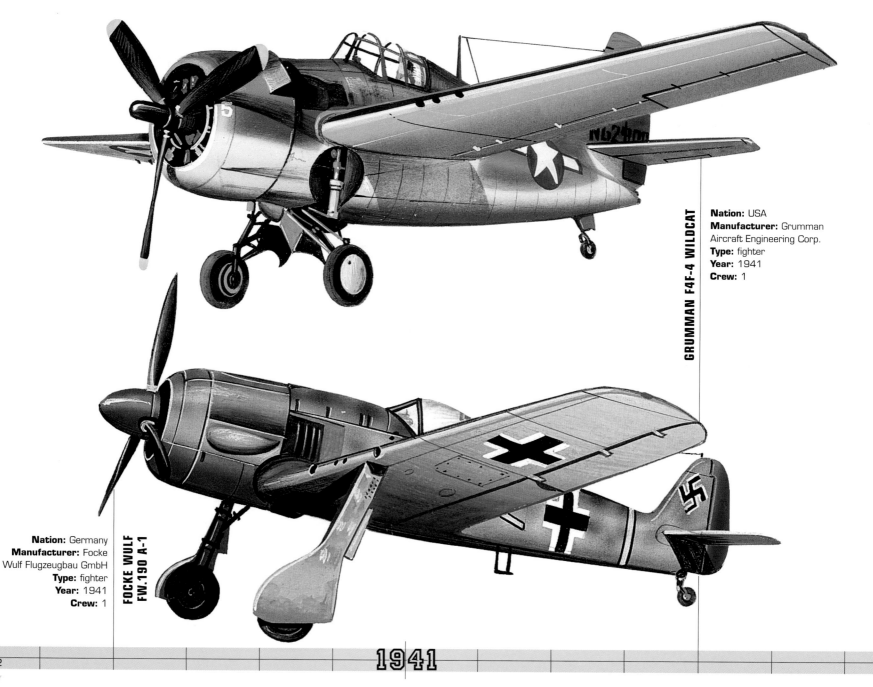

GRUMMAN F4F-4 WILDCAT

Nation: USA
Manufacturer: Grumman Aircraft Engineering Corp.
Type: fighter
Year: 1941
Crew: 1

Nation: Germany
Manufacturer: Focke Wulf Flugzeugbau GmbH
Type: fighter
Year: 1941
Crew: 1

FOCKE WULF FW.190 A-1

1941

Britain, with the threat to its cities and civilian population eliminated, the doctrine of air superiority took on a new aspect. It was no longer a question of defending, but of attacking. And so the RAF's most prestigious planes were born: the Beaufighter, the Mosquito, the newer and more powerful versions of the Spitfire, and the big long-range Stirling, Lancaster and Halifax bombers. It was these latter upon which Britain leaned most heavily from 1940 onward to penetrate continental airspace and strike German positions. More than 15,000 four-engine bombers rolled off the assembly lines during the course of the war, and this enormous demand naturally had a positive influence on the evolution of production technology and logistics. The raids on Germany became more and more devastating and incessant, to the extent that by the end of the war British and American planes were hitting German territory all day and all night without interruption, with absolute air superiority firmly in their grasp. As history demonstrates, the saturation bombing strategy worked.

A NEW WORLD POWER

The Japanese attack on Pearl Harbor on December 7, 1941 stunned the world. But not so much for its efficiency and perfection of execution, or even the incalculable blow it inflicted on

MITSUBISHI G4M1

Nation: Japan
Manufacturer:
Mitsubishi Jukogyo K.K.
Type: bomber
Year: 1941
Crew: 7

NORTH AMERICAN B-25A MITCHELL

Nation: USA
Manufacturer: North American Aviation Inc.
Type: bomber
Year: 1941
Crew: 3-6

THE DAIMLER BENZ DB 605

Base characteristics: 12-cylinder 60-degree inverted V, 4 valves per cylinder, overhead cam, pressure-cooled, direct fuel injection with supercharger, 1,475 horsepower, 2,800 rpm. The DB 605 first appeared in 1941as the successor of the DB 600, DB 601 and DB 603. Subsequent versions reached an output of 2,000 horsepower. The engines of the Daimler Benz 600 series, along with the Junkers Jumo and BMW's various radial engines, were literally the driving force of the Luftwaffe, produced in enormous quantities and used in virtually all of the most important German aircraft of World War II.

American military might, which shaped the entire first year of the war in the Pacific. It was stunning above all because it revealed to the world a military machine until that moment practically unknown. In particular, the attack demonstrated the quality and efficacy of the Japanese air force, which western observers had evidently grossly underestimated. Japan had always been considered an industrially weak nation, lagging far behind the West in aeronau-

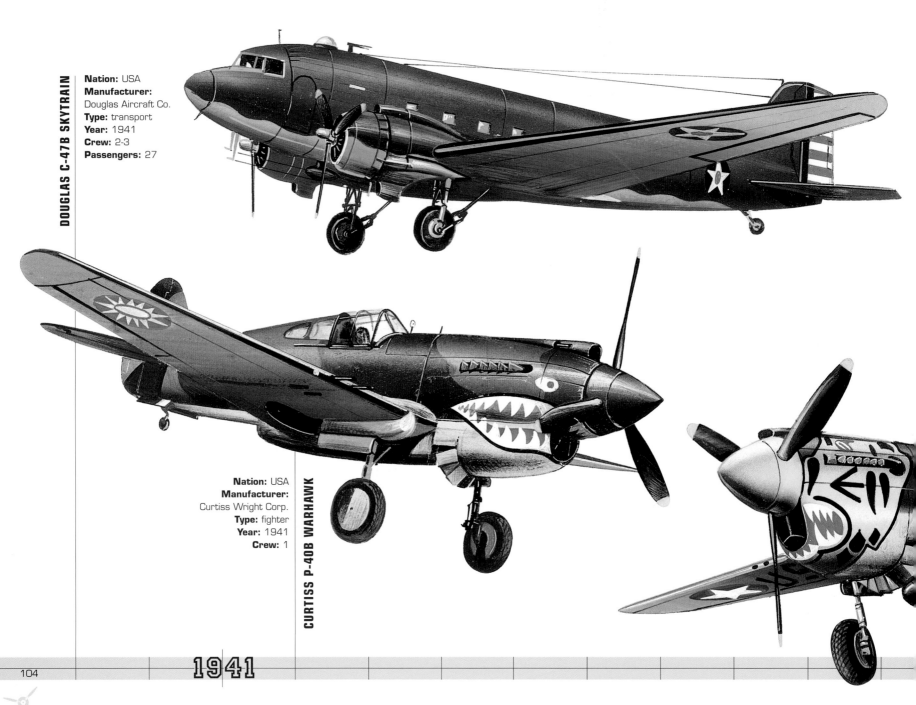

Nation: USA
Manufacturer:
Douglas Aircraft Co.
Type: transport
Year: 1941
Crew: 2-3
Passengers: 27

Nation: USA
Manufacturer:
Curtiss Wright Corp.
Type: fighter
Year: 1941
Crew: 1

1941

tics, designing planes obsolete even before they were built, or at best building foreign planes and engines under license. In truth, since 1910, Japan had been developing an efficient industrial infrastructure. Companies like Nakajima, Kawasaki and Mitsubishi began to appear toward the end of World War I, gradually creating a foundation for an industrial expansion more formidable than anyone had imagined.

This uniquely Japanese system reached

maturity in the early '30s, driven by demand from the Army and Navy for a new generation of Japanese-made warplanes. The results were excellent: planes like the Mitsubishi Ki-21 and G3M bombers, and the Nakajima Ki-27 and Mitsubishi A5M fighters were in many ways superior to their western counterparts. The next generation was even more competitive, the star achievement being the Mitsubishi A6M Reisen. Better known as the Zero, this deadly

fighter dominated the war in the Pacific f during America's long recovery from Pearl Harbor.

Japan exploited its war with China just as Germany had exploited the Spanish Civil War, using it as a test ground for more sinister and ambitious plans. Meanwhile, Japan's industrial apparatus was expanding both qualitatively and quantitatively, always operating at maximum capacity. In 1938, 3,201 aircraft of all types were produced; in 1941 5,088. The numbers grew:

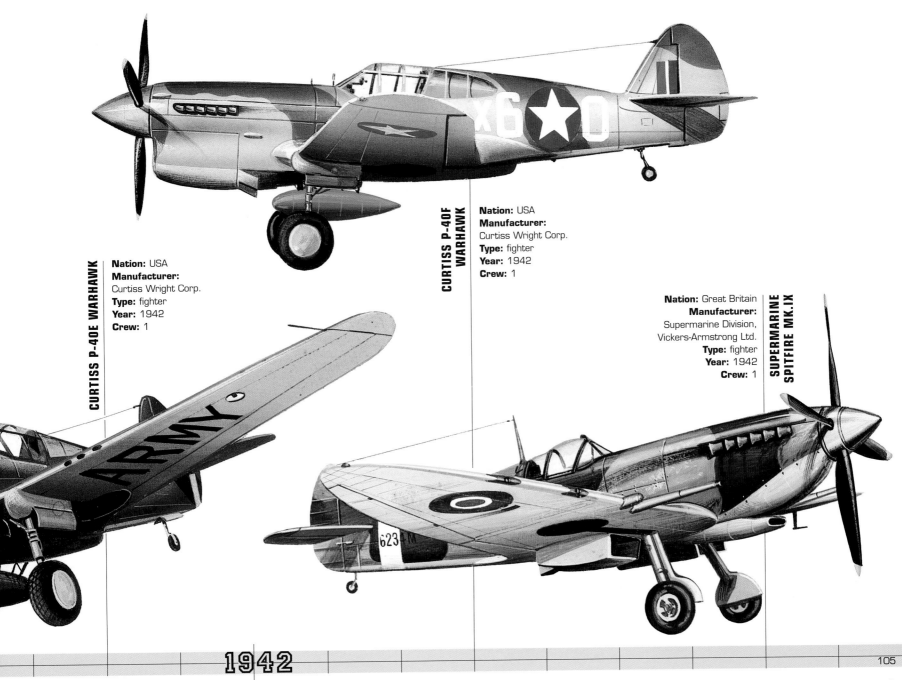

CURTISS P-40E WARHAWK

Nation: USA
Manufacturer:
Curtiss Wright Corp.
Type: fighter
Year: 1942
Crew: 1

CURTISS P-40F WARHAWK

Nation: USA
Manufacturer:
Curtiss Wright Corp.
Type: fighter
Year: 1942
Crew: 1

SUPERMARINE SPITFIRE MK.IX

Nation: Great Britain
Manufacturer:
Supermarine Division,
Vickers-Armstrong Ltd.
Type: fighter
Year: 1942
Crew: 1

1942

between January1944 and June 1945, Japan built an incredible 39,266 airplanes, almost as many as Germany did in that same period.

In December 1941, Japan had the numbers it needed. The Imperial Army Air Force boasted 1,500 warplanes, the Navy 1,400, these latter being the spearhead of the campaign to extend the Empire throughout the vast Pacific. Until about mid-1942, the Japanese enjoyed air superiority in the Pacific theater,

suffering only occasional setbacks at the hands of the hard-hit Allied forces. But America, the wounded giant, was about to reawaken. The era of Japanese air superiority ended with the great air and sea battles of the spring and summer of 1942, particularly the Battle of Midway. For the next three long and bloody years, Japan was restricted to defending first the territory conquered during its expansion (Malaysia, Burma, Java, the Philippines), and fi-

nally Japan itself, hard hit in 1944 by devastating waves of American B-29 bombers, and eventually by atomic bombs in 1945.

AMERICA REAWAKENS

Pain, disbelief and anger were just a few of the powerful emotions provoked by the surprise attack on Pearl Harbor. Pain for the loss of life (2,403 dead, 1,778 wounded); disbelief at the force of the blow struck by a totally underesti-

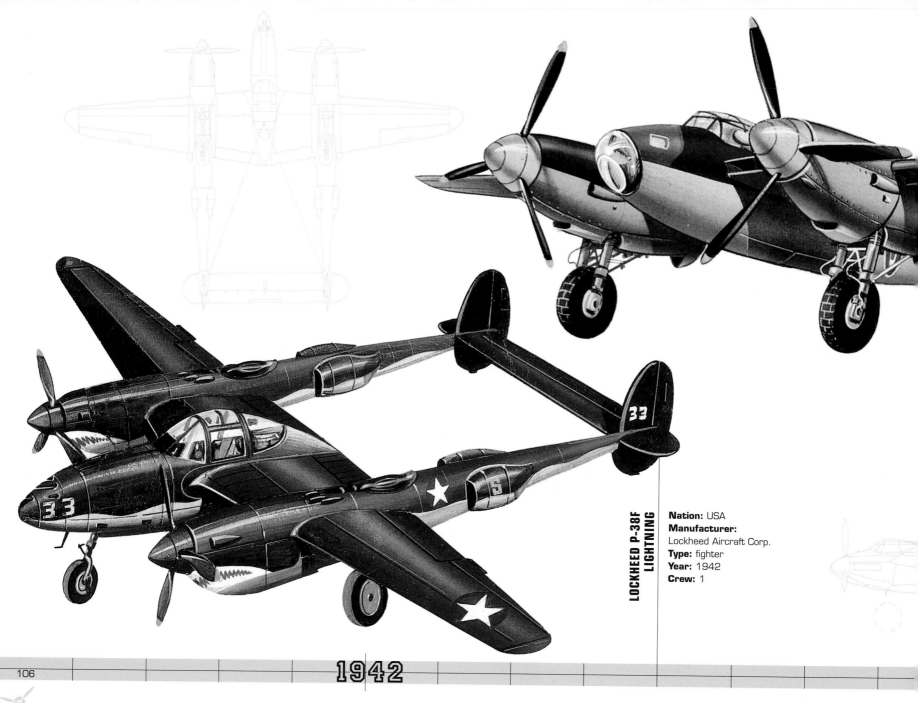

LOCKHEED P-38F LIGHTNING

Nation: USA
Manufacturer: Lockheed Aircraft Corp.
Type: fighter
Year: 1942
Crew: 1

1942

mated adversary; and anger at having to wait, with the Pacific Fleet utterly crippled, to exact revenge. But the nation that Churchill called 'the sleeping giant' turned these difficult emotions to its advantage as it readied itself to fight and win two wars on opposite sides of the globe, an extraordinary feat. The ramifications would go well beyond military victory. Indeed, Pearl Harbor might be considered the event that marks the transformation of the United

States from an important industrial power to undisputed world leader.

The reaction to the surprise attack was not, however, immediate. When war broke out in Europe in 1939, American military aviation was by no means ready for conflict. Like France and Britain, the US had long neglected military aviation, ignoring the protests of General William 'Billy' Mitchell. Commander of the American Expeditionary Force sent to Europe

during World War I. Mitchell had developed a doctrine similar to that of Giulio Douhet concerning the airplane's strategic role. But no one was listening. This political myopia eventually came to condition America's entire industrial apparatus which, by preferring to serve the civilian market, had lost the ability to make good warplanes. Only in July 1926, with the creation of the US Army Air Corps (USAAC), did America begin thinking about improving its

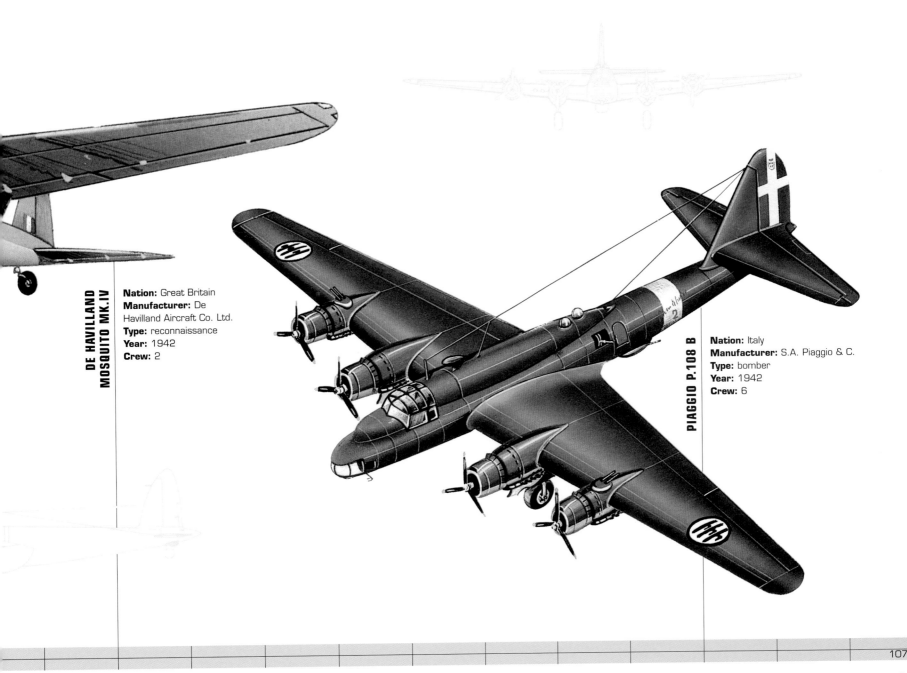

DE HAVILLAND MOSQUITO MK.IV

Nation: Great Britain
Manufacturer: De Havilland Aircraft Co. Ltd.
Type: reconnaissance
Year: 1942
Crew: 2

PIAGGIO P.108 B

Nation: Italy
Manufacturer: S.A. Piaggio & C.
Type: bomber
Year: 1942
Crew: 6

military readiness. The process was long and slow, and even by the mid-1930s American military aviation remained underfunded and underdeveloped by comparison to the incredible progress being made in the commercial sector.

The first important step toward remedying the situation was taken in September 1939, when America sanctioned its indirect

One of the earliest Piaggio P.108 Bs with camouflage.

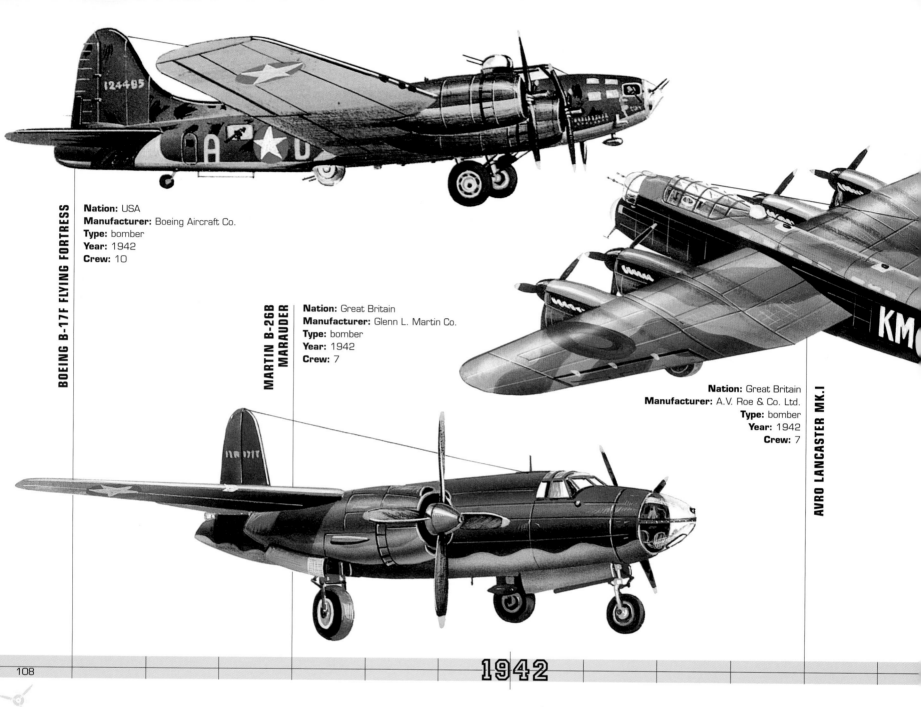

Nation: USA
Manufacturer: Boeing Aircraft Co.
Type: bomber
Year: 1942
Crew: 10

Nation: Great Britain
Manufacturer: Glenn L. Martin Co.
Type: bomber
Year: 1942
Crew: 7

Nation: Great Britain
Manufacturer: A.V. Roe & Co. Ltd.
Type: bomber
Year: 1942
Crew: 7

1942

participation in the European conflict. Overriding the strict conditions of the Neutrality Act of 1935, which prohibited the export of military goods, America began building arms for its European friends. The second important step came in 1941 with the passing of the Lend-Lease Act, which gave carte blanche to President Roosevelt in the sale, transfer or leasing of any and all types of goods and equipment to nations requiring help in defending themselves

against Axis aggression. These decisions, made in response to desperate pleas from France and Britain, gave American industry a powerful boost. A fortunate collateral effect was the gradual reinforcement of the Army and Navy air forces, though only to a bare minimum level of competitiveness. On the day war was declared, the Army Air Corps (which became the US Army Air Forces (USAAF) in June 1941) had 3,305 planes and the Navy about

3,000. Though perhaps acceptable numbers on paper, they proved to be thoroughly inadequate against Japan's massive aerial strength.

American inferiority lasted throughout most of 1942, a terrible year, a blood-drenched juggling act in which the US tried, largely in vain, simultaneously to stop Japanese expansion in the Pacific and German expansion in Europe. But the scales gradually tilted back in the Allies' favor, thanks to the intro-

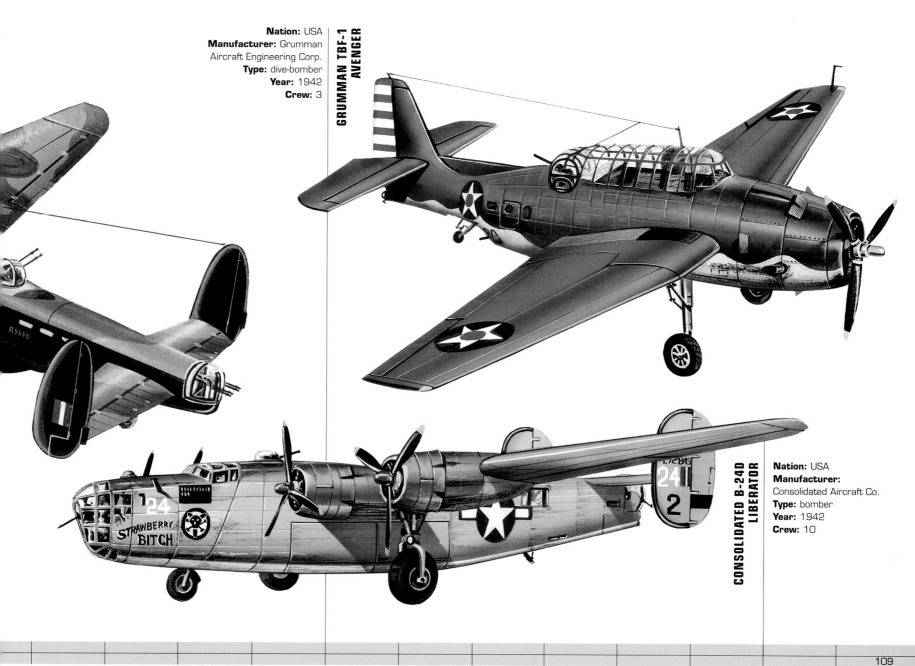

Nation: USA
Manufacturer: Grumman
Aircraft Engineering Corp.
Type: dive-bomber
Year: 1942
Crew: 3

Nation: USA
Manufacturer:
Consolidated Aircraft Co.
Type: bomber
Year: 1942
Crew: 10

duction of some exceptional fighter planes that were destined to make history. The P-47 Thunderbolt, the P-38 Lightning, the P-51 Mustang, the F-4U Corsair, and the F6F Hellcat were not merely warplanes that dominated the skies on all fronts, but major landmarks in the history of both aviation technology and military tactics. Equally important were the B-17 and B-24 bombers, decisive in defeating the Third Reich, products of a strategic approach

that culminated in the B-29, the only plane ever to have dropped an atomic bomb. Any remaining doubts as to the validity of Douhet and Mitchell's theories were brutally erased at Hiroshima and Nagasaki in August 1945.

It was as much America's unparalleled industrial capacity as the quality of its planes that decided the war's outcome. From 1941 to 1945, a total of 789,947 engines and 297,211 airplanes were built. Of these,

99,742 were fighters, and 97,592 bombers (which can be further subdivided into 35,743 four-engine and 35,369 twin-engine planes). On January 1, 1945, a total of 86,000 active warplanes made the United States the world's number one aeronautical power, a role that has remained unchallenged ever since.

ITALY'S FAILURE

Among the Axis countries, Italy was the weak

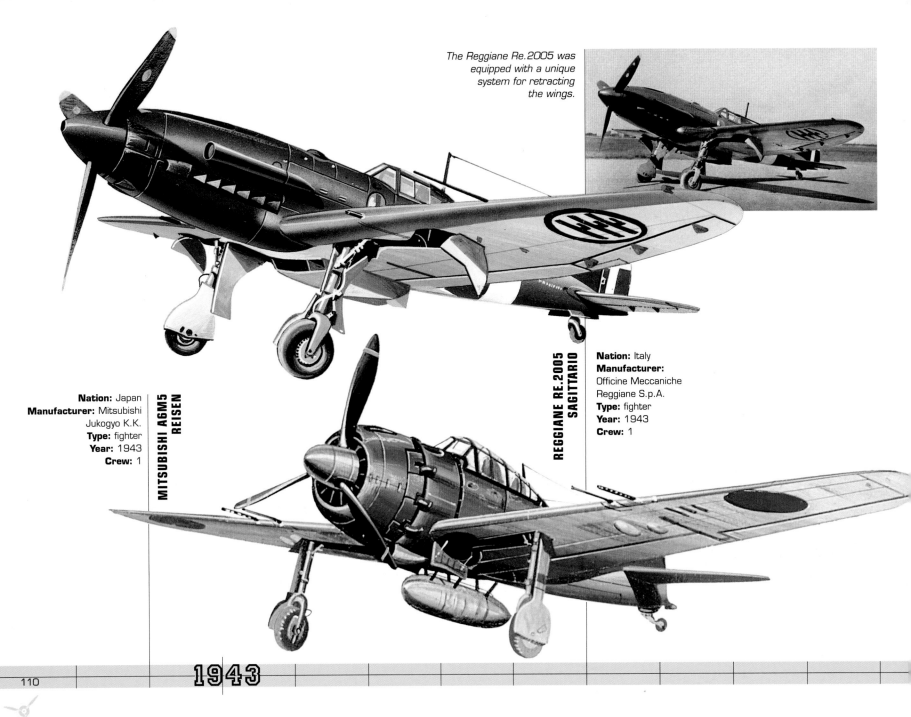

The Reggiane Re.2005 was equipped with a unique system for retracting the wings.

Nation: Italy
Manufacturer: Officine Meccaniche Reggiane S.p.A.
Type: fighter
Year: 1943
Crew: 1

Nation: Japan
Manufacturer: Mitsubishi Jukogyo K.K.
Type: fighter
Year: 1943
Crew: 1

1943

link. The halcyon days of the '20s and '30s, of Italian competition victories and endurance records and spectacular transoceanic raids, ended abruptly with the outbreak of war. The formidable image of Italian air power turned out to be false. Beneath Mussolini's rhetoric lay the fact that Italian air forces had never really been tested: the Ethiopian campaign and participation in the Spanish Civil War had been conducted against adversaries too weak to

THE BEST ENGINE FOR THE BEST PLANES

Developed from the Wasp engines of the 1930s, the Pratt & Whitney R-2800 Double Wasp was probably the best airplane engine of its time. An 18-cylinder double-row radial, it was putting out 2,000 hp in 1939, years before other manufacturers were able to reach that mark. It powered many of America's best planes: the Republic P-47 Thunderbolt, the Grumman F6F Hellcat, the Vought F4U Corsair, and the Northrop P-61 Black Widow.

VOUGHT F4U-1 CORSAIR

Nation: USA
Manufacturer: United Aircraft Corp.
Type: fighter
Year: 1943
Crew: 1

A formation of US Navy F4U-1 Corsairs.

YAKOVLEV YAK-9

Nation: USSR
Manufacturer: State Industries
Type: fighter
Year: 1943
Crew: 1

test Italian strength. Politicians and military strategists therefore deceived themselves into overestimating Italy's military might. Historians also note that the Italian high command had largely ignored General Douhet in the decades prior to WWII, preferring to believe that any war would be primarily land-based, against neighboring countries, and largely defensive.

The new conflict immediately displayed the extent to which the Regia Aeronautica

(founded on March 28, 1923) had been resting on past accomplishments, blind to the reality of Italian vulnerability and unpreparedness. On June 10, 1940, when Italy joined Germany in the war, it had 3,296 planes, about half were combat aircraft: 783 bombers, 594 fighters, and 419 surveillance/reconnaissance planes. In theory this force made Italy an effective power; in practice it was an ineffective one, severely compro-

mised by its planes' poor quality. More than half the fighters, for example, where obsolete Fiat C.R.42 biplanes. Though the remainder were modern monoplanes – the Fiat G.50 and the Macchi M.C.200 – in armaments and performance they trailed their counterparts from other nations. The bombers were slightly better, but they did not improve during the war, and were obsolete by the time it ended.

The Regia Aeronautica's inadequate

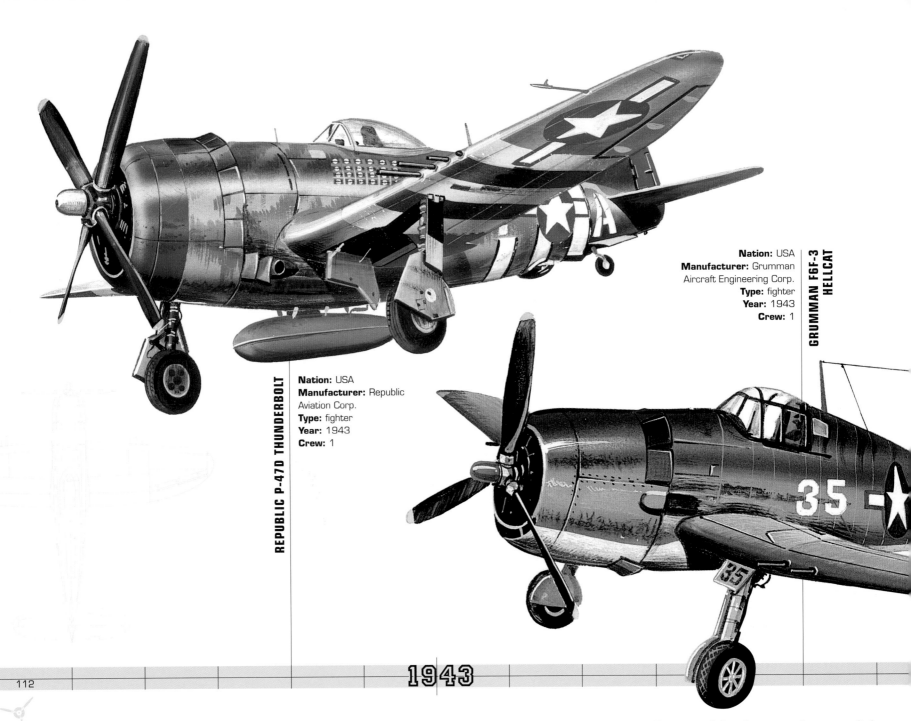

Nation: USA
Manufacturer: Grumman Aircraft Engineering Corp.
Type: fighter
Year: 1943
Crew: 1

GRUMMAN F6F-3 HELLCAT

Nation: USA
Manufacturer: Republic Aviation Corp.
Type: fighter
Year: 1943
Crew: 1

REPUBLIC P-47D THUNDERBOLT

1943

1937-1945

preparation is best illustrated by the experience of the Italian Air Corps in Belgium, late in the Battle of Britain, between October 1940 and January 1941. The 13th and 43rd bomber wings, the 56th fighter wing and a squadron of reconnaissance craft, the 179th, were assigned to support to the Luftwaffe's operations against Great Britain. The German field command strongly objected to Italian participation, and was soon proved right. During

those few months of battle on the Channel front, the best planes and pilots that the Regia Aeronautica had to offer revealed their many limits in a tragically useless expenditure of blood, spilled in the name of political necessity and the conviction that the war would soon be over. The Axis was totally mistaken: the war expanded rapidly, eventually encompassing the entire Mediterranean basin and the immensity of the Soviet Union.

Devastated by the turn of events, Italy struggled to recover and adapt to the realities for which it had been so unprepared. Germany assisted Italy by allowing the country to build its excellent Daimler Benz engines under license, thereby filling the void in engine production, which had been the primary impediment to building competitive warplanes. Italian aeronautical production, especially in terms of fighters, immediately made a qualitative leap. The

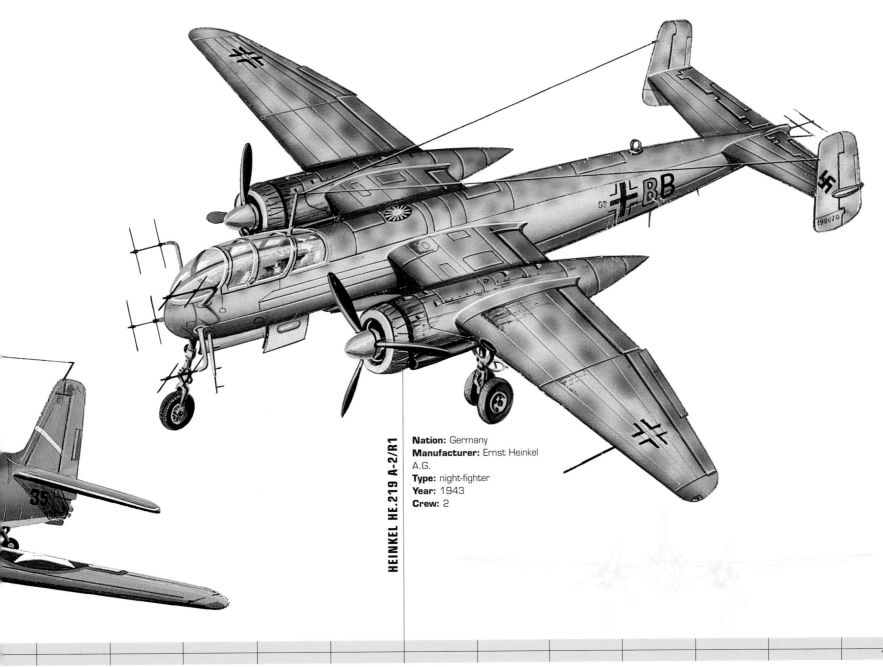

HEINKEL HE.219 A-2/R1

Nation: Germany
Manufacturer: Ernst Heinkel
A.G.
Type: night-fighter
Year: 1943
Crew: 2

Macchi M.C.202 of 1941, Italy's most famous and widely used fighter of its day, was the first felicitous result. With the next generation, the

so-called 'Series 5' planes – the Macchi M.C.205, Fiat G.55, and Reggiane Re.2005 – Italy could finally stand up to its adversaries.

But the effort was ultimately futile. Supply lines were cut off, raw materials were scarce, and factories were under continuous bombardment, making it impossible for Italy to maintain effective production levels. In fact, at no point during the war was Italian industry able to produce large numbers of aircraft. A respectable 3,257 were built in 1940, a handful more in

The Heinkel He.219 was the first German plane with landing gear in a 'tricycle' configuration.

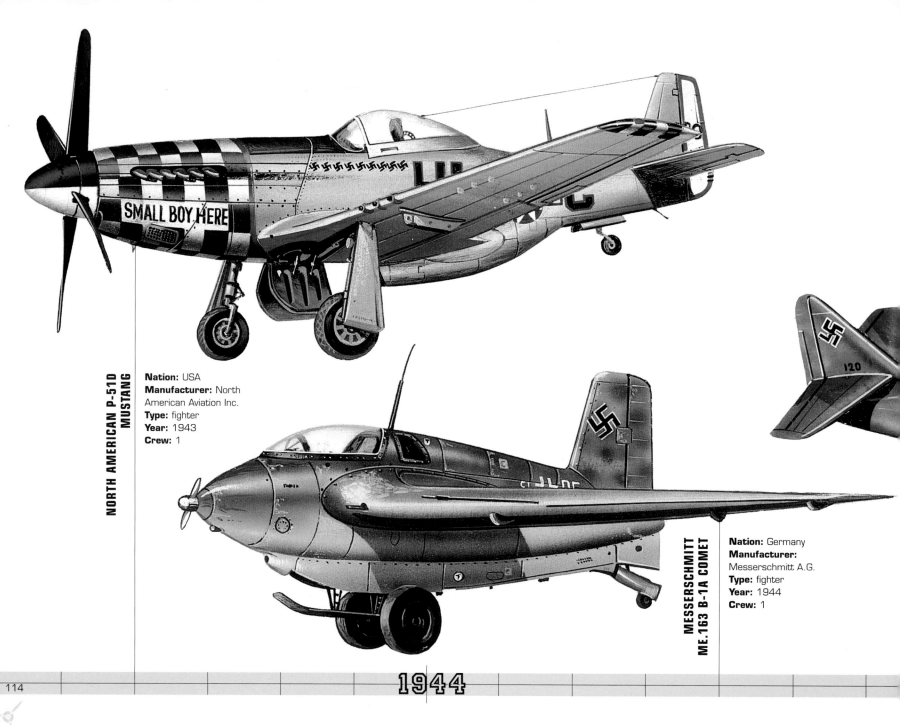

NORTH AMERICAN P-51D MUSTANG

Nation: USA
Manufacturer: North American Aviation Inc.
Type: fighter
Year: 1943
Crew: 1

MESSERSCHMITT ME.163 B-1A COMET

Nation: Germany
Manufacturer: Messerschmitt A.G.
Type: fighter
Year: 1944
Crew: 1

1944

1941. But unlike other nations, the trend spiraled downward thereafter: 2,818 in 1942, 1,930 in the first eight months of 1943, then none. On September 8, 1943 (the day of the armistice with the Allies), the Italian air forces had 877 planes. More than 10,000 had been lost since June 1940. An enormous price for defeat, paid on every front, from Africa to the Mediterranean, from the Aegean to the Balkans, from the English Channel to the Russian tundra. But it wasn't over. The Regia Aeronautica had been dissolved, and its resources were divided between a newly constituted air force that fought on the side of the Allies under the banner of the Balkan Air Force and the exiled Mussolini's Republic of Salò, still allied with the Germans. And so it was that the last two years of the war saw Italian pilots fighting on both sides, each in the cause to which he was bound, be it right or wrong. The final act of the tragedy was enacted in the skies over Lombardy, the Veneto, Albania and Yugoslavia.

THE EMERGENCE OF THE SOVIET UNION

The Soviet Union, the third major Allied power, was not prepared for the German invasion. When Hitler launched Operation Barbarossa, no one imagined that the Luftwaffe would need only a few days to defeat what was considered one of the world's most powerful air forces. But once

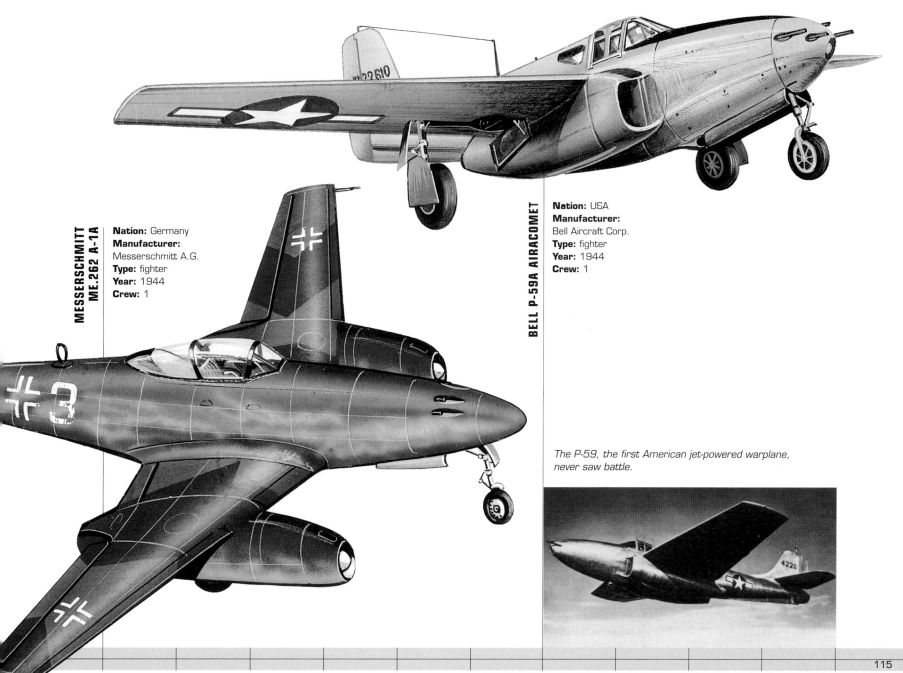

MESSERSCHMITT ME.262 A-1A

Nation: Germany
Manufacturer:
Messerschmitt A.G.
Type: fighter
Year: 1944
Crew: 1

BELL P-59A AIRACOMET

Nation: USA
Manufacturer:
Bell Aircraft Corp.
Type: fighter
Year: 1944
Crew: 1

The P-59, the first American jet-powered warplane, never saw battle.

again, reality differed dramatically from perception. The Soviet military build-up of the 1930s, which showcased large numbers of advanced aircraft like the Polikarpov I-16 fighter and the Tupolev SB-2 bomber – planes that had performed brilliantly in the Spanish Civil War – represented the maximum limit of Soviet industrial capacity. When Germany invaded, the VVS (Voenno-Vozdushnye Sili, or Russian Air Force) was still in the midst of a massive restructuring.

Faced with Germany's vast organizational and technological superiority, Soviet planes and pilots were swatted from the air like so many flies.

And yet Soviet aviation had progressed steadily and strongly since the 1917 Revolution. During the tsarist era Russia had always lagged behind the rest of Europe in aeronautical production, with the sole exception of Igor Sikorsky's incomparable multi-engine bombers. But in 1918 the decision was taken to liberate the

country from dependency on foreign equipment and to develop a self-sufficient, all-Soviet air force. And thus the Central Aerohydrodynamics Institute (TsAGI) was born, a centralized research and engineering facility charged to design engines and aircraft, develop and test new technologies, and train engineers and technicians. By 1920 the apparatus was in place, and an ambitious expansion plan was launched. This period saw the production of the first original creations

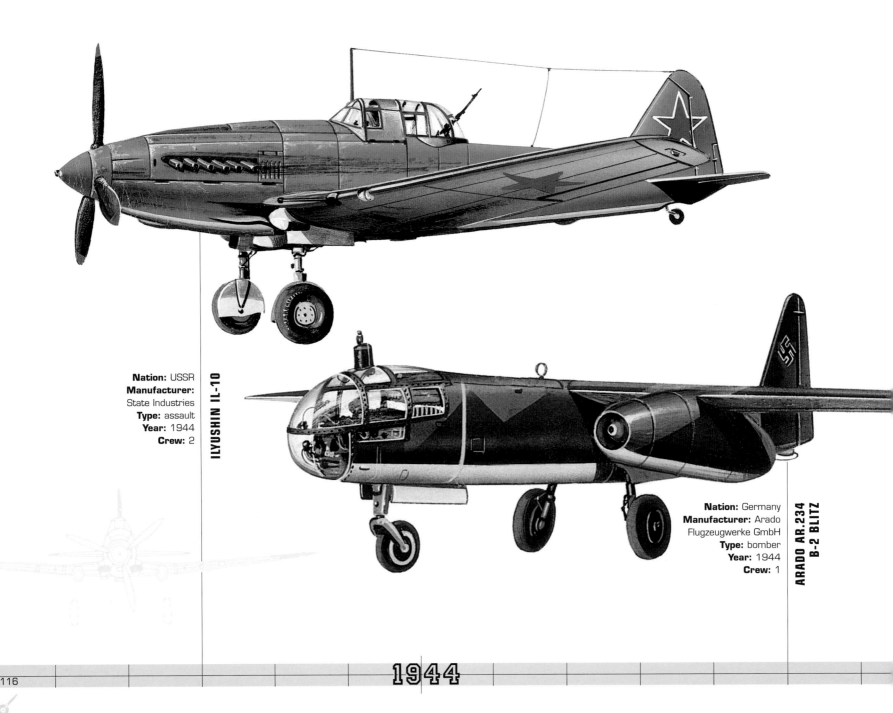

Nation: USSR
Manufacturer: State Industries
Type: assault
Year: 1944
Crew: 2

ILYUSHIN IL-10

Nation: Germany
Manufacturer: Arado Flugzeugwerke GmbH
Type: bomber
Year: 1944
Crew: 1

ARADO AR.234 B-2 BLITZ

1944

of the great Soviet aircraft designers: Tupolev, Polikarpov, Yakovlev, names whose fame survives to this day.

Like the US after Pearl Harbor, the Soviet Union took a while to recover from the devastating German attack. In a colossal and heroic effort, the Soviets managed to rebuild their air forces and increase aircraft production capacity in just over a year. During the winter of 1941, hundreds of engine and aircraft facto-

ries were moved to areas far away from the battlefront; research and testing facilities were relocated to relatively safe regions – the Volga valley, the Urals and western Siberia. Though begun as an enterprise driven by a sense of emergency and desperation, in the end dispersion proved to have been a wise move.

The Allies contributed significantly to the Soviet recovery through their constant provision of equipment and arms. Between 1942

and 1944, the US and Great Britain supplied the Soviets with 14,833 aircraft of every type and class, not to mention machinery, steel, copper and aluminum. This assistance, together with a lull in Axis operations, allowed the Soviets to make up for lost time, and soon they were producing effective new aircraft in numbers that outstripped German production. The best of these aircraft tended to be fighters and assault planes.

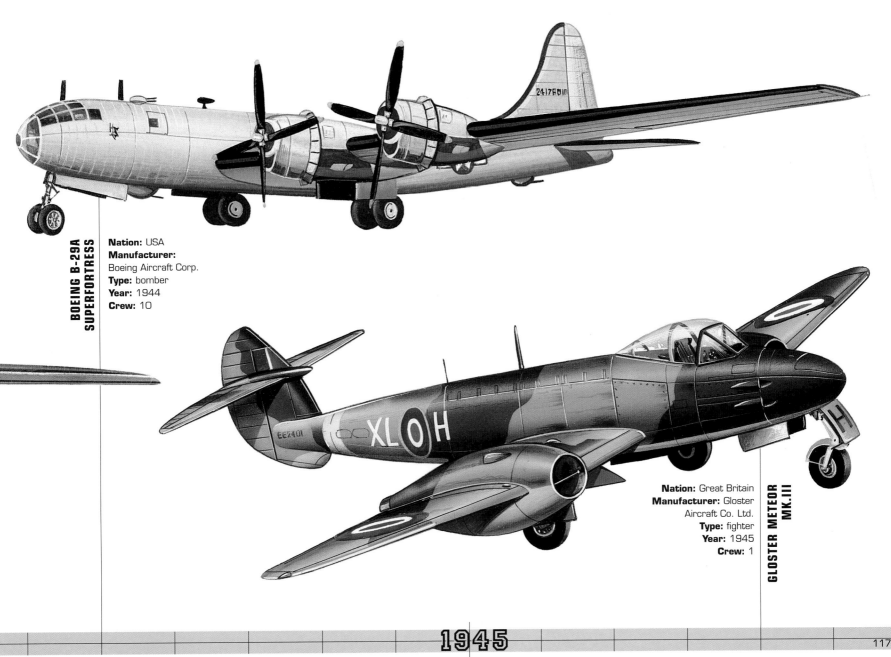

BOEING B-29A SUPERFORTRESS

Nation: USA
Manufacturer:
Boeing Aircraft Corp.
Type: bomber
Year: 1944
Crew: 10

GLOSTER METEOR MK.III

Nation: Great Britain
Manufacturer: Gloster
Aircraft Co. Ltd.
Type: fighter
Year: 1945
Crew: 1

1945

The last two years of the war were characterized by the gradual dissolution of German power and a dramatic increase in that of the Soviets. Not only had all of the initial obstacles been overcome, but a gargantuan military production machine had been set into motion, and wouldn't run down for many decades to come. Approximately 125,000 airplanes were built during the course of the conflict, the high points being 1944 (40,300 units) and 1945 (41,800). The USSR was now positioned to compete head-to-head with the United States in that seemingly interminable race for global military supremacy known as the Cold War.

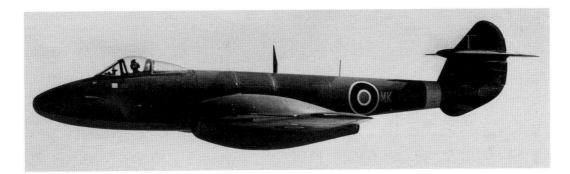

The Gloster Meteor MkIII was the only jet-powered plane fighting at the front in the closing days of the war.

F-15C Eagles of the 58th Tactical Fighter Squadron taking off during Operation Desert Shield, first Gulf War.

Opposite page: the British Electric Lightning fighter.

1946

THE ERA OF THE MILITARY JET

THE NEW MEANS OF PROPULSION DEVELOPED DURING WORLD WAR II SIGNALS THE DAWN OF MODERN MILITARY AVIATION, PROVING GROUND OF MUCH OF TODAY'S ADVANCED TECHNOLOGY

2003

November 1950. The 'jet age,' the Germans had prefigured late in WWII definitely arrived in Korea. History's first jet-powered aircraft fight occurred on the Korean conflict's 8th day, near the River Yalu. Lieutenant Russell J. Brown, piloting a USAF Lockheed F-80, engaged a Soviet MiG-15 in combat. Brown, despite his plane's inferiority – less agile and less power-ful than a MiG-15 – emerged victorious.

WWII ended in 1945, yet barely five years later another conflict was claiming headlines and lives. The Korean War appeared on the surface to be a localized political dispute; however, it was a much larger contest between the two new 'superpowers,' the Soviet Union and the United States, somehow now archenemies just five years after being allies against Hitler. At stake was not only military superiority, but ideo-logical supremacy and, by extension, total glob-al domination. The world had been divided, and nations were compelled, often forcibly, to take one side or the other. The ensuing rivalry be-tween the two blocs and the frantic arms race that would characterize the next forty years of global relations, was founded on a disturbing paradox: the only way to ensure peace was re-ciprocally to maintain such overwhelming mili-tary might that neither enemy would contem-

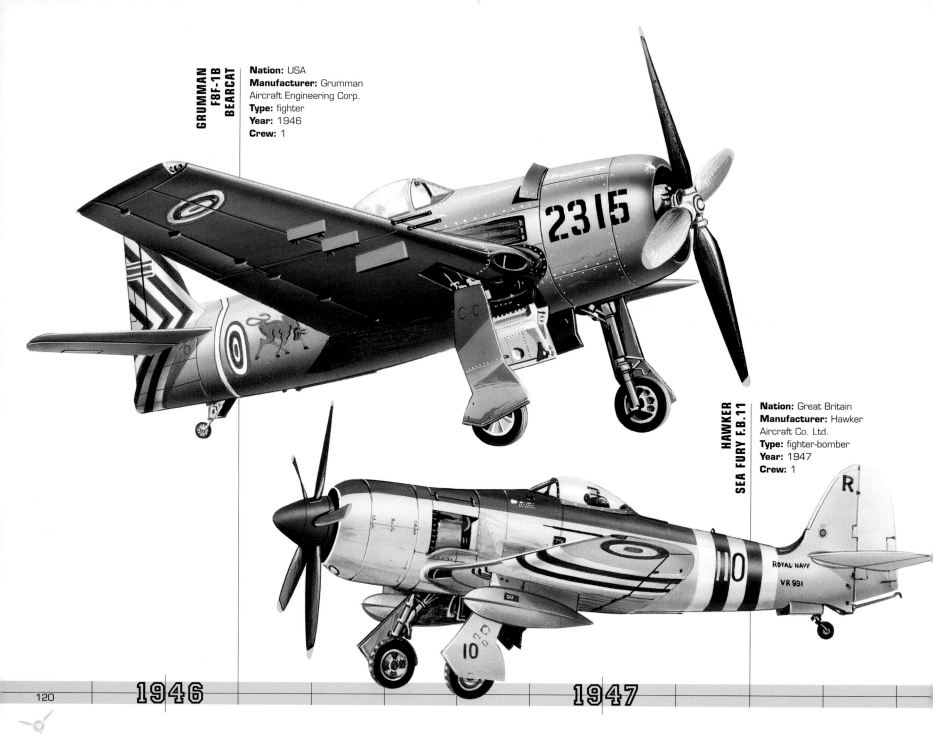

Nation: USA
Manufacturer: Grumman
Aircraft Engineering Corp.
Type: fighter
Year: 1946
Crew: 1

Nation: Great Britain
Manufacturer: Hawker
Aircraft Co. Ltd.
Type: fighter-bomber
Year: 1947
Crew: 1

1946-2003

plate war. Naturally, this situation made the role of aviation more central than ever. And so for the next four decades, aeronautical technology grew at the same frenetic pace as the ordnance of destruction it was designed to carry. The Cold War ended with the collapse of the Soviet empire in the early 1990s, but new perceived threats to global stability continue to fuel the development of ever more sophisticated and deadly military aircraft.

POST-WAR AMERICA

The United States' defeat of Germany and Japan elevated it to undisputed world leadership. Peace reigned, thanks in part to the enormous American contribution. But the war had taught the world that sometimes peace can be achieved only through the use of force, and when the Soviet Union revealed its true geopolitical ambitions by absorbing neighboring nations, that lesson could not be ignored.

The peace-through-force premise shaped development of military aviation in post-war America. The need to maintain a balance of forces, to prevent the adversary from possessing weapons more powerful or efficient than one's own – a doctrine known as 'the balance of terror' – led to a process of unprecedented qualitative evolution in the airplane. America's enormous industrial apparatus, which through the sheer momentum of the

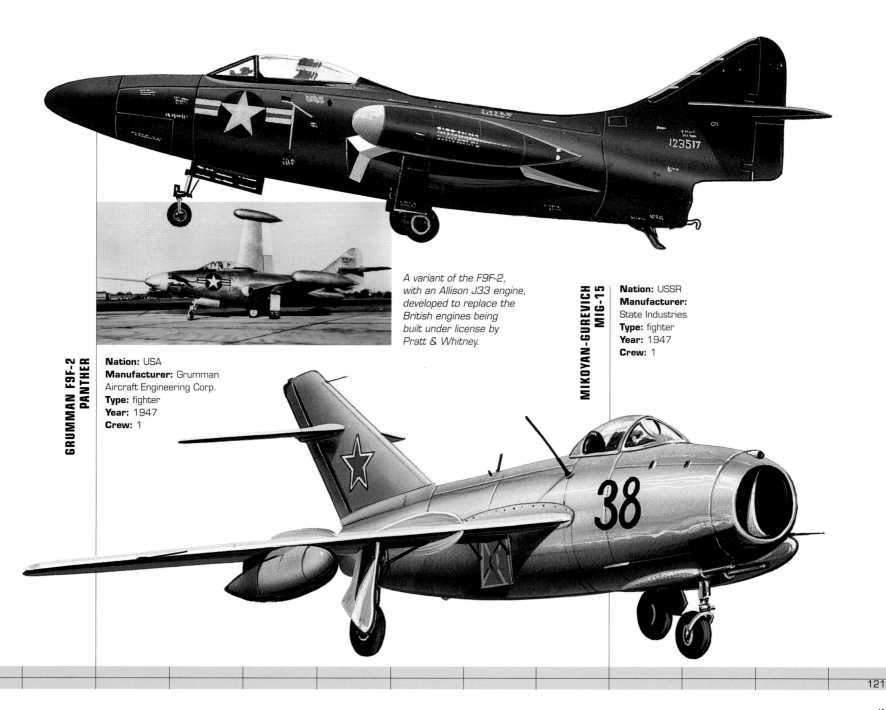

A variant of the F9F-2, with an Allison J33 engine, developed to replace the British engines being built under license by Pratt & Whitney.

GRUMMAN F9F-2 PANTHER

Nation: USA
Manufacturer: Grumman Aircraft Engineering Corp.
Type: fighter
Year: 1947
Crew: 1

MIKOYAN-GUREVICH MIG-15

Nation: USSR
Manufacturer: State Industries
Type: fighter
Year: 1947
Crew: 1

war effort had kept operating at full capacity long after victory, fully agreed with the politicians and military strategists. Naturally victory had reduced the urgency of certain programs: some were downscaled, others abandoned. But the inexorable march of progress was not affected. The jet engine, new protagonist in the world of aviation, had entered the scene with a bang – and all technological and economic resources would be

dedicated to its development so America could catch up with the European competition.

Germany and Britain had already crossed the finish line before war's end, so the United States was last in the race toward jet propulsion. In fact, Britain had put the Gloster Meteor into production a full year before war ended; Germany was so far ahead as to have sent Messerschmitt ME.262 jet fighters into battle. Meanwhile the Bell P-59 Airacomet,

the first USAF jet, was still mired in the prototyping phase. Initially, American inferiority in jet propulsion was as dramatic as its superiority would be later. The tables quickly turned. The Lockheed F-80 Shooting Star of 1948, America's first true combat jet, had an immediate global impact. The US military's introduction of this plane initiated a massive campaign of rearmament, expansion and modernization that rapidly generated

The era of the military jet

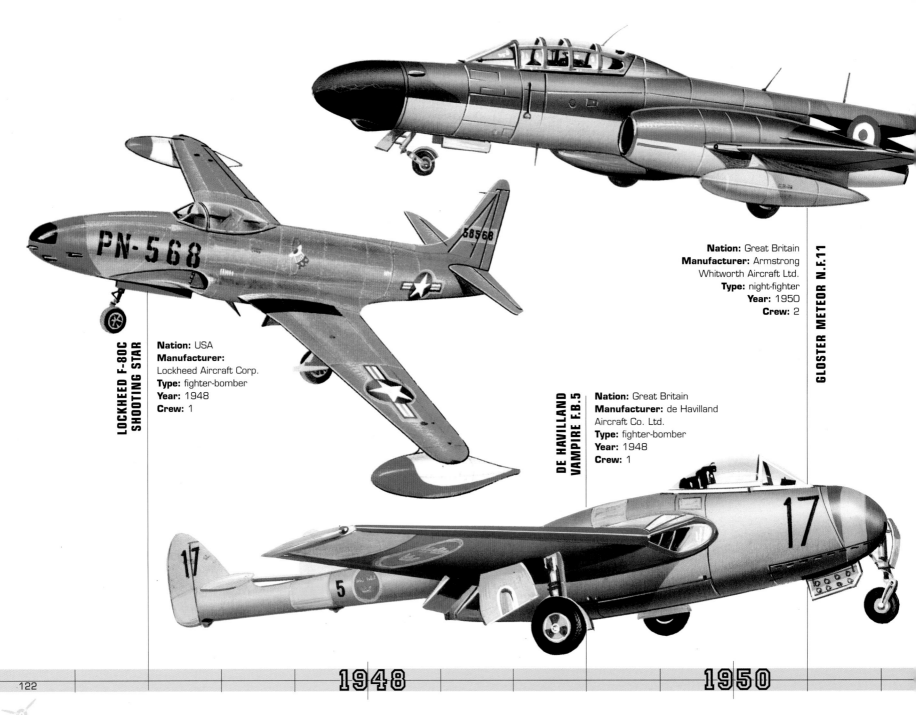

Nation: Great Britain
Manufacturer: Armstrong Whitworth Aircraft Ltd.
Type: night-fighter
Year: 1950
Crew: 2

GLOSTER METEOR N.F.11

LOCKHEED F-80C SHOOTING STAR

Nation: USA
Manufacturer: Lockheed Aircraft Corp.
Type: fighter-bomber
Year: 1948
Crew: 1

DE HAVILLAND VAMPIRE F.B.5

Nation: Great Britain
Manufacturer: de Havilland Aircraft Co. Ltd.
Type: fighter-bomber
Year: 1948
Crew: 1

1948

1950

numerous other combat jets of a quality unrivalled in the western bloc.

A major organizational and operational advance resulted from the decision to grant full autonomy to the air forces, liberating them from their historical subordination to the US Army. On September 18, 1947, the USAAF of WWII glory days passed the aeronautical baton to the newborn United States Air Force, today's USAF. The Navy followed an analogous path, though without separating out its air forces. It developed new aircraft and upgraded existing ones, often in direct competition with the USAF, eventually launching the era of the carrier-based jet with the McDonnell FH Phantom, the first of an illustrious family of fighters, including the more famous Phantom II of the 1950s.

The first generation of combat jets were developed in this climate: the Republic F-84 Thunderjet and the North American F-86 Sabre for the US Air Force; the Grumman F9F Panther and the McDonnell F2H Banshee for the US Navy. Some overlap occurred during the piston engine's waning era: these new jets trained and fought for some years alongside the final versions of WWII prop planes. In other cases, aircraft like the gigantic Convair B-36 strategic bomber used both types of engines simultaneously, epitomizing this period

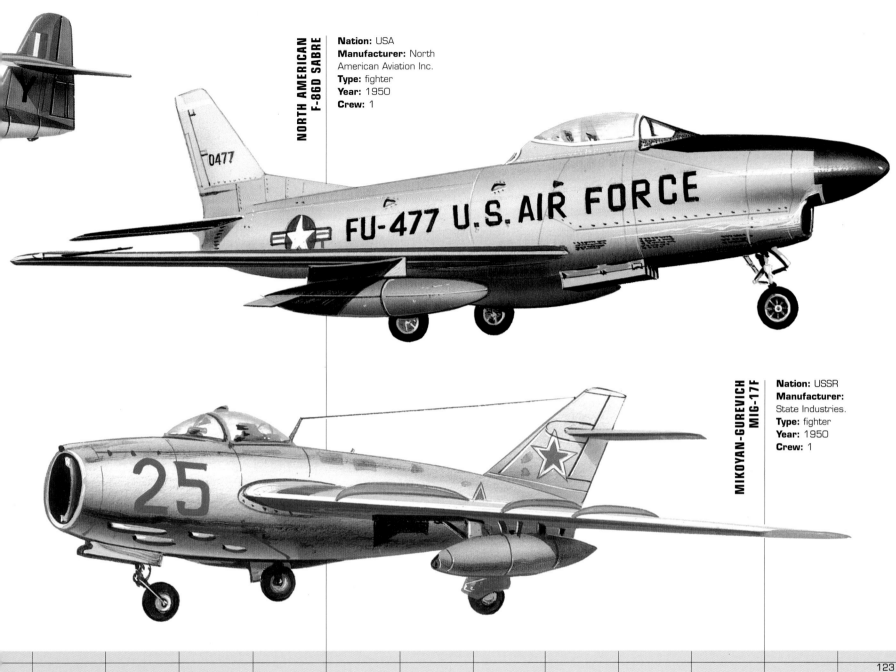

NORTH AMERICAN F-86D SABRE

Nation: USA
Manufacturer: North American Aviation Inc.
Type: fighter
Year: 1950
Crew: 1

MIKOYAN-GUREVICH MIG-17F

Nation: USSR
Manufacturer: State Industries.
Type: fighter
Year: 1950
Crew: 1

of transition. But the transition from propeller to jet propulsion was final and irreversible.

USSR: A CHANGE OF STANCE

In 1945, Soviet military aviation was in a position of marked qualitative inferiority compared to its former allies. But Stalin's expansionist aims drove Soviet industry to close the

An F-86D armed with a retractable carriage for 24 air-to-air missiles, to be fired singly or together.

The era of the military jet

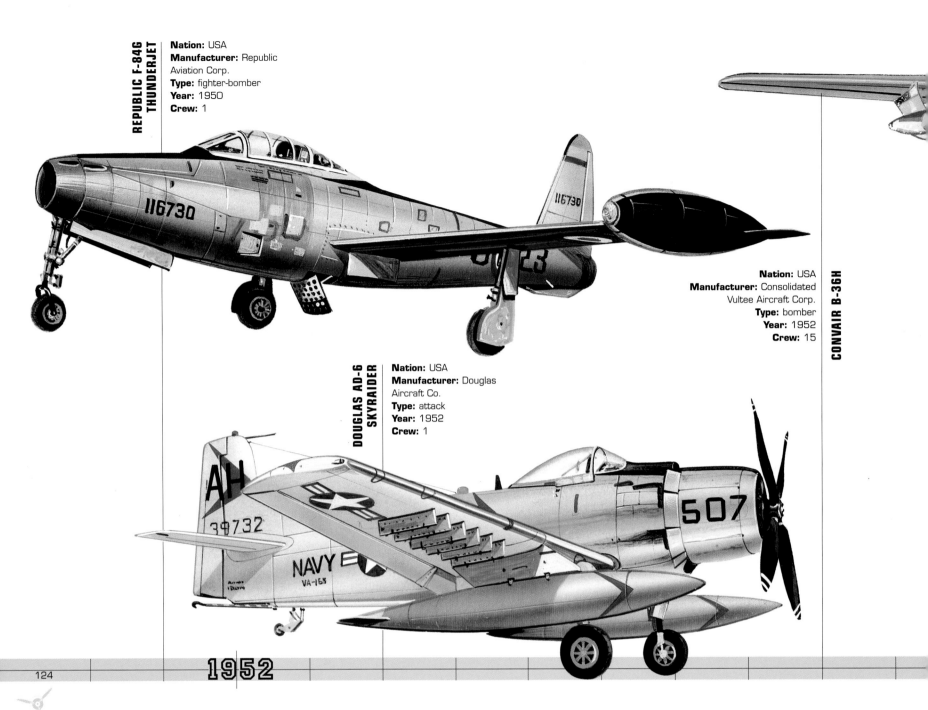

Nation: USA
Manufacturer: Republic Aviation Corp.
Type: fighter-bomber
Year: 1950
Crew: 1

116730

116730

Nation: USA
Manufacturer: Consolidated Vultee Aircraft Corp.
Type: bomber
Year: 1952
Crew: 15

Nation: USA
Manufacturer: Douglas Aircraft Co.
Type: attack
Year: 1952
Crew: 1

AH
39732
NAVY
VA-165
507

1952

gap in record time. The USSR, observing the relative calm of the American and British aeronautical industries in the 1946-47 period, took the exact opposite stance. The Soviet arms industry did not even pause to breathe after WWII. On the contrary, it accelerated both production and research, riding the wave of the progress made in the final phase of the war in Europe. The obstacles were formidable, however, especially in the development of jet engine technology, in which the USSR was effectively without autonomous experience.

The first step was taken while the war was still underway: Stalin's troops had captured and brought to the USSR many German aeronautical engineers and technicians, along with huge quantities of material and documentation. These specialists were set to work on a massive program to advance Soviet aeronautical technology. The captured men included engineers who had designed and built the revolutionary BMW and Junkers Jumo turbine engines, which had powered the Luftwaffe's best combat aircraft. Others had helped develop new jet engines. The results were not outstanding: what the Soviets managed to produce were basically reproductions of the earliest German experiments with turbojets, or derivations thereof – and they were not especially promising. Nonetheless, these early

Nation: France
Manufacturer: Avions Marcel Dassault
Type: fighter-bomber
Year: 1952
Crew: 1

Nation: USSR
Manufacturer: State Industries
Type: fighter
Year: 1953
Crew: 1

1953

turbojets were installed in prototype after prototype, dozens in the end, some of which even reached operational status. These could not be termed anything more than experiments. However, a significant outcome resulted: the formation of a nucleus of work teams headed by the men who became the USSR's most famous aeronautical giants: Tupolev, Ilyushin, Yakovlev, Sukhoi, and the inseparable Mikoyan and Gurevich, from whom the legendary MiG

took its name.

With the West absorbed in post-war reconstruction and political healing, few observers recognized or analyzed what was going on behind the Iron Curtain at that time. The furious Soviet rearmament program went, if not completely unnoticed, then certainly underestimated. In fact, the West ingenuously handed the Soviets their first success in the jet propulsion field on a silver

platter. In 1946, Great Britain licensed Soviet production of its most advanced turbojet, the Rolls-Royce Nene, even supplying several engines for reference. Thus, in one fell swoop, the Soviets closed the yawning technological gap between East and West, and made up for a good deal of lost time. They immediately exploited this incredible windfall to the maximum: in just a few months, the first modern Soviet jet fighter, the MiG-15, was designed

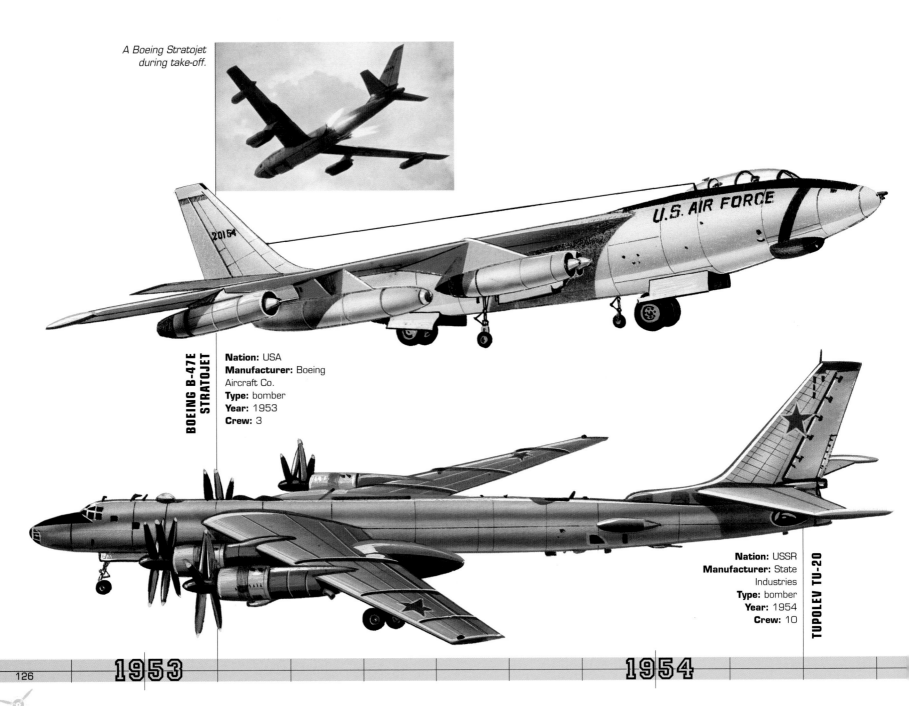

A Boeing Stratojet during take-off.

BOEING B-47E STRATOJET

Nation: USA
Manufacturer: Boeing Aircraft Co.
Type: bomber
Year: 1953
Crew: 3

Nation: USSR
Manufacturer: State Industries
Type: bomber
Year: 1954
Crew: 10

TUPOLEV TU-20

1953   **1954**

and built around the superb English engine. Ironically, in the Korean War's early phases, this simple and powerful machine proved decidedly superior to anything in the USAF or Navy arsenal. The conquest of aeronautical autonomy set into motion an unstoppable forward momentum. Soviet industry increased both its pace and scope and quickly became not only competitive in every aeronautical area, but in many cases superior to

the West. The MiG had already proven its worth, but even in the medium and heavy bomber sector, the cutting-edge designs of Yakovlev and Tupolev thoroughly outclassed their American and British counterparts in the early years of the 'jet age.'

SECOND- AND THIRD-GENERATION FIGHTERS

Progress in jet propulsion and electronics were key factors in the rapid evolution of the

fighter plane, combat aircraft par excellence, during the 1950s. The Korean War experience provided the impetus for the development of a new generation of jet fighters, with basically similar results on both the Soviet and American sides. The shift from the first to the second generation was anything but gradual. With the new engines, fighter performance improved dramatically. The resolution of long-standing aerodynamic problems and resolu-

CONVAIR F-102A DELTA DAGGER

Nation: USA
Manufacturer: Convair Division of General Dynamics
Type: fighter
Year: 1954
Crew: 1

TUPOLEV TU-16A

Nation: USSR
Manufacturer: State Industries
Type: bomber
Year: 1954
Crew: 7

An F-102A landing using parachute brake and airbrakes.

tion of new construction issues were both important factors contributing to the fighter plane's radical improvement. With the advent of the missile, fighters became even deadlier, while the incorporation of electronics not only facilitated flight and combat by making the plane an extension of the pilot's will, but made it possible for a single aircraft to perform a variety of functions previously requiring separate planes. The new fighters set the standard for the next two decades: planes capable of operating at velocities exceeding the speed of sound, powerfully armed, outfitted with the most sophisticated technology, and constructed with the most advanced materials. On the American side, this second generation's avant-garde was represented by the North American F-100 Super Sabre, the Convair F-102 Delta Dagger, the Lockheed F-104 Starfighter, the Republic F-105 Thunderchief (USAF), the LTV F-8 Crusader and the Mc-Donnell F-4 Phantom II (USN). These planes enabled the United States to enter the 1960s boasting the most powerful air force in the western world. With these planes America entered into its second post-war conflict, this time in Vietnam.

Progress on the Soviet side was right in step with that of the Americans. Among the many exceptional aircraft built during those

The era of the military jet

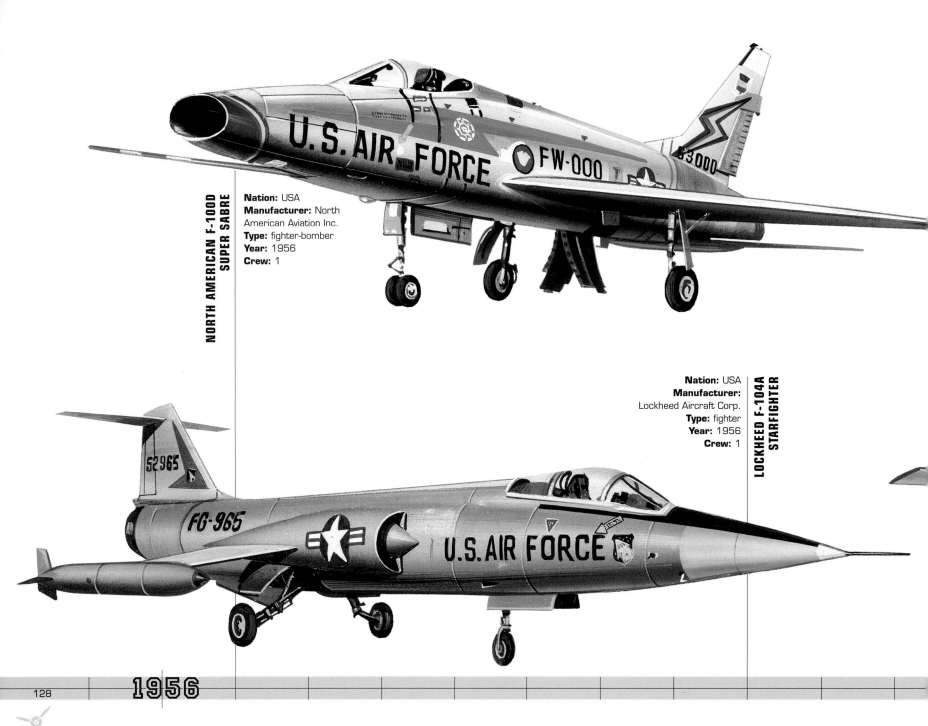

Nation: USA
Manufacturer: North American Aviation Inc.
Type: fighter-bomber
Year: 1956
Crew: 1

Nation: USA
Manufacturer: Lockheed Aircraft Corp.
Type: fighter
Year: 1956
Crew: 1

1956

years, the MiG is the plane that best represents the continuity and rapidity of that progress: from the aforementioned MiG-15 to the 17 to the powerful twin-turbojet MiG-19 of 1953, and finally to the MiG-21 of 1956, which operated at Mach 2, twice the speed of sound. These planes were built in the tens of thousands, not only to serve the forward guard of the motherland, but also to arm the ever-increasing number of Soviet satellite

countries. The extraordinary improvements in the quality and power of the aircraft themselves were accompanied in the 1960s by an intelligent restructuring of the air forces aimed at optimizing the priority role the 'balance of terror' doctrine had assigned to them. Three new Soviet air arms developed from the old VVS: the IAPVO (Aviatsiya Protivovozdushnoi Oborony Strany), which defended the national territory; the FA (Frontovaya Aviat-

siya), or tactical wing; and the ADD (Aviatsiya Dalnovo Deistviya), the long-range strike force. To them was added the VVSMF (Mosdkaya Aviatsiya), the land-based branch of the Soviet Navy assigned to maritime reconnaissance, coastal patrol and anti-submarine missions.

The ever more fervent quest for military superiority during the 1970s gave rise to the third generation of combat aircraft. More powerful and sophisticated than ever, fighter

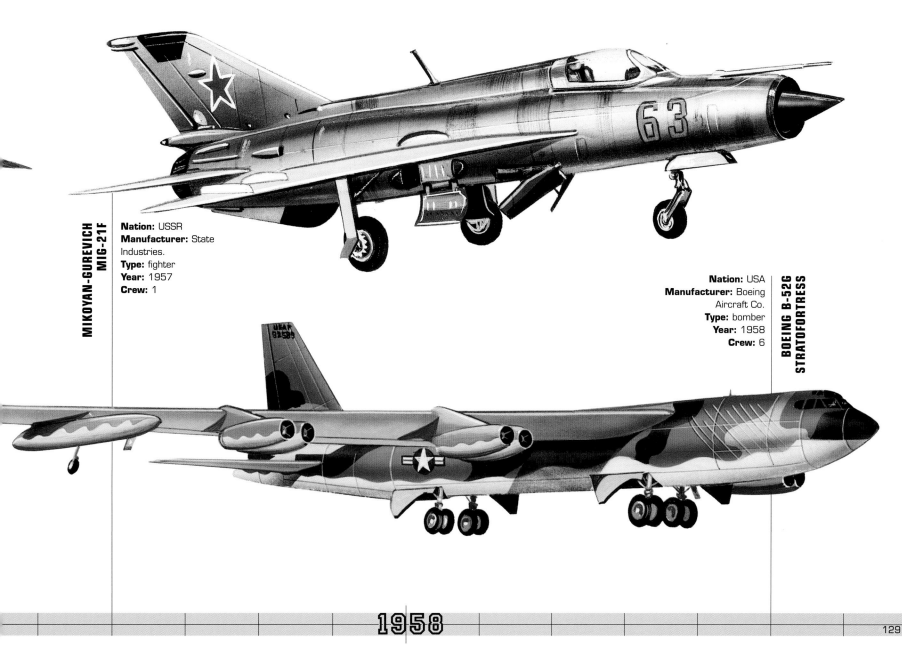

MIKOYAN-GUREVICH MIG-21F

Nation: USSR
Manufacturer: State Industries.
Type: fighter
Year: 1957
Crew: 1

BOEING B-52G STRATOFORTRESS

Nation: USA
Manufacturer: Boeing Aircraft Co.
Type: bomber
Year: 1958
Crew: 6

1958

planes essentially became airborne weapons systems, integrated with the most advanced avionics. Once again, the two superpowers remained neck-to-neck, progressing at the same insidious pace. With carrier-based fighters the US Navy gained a decisive advantage, first with the Grumman F-14 Tomcat, a powerful interceptor with variable-sweep wings,

A B-52G Stratofortress being refueled in midair during the first Gulf War.

The era of the military jet

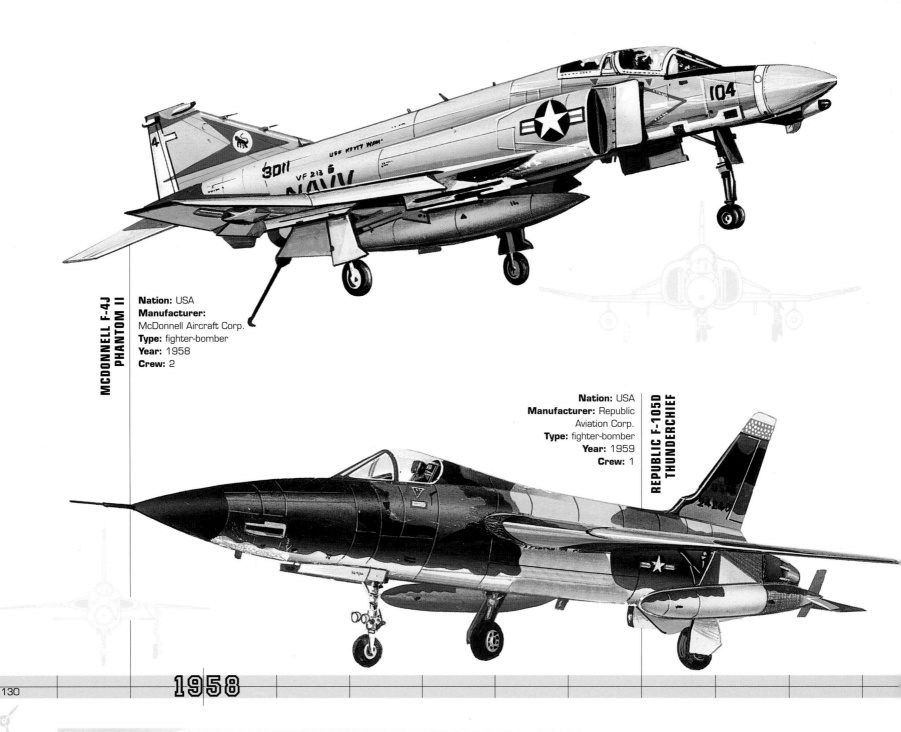

MCDONNELL F-4J PHANTOM II

Nation: USA
Manufacturer:
McDonnell Aircraft Corp.
Type: fighter-bomber
Year: 1958
Crew: 2

REPUBLIC F-105D THUNDERCHIEF

Nation: USA
Manufacturer: Republic
Aviation Corp.
Type: fighter-bomber
Year: 1959
Crew: 1

1958

then with the multirole A/F-18 Hornet, which replaced the F-4 Phantom II. The US Air Force introduced two equally fine machines: the McDonnell-Douglas F-15 Eagle interceptor, and the multirole General Dynamics F-16 Fighting Falcon.

The Soviet fighters of the epoch, though less sophisticated than the American and of-

An F-4E Phantom II of the 81st Tactical Fighter Squadron releasing its bomb load.

ENGLISH ELECTRIC LIGHTNING F.1

Nation: Great Britain
Manufacturer: English Electric Aviation Ltd.
Type: fighter
Year: 1959
Crew: 1

DASSAULT MIRAGE 3

Nation: France
Manufacturer: Avions Marcel Dassault
Type: multirole
Year: 1960
Crew: 1

ten built as needed responses to the enemy's tenacious progress, were every bit as powerful and well-armed. Standout models include the swept-wing MiG-23, the Mach 3 MiG-25, the formidable MiG-29, the Sukhoi Su-15 interceptor and the multirole Su-24 and Su-27.

THE STRATEGIC BOMBER

The long-range bomber gained incalculable new strategic importance with the existence of nuclear weapons, which had already proved decisive in WWII. Indeed, it was beneath the ominous shadow of such armaments that, prior to the advent of the intercontinental ballistic missile, the world trembled in fear of nuclear holocaust. People knew all too well that what had happened at Hiroshima and Nagasaki in 1945 was nothing in comparison to what could happen now: the warheads were a hundred times more powerful, and there were thousands more of them. And if such a warhead were to be dropped, it would be a long-range bomber that dropped it.

The bomber's development proceeded throughout the 1960s before ballistic missiles eventually rendered it less necessary. Alongside the usual adversaries, Great Britain inserted itself as the third great protagonist in this sector. The US enjoyed an ini-

DOUGLAS A-4E SKYHAWK

Nation: USA
Manufacturer: Douglas Aircraft Co.
Type: attack
Year: 1961
Crew: 1

An A-4E Skyhawk of the Kuwaiti air forces taxiing during the first Gulf War. 'Free Kuwait' is painted on the engine cowling.

tial advantage of having excellent prototypes upon which to build, particularly the Boeing B-29, which had put an end to the war with Japan. With its enemy well identified and defined, the USAF took the B-29 as its starting point, augmenting both its performance and its destructive power. The direct successor of the B-29 and the B-50 variant was the Convair B-36, introduced in 1947. The last of its class to be powered by piston engines, the B-

36 was a veritable colossus, capable of carrying nearly 40 tons of bombs for a distance of 6,200 miles. The B-36 is also an apt symbol of the transition to the jet age: the D version of 1949 was outfitted with four turbojets in addition to its six enormous radial engines, significantly augmenting its performance. The next step came quickly: in late 1950 the USAF introduced its first effective jet bomber, the Boeing B-47 Stratojet. Seven years later

the Strategic Air Command added to its arsenal the plane that today remains even today an important symbol of conventional air power: the Boeing B-52 Stratofortress, an aircraft of such irrefutable quality and versatility that even the more modern bisonic Convair B-58 Hustler of 1959 has not displaced it.

As ever, the Soviet Union was never far behind in developing the same sector, sometimes it was ahead. Like the Americans,

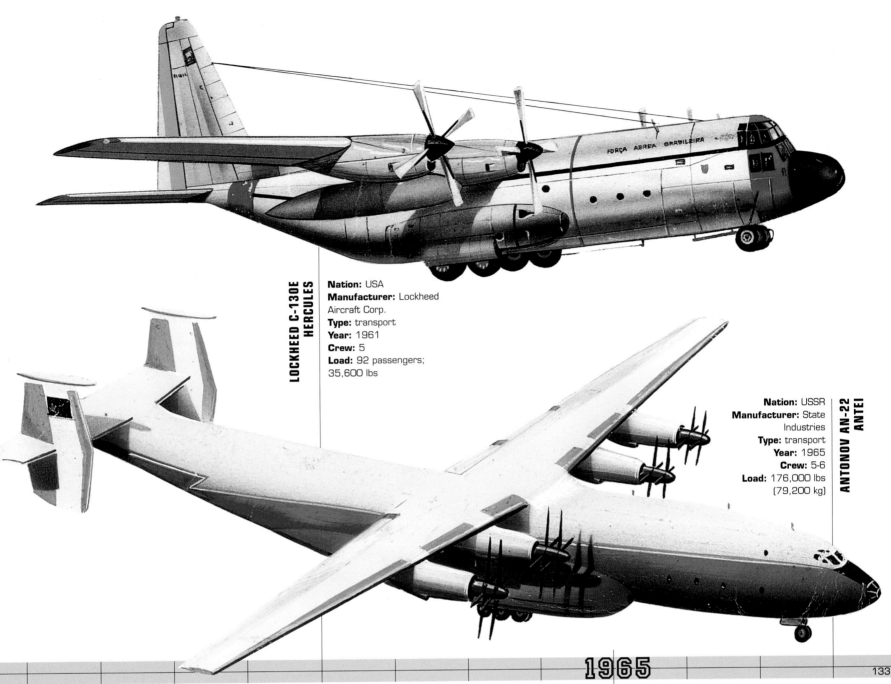

LOCKHEED C-130E HERCULES

Nation: USA
Manufacturer: Lockheed Aircraft Corp.
Type: transport
Year: 1961
Crew: 5
Load: 92 passengers; 35,600 lbs

ANTONOV AN-22 ANTEI

Nation: USSR
Manufacturer: State Industries
Type: transport
Year: 1965
Crew: 5-6
Load: 176,000 lbs (79,200 kg)

1965

Soviet bombers tended toward gigantism in the years preceding the intercontinental ballistic missile (ICBM). The most significant exponents of this category were the Myasischev Mya-4, the Tupolev Tu-20 turboprop, the Tu-16 and the supersonic Tu-22, which appeared in 1960 as a direct response to the American B-58.

Great Britain inserted itself brilliantly into the race with its three great strategic bombers of the so-called 'V' class, all of them developed as part of the intensive rearmament of the early '50s: the Vickers Valiant of 1953, the Avro Vulcan of 1955, and the Handley Page Victor of 1956. The best of the three was the Vulcan, the world's first delta-wing bomber, which remained in service until the 1980s.

Meanwhile the United States had defined a new objective: integration of the most recent advanced weapons system – the cruise missile – into the traditional bomber. The result was the Rockwell International B-1, one of the most controversial military projects of recent decades. This sophisticated strategic bomber, a veritable flying computer, was capable of carrying 22 cruise missiles and had a range that permitted it reach any point on the globe. The project was initiated in the late '60s with the intention of replacing

SUKHOI SU-17

Nation: USSR
Manufacturer: State Industries
Type: attack
Year: 1967
Crew: 1

1967

1946-2003

the B-52. But enormous cost overruns compelled President Carter to suspend the B-1 program in 1977.

The traditional bomber's final evolution took place in the 1980s, fueled by the renewed intensification of the arms race provoked by the Reagan administration. Among the consequences of the new policy was the reactivation of the Rockwell B-1. Though brought to a successful conclusion,

VERTICAL FLIGHT

The aeronautics industry has always imagined the possibility of a conventional airplane that would incorporate a key feature of the helicopter: vertical takeoff and landing. Carrier-based fighters and certain military transport planes, classified as STOL aircraft (short takeoff and landing), have long been able to operate on relatively short runways. But the dream of VTOL (vertical takeoff and landing) or STOVL (short takeoff, vertical landing) seemed an impossible dream until the introduction of the Harrier fighter, nicknamed 'jump jet,' the first combat plane capable of vertical flight. Conceived in Great Britain in the 1950s, the research and development process was as long as it was controversial. But the revolutionary Harrier has amply demonstrated its enormous strategic and logistical potential, both in the ground-based operations for which it was originally conceived and in the carrier-based role it has since assumed.

From a strictly technological point of view, the key to the Harrier's success lies in the original propulsion system, wherein the engine is equipped with four multi-directional thrust-vectoring nozzles which give the plane its unique ability to hover, and give the pilot an exceptional degree of control on the vertical axis. This original configuration has remained unaltered throughout the Harrier's long evolution, the most important phase of which took place in the 1970s after the US Marine Corps, impressed with the plane's potential, arranged for McDonnell-Douglas to build it on license in the

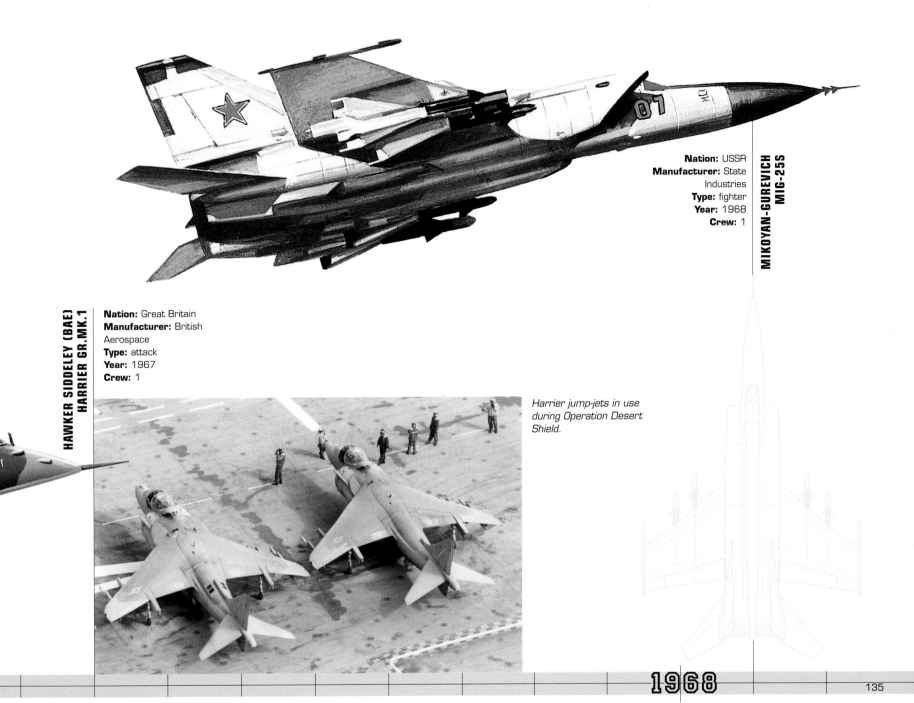

MIKOYAN-GUREVICH MIG-25S

Nation: USSR
Manufacturer: State
Industries
Type: fighter
Year: 1968
Crew: 1

HAWKER SIDDELEY (BAE) HARRIER GR.MK.1

Nation: Great Britain
Manufacturer: British
Aerospace
Type: attack
Year: 1967
Crew: 1

Harrier jump-jets in use
during Operation Desert
Shield.

1968

135

The era of the military jet

United States. Up to this point, the plane had been considered by many as not much more than a bizarre experimental toy. Then McDonnell-Douglas completely redesigned the plane, tailoring it to the specific needs of the Marines. Dubbed the AV-8B Harrier II, the jump jet was now not merely a great idea with great potential, but a mature and battle-ready fighter plane. After a promising debut in the Falkland Islands conflict of 1982, the Harrier definitively proved its mettle in the first Gulf War. With the STOVL concept's increasing importance in modern warfare combat operations, and in continuous tactical and reconnaissance missions launched from continuously changing positions, the Harrier revealed itself to be indispensable.

Vertical flight, innovation and high technology are also the guiding principles behind another ambitious initiative of American industry, the 'convertiplane' project that gave rise to the Bell-Boeing V-22 Osprey. A cross between a helicopter and an airplane, the Osprey has been ordered by the US Marine Corps, the US Navy and the USAF. Design began in 1982 and the first cycle of test flights in 1989. But the project has been and continues to be fraught with long delays, cost overruns and numerous accidents which have placed the dependability of the aircraft in serious question. The distinguishing feature of the convertiplane is a wing which rotates on the horizontal axis, allowing the two oversized propellers to assume different positions: parallel to the ground in the takeoff and landing phases, perpendicular in forward flight. The Osprey is scheduled to enter service in 2005.

far fewer were produced than originally planned, and the B-1 did not succeed in replacing the venerable B-52.

EUROPEAN FIGHTERS AND MULTI-ROLES

Europe was by no means immune to 'Cold War fever.' During the 45 years of the Soviet-American arms race, the Old Continent found both the motivation and the resources to maintain its aeronautical industry at the same

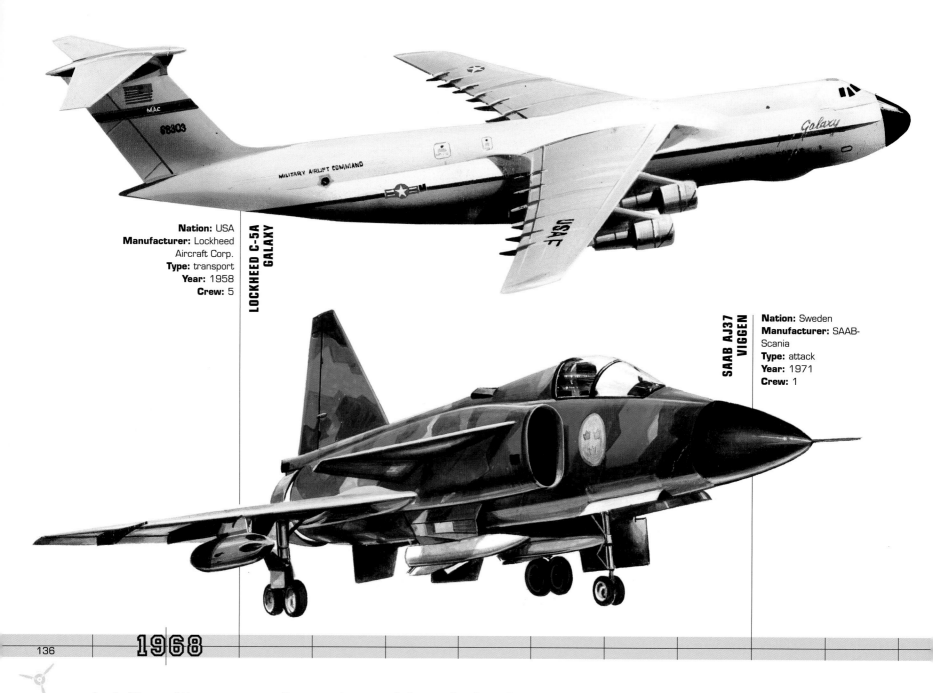

Nation: USA
Manufacturer: Lockheed Aircraft Corp.
Type: transport
Year: 1958
Crew: 5

LOCKHEED C-5A GALAXY

Nation: Sweden
Manufacturer: SAAB-Scania
Type: attack
Year: 1971
Crew: 1

SAAB AJ37 VIGGEN

1968

1946-2003

level of those of the superpowers. France and Britain, Europe's traditional aeronautical leaders, developed some of the best combat planes ever built. And they were joined by a third, and unexpected power: Sweden.

As in the States, British participation in the Korean War both stimulated the aviation industry and underscored to need to maintain a competitive air force. Consequently, research and production received the boost

needed to awaken from the post-war lull.

The second generation of British fighters appeared at the end of the '40s; the best of them were the RSF's powerful bisonic English Electric Lightning interceptor and the Fleet Air Arm's advanced Supermarine Scimitar and Hawker Siddeley Sea Vixen. But British ingenuity's greatest success was the revolutionary Harrier, the first fixed-wing aircraft capable of vertical takeoff and landing, a machine so

innovative as to have changed some of air warfare's most basic tactical tenets. After its extremely lengthy gestation, the Harrier was chosen by the US Marine Corps. A licensing agreement was negotiated with McDonnell-Douglas, which then proceeded develop even more advanced and powerful versions of the already supremely advanced 'Jump Jet.'

In France, the enterprising Marcel Dassault's new aeronautical firm dominated the

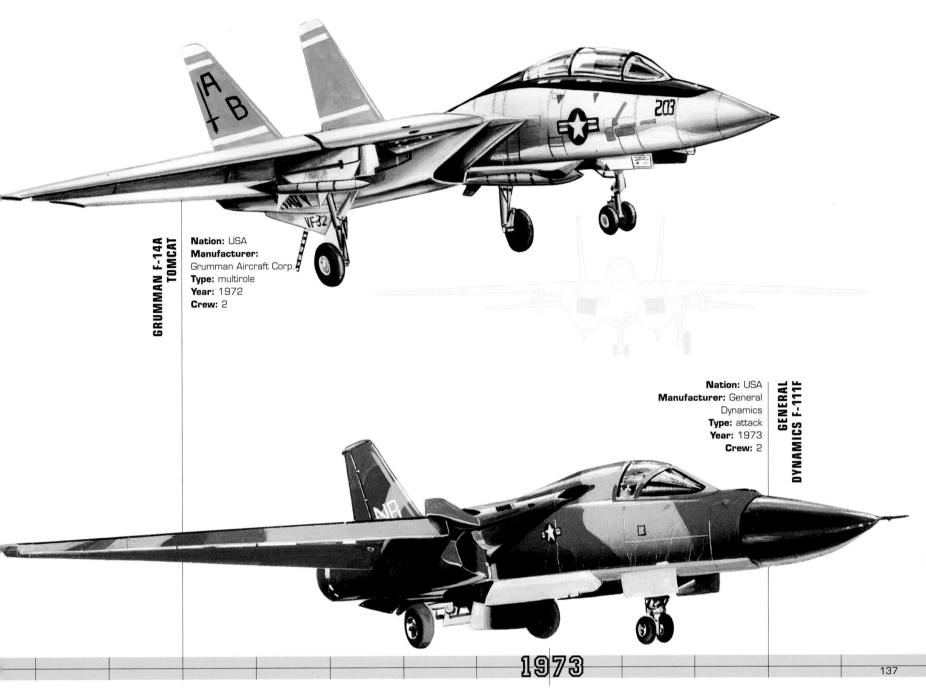

GRUMMAN F-14A TOMCAT

Nation: USA
Manufacturer:
Grumman Aircraft Corp.
Type: multirole
Year: 1972
Crew: 2

GENERAL DYNAMICS F-111F

Nation: USA
Manufacturer: General
Dynamics
Type: attack
Year: 1973
Crew: 2

1973

1950s. After the success of his Ouragan of
1949 – the first French jet fighter – came that
of the supersonic Dassault Mystère and
Super Mystère, and the carrier-borne Éten-
dard. From these early experiences the most
famous Dassault fighter, the Mirage, was
developed. The base version, the Mirage III,
gave rise to a long line of variants that many

*An F-14A Tomcat bristling with missiles: an AIM-7
Sparrow, an AIM-9 Sidewinder, and an AGM-54 Phoenix.*

The era of the military jet

Nation: USA
Manufacturer: McDonnell
Aircraft Corp.
Type: multirole
Year: 1974
Crew: 1

Maintenance inspectors
decontaminate an F-15E
Eagle during Operation
Desert Shield.

USAF
10291
F-15

1974

nations' air forces eagerly acquired in great numbers. France's ambition to become the world's third military power corresponded with Dassault's ambition to build the world's best fighter jets. And with the last two versions of the Mirage – the multirole 2000 and Super Mirage 4000 of the 1980s – and the extraordinary Rafale of the 1990s, it would be difficult to argue that France didn't succeed.

One of the more interesting military phenomena of the post-war era was the Swedish aeronautical industry's unexpectedly rapid evolution – which immediately becomes more understandable, however, if one considers the country's proximity to the USSR and the consequent need to defend its borders. The effective but not exceptional Saab 32 Lansen entered into service in 1955. Then, just a few months later, the world military establishment was stunned by the power and

sophistication of the Saab 35 Draken, undeniably one of the finest interceptors of its time. The Swedes repeated their success in subsequent evolutions, most notably the Saab 37 Viggen and the 39 Gripen, this latter a multirole combat plane that could stand with the best aircraft being built by any of the traditional giants of aviation.

Recognizing the immense financial and industrial resources that development of a

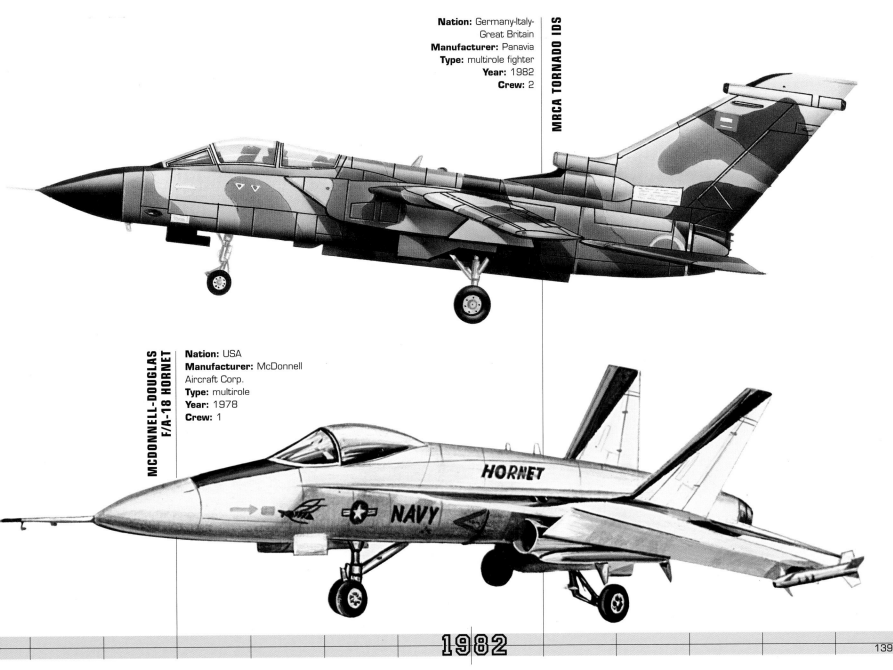

Nation: Germany-Italy-
Great Britain
Manufacturer: Panavia
Type: multirole fighter
Year: 1982
Crew: 2

Nation: USA
Manufacturer: McDonnell
Aircraft Corp.
Type: multirole
Year: 1978
Crew: 1

1982

139

SMART BOMBS

The so-called 'smart bomb' was one of the many great surprises of the 1991 Gulf War. During the 42 days of Operation Desert Storm (January 17 February 28) conducted by an international US-led coalition, the devastating precision of these weapons was witnessed by the world as command centers, bunkers, industrial installations and missile-launching sites were destroyed with a 'surgical' efficiency never before seen in the history of aerial bombardment. The American arsenal divides them into two major families: LGBs (laser-guided bombs) and HOBOS (homing bomb system), these latter either electro-optical or infrared guided. In addition to bombs built specifically for these purposes, there also exist conversion kits that can be applied to the various types of free-fall, or 'dumb' bombs. Once launched, smart bombs respond with sensors to the laser, TV or infrared commands emitted by the delivery aircraft, maneuvering their small guide fins to alter trajectory and direct themselves to the target. The speed and distance they can reach depend exclusively on the altitude at which they are launched. In the case of electro-optical guided ordnance, known as 'fire-and-forget' bombs, the target is acquired through a TV link with the delivery plane and reached by 'memorizing' the contrast between the target and the surrounding environment. With laser-guided bombs, on the other hand, the target must be continuously 'lit up' by a laser designator, which can be aimed from the delivery aircraft, from another plane, or even from the ground.

modern airplane required, a number of European countries decided to optimize those resources by working together. The resulting international consortium comprising Great Britain, Italy and Germany thus created the MRCA Tornado, a multirole jet with variable-sweep wings intended for the three participating nations' air forces. The Tornado's success led to the Eurofighter program, which saw the inclusion of Spain in the consortium.

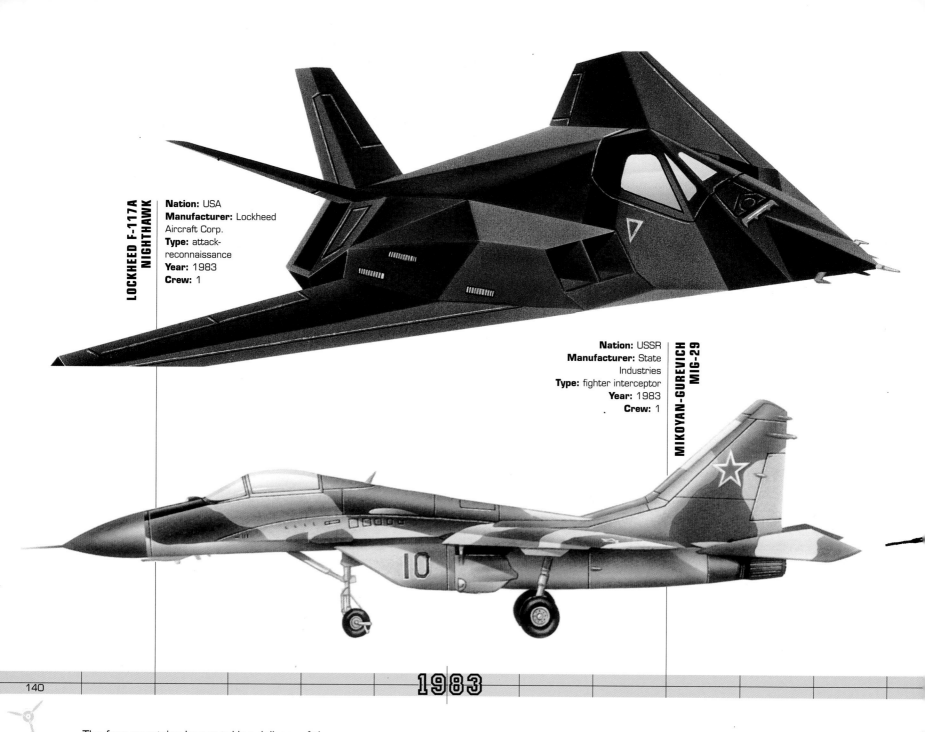

LOCKHEED F-117A NIGHTHAWK

Nation: USA
Manufacturer: Lockheed Aircraft Corp.
Type: attack-reconnaissance
Year: 1983
Crew: 1

MIKOYAN-GUREVICH MIG-29

Nation: USSR
Manufacturer: State Industries
Type: fighter interceptor
Year: 1983
Crew: 1

1983

The four countries began taking delivery of the first Eurofighter Typhoons (the plane was interestingly classified as an 'air-superiority fighter') in 2002; production is scheduled to continue through 2018.

NEW TECHNOLOGIES

From the 1990s onward, neither the remnant of the once titanic Soviet aeronautical industry nor the important European contributions to

INVISIBLE AIRPLANES

'Stealth': an intriguing name for an intriguing new development in the world of military aviation. The latest challenge faced by aeronautical technology is so ambitious as to be nearly preposterous: to build an 'invisible' combat plane capable of eluding not only traditional optical means, but above all the ever more sensitive and sophisticated radar, infrared and electromagnetic detection systems. During the 1980s and '90s, the American aerospace industry invested untold billions of dollars on this research to become the unchallenged leader in the field. The first two exponents of this new breed of stealth aircraft – the Lockheed F-117 tactical fighter and the Northrop B-2 strategic bomber – have both demonstrated their absolute validity on the field of battle to the extent that, from the moment of their introduction in the first Gulf War, traditional air war tactics and strategies have changed definitively and forever.

The first aspect of the F-117's 'invisibility' derives from the form itself: the plane is an unusual configuration of angular lines and polyhedric surfaces, at first glance awkward and arbitrary but in reality carefully designed to fracture the radar signature. The entire structure, which makes extensive use of advanced materials such as Kevlar, carbon fiber and titanium, obeys a sort of zig-zag compositional principle, with all angles larger than 30 degrees with

F-16 Fighting Falcons of the 157th Tactical Fighter Wing lined up on the runway during the first Gulf War.

Nation: USA
Manufacturer: General Dynamics
Type: multirole fighter
Year: 1984
Crew: 1

1984

respect to the vertical, following this same logic down the finest details. The deflection of radar waves is further ensured by the exterior sheathing, which is made of special materials that absorb electromagnetic energy. No less attention was given to the suppression of the other most important sources of instrument visibility: heat and noise. The intake valves of the engines are covered by tight rectangular grilles that muffle the noise of the fans, making the plane as quiet as a luxury automobile. The exhaust valves are configured so as to send the hot air upwards where it is mixed with a jet of cold air, thereby 'hiding' the engine's heat above the plane where ground-based instrumentation cannot detect it.

The same technological and operational philosophy underlies the B-2 bomber, the unexpected form of which derives directly from the 'flying wings' developed by Northrop in the immediate post-war years. The result of these technologies pushes the limits of credulity. The gigantic B-2, with a wingspan just slightly less than that of a 747, disperses its own massive electromagnetic image in millions of illegible 'echoes' and becomes effectively invisible. The point is somewhat debatable. Some claim that the total surface area visible to instrumentation is not more than one third of a square foot – that is, the size of a postcard. Others insist that in reality these planes are detectable, but at such close distances (10-15 miles) as to render the enemy's timely preparation of defenses impossible.

furthering military aviation could touch the United States' absolute supremacy. On the geopolitical level, the end of the Cold War and the reestablishment of cordial diplomatic ties between East and West inaugurated a new phase in the global balance of power, with America as the sole and undisputed superpower. The end of the arms race did not eliminate the specter of war; despite the absence of hostile colossi, there remains the possibility of regional

Nation: USSR
Manufacturer: State Industries
Type: multirole-training
Year: 1984
Crew: 2

Nation: France
Manufacturer: Dassault-Breguet
Type: attack
Year: 1987
Crew: 2

1984

conflicts no less bloody and violent than the wars of the past and capable of sparking dangerous political chain reactions. And of course there is danger of supra-regional ideological conflict, as evidenced by September 11, 2001, when the world met a new enemy without country or government: international terrorism. Humanity has not been liberated

From this angle the Soviet fighter Su-27 shows its resemblance to the F-15 and the MiG-29.

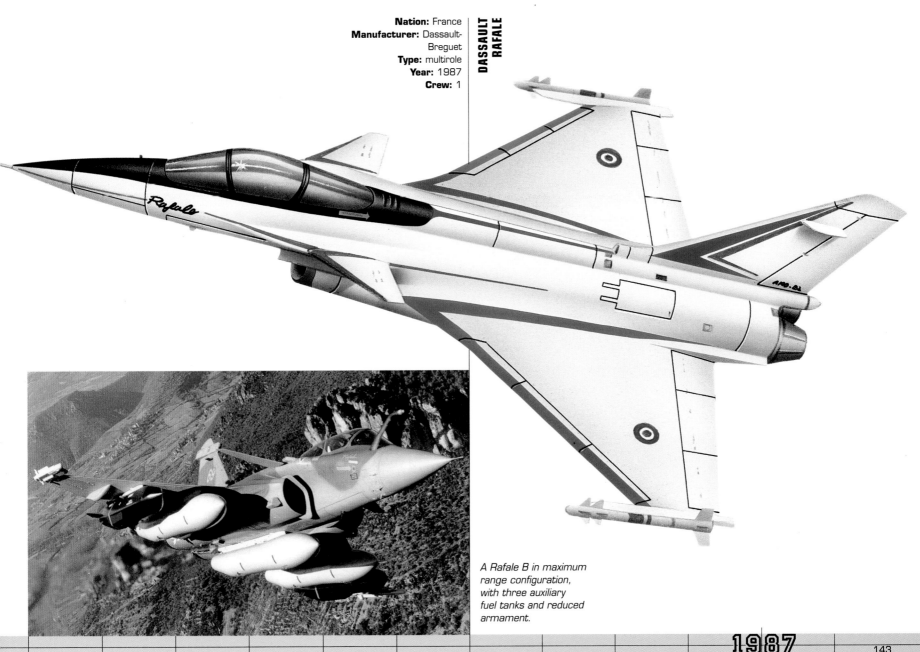

Nation: France
Manufacturer: Dassault-Breguet
Type: multirole
Year: 1987
Crew: 1

DASSAULT RAFALE

A Rafale B in maximum range configuration, with three auxiliary fuel tanks and reduced armament.

from war: in 1991 it ravaged the Persian Gulf; in 1999, the Balkans; in 2002, Afghanistan, and now it devastates Iraq. The images of contemporary warfare are burned forever into our minds: the merciless precision of so-called 'surgical' air strikes, the devastating incursions of cruise missiles launched from ships, aircraft, even submarines positioned thousands of miles away. It is no accident that 'air superiority' is by now a concept familiar to

everyone; indeed, it determined the outcome of all the aforementioned conflicts.

The new millennium's geopolitical scenario thus foresees an even more important role for the airplane. Modern military aviation continues to evolve at an incredible pace, particularly with regard to advanced materials and electronics. The enormity of this progress is confirmed by projects undertaken in recent years, from those aimed at optimizing 'traditional' aircraft

(i.e., aircraft still having recognizable features such as wings!), to those designed for hypothetical future wars, aircraft that breach the threshold between comprehensible reality and science fiction. One such project is the Northrop B-2 Spirit, unquestionably the most innovative and sophisticated bomber ever built. The B-2's distinctive 'flying wing' design is merely the most apparent outcome of the program's underlying objective: to create a long-range

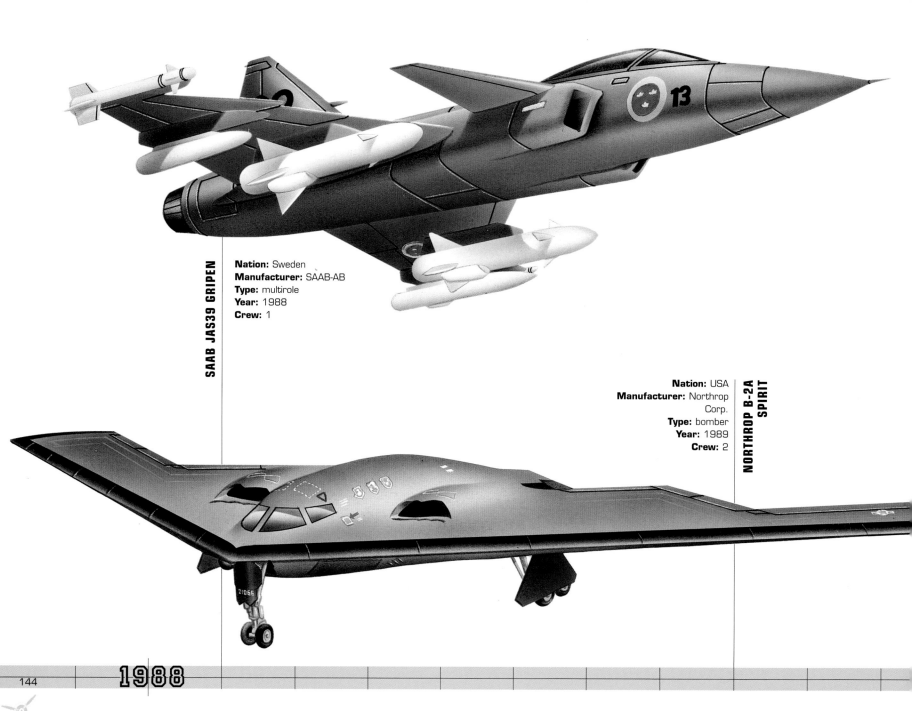

SAAB JAS39 GRIPEN

Nation: Sweden
Manufacturer: SAAB-AB
Type: multirole
Year: 1988
Crew: 1

NORTHROP B-2A SPIRIT

Nation: USA
Manufacturer: Northrop Corp.
Type: bomber
Year: 1989
Crew: 2

1988

bomber with reduced infrared, radar, electromagnetic, acoustic and visual signatures in order to remain 'invisible' to enemy defenses. The costs for the program were so enormous as to be unimaginable, but the resulting technology, known as 'stealth,' represents one of the great milestones in aviation history.

No less futuristic is the fourth-generation

The ultra-sophisticated B-2 bomber preparing for its first flight.

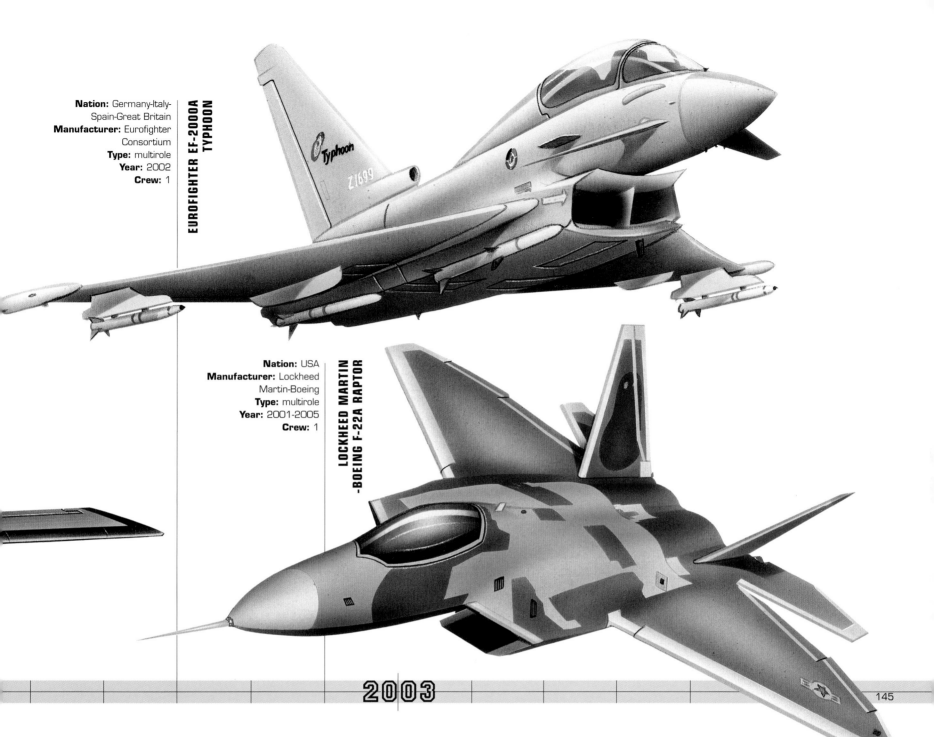

Nation: Germany-Italy-
Spain-Great Britain
Manufacturer: Eurofighter
Consortium
Type: multirole
Year: 2002
Crew: 1

EUROFIGHTER EF-2000A TYPHOON

Nation: USA
Manufacturer: Lockheed
Martin-Boeing
Type: multirole
Year: 2001-2005
Crew: 1

LOCKHEED MARTIN -BOEING F-22A RAPTOR

2003

'air-superiority' fighter developed by Lockheed-Martin-Boeing, the spectacular F-22A Raptor. Designed in the early '90s and finally produced in 2001, the F-22A pushes the B-2's stealth technology yet further, adapting it to different operational needs.

Superiority in armaments and munitions also belongs to America, which has gradually developed a doctrine whereby the aircraft is conceived as a courier, designed to deliver ever more sophisticated and costly weapons in the most efficient way possible. Today, between guided missiles and 'smart bombs,' on-board weapons management and automated countermeasure systems, a modern combat plane is essentially a computer terminal with wings. The pilot assumes the role of supervisor, whose task it is monitor the workings of the system and whose intervention is necessary only in the ever less likely event of unforeseen circumstances. This new reality makes the images and accounts of wars gone by seem farther away in the past than they actually are. For it was only two or three generations ago when it was man who dominated machine, when aviators challenged one another face-to-face, one-on-one like knights of yore, with only their wits and skill and intimate knowledge of the peculiarities of their own trusted plane to determine a battle's outcome.

The Airbus family will soon include a new 800-passenger superliner, the A-380.

Opposite page: An L-188A Electra turboprop, one of Lockheed's less fortunate contributions to civil aviation.

1940

THE JET AND CIVIL AVIATION

THE RACE TO DEVELOP THE FIRST JET LINER
SETS THE PACE FOR THE EVOLUTION
OF MODERN COMMERCIAL AIR TRANSPORT,
ONE OF HUMANKIND'S GREATEST ACHIEVEMENTS.

2003

With a century having passed since the airplane's birth, it might be thought that the world's problems had been resolved. Many have, but others have arisen. In recent years terrorism, war, and epidemics, to name a few, have caused inestimable damage to global commercial aviation. In the fiscal year 2001-2002 the civil air transport industry reported cumulative losses of $25 billion, with 400,000 jobs lost. Venerable airlines like TWA, Sabena and Ansett have folded, crushed by debt; others such as Swissair, United, and American Airlines are in deep financial crisis. In addition to problems caused by excessive deregulation, pitiless competition, and astronomical cost increases, terrorism is a factor. The events of September 11, 2001 halved passenger traffic, and it had barely recovered before war was declared on Iraq. Concurrently, the SARS epidemic broke out in China, and the world was afraid of anyone arriving by airplane from anywhere.

This grim portrait of the state of commercial aviation, painted by the IATA (International Air Transport Association) in June 2003, describes a single, particularly bad year. But civil transport has seen many others. In recent decades, it has become an extremely complex and dynamic system, more subject

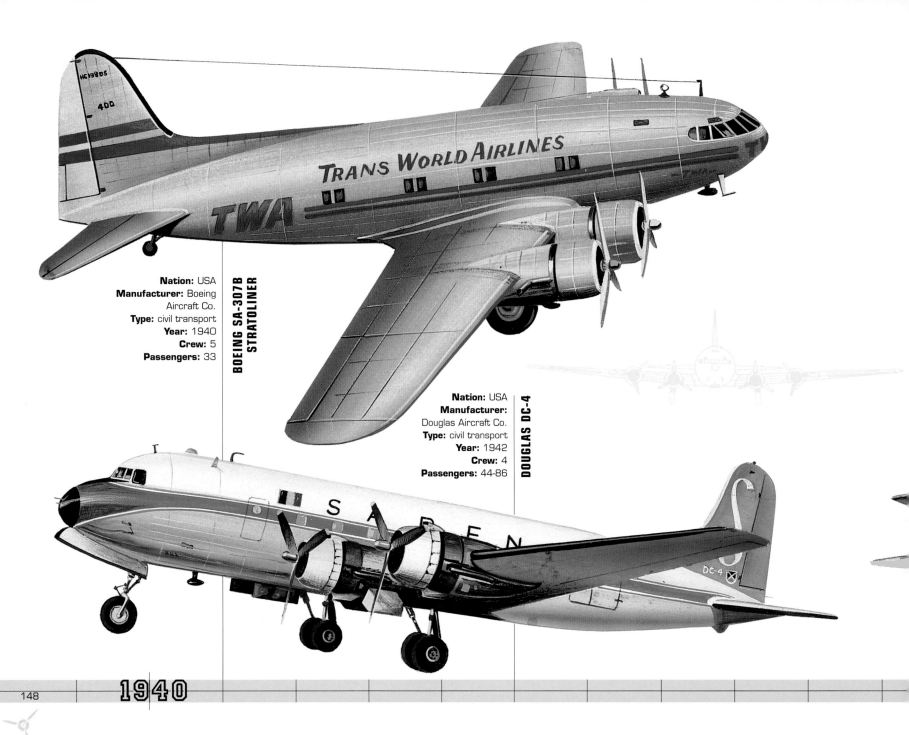

Nation: USA
Manufacturer: Boeing Aircraft Co.
Type: civil transport
Year: 1940
Crew: 5
Passengers: 33

BOEING SA-307B STRATOLINER

Nation: USA
Manufacturer: Douglas Aircraft Co.
Type: civil transport
Year: 1942
Crew: 4
Passengers: 44-86

DOUGLAS DC-4

1940

1940-2003

than other systems to external variables, such that economic crises, energy shortages, military conflicts and geopolitical tensions have heavily conditioned commercial aviation's development. However, bad years aside, the overall tendency has been toward expansion and progress, and nothing has ever stopped commercial air travel from playing a determining role in the evolution of modern society. The vast network of air traffic routes that wraps

the planet is only the most evident sign of a need for mobility that only the airplane can fulfill. A few key numbers help explain the dimensions of the phenomenon.

According to the ICAO (International Civil Aviation Organization), between 1982 and 1991 the number of passengers transported annually by commercial airlines grew from 766 million to nearly 1.1 billion. Recent events have flattened the growth curve somewhat,

but nonetheless, 1.6 billion passengers took to the skies in 2002, accounting for 40% of global trade in the aeronautical sector. The IATA foresees increases to 2.3 billion in 2010 and 3 billion by 2015. The European market, with 130 active airlines as of 2003 and around 300 million passengers served annually, is growing especially fast, and is expected to double by 2020. The outlook of the aerospace industry itself is another important factor to

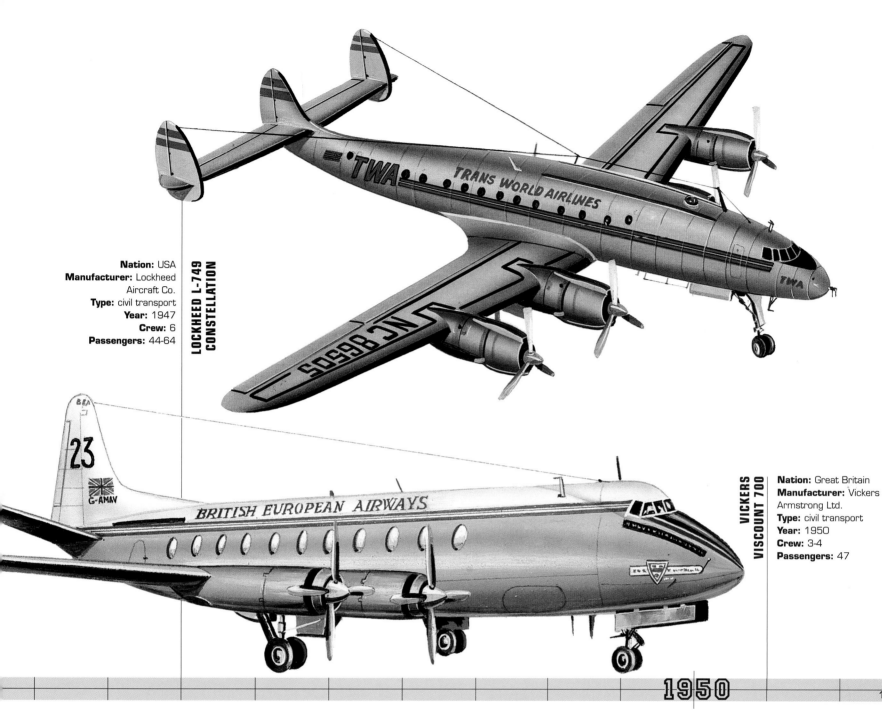

Nation: USA
Manufacturer: Lockheed
Aircraft Co.
Type: civil transport
Year: 1947
Crew: 6
Passengers: 44-64

VICKERS VISCOUNT 700

Nation: Great Britain
Manufacturer: Vickers
Armstrong Ltd.
Type: civil transport
Year: 1950
Crew: 3-4
Passengers: 47

1950

consider, and is perhaps an even more concrete indicator than projected traffic figures, as it costs a lot more to build a jetliner than to fly in one. Airbus Industrie, to name just one manufacturer, estimates that it alone will have to build no fewer than 18,000 new passenger aircraft by 2020 to keep up with demand. The civil air transport revolution, perhaps the most conspicuous achievement of the modern era, has in many ways only just begun. It is useful

to retrace the milestones of this revolution through the period of its greatest progress, from the end of WWII to the present.

THE LAST PISTON-ENGINE AIRLINERS

The jet engine, born of the exigencies of war, became the great protagonist of aviation in the 1950s. While the revolutionary new technology had an immediate impact in the military sector, it took a while longer to affect civil

transport. The early post-war years saw commercial aviation in a transitional phase, still fully reliant on what would turn out to be the last generation of piston-driven engines, yet nevertheless expanding at an unprecedented rate. First in line were the United States, Great Britain and the Soviet Union, the nations that had won the war. And alongside them stood, surprisingly, France, whose aeronautical industry had been at a standstill since

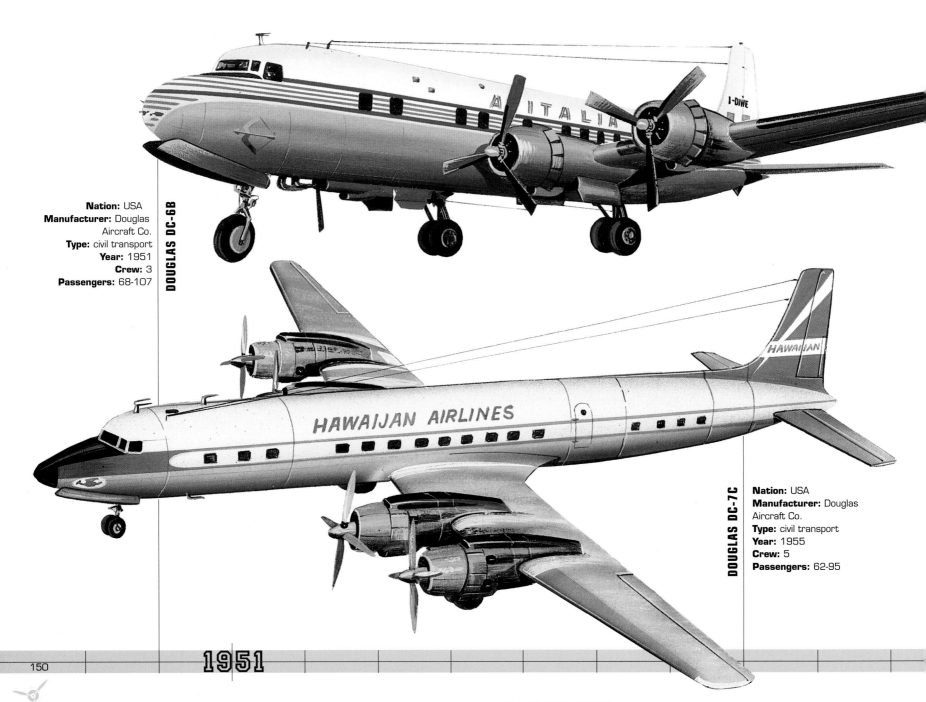

Nation: USA
Manufacturer: Douglas Aircraft Co.
Type: civil transport
Year: 1951
Crew: 3
Passengers: 68-107

DOUGLAS DC-6B

DOUGLAS DC-7C

Nation: USA
Manufacturer: Douglas Aircraft Co.
Type: civil transport
Year: 1955
Crew: 5
Passengers: 62-95

1951

1940-2003

the German occupation. But by 1945 significant signs of progress had already begun to show, and France gradually regained its confidence and autonomy such that European aeronautics, with France and Great Britain as the spearhead, was soon challenging American supremacy. This was due in large part to the nationalization of the airlines that had

In the version built for Alitalia, the four-engine DC-6B carried 69 passengers.

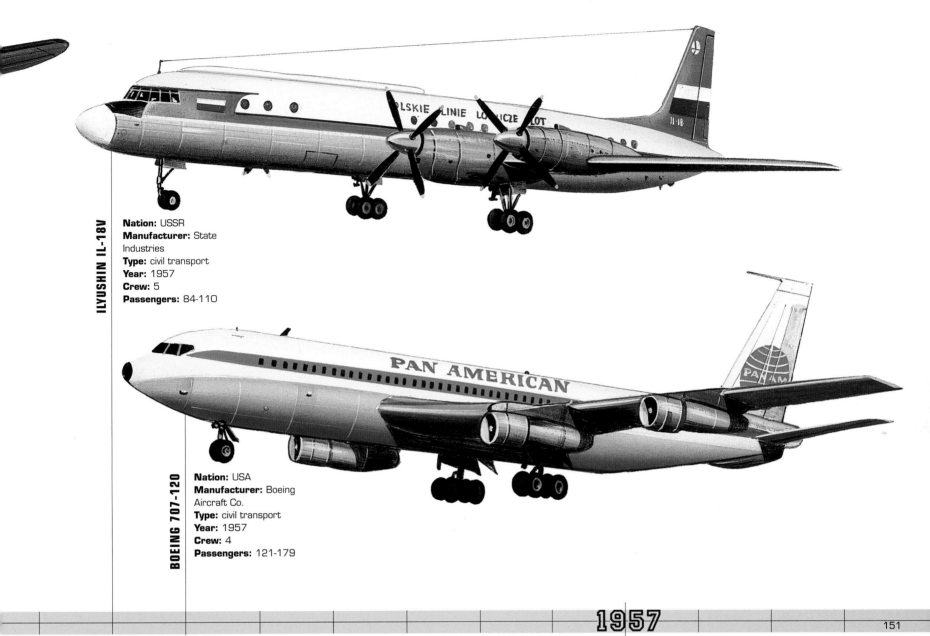

ILYUSHIN IL-18V

Nation: USSR
Manufacturer: State
Industries
Type: civil transport
Year: 1957
Crew: 5
Passengers: 84-110

BOEING 707-120

Nation: USA
Manufacturer: Boeing
Aircraft Co.
Type: civil transport
Year: 1957
Crew: 4
Passengers: 121-179

1957

151

The jet and civil aviation

survived the war. On January 1, 1946, Air France, which had dominated European civil transport throughout the 1930s, re-appeared: with the company back in business, so too was France. A well-designed incentive program also helped French industry to return to its usual level of excellence.

An analogous process of nationalization was taking place in Britain, with the creation on August 1, 1946 of the British European Airways Corporation (BEA), conceived to cover the European routes in support of the existing BOAC (founded April 1940), which had been operating the international routes during the war years. At the industrial level, apart from the success of a few medium-range airliners designed for the shorter European routes, British efforts to best the Americans at building long-range transcontinental liners were for the most part futile.

Important initiatives such as the Avro 688 and 689 Tudor of 1945-46 were abandoned for economic reasons, while others such as the Handley Page H.P.81 of 1948 failed to live up to expectations.

The French or British could do little to challenge the quality and quantity of aircraft produced by the larger American manufacturers. The US, it must be stated, had spent the war years fighting overseas, while its own

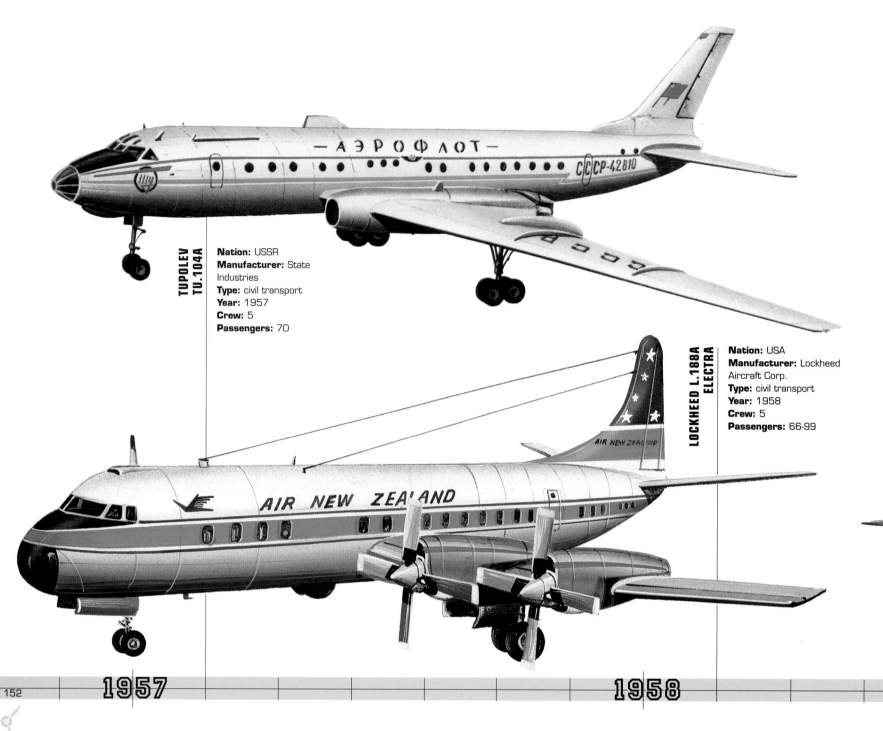

TUPOLEV TU.104A

Nation: USSR
Manufacturer: State Industries
Type: civil transport
Year: 1957
Crew: 5
Passengers: 70

LOCKHEED L.188A ELECTRA

Nation: USA
Manufacturer: Lockheed Aircraft Corp.
Type: civil transport
Year: 1958
Crew: 5
Passengers: 66-99

1957

1958

1940-2003

territory remained untouched. Consequently, while many nations saw their cities burn, American commercial aviation had been steadily evolving in relative tranquility since 1941, with a continental-sized country as its testing ground. The facts speak. In 1945, while a devastated Europe was facing the grim task of reconstruction, the American domestic passenger fleet had carried 6 million customers, an increase of 50 percent over

1941. So, already riding a wave of expansion, it was not difficult to simply move forward in the post-war years. Aeronautical production easily covered all the needs of the growing market: the dependable Martin and Convair twin-engines, worthy successors of the DC-3, filled the short- to medium-range niche, while the four-engine Boeing Stratocruiser and Lockheed Constellation joined the Douglas DC-4 to dominate the ever more competitive

transatlantic market. The North Atlantic route was of course the most significant at the international level, since it involved the interests of both Europe and America. But there was little to be done: in 1948, 148,000 of the 240,000 transatlantic passengers flew with TWA, Pan American and American Overseas. Two years later the ratio was slightly greater: of the 311,000 passengers who crossed the Atlantic in 1950, 174,000 of them did so on

Nation: Great Britain
Manufacturer: de Havilland
Aircraft Co. Ltd.
Type: civil transport
Year: 1958
Crew: 4
Passengers: 81

DE HAVILLAND D.H.106 COMET 4

Nation: USA
Manufacturer: Douglas
Aircraft Corp.
Type: civil transport
Year: 1958
Crew: 5
Passengers: 112-173

DOUGLAS DC-8-20

American planes. By 1951 it was no contest: the four US giants – Eastern, American, United and TWA – were cumulatively transporting 13.6 million passengers annually, Capital was close to 2 million, and seven other companies had broken the 500,000 mark. The planes themselves, the aircraft that signaled the end of a fascinating and unrepeatable era, were the last versions of the Constellation and the legendary Douglas DC-6 and DC-7.

Behind the Iron Curtain, the Soviets proceeded largely in isolation, preferring to expand their enormous domestic market as well as to hide behind a veil of secrecy as they worked with their captured German scientists on the development of the jet engine.

THE RACE TO BUILD THE FIRST JET LINER

British industry, the early leader in the development of the jet engine for military use, was the first to first introduce the revolutionary technology to the civil transport sector, in the early 1950s. Two dates are fundamental: July 16, 1948, debut of the Vickers Viscount, the first turbo-prop passenger plane, and July 27, 1949, maiden flight of the de Havilland Comet, the world's first commercial jet. The Comet had a disastrous infancy, however. After entering officially into service in May 1952, it was involved in two terrible accidents

The jet and civil aviation

Nation: France
Manufacturer: Sud-Aviation
Type: civil transport
Year: 1959
Crew: 4
Passengers: 64-99

SUD-AVIATION SE-210 CARAVELLE III

The sharp, clean line of the Caravelle III, a successful French airliner that remained in service until 1979.

1959

1940-2003

(January and April of 1954); they resulted in the giant four-engine jetliner being grounded for the next four and a half years. The Viscount seemed the winning card, and in fact turned out to be just that. BEA, which inaugurated the big turboprop on July 29, 1950, grew to become Europe's No. 1 airline by 1955. But British supremacy didn't last long as competition soon became both wider and more heated. On September 15, 1956 the

Soviets flew their first commercial jet, the Tupolev Tu-104, on the Moscow-Omsk-Irkutsk route. In October of 1958 BOAC revived the Comet and made the first transatlantic jetliner flight, beating out Pan American – the first US company to fly that mother of all American passenger planes, the Boeing 707 – by 14 days. Then in May 1959 Air France introduced the Caravelle, a versatile twin-engine jet with a structural formula that would become

the standard for most short- to medium-range passenger aircraft. After these historic milestones, the challenge shifted from the technological sphere to the commercial one, and the Americans immediately seized the lead. Boeing's first passenger jet, the 707, dared to take on its direct rival, the Douglas DC-8, and the battle was fierce. But it was precisely this competition between the two American giants that led to the virtual obliteration of all

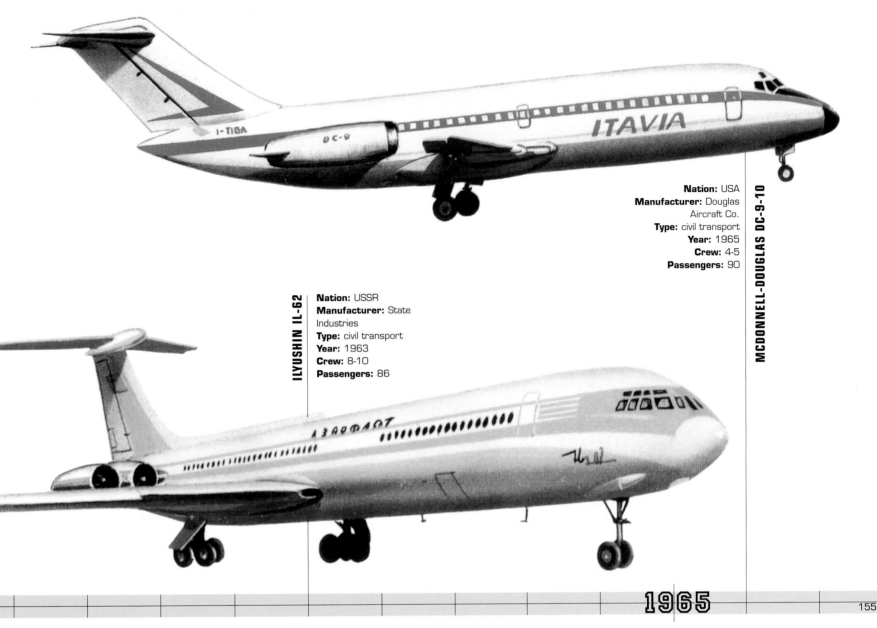

ITAVIA

Nation: USA
Manufacturer: Douglas
Aircraft Co.
Type: civil transport
Year: 1965
Crew: 4-5
Passengers: 90

MCDONNELL-DOUGLAS DC-9-10

I-TIGA

DC-9

ILYUSHIN IL-62

Nation: USSR
Manufacturer: State
Industries
Type: civil transport
Year: 1963
Crew: 8-10
Passengers: 86

1965

other challengers. The Soviet domestic monopoly notwithstanding, a period began in which the world passenger plane market consisted of two names: Boeing and Douglas.

This is not to brush the Soviet market aside, however. During the 1950s, Aeroflot was the largest airline in the world, the result of a massive program of expansion that had been underway since 1946 with the goal of rendering the Soviet empire completely

autonomous. And this political self-sufficiency was seconded by Soviet industry, which was building airplanes every bit as good as those in the West. In 1950 the Soviet civil transport network covered 186,750 miles, with 1.6 million passengers and 200,000 tons of cargo and mail carried; ten years later those numbers had grown to 200,000 miles, 2.5 million passengers, and 285,000 tons.

The progress of these four leader

nations drew the rest of the world along in its wake. In Germany, historic Lufthansa was back on its feet and prospering, while in Italy LAI (Linee Aeree Italiane) and Alitalia (Aerolinee Internazionali Italiane) led the field during these difficult years of reconstruction. Italian aviation would receive an important boost ten years later when the two companies merged to form the national airline, which retained the name Alitalia.

Nation: USA
Manufacturer: Boeing
Commercial Airplane Co.
Type: civil transport
Year: 1967
Crew: 6-7
Passengers: 189

N7287D

UNITED

The Boeing 727 took a leading role in commercial aviation as the largest-selling passenger plane of its time.

1967

1940-2003

THE ERA OF THE WIDE-BODY

The Sixties and Seventies saw commercial aviation's most intense growth. While the battle between American manufacturers to conquer the world market not only for long-range jets but for short- to medium-range ones as well (McDonnell-Douglas DC-9 vs Boeing B-727 and 737) was being fought, a new concept had taken root: the high-capacity, or 'wide-body' passenger jet. With

traffic demand constantly increasing, airlines had begun asking for larger planes that could carry more passengers over greater distances in order to optimize cost and profit parameters. As usual, the strongest input on both the technological and commercial levels came from the United States, from Boeing specifically. The era of the wide-body was inaugurated on February 8, 1969 with the first flight of the B-747, the largest commer-

cial aircraft in the world. With a capacity of more than 400 passengers, the 747 became immediately known by the nickname 'Jumbo Jet.' The impact that this graceful giant had on the global market was enormous. For long-range passenger flights, the 747 represented a revolutionary new standard, and so literally from one day to the next, the world aviation industry had to come to terms with a new reality. And in fact, not

BOEING 737-200

Nation: USA
Manufacturer: Boeing Commercial Airplane Co.
Type: civil transport
Year: 1967
Crew: 5
Passengers: 115-130

Nation: USA
Manufacturer: Boeing Commercial Airplane Co.
Type: civil transport
Year: 1969
Crew: 10-13
Passengers: 400

BOEING 747-200

1969

long after Pan American became the first company to put the miraculous new machine in service (January 22, 1970, New York-London), the extremely long waiting list for delivery of new Jumbos was essentially a list of all the world's major airlines.

The gauntlet Boeing threw down was picked up by the other great American manufacturers, McDonnell-Douglas first among them: in 1971 its tri-engine DC-10 entered service under the flag of American Airlines. A year later, Eastern began serving its domestic routes with the third principal exponent of this new generation of passenger planes, the

The 747, archetype of the wide-body airliner, was nicknamed the 'Jumbo Jet.'

The jet and civil aviation

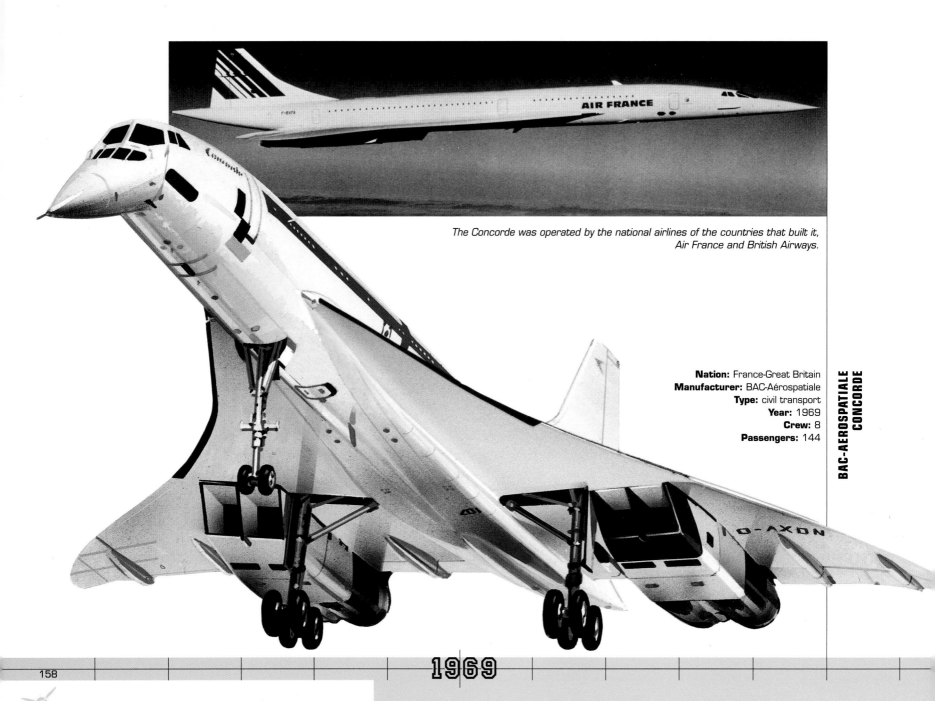

The Concorde was operated by the national airlines of the countries that built it, Air France and British Airways.

Nation: France-Great Britain
Manufacturer: BAC-Aérospatiale
Type: civil transport
Year: 1969
Crew: 8
Passengers: 144

1969

1940-2003

Lockheed L-1011 Tristar, another tri-engine jet that had been under development since 1968. These latter two models did not, however, enjoy anything like the same success as the 747, in part because Boeing had had the wisdom to produce it in constantly evolving variants, each optimized for the specific needs of the client airline, each better and more powerful than its predecessor.

The USSR waited a decade to develop its

AN ILL-FATED DREAM: SUPERSONIC CIVIL TRANSPORT

Of the myriad 'races' that have characterized the history of aviation, surely one of the most engrossing was the one which pitted the four great aeronautical powers – USA, USSR, France, and Britain – against one another to build the first supersonic passenger jet. There was much at stake: not only the conquest of new technologies and potentially huge economic benefits, but also and above all prestige. The competition, conditioned more by questions of cost than of technology, generated three distinct results, none of which can in the end be considered entirely successful. The Soviet Tupolev Tu-144 was the first supersonic airliner (December 13, 1968), but it remained more or less in the experimental stage for ten years before eventually being abandoned. The Anglo-French Concorde had better luck. After making its maiden flight on March 2, 1969 and a subsequent hiatus of nearly seven years (it wasn't easy creating a market niche for the innovative aircraft), the Concorde entered service with the colors of Air France and British Airways on January 21, 1976. The great failure was instead the American SST. The program, launched in October 1968 by Boeing, ground to a halt three years later when the US Senate refused to approve the astronomical expenditures necessary for developing the plane.

However, the Concorde, shining achievement of European industry, was in reality but an end in itself: this

Nation: USA
Manufacturer:
McDonnell-Douglas Corp.
Type: civil transport
Year: 1972
Crew: 13
Passengers: 255-380

Nation: USSR
Manufacturer: State
Industries
Type: civil transport
Year: 1976
Crew: 8-10
Passengers: 350

Nation: France-Germany-Spain-
Great Britain
Manufacturer: Airbus Industrie
Type: civil transport
Year: 1977
Crew: 8-10
Passengers: 253

1976

futuristic beauty capable of cutting the flight time between Europe and America in half proved to be an economic disaster. Boycotted by the Americans (who went so far as to ban it from their airports for environmental reasons) and crippled by exorbitant operational costs, the Concorde quickly assumed the role of luxury liner, an airborne limousine for VIPs that the two airlines kept in service purely for reasons of 'image.' Nonetheless, the career of the Concorde was relatively long and illustrious: in 25 years the fourteen planes in service carried more than 3 million intercontinental passengers. Then, on July 25, 2000, the myth of the 'Queen of the Skies' was shattered when a 203-series Concorde, Air France flight AF4590, crashed during takeoff from Paris's Charles de Gaulle Airport, killing all 109 passengers and claiming an additional four victims on the ground. The lengthy inquest determined after fourteen months that the cause of the tragedy was not structural, but rather the result of an unfortunate combination of external events. The Concorde resumed service in November 2001, in the hopes that it could reclaim its limited but prestigious position. But after the crisis of 9/11 Air France and British Airways decided that maintaining the now injured image of the world's only supersonic airliner was counterproductive. And so, on April 10, 2003 the two airlines announced the end: the last flight of the French Concorde took off from Paris on May 31, followed by its British sister on September 30. A chapter had been closed, an era had ended. And no one expected another to open. In the end, the only clamor surrounding the remaining Concordes was that made by the world's various aeronautical museums.

first wide-body passenger liner. It wasn't until December 26, 1980 that the Ilyushin Il-86, with a capacity of around 350, made its first flight under the Aeroflot colors.

ENERGY CRISIS AND DEREGULATION

The last century's final two decades belong not to the history of aviation but to its present. The generation of commercial aircraft now so much a part of our lives was born of two key

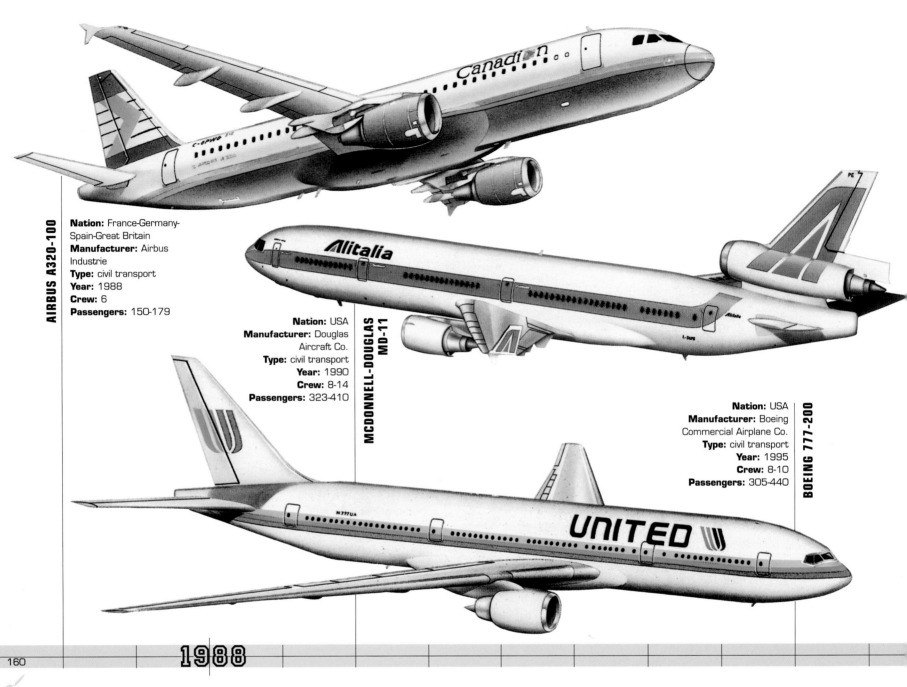

AIRBUS A320-100

Nation: France-Germany-Spain-Great Britain
Manufacturer: Airbus Industrie
Type: civil transport
Year: 1988
Crew: 6
Passengers: 150-179

MCDONNELL-DOUGLAS MD-11

Nation: USA
Manufacturer: Douglas Aircraft Co.
Type: civil transport
Year: 1990
Crew: 8-14
Passengers: 323-410

BOEING 777-200

Nation: USA
Manufacturer: Boeing Commercial Airplane Co.
Type: civil transport
Year: 1995
Crew: 8-10
Passengers: 305-440

1988

factors: the great energy crisis of the early '80s, and the imposing entrance onto the world stage of Airbus Industrie, the European consortium (France, Germany, Great Britain, Spain), which has changed the face of the world aeronautical market. After years of increasing subordination to the United States, the Old Continent had begun during the 1970s to experiment with cooperative, transnational programs, merging technological, financial and

industrial resources in an attempt to break the grip of what had become an American monopoly. And the experiments worked. The Airbus consortium quickly took a significant piece of the pie from the American giants in its early years, then that piece continued to grow larger and larger, to the point where today Europe sells more passenger airplanes than the United States. Airbus's expansion continues, encompassing every segment of the commer-

cial transport sector, and very soon we will witness perhaps its greatest coup of all: the doubling of the capacity of today's long-range widebodies. In fact, the Airbus A-380, scheduled to enter into service in 2006, will boast the astonishing capacity of up to 840 passengers.

This new market dynamic has somehow survived the evolution of commercial aviation's most recent phase, characterized above all by the twin problems of high energy costs and

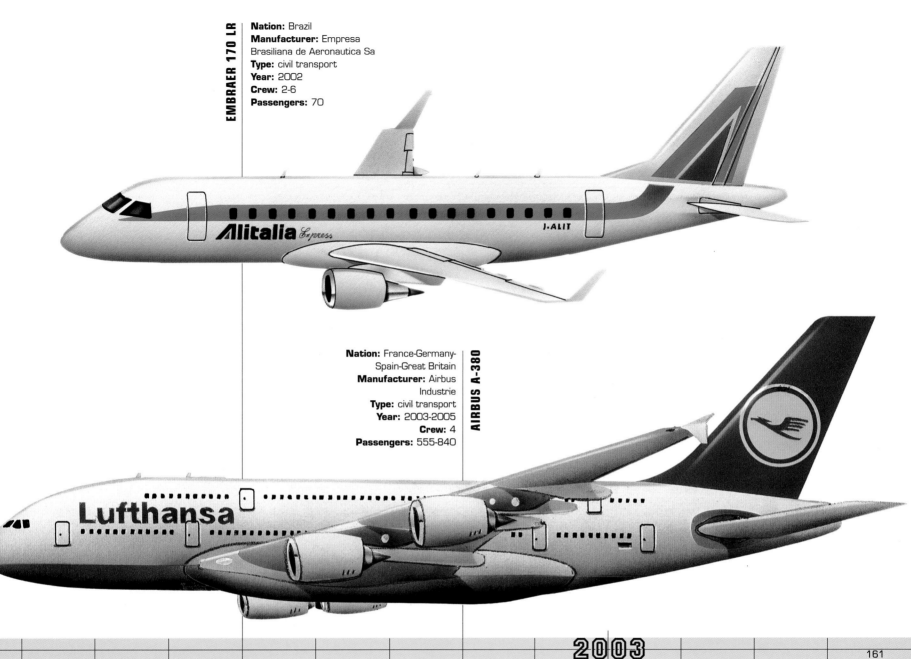

EMBRAER 170 LR

Nation: Brazil
Manufacturer: Empresa Brasiliana de Aeronautica Sa
Type: civil transport
Year: 2002
Crew: 2-6
Passengers: 70

AIRBUS A-380

Nation: France-Germany-Spain-Great Britain
Manufacturer: Airbus Industrie
Type: civil transport
Year: 2003-2005
Crew: 4
Passengers: 555-840

2003

increasing deregulation. The first has had the effect of ensuring that the latest generation of aircraft, from the smallest short-range courier to the largest transoceanic wide-body, can offer maximum energy efficiency and operational flexibility, and by extension, maximum economic performance. The second problem, rather more complex, has traumatized the airline industry. The seemingly unstoppable process of liberalization, born in the United States and now migrated to Europe, has all but obliterated the system of rigid tariff and traffic regulations that, for decades, had helped maintain relative equilibrium in the commercial aviation market. The new laws – or rather, the absence thereof – have created an unprecedented level of competition, an all-out price war, with no holds barred and no discount too low. New 'budget' airlines are born as quickly as others fold, and the air traffic network has sprung thousands of new routes and connections as companies scramble to fill every possible territorial void. From one point of view, deregulation can be seen as a powerful engine of growth, a generator of opportunity. From another, it is the mechanism behind the collapse of venerable giants like Pan Am, TWA and Sabena, and is responsible for placing the financial health of those airlines which have managed to survive in a continuous state of grave risk.

The jet and civil aviation

One of the many
different types of
experimental 'X' planes
being moved from
its hangar.

Opposite page:
The Bell X-2

692

X-3

1946

THE FINAL FRONTIER

THE QUEST TO FLY EVER HIGHER, FASTER, FARTHER

AND THE EXPERIMENTAL AIRCRAFT THAT DID SO

LED TO CROSSING OF THE LAST THRESHOLD:

OUTER SPACE.

2003

Ever since its birth one hundred years ago, war's exigencies have driven aviation's most significant advances. But since the end of World War II, strictly military aims have existed alongside another, equally influential force: aerospace research. The desire to conquer the cosmos, to cross the final barriers, has led to innumerable milestones in the history of flight, each one taking its place along the inexorable path that connects the Wright brothers' 'heavier-than-air' craft directly to whatever technological miracles the future might hold.

The Space Shuttle, which since the early 1980s has been instrumental in shaping a new phase in space travel, represents the highest expression of traditional aviation. Unlike other means of space travel such as the rocket, its derivation from the airplane is evident, both functionally and operatively. Just as a 'normal' airplane moves its payload – be it cargo, mail or passengers – from one airport to another, then turns around and does it again, so does the Shuttle move its various payloads back and forth between Earth and space. And even though it is launched like a rocket and remains in orbit like a satellite, it performs what is per-

Nation: USA
Manufacturer: Bell Aircraft Corp.
Type: experimental
Year: 1946
Crew: 1

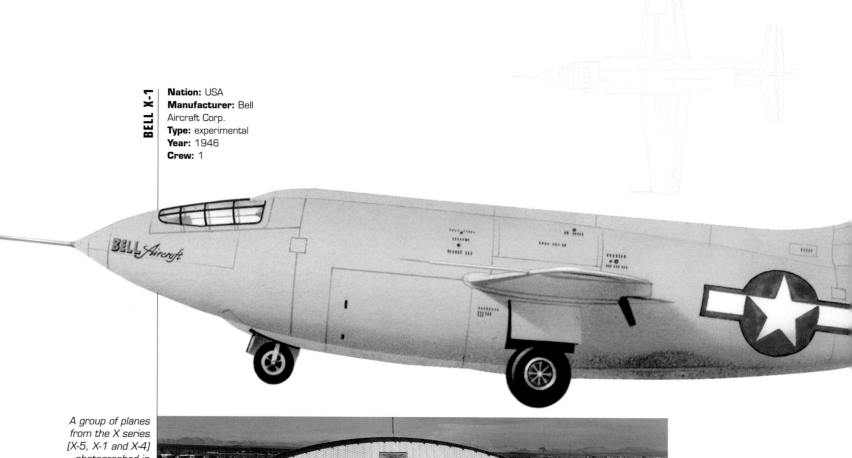

A group of planes from the X series (X-5, X-1 and X-4) photographed in front of a hangar at Dryden Flight Research Center, 1962.

1946

haps the most difficult and important phase of its mission – reentry and landing – exactly like an airplane. Or to be more precise, like a very heavy and extremely expensive glider.

The perfect synthesis of aeronautical and aerospace technology represented by the Shuttle is the product of decades upon decades of research into structures, materials, avionics, aerodynamics and propulsion

systems, the results of which have often gone well beyond the specific objective of flying in space. The history of experimental aircraft, the original protagonists of the arduous march toward outer space, is a history that runs parallel to, though somewhat in the shadow of military and commercial aviation. Its names and dates and places and heroes are less well known, but its achievements are no less extraordinary.

The project that is central to this history was as daring as it was successful. Launched in the United States way back in 1942 under the name Experimental Research Aircraft Program, it gave birth to the famous series of 'X-planes,' amazing machines designed for pure research into the limits of possibility which had a direct influence on military production and on the evolution of commercial aviation. The im-

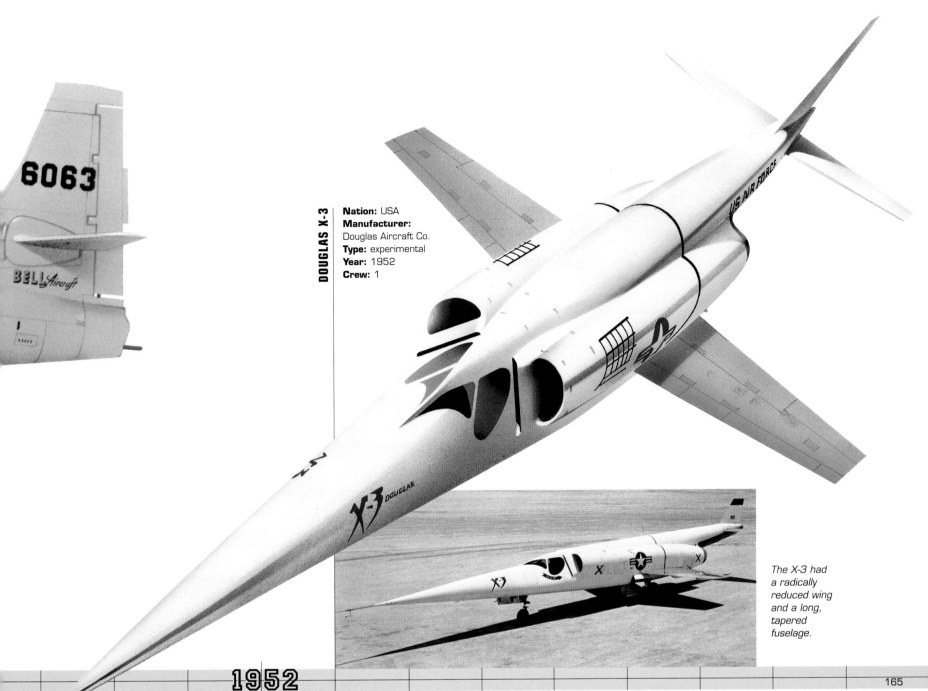

Nation: USA
Manufacturer: Douglas Aircraft Co.
Type: experimental
Year: 1952
Crew: 1

The X-3 had a radically reduced wing and a long, tapered fuselage.

1952

mensity of the technological contributions of the X-plane program can be grasped through itc many 'firsts': first to break the sound barrier, first to use variable-sweep wings, first to reach altitudes upwards of 300,000 feet, first to fly at six times the speed of sound, first to be built from sophisticated metals, first to use rocket engines, first to experiment with revolutionary aerodynamic forms. The list goes on.

The three most famous of the X-planes are the Bell X-1 and X-2, and the North American X-15. The X-1, ancestor of the entire series, was the first American aircraft to employ a rocket engine for the purpose of researching the problems of supersonic flight. This historic milestone was reached on October 14, 1947 by Charles 'Chuck' Yeager. Ferried to 30,000 feet by a B-29, the X-1 was released, and

reached 670 miles per hour in horizontal flight. The next big record was set in August 1949 by Frank Everest, who brought the X-1 to an altitude of 71,930 feet. In December 1953 Yeager flew a more powerful version of the X-1 at the then astonishing speed of 1,649 mile an hour. But this wasn't fast enough, or high enough. The Bell X-2 was developed, and its larger backswept wings helped it break both the

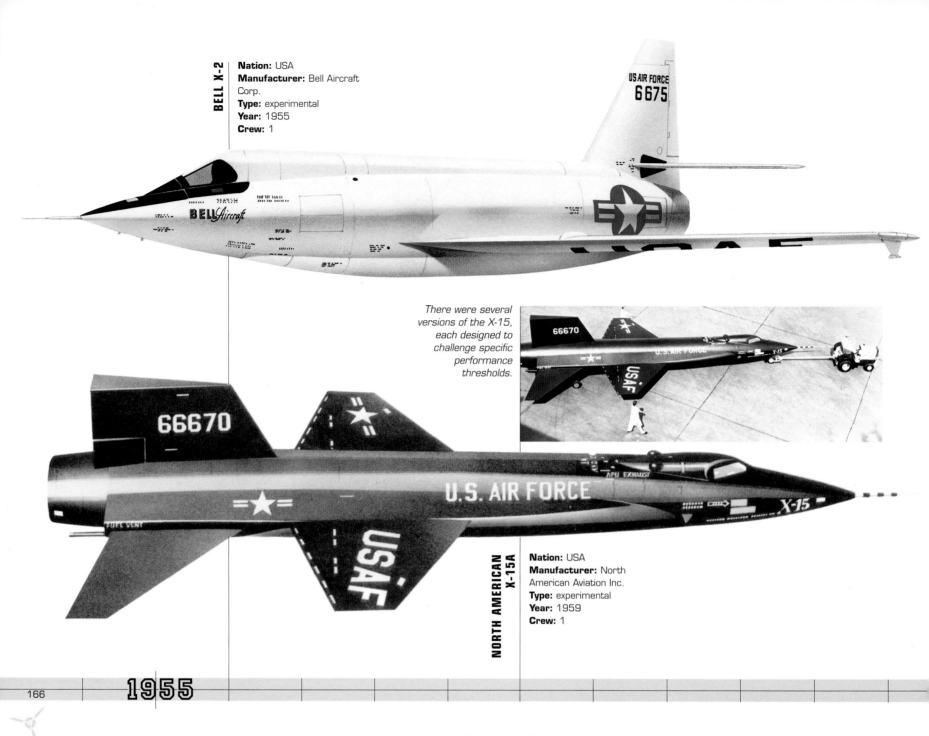

Nation: USA
Manufacturer: Bell Aircraft Corp.
Type: experimental
Year: 1955
Crew: 1

US AIR FORCE
6675

BELL Aircraft
USAF

There were several versions of the X-15, each designed to challenge specific performance thresholds.

66670
U.S. AIR FORCE
USAF
X-15
APU EXHAUST
FUEL VENT

NORTH AMERICAN X-15A

Nation: USA
Manufacturer: North American Aviation Inc.
Type: experimental
Year: 1959
Crew: 1

1955

An X-2 takes flight after being released by the 'mother ship,' a Boeing B-29.

altitude and speed records right away: on September 7, 1956 Iven Kincheloe reached 120,170 feet; 20 days later Captain Milburn Apt crashed and died in his X-2, but not before having pushed it to 2,094 mph, Mach 3.2, more than three times the speed of sound.

Next came the Douglas X-3, designed to study aerodynamic and structural behavior in prolonged supersonic flight, but the project failed. However, the North American X-15 of 1959 surpassed by ample margins the X-1 and X-2's records, reaching such altitudes as to blur the distinction between flight and space flight. The idea was to build a rocket-powered plane capable of operating at altitudes between 60,000 and 260,000 feet, at speeds between four to ten times

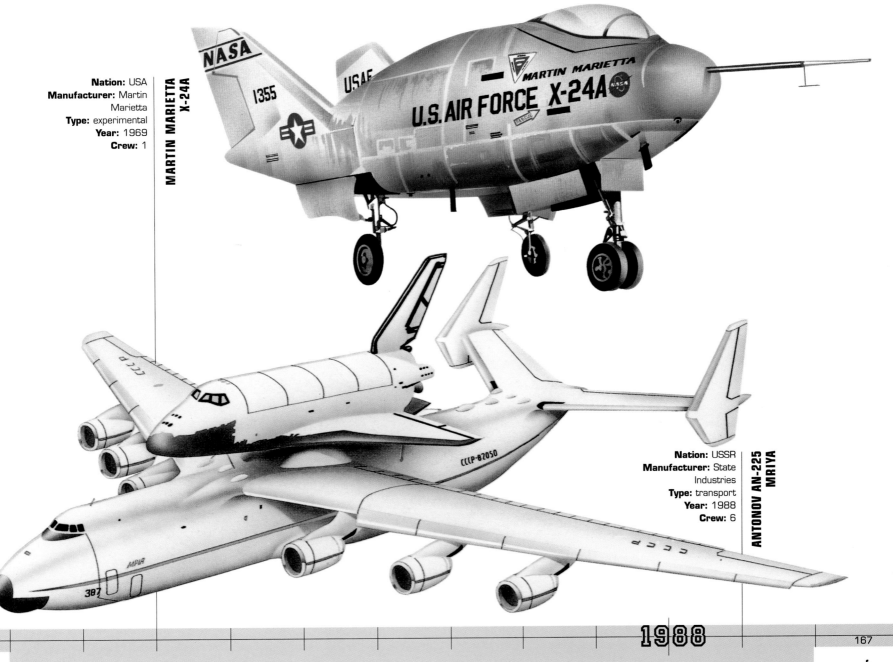

Nation: USA
Manufacturer: Martin
Marietta
Type: experimental
Year: 1969
Crew: 1

MARTIN MARIETTA X-24A

Nation: USSR
Manufacturer: State
Industries
Type: transport
Year: 1988
Crew: 6

ANTONOV AN-225 MRIYA

1988

167

The final frontier

BURAN, THE UNLUCKY SOVIET SHUTTLE

The ferocious United States-Soviet Union rivalry during the Cold War led the Soviets to challenge the U.S. not only in the military sector, but in aerospace as well. The development of the Soviet shuttle, called Buran ('Snowstorm' in Russian) was authorized in 1976 in direct response to the American initiative. In 1980, the construction program was initiated, which was to generate five operational shuttles and six reduced-scale models for testing the entire system. The first of these tests, a suborbital flight, was flown in July 1983. The next year saw the beginning of the aerodynamic testing of the finished spacecraft, which

went on until April 1988. The Buran's first – and only – orbital launch took place at the Baikonur cosmodrome on November 15 of that year. No crew was on board, since much of the avionics had not yet been installed and the life-support system remained untested. The shuttle was launched with a powerful Energia vector rocket to an altitude of approximately 155 miles, where the vehicle completed two earth orbits before igniting its reentry rockets. The flight lasted exactly 3 hours and 25 minutes. Its limited scope notwithstanding, the flight demonstrated the Buran to be a valid machine. Particularly positive results

came from the autopilot system, which landed the shuttle perfectly despite 40-mile-an-hour crosswinds, and from the thermal sheathing: examination revealed that only 5 of the 38,000 insulation tiles had come loose during reentry. The Buran was proudly exhibited in June 1989 at France's Le Bourget aerospace fair, installed on the back of a gargantuan transport plane built expressly for the purpose, the Antonov An-225 Mriya ('Dream' in Russian). The collapse of the Soviet Union, however, instantly dried up the funding for the Buran program, which was officially cancelled in 1993.

Nation: USA
Manufacturer:
Rockwell International
Type: space shuttle
Year: 1977-2003

NASA/ROCKWELL INTERNATIONAL
SPACE SHUTTLE

The explosive takeoff of the Space Shuttle, with booster engines at full thrust.

2003

1946-2003

that of sound. The primary challenges were to find sheathing materials that would withstand extreme temperatures, and developing a rocket engine three times more powerful than anything yet built. The first X-15 left the factory on October 15, 1958 for extensive testing. In fact, the first of the 199 missions flown by the X-15 occurred only in November 1960. For the next eight years speed and altitude records fell like dominoes: 4,093 mph in 1961 (November 9, Bob White); 354,109 feet in1963 (August 22, Joe Walker); 4,519 mph in 1967 (October 3, William Knight).

The Space Shuttle, the world's operative transatmospheric aircraft and the crowning glory of these bold experiments, has remained an isolated case since its introduction in April 1981. Analogous projects in the former Soviet Union and France were never concluded, while the British HOTOL and American TAV programs, begun back in the '80s, are still in the research phase.

Now, after the tragic loss of the Columbia and its crew in February 2003, the Shuttle program itself risks being downsized, if not terminated outright. The quest to find its successor is only one of the new millennium's many challenges.

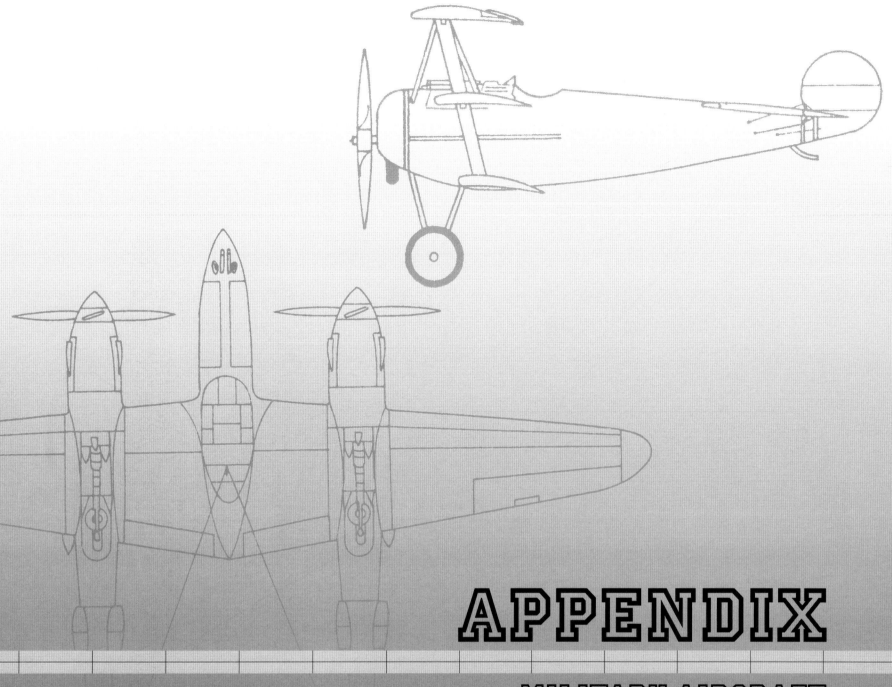

APPENDIX

MILITARY AIRCRAFT

■ ALBATROS D.III

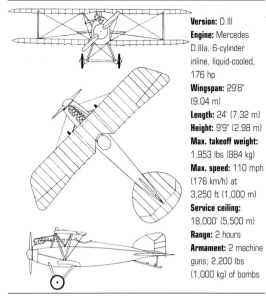

Version: D.III
Engine: Mercedes D.IIIa, 6-cylinder inline, liquid-cooled, 176 hp
Wingspan: 29'8" (9.04 m)
Length: 24' (7.32 m)
Height: 9'9" (2.98 m)
Max. takeoff weight: 1,953 lbs (884 kg)
Max. speed: 110 mph (176 km/h) at 3,250 ft (1,000 m)
Service ceiling: 18,000' (5,500 m)
Range: 2 hours
Armament: 2 machine guns; 2,200 lbs (1,000 kg) of bombs

The D.III version was the best of the Albatros fighters, and from the moment of its introduction in January 1917 it began displacing the D.I and D.II models from the German ranks, to the extent that there were already 446 of them operating at the front by November of that same year. The Albatross D.III was the plane that helped pilots like Manfred von Richthofen, Werner Voss, Ernst Udet, Eduard von Schleich and Bruno Lorzer to tally up the innumerable victories that have memorialized them as the greatest German aces of the First World War. It was the impressive performance of the French Nieuport 17 that moved the Germans to improve the D.II to create the D.III: its sesquiplane wing with V-struts was borrowed from the French fighter, and the fuselage was modified to incorporate a more powerful engine.

■ ANTONOV AN-22 ANTEI

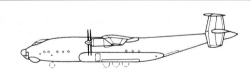

Engine: 4 Kuznetsov NK-12MA turboprops, 15,000 hp each – **Wingspan:** 211'4" (64.40 m) – Length: 190' (57.90 m) – **Height:** 41'1" (12.53 m) – **Max. takeoff weight:** 550,000 lbs (250,000 kg) – **Max. speed:** 460 mph (740 km/h) at sea level – **Range:** 6,850 miles (10,950 km)

On the basis of the experience acquired building the Antonov An-10 and An-12 (large quadrimotor turboprop transport planes for civil and military use), the even larger An-22 was developed. When it was presented at the Paris Aeronautical Fair in 1965, it was the largest and heaviest plane built to date. Baptized Antei (or Antaeus, for its extraordinary load-bearing capacity), a prototype of the An-22 flew its maiden flight on February 27 of that same year. Production began in 1967, with about 50 units

completed by 1974. It served both the civilian airline Aeroflot and the Soviet Air Force. The codename given the An-22 by NATO was COCK.

■ ARADO AR.234

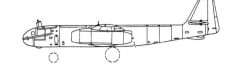

Version: Ar.234 B-2 – **Engine:** 2 Junkers Jumo 0048 jets, 1,990 lbs (900 kg) thrust each – **Wingspan:** 46'3" (14.10 m) – **Length:** 41'6" (12.65 m) – **Height:** 14'2" (4.30 m) – **Max. takeoff weight:** 18,500 lbs (8,410 kg) – **Max. speed:** 465 mph (742 km/h) at 19,700 ft (6,000 m) – **Service ceiling:** 32,800' (10,000 m) – **Range:** 1,020 miles (1,630 km) – **Armament:** 2 20mm cannons, machine guns; 3,300 lbs (1,500 kg) bombs

The German Ar.234 was the world's second jet-powered airplane, and the first operative bomber jet. Only a couple of hundred were built, however, and very few of them ever saw any combat. The first flight of the Arado Ar.234 VI took place on June 15, 1943, and it demonstrated itself to be an excellent plane with no major defects. On March 10, 1944 the prototype of the V9 was successfully tested, and became the departure point for the Ar.234 B series, destined to become the most extensively produced of all. The first batch of test planes was delivered in June of that year and were used largely for reconnaissance missions, after which five sub-series were designed: the B-1 photo-recon version, the B-2 bomber, the B-2/1 target finder, the B-2/b modified recon model, and the long-range B-2/r, notable for its auxiliary fuel tanks The bomber version carried 3,300 lbs of ordnance, not in the traditional bomb bay but in a unique external rack assembly beneath the engine gondolas. All versions shared the same standardized defensive armament of two rear-firing MG 151 20mm cannons installed in a belly turret near the tail section.

■ AVRO LANCASTER

During the course of World War II, Lancasters flew 156,000 missions and dropped 608,612 tons of bombs, more than twice as many as the Handley Page Halifax. From the end of 1941 to the early months of 1946, 7,366 Lancasters were produced, 442 of them in allied Canada. Among the plane's more prestigious feats: the sinking of the *Tirpitz* as it hid in a Norwegian fjord on November 12, 1944, and the daring raid into the Ruhr valley on the night of May 16-17, 1943, which destroyed the Mohne, Eder and Sorpe dams. One of the bomber's greatest features was its ability to carry ordnance of ever-increasing size and weight. On the night of April 10, 1942 a Lancaster carried the world's first 8,000-lb bomb; on September 15, 1943, it carried "Tallboy," a 12,000-pounder; and on March 14, 1945, it hauled and dropped the 20,000-lb "Grand Slam." But despite its being unanimously considered one of the safest bombers to fly, the Lancaster suffered a very high loss rate. In fact, more than half of the units produced were lost (3,349 planes never returned, 487 irreparably

damaged), numbers which give an idea of the extent to which the Allies depended on this noble bomber.

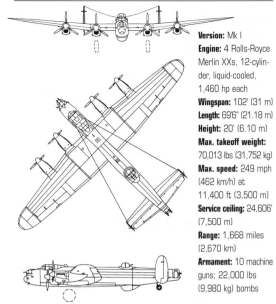

Version: Mk I
Engine: 4 Rolls-Royce Merlin XXs, 12-cylinder, liquid-cooled, 1,460 hp each
Wingspan: 102' (31 m)
Length: 69'6" (21.18 m)
Height: 20' (6.10 m)
Max. takeoff weight: 70,013 lbs (31,752 kg)
Max. speed: 249 mph (462 km/h) at 11,400 ft (3,500 m)
Service ceiling: 24,606' (7,500 m)
Range: 1,668 miles (2,670 km)
Armament: 10 machine guns; 22,000 lbs (9,980 kg) bombs

■ BELL P-59 AIRACOMET

The Bell P-59 Airacomet is most notable for having ushered in the age of the jet engine. The USAF began the project in 1941, put the plane in production in 1944, but it never saw combat. The Airacomet was a monoplane of traditional line and structure. What was unique about it was its motors. The first 20 units, called the P-59A, had twin jet engines with 2,000 lbs of thrust per engine. In the 30 P-59Bs built subsequently, the engines were modified. The planes ended up being used as training aircraft, and as 'guinea pigs' for experimentation with new engine types.

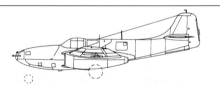

Version: P-59A – **Engine:** 2 General Electric J-31-GE5s, 2,000 lb thrust each – **Wingspan:** 44'2" (13.87 m) – **Length:** 38'6" (11.84 m) – **Height:** 12'4" (3.76 m) – **Max. takeoff weight:** 13,702 lbs (6,214 kg) – **Max. speed:** 415 mph (665 km/h) at 30,000 ft (9,150 m) – **Service ceiling:** 46,250' (14,100 m) – **Range:** 400 miles (644 km) – **Armament:** 1 37mm cannon, 5 machine guns

■ BOEING B-17 FLYING FORTRESS

Flying Fortress: the name alone captures the myths and legends surrounding the indomitable B-17, of which some 12,731 units in various versions were built. The Fortress first saw action in Europe on August 17, 1942, hitting German positions in daytime raids, and on January 27, 1943 it began its famously bold penetrations into German territory. The first prototype was launched on July 28, 1935, but the first production order – for 39 B-17Bs, an improved version of the original – didn't come until 1938. A second order for 38 further improved B-17Cs came the next year; and 42 B-17Ds, virtually identical to their predecessors, were ordered in 1940. A great leap forward was made in 1941 with the appearance of the B-17E. The entire tail section was overhauled, giving the plane greater stability at high altitudes and allowing the incorporation of a gun turret to defend the stern. In all, 512 B-17Es were produced, the first units sent to the Pacific in early 1942, then eventually to Europe in July of that year. The subsequent version was the B-17F of 1942, an even more powerful and well-armed craft, of which 3,400 were built. The series closed with the massive production – nearly 7,000 units – of the most evolved version of all, the B-17G.

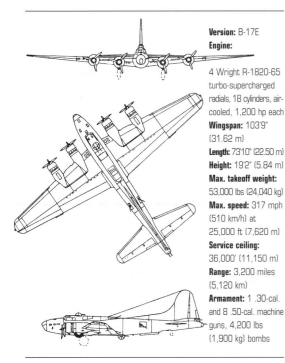

Version: B-17E
Engine:
4 Wright R-1820-65 turbo-supercharged radials, 18 cylinders, air-cooled, 1,200 hp each
Wingspan: 103'9" (31.62 m)
Length: 73'10" (22.50 m)
Height: 19'2" (5.84 m)
Max. takeoff weight: 53,000 lbs (24,040 kg)
Max. speed: 317 mph (510 km/h) at 25,000 ft (7,620 m)
Service ceiling: 36,000' (11,150 m)
Range: 3,200 miles (5,120 km)
Armament: 1 .30-cal. and 8 .50-cal. machine guns, 4,200 lbs (1,900 kg) bombs

■ BOEING B-29 SUPERFORTRESS

The B-29 was irrefutably the best strategic bomber of WWII, the Allies' number one weapon in both Europe and the Pacific. Pride of the American aeronautical industry, the B-29 was the culmination of all the technological and battlefield experience accumulated to that point, and would enjoy a career lasting well beyond the close of the war. In all, 3,970 B-29s were produced (2,000 between 1943 and 1945), many of which went on to participate in the Korean conflict and remaining in service throughout the 1950s, even beyond. Indeed, it was the admiration commanded by the B-29 that helped reestablish the balance of strategic air power between the US and USSR at the height of the Cold War. The Superfortress was a large monoplane of medium wingspan, with a circular section fuselage that was completely pressurized (except the bomb bay). Its defensive armament was formidable: 12 heavy machine guns and a 20mm cannon distributed among 4 remote-controlled turrets and a manually operated tail turret. One of the more important modifications of the B-29A with respect to its predecessor was the heavily armed top forward turret, outfitted with four machine guns.

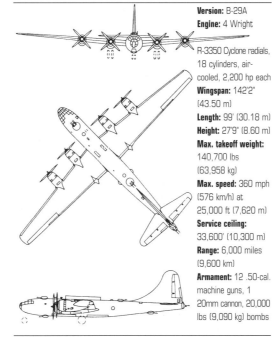

Version: B-29A
Engine: 4 Wright R-3350 Cyclone radials, 18 cylinders, air-cooled, 2,200 hp each
Wingspan: 142'2" (43.50 m)
Length: 99' (30.18 m)
Height: 27'9" (8.60 m)
Max. takeoff weight: 140,700 lbs (63,958 kg)
Max. speed: 360 mph (576 km/h) at 25,000 ft (7,620 m)
Service ceiling: 33,600' (10,300 m)
Range: 6,000 miles (9,600 km)
Armament: 12 .50-cal. machine guns, 1 20mm cannon, 20,000 lbs (9,090 kg) bombs

■ BOEING B-47 STRATOJET

The B-47 was the USAF's first true jet-powered bomber, and the first ever with a back-flaring wing design. The 1,800 B-47s produced between 1946 and 1957 remained in service through the mid-60s. The project began in late 1945; the first of two prototypes flew its maiden voyage on December 17, 1947. The first B-47A took to the skies on June 21, 1950, and in April 1951 the B-47B was introduced; 380 were built. The definitive E version appeared in January 1953, and much greater numbers were built. All these B-47 variants operated as bombers until 1957, and were then converted to reconnaissance and training aircraft. The last B-47s were retired from service in 1966.

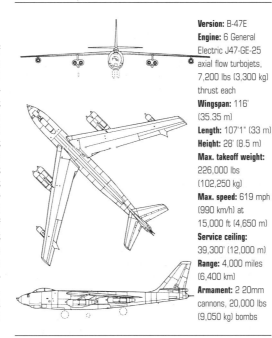

Version: B-47E
Engine: 6 General Electric J47-GE-25 axial flow turbojets, 7,200 lbs (3,300 kg) thrust each
Wingspan: 116' (35.35 m)
Length: 107'1" (33 m)
Height: 28' (8.5 m)
Max. takeoff weight: 226,000 lbs (102,250 kg)
Max. speed: 619 mph (990 km/h) at 15,000 ft (4,650 m)
Service ceiling: 39,300' (12,000 m)
Range: 4,000 miles (6,400 km)
Armament: 2 20mm cannons, 20,000 lbs (9,050 kg) bombs

■ BOEING B-52 STRATOFORTRESS

Still today, as demonstrated by its current use in Iraq, the Boeing B-52 Stratofortress retains its status as an unparalleled long-range strategic bomber. Despite the enormous technological progress of recent decades, no newer aircraft has been able to completely replace the indispensable B-52.

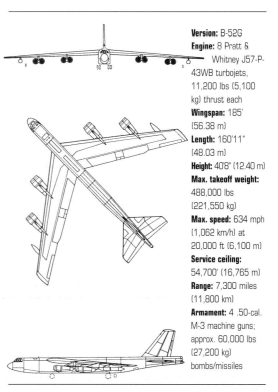

Version: B-52G
Engine: 8 Pratt & Whitney J57-P-43WB turbojets, 11,200 lbs (5,100 kg) thrust each
Wingspan: 185' (56.38 m)
Length: 160'11" (48.03 m)
Height: 40'8" (12.40 m)
Max. takeoff weight: 488,000 lbs (221,550 kg)
Max. speed: 634 mph (1,062 km/h) at 20,000 ft (6,100 m)
Service ceiling: 54,700' (16,765 m)
Range: 7,300 miles (11,800 km)
Armament: 4 .50-cal. M-3 machine guns; approx. 60,000 lbs (27,200 kg) bombs/missiles

Protagonist through nearly 50 years of military history – from Vietnam to the Gulf War and the Balkan, Afghanistan and Iraq conflicts – the B-52 is a unique weapon in the American arsenal. Of the 744 B-52s built between 1954 and 1962, 85 were still on front-line operational status at the end of 2001, with 9 more on reserve. Their active life is far from over; the USAF plans to retain them in service until 2045. In addition to being strategic bombers, these planes are also used in low-altitude raids and sea interdiction. The B-52's armament is a veritable catalogue of the Air Force's range of weapons, running from conventional bombs to mines to cruise and anti-ship missiles to nuclear ordnance.

■ BRISTOL BEAUFIGHTER

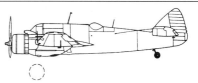

Version: Mk.IF – **Engine:** 2 Bristol Hercules XI radials, 14 cylinders, air-cooled, 1,400 hp each – **Wingspan:** 57'10" (17.63 m) – **Length:** 41'3" (12.50 m) – **Height:** 15'10" (4.83 m) – **Max. takeoff weight:** 21,000 lbs (9,500 kg) – **Max. speed:** 320 mph (516 km/h) at 15,700 ft (4,800 m) **Service ceiling:** 26,100' (8,000 m) – **Range:** 1,180 miles (1,890 km) – **Armament:** 4 20mm cannons, 6 machine guns

'Whispering Death' was the darkly poetic name the Japanese gave to the fearsome Bristol Beaufighter. A multipurpose plane – fighter-bomber, night raider, torpedo bomber, dive-bomber – fully 5,562 of them were built in numerous versions between 1939, year of its maiden flight, and September 1945. First came the Mk.IF, illustrated here. The Mk.IIF replaced the original engines with two Rolls-Royce Merlin XXs. With the Mk.VI, the Beaufighter returned to a radial-type motor, two 1,650-horsepower Hercules, with 1,832 units built in two variants, the Mk.VIF for the Fighter Command and the Mk.VIC for the Coastal Command. The last Beaufighter series, the Mk.X, specially designed for torpedo bombing and dive-bombing, first flew in spring 1943, and continued through to the end of the war.

■ BRISTOL F.2

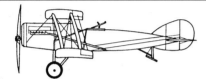

Version: F.2b – **Engine:** Rolls-Royce Falcon III V-12s, liquid-cooled inline, 275 hp – **Wingspan:** 39'3" (11.97m) – **Length:** 25'10" (7.87 m) – **Height:** 9'9" (2.97 m) – **Max. takeoff weight:** 2,779 lbs (1,261 kg) – **Max. speed:** 122 mph (196 km/h) at 5,000 ft (1,524 m) – **Service ceiling:** 19,900' (6,096 m) – **Range:** 3 hours – **Armament:** 3 machine guns, 240 lbs (109 kg) bombs

The Bristol F.2, though created to be a reconnaissance plane, proved to be more than capable of holding its own against the most ferocious enemy fighters. The prototype of the first version, the F.2a, flew on September 9, 1917. The superior F.2b, with its more powerful engine and greater range, was introduced in the summer of 1917. A total of 3,101 were built during the war, but production went ahead afterwards until reaching 5,500 units.

■ CAPRONI CA.46

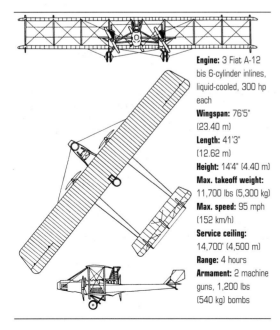

Engine: 3 Fiat A-12 bis 6-cylinder inlines, liquid-cooled, 300 hp each
Wingspan: 76'5" (23.40 m)
Length: 41'3" (12.62 m)
Height: 14'4" (4.40 m)
Max. takeoff weight: 11,700 lbs (5,300 kg)
Max. speed: 95 mph (152 km/h)
Service ceiling: 14,700' (4,500 m)
Range: 4 hours
Armament: 2 machine guns, 1,200 lbs (540 kg) bombs

The line of bombers developed by Caproni during the course of the First World War brought Italy to the avant-garde of world aviation, rivaled only by Russia and its gigantic aircraft built by Igor Ivanovich Sikorsky. The founding model of the Caproni lineage, the Ca.30, first appeared in 1913 and was followed by a series of increasingly efficient versions. Those that fall under the military denomination Series 5 (Ca.44, 45 and 46) were introduced in early 1918 and turned out to be the best, thanks to significant modifications to the structure and engines, which made for excellent overall performance. Of these three versions 225 units were produced up until the end of the conflict, after which manufacturing rights were ceded to France, Great Britain, and the United States.

■ CONSOLIDATED B-24 LIBERATOR

A vast number of Liberators – a total of 18,188 were built – performed a wide range of roles throughout WWII, from maritime reconnaissance to anti-submarine missions to transport operations. But the Liberator made its greatest contribution as a fighter-bomber, unloading 635,000 tons of ordnance and shooting down 4,189 enemy planes during its three years of operation. The first version to play a significant role was the B-24D, of which 2,738 were produced, largely for use in the North African and Pacific theaters. Subsequent versions were the B-24E, G and H, which vaunted no major improvements, but which nonetheless eventually evolved into the B-24J, the most extensively produced of the Liberator series. The final versions in the series, the B-24L and the B-24M, of which 1,667 and 2,593 were built respectively, where characterized by significant modifications in the gun configurations. Production of the Liberator ceased on May 31, 1945.

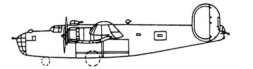

Version: B-24D – **Engine:** 4 Pratt & Whitney R-1830-43 Twin Wasp radials, 14-cylinder, air-cooled, 1,200 hp each – **Wingspan:** 110' (33.52 m) – **Length:** 66'4" (20.22 m) – **Height:** 17'11" (5.46 m) – **Max. takeoff weight:** 60,000 lbs (27,216 kg) – **Max. speed:** 305 mph (488 km/h) at 25,000 ft (7,620 m) – **Service ceiling:** 31,800' (9,750 m) – **Range:** 2,865 miles 4,585 km) – **Armament:** 11 .50-cal. machine guns, 8,000 lbs (3,620 kg) bombs

■ CONVAIR B-36

The concept of the strategic bomber saw its first expression in the post-WWII era in the Convair B-36, an imposing giant propelled by 6 piston-driven engines. In later versions, starting with the B-36D of 1949 and ending in 1953 with the H and J, an additional 4 jet engines were incorporated. This aircraft, at the time the largest ever built for the USAF, was conceived during the height of the war as a solution to the problem of secure Allied airbases in Europe: departing from the American continent, the B-36 would be able to strike German positions. The project wasn't completed in time for war use, the first prototype making its maiden flight on August 8, 1946. But with

the onset of the Cold War, the B-36 became the symbol of American air power; and in a sense the first 'psychological deterrent' in the balance of power between East and West during the era preceding the intercontinental ballistic missile. It was a role that the B-36 maintained until 1957, when the 363 units that had been built began to be decommissioned by the Strategic Air Command.

Version: B-36H – **Engine:** 6 Pratt & Whitney R-4360-53 Wasp Major radials, 28-cylinder, air-cooled, 3,800 hp each; 4 General Electric J47-GE-19 turbojet, 5,200 lbs (2,358 kg) thrust each – **Wingspan:** 230' (70.10 m) – **Length:** 162' (49.40 m) – **Height:** 46'8" (14.22 m) – **Max. take-off weight:** 411,000 lbs (185,976 kg) – **Max. speed:** 416 mph (661 km/h) – **Service ceiling:** 44,000' (13,500 m) – **Range:** 7,700 miles (12,320 km) – **Armament:** 16 20mm cannons, 86,000 lbs (38,900 kg) bombs

■ CONVAIR F-102 DELTA DAGGER

The first supersonic interceptor with a 'delta' wing design, and the first armed exclusively with air-to-air missiles, the Convair F-102 Delta Dagger flew as a prototype on October 24, 1953. Fine-tuning to resolve aerodynamic faults caused delay, but the Dagger assumed its definitive form in 1954. The first deliveries to various Air Defense Command squadrons began in mid-1956, and production blazed ahead until April 1958, with a total of 975 units rolling off the assembly line. The Air Force also bought 111 modified Daggers, the TF-102 A, for training purposes. The planes remained in intensive service for nearly two decades; it wasn't until 1974 that they were taken from the front lines and consigned to the Air National Guard. A number of units were given to Turkey and Greece, in accordance with NATO foreign assistance programs.

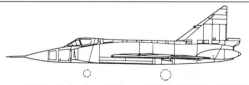

Version: F-102A – **Engine:** Pratt & Whitney J57-P-23, 17,000 lbs (7,711 kg) thrust – **Wingspan:** 38' (11.61 m) – Length: 68'4" (20.83 m) – **Height:** 21'2" (6.45 m) – **Max. takeoff weight:** 31,570 lbs (14,288 kg) – **Max. speed:** 830 mph (1,327 km/h) at 35,700 ft (10,975 m) – **Service ceiling:** 53,600' (16,460 m) – **Range:** 1,350 miles (2,170 km) – **Armament:** 24 unguided 2.75-inch rockets, 6 air-to-air guided missiles

■ CURTISS P-40B WARHAWK

This single-prop workhorse was America's most important fighter during WWII's first two years, not so much for its quality as for the sheer number produced, which made it possible to stall the adversary on all fronts while waiting for the next, hopefully better plane. The P-40 in its many variants fought throughout the Pacific, European, African and Russian campaigns, distributed like candy to the Allies by the Americans. Design work began in 1939, and in 1941 the 'B' version (known as Tomahawk Mk.II in the RAF) was the first to see combat. It fought at Pearl Harbor, in Africa – and even in China, under the banner of the American Volunteer Group's "Flying Tigers."

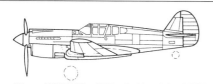

Engine: Allison V-1710-33, V-12, liquid-cooled, 1,040 hp – **Wingspan:** 37' (11.38 m) – **Length:** 31'6" (9.68 m) – **Height:** 10'6" (3.23 m) – **Max. takeoff weight:** 7,590 lbs (3,450 kg) – **Max. speed:** 355 mph (566 km/h) at 14,850 ft (4,572 m) – **Service ceiling:** 32,100' (9,875 m) – **Range:** 935 miles (1,500 km) – **Armament:** 4 machine guns

■ CURTISS P-40E WARHAWK

After building 131 P-40Bs, a handful of Cs and 582 P-40Ds – the great majority of which went to the RAF with the designation Kittyhawk I – Curtiss began producing the E, which became operative in 1942. It incorporated significant improvements, above all in its defense and attack capabilities. These were the first P-40s to serve the USAF in the Mediterranean theater. In all, 2,300 units of the P-40E were built.

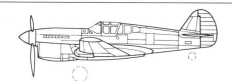

Engine: Allison V-1710-39, V-12, liquid-cooled, 1,186 hp – **Wingspan:** 37' (11.38 m) – **Length:** 30'10" (9.50 m) – **Height:** 10'6" (3.23 m) – **Max. take-off weight:** 8,200 lbs (3,723 kg) – **Max. speed:** 357 mph (570 km/h) at 14,850 ft (4,572 m) – **Service ceiling:** 28,730' (8,840 m) – **Range:** 705 miles (1,126 km) – **Armament:** 6 machine guns, 720 lbs (327 kg) bombs

■ CURTISS P-40F WARHAWK

The urgent need to improve the performance of the P-40 led to the development in 1941 of a version equipped with a Rolls-Royce Merlin engine in place of the Allison V-12, built through a licensing agreement with RR by the American firm Packard. The P-40F was superior to its predecessors, but its production – only 1,311 units – was hindered by the chronic scarcity of Merlin engines, which had been prioritized for use in the P-51 Mustang. The final version was the N of 1943 (5,219 units built), which brought the grand total of P-40s to an amazing 13,733.

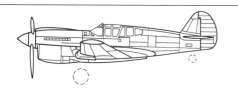

Engine: Packard V-1650-1, V-12, liquid-cooled, 1,300 hp – **Wingspan:** 37' (11.38 m) – **Length:** 33' (10.16 m) – **Height:** 10'6" (3.23 m) – **Max. takeoff weight:** 8,200 lbs (4,241 kg) – **Max. speed:** 365 mph (585 km/h) at 19,825 ft (6,100 m) – **Service ceiling:** 34,075' (10,485 m) – **Range:** 377 miles (603 km) – **Armament:** 6 machine guns, 500 lbs (227 kg) bombs

■ DASSAULT MIRAGE 2000

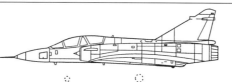

Version: 2000N – **Engine:** Snecma M-53-P2 turbofan, 21,650 lbs (9,798 kg) thrust, with afterburner – **Wingspan:** 30'1" (9.26 m) – **Length:** 47'4" (14.55 m) – **Height:** 16'9" (5.15 m) – **Max. takeoff weight:** 35,600 lbs (17,000 kg) – **Max. speed:** 1,327 mph (2,124 km/h) at 39,000 ft (12,000 m) – **Service ceiling:** 65,000' (20,000 m) – **Range:** 875 miles (1,400 km) – **Armament:** 1 ASMP air-to-surface nuclear missile

The N is the final evolution of the Mirage 2000, a series of powerful and sophisticated combat vehicles that earned France a major military presence in the 1980s. Production began in 1979 with the 2000C interceptor, which became operative in 1984. Improvements to the propulsion and avionics systems characterized the next version, the 2000E. The variant illustrated here, designed for nuclear air-to-surface strikes, is an evolution of the two-seater 2000B training jet, the prototype of which first appeared on February 3, 1983. As of year 2000, a total of 587 units had been built, with 350 enlisted for service in France's Armée de l'Air and the remainder exported to other nations.

■ DASSAULT MIRAGE III

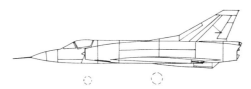

Version: III-C – **Engine:** Snecma Atar 9B turbojet, 13,200 lbs (6,000 kg) thrust – **Wingspan:** 26'9" (8.22 m) – **Length:** 48' (14.77 m) – **Height:** 13'10" (4.25 m) – **Max. takeoff weight:** 26,080 lbs (11,800 kg) – **Max. speed:** 1,395 mph (2,230 km/h) at 35,750 ft (11,000 m) – **Service ceiling:** 56,625' (16,500 m) – **Range:** 750 miles (1,200 km) – **Armament:** 2 30mm cannons, 3,000 lbs (1,360 kg) mixed ordnance

Among the finest combat planes ever built, the Mirage stands as Europe's most successful fighter jet. In service since 1960, it evolved through numerous versions, each more powerful than the last, which are still in use today in the air forces of twenty or so nations. The program began in 1953 and the first version, the III-A, flew on May 12, 1958. This was followed by the III-B training plane (October 20, 1959) and the III-C interceptor (October 9, 1960), after which the Mirage was immediately put to use in the Armée de l'Air. Further versions were developed: the III-D two-seater, designed for tactical support; the III-E multirole fighter (first flight April 21, 1961); the III-R, outfitted for photo-reconnaissance (October 31, 1961). This exceptional French plane enjoyed instant success abroad, and as such many sub-models were built to accommodate the numerous foreign buyers. In fact, the Mirage 5 (May 1, 1967), a simplified

version of the III-E, was designed explicitly for export to the Middle Eastern countries. More than 1,400 French-built Mirage III-5s were sold, and many more were manufactured through license agreements with four other countries.

■ DASSAULT MYSTÈRE

Version: IV-A – **Engine:** Hispano Suiza Verdon 350 turbojet, 7,700 lbs (3,500 kg) thrust – **Wingspan:** 36'6" (11.12 m) – **Length:** 42'2" (12.85 m) – **Height:** 15' (4.60 m) – **Max. takeoff weight:** 16,500 lbs (7,500 kg) – **Max. speed:** 700 mph (1,120 km/h) at sea level – **Service ceiling:** 44,950' (13,700 m) – **Range:** 1,060 miles (1,690 km) – **Armament:** 2 30mm cannons, 2,000 lbs (905 kg) mixed ordnance

The first European fighter with a delta-wing design and supersonic characteristics was the Dassault Mystère, a plane that consolidated the position France had gained at the cutting edge of post-WWII aviation technology with Dassault's first jet, the M.D.450 Ouragan. The prototype first flew on February 23, 1951. After a limited run of the original version, the II-C, production focused on the definitive version, the IV-A. A total of 483 units were built, the last in 1958, for the French, Indian and Israeli air forces. The adoption of a turbojet with afterburner and marked improvements in overall performance distinguished the subsequent version, the IV-B (first flight December 1953), from which evolved the Super Mystère of 1955. This final version re-mained in production until October 1959 and wasn't retired from service until the middle of the 1970s.

■ DASSAULT RAFALE

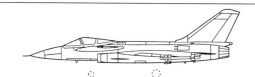

Version: A – **Engine:** 2 General Electric F404-GE-400 turbofans, 16,000 lbs (7,258 kg) thrust each – **Wingspan:** 36'9" (11.20 m) – **Length:** 51'10" (15.80 m) – **Height:** 17' (5.20 m) – **Max. takeoff weight:** 44,100 lbs (20,000 kg) – **Max. speed:** 1,335 mph (2,135 km/h) – **Service ceiling:** 59,450' (18,290 m) – **Range:** 1,155 miles (1,850 km) – **Armament:** 1 30mm cannon, 7,700 lbs (3,500 kg) mixed ordnance

The Rafale (which means 'burst' in French) is the most recent addition to the dynasty of combat planes built by Dassault. This sophisticated Mach 2 twin turbo craft, developed to compete with the European Typhoon fighter, is today one of the most advanced multirole fighter planes in the world. After France's withdrawal from the Eurofighter program in 1985, the Rafale project slowed down radically due to excessive costs, now borne alone. The first two prototypes (C for the Armée de l'Air and M for the naval branch) flew respectively on

D
D

May 19 and December 12, 1991; full-scale production on the Rafale B didn't begin until December of 1998. A total of 109 units, not counting the 13 existing test models, have been ordered. Full operational readiness is scheduled for 2005.

■ DE HAVILLAND MOSQUITO

The de Havilland Mosquito was perhaps the most versatile combat vehicle of World War II. When used as a photo-recon plane it did not require armament, for its speed and altitude rendered it practically invulnerable. When outfitted as a bomber, and therefore weighed down, it was still the fastest plane in the Bomber Command. As a long-range fighter, it operated with the same deadly efficiency whether by day or by night, equally as effective against the German night fighters as against incoming rockets. From 1941 to 1950, Great Britain built 6,439 Mosquitos in a dozen versions; another 1,342 units were produced in Canada and Australia. The success of this airplane is even more extraordinary when one considers that it was made entirely of wood. The Mosquito was a slim and elegant twin-engine monoplane, the peerless performance of which was owed to a number of factors, foremost among them being the extreme reduction of the housings for the two Merlin engines, the exquisite accuracy of its aerodynamics, and an exceptionally favorable power-to-weight ratio.

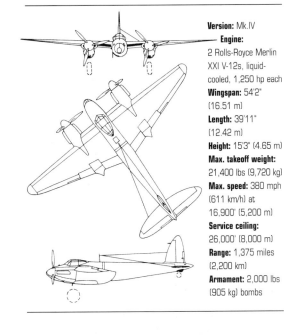

Version: Mk.IV – **Engine:** 2 Rolls-Royce Merlin XXI V-12s, liquid-cooled, 1,250 hp each **Wingspan:** 54'2" (16.51 m) **Length:** 39'11" (12.42 m) **Height:** 15'3" (4.65 m) **Max. takeoff weight:** 21,400 lbs (9,720 kg) **Max. speed:** 380 mph (611 km/h) at 16,900' (5,200 m) **Service ceiling:** 26,000' (8,000 m) **Range:** 1,375 miles (2,200 km) **Armament:** 2,000 lbs (905 kg) bombs

■ DE HAVILLAND VAMPIRE

Preceded by the Gloster Meteor, the de Havilland Vampire was the second jet-powered fighter to serve Britain's RAF. It was completed too late to participate in WWII, but in the postwar years it was use as a fighter, fighter-bomber, night fighter and training plane by the air forces of more than thirty countries. In addition to the huge numbers of Vampires produced in Great Britain until 1958, it was also built under license in India, Australia, France and Italy. Indeed, in 1950 the de Havilland fighter become the first jet used in the Aeronautica Militare Italiana. The prototype flew on September 26, 1943; the most successful version, the FB.5, made its first appearance on June 23, 1948. Production eventually surpassed 4,000, and many Vampires remained in service as training planes until the 1970s.

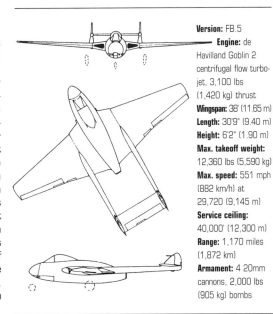

Version: FB.5 **Engine:** de Havilland Goblin 2 centrifugal flow turbojet, 3,100 lbs (1,420 kg) thrust **Wingspan:** 38' (11.65 m) **Length:** 30'9" (9.40 m) **Height:** 6'2" (1.90 m) **Max. takeoff weight:** 12,360 lbs (5,590 kg) **Max. speed:** 551 mph (882 km/h) at 29,720 (9,145 m) **Service ceiling:** 40,000' (12,300 m) **Range:** 1,170 miles (1,872 km) **Armament:** 4 20mm cannons, 2,000 lbs (905 kg) bombs

■ DORNIER DO.17

Baptized the 'Flying Pencil' by its own designers in the prototype phase, the Dornier Do.17 was one of the best known and most commonly used bombers of the Luftwaffe. It went through numerous evolutions and remained in production for the entire course of WWII. The Dornier Do.17 Z was the last and most important of the 17s, with just over 500 units produced up until the summer of 1940. The Germans then moved onto the 217, a larger and more powerful aircraft. The Dornier Do. in all its various manifestations proved to be a reasonably good plane, though certainly not exceptional.

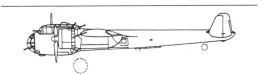

Version: Do.17 Z-2 – **Engine:** 2 Bramo 323P radials, 9-cylinder, air-cooled, 1,000 hp each – **Wingspan:** 58'6" (18 m) – **Length:** 51'4" (15.80 m) – **Height:** 14'9" (4.55 m) – **Max. takeoff weight:** 19,500 lbs (8,590 kg) – **Max. speed:** 256 mph (410 km/h) at 13,000' (4,000 m) – **Service ceiling:** 26,650' (8,200 m) – **Range:** 721 miles (1,160 km) – **Armament:** 6 machine guns, 2,000 lbs (910 kg) bombs

■ DOUGLAS A4 SKYHAWK

The Skyhawk was developed in response to a specific request from the US Navy: to create an attack jet capable of replacing the Douglas AD Skyraider. The challenge was duly met by the A4, a powerful and dependable attack plane of which some 2,960 units were built between 1954 and 1979. After the A4-A of 1954 and A4-B of 1956, the Skyhawk found its optimal early configuration, thanks to a bigger engine and numerous structural modifications, in the A4-E, whose prototype flew on July 12, 1961. The 1970s was the decade of the A4-M, or Skyhawk II, which first flew on April 10, 1970. In addition to Israel, Douglas's second-best customer after the US Navy and Marines, the Skyhawk was purchased in significant numbers by Australia, New Zealand, Singapore, Kuwait and Argentina.

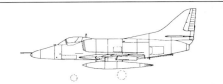

Version: A4-E – **Engine:** Pratt & Whitney J52-P-6 turbojet, 8,520 lbs (3,855 kg) thrust – **Wingspan:** 27'3" (8.38 m) – **Length:** 39'8" (12.21 m) – **Height:** 15'6" (4.77 m) – **Max. takeoff weight:** 24,560 lbs (11,113 kg) – **Max. speed:** 690 mph (1,102 km/h) at sea level – **Service ceiling:** 48,540' (14,935 m) – **Range:** 925 miles (1,480 km) – **Armament:** 2 20mm cannons, 8,220 lbs (3,719 kg) mixed ordnance

■ DOUGLAS AD SKYRAIDER

Version: AD-6 – **Engine:** Wright R-3350-26W Cyclone radial, 18-cylinder, air-cooled, 2,700 hp – **Wingspan:** 49'6" (15.24 m) – **Length:** 39'8" (11.83 m) – **Height:** 15'6" (4.77 m) – **Max. takeoff weight:** 24,973 lbs (11,340 kg) – **Max. speed:** 323 mph (518 km/h) at 17,800' (5,486 m) – **Service ceiling:** 28,500' (8,690 m) – **Range:** 1,150 miles (1,840 km) – **Armament:** 4 20mm cannons, 8,000 lbs (3,628 kg) mixed ordnance

Versatile and sturdy, the powerful Douglas Skyraider was the last great piston-engine combat plane. Created in response to the mounting pressures of the closing years of WWII (the prototype flew on April 18, 1945), the Skyraider didn't make it off the assembly line in time to participate. But it got a chance to show its extraordinary mettle in the next two major American conflicts – Korea and Vietnam – where it was utilized as a dive-bomber, very often proving itself to be more efficient than the sophisticated modern jets of that epoch. Between 1945 and 1957, seven versions were produced (3,180 units total) in 28 different series, with specializations ranging from recon to electronic interference, from submarine detection to advanced aerial surveillance, from night raids to bombing runs. The career of the Skyraider ended on April 10, 1968, the day a grateful US Navy officially retired it from service.

■ DOUGLAS C-47 SKYTRAIN

The C-47 is essentially the military evolution of the hugely successful commercial airliner, the Douglas DC-3. The twin-engine passenger plane first appeared in 1935, and in 1940 Douglas was asked to develop a version for use in the USAF, the denomination of which was changed to C-47. With America's entry into the war, production of the C-47 was radically accelerated, and it quickly became the principal military transport plane of the Allied forces, carrying cargo, personnel and paratroops. The most important versions used by the Air Force were the C-47 Skytrain and the C-53 Skytrooper, while the US Navy used the code R4D. The Royal Air Force gave it yet another name, Dakota. All in all, 10,123 units were built, many of which remained in service through the Vietnam War, where it even did duty as a gunship.

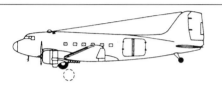

Version: C-47B – Engine: 2 Pratt & Whitney R-1830-92 Twin Wasp radials, 14-cylinder, air-cooled, 1,200 hp each – Wingspan: 95'6 (29.10 m) – Length: 63'8" (19.43 m) – Height: 17' (5.18 m) – Max. takeoff weight: 26,000 lbs (11,793 kg) – Max. speed: 231 mph (370 km/h) – Service ceiling: 30,000' (7,315 m) – Range: 1,600 miles (2,574 km)

■ ENGLISH ELECTRIC LIGHTNING

The Royal Air Force's crown jewel for more than twenty years, the Lightning was a powerful bisonic interceptor whose design roots reach back to 1949. The plane required a lengthy development phase, and didn't become operative until June of 1960. But from that moment on, it remained at the front line of British defense until the 1980s, when it was replaced by the more sophisticated Tornado. The first version of the Lightning that went to production was the F-1, but it didn't reach its ideal configuration until the F.3, which appeared on June 16, 1962. The last of the series was the F.6 of 1964. A total of 338 units were built, including two series of two-seater training planes and a number of variants designed for export to Saudi Arabia and Kuwait.

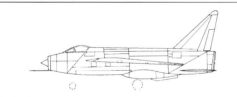

Version: F.1 – Engine: 2 Rolls-Royce Avon 21 turbojets, 14,350 (6,545 kg) thrust each – Wingspan: 49'6 (10.61 m) – Length: 39'8" (16.84 m) – Height: 15'6" (5.97 m) – Max. takeoff weight: 24,973 lbs (18,915 kg) – Max. speed: 323 mph (2,414 km/h) at 17,800' (10,970 m) – Service ceiling: 28, 500' (18,920 m) – Range: 1,150 miles (1,440 km) – Armament: 2 30mm cannons, 2 air-to-air missiles.

■ EUROFIGHTER EAP TYPHOON

The Eurofighter Typhoon is the most recent and advanced European combat aircraft. After a long gestation period that began in the 1970s, this sophisti-

cated multirole fighter-bomber entered into service in 2002 as the principal plane of the British, German, Spanish and Italian forces. The production figures for the four partners total 620 units and are distributed as follows: Great Britain 232 (37 two-seat trainers), Germany 180 (33), Italy 121 (5) and Spain 87 (15). Construction has been entrusted to two international consortia – Eurofighter for the shell, and Eurojet for the engines. Though final delivery isn't scheduled until 2018, the first units should be fully operational by 2005-06. The Typhoon is a twin-jet, single-pilot plane, designed to specialize in air-to-air combat. It has a 'canard' wing configuration (i.e., tailplane forward of the main delta wing) for greater agility and can operate at Mach 2. Every aspect of the plane is an expression of the highest technology, from its carbon-fiber structure to its components in lithium, magnesium and titanium compounds, to its voice-commanded digital flight and armament cycling controls.

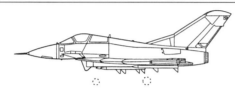

Engine: 2 Eurojet EJ200 turbofans, 20,285 lbs (9,180 kg) thrust each – Wingspan: 34'6" (10.50 m) – Length: 47'6" (14.50 m) – Height: 21' (6.40 m) – Max. takeoff weight: 46,400 lbs (21,000 kg) – Max. speed: 1,288 mph (2,060 km/h) at 39,360' (12,000 m) – Service ceiling: 60,000' (18,290 m) – Range: 695 miles (1,112 km) – Armament: 1 27mm cannon, 14,365 lbs (6,500 kg) mixed ordnance

■ FIAT C.R.42 FALCO

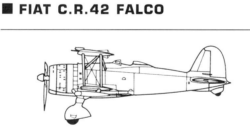

Engine: Fiat A.74 RC 38 radial, 14 cylinders, air-cooled, 840 hp – Wingspan: 32' (9.70 m) – Length: 27'3" (8.26 m) – Height: 9'9" (3.30 m) – Max. takeoff weight: 5,050 lbs (2,295 kg) – Max. speed: 272 mph (440 km/h) at 19,800' (6,000 m) – Service ceiling: 34,650' (10,500 m) – Range: 486 miles (785 km) – Armament: 2 machine guns

Between February 1939 and June 1943, Fiat produced 1,781 Falcos. The prototype first flew on May 23, 1938, and performed admirably. This single-seat biplane had an entirely metallic structure, sheathed partly in Duralumin and partly in canvas. After the Italian air command's first large order of 200 planes, the Hungarian, Belgian and Swedish military establishments soon followed suit. When Italy entered WW II, approximately 300 operative Falcos were in service. This little fighter saw the most action on the African front, where it had to struggle against the enemy planes' superiority and the severe conditions of this war theater. The Falco eventually assumed other roles: bomber escort, reconnaissance, surveillance, dive-bombing and night-fighting.

■ FOCKE WULF FW.190

The Fw.190 fighter-bomber distinguished itself on all fronts until the Third Reich's final day. Indeed, it was such a fine plane that the Germans built 13,367 of them. A small monoplane with a low-mounted wing and retractable landing gear, its most advanced feature was its aerodynamic line. The inverted V motor was cooled by a 10-bladed fan; the canopy was made entirely of Plexiglas and allowed the pilot a 360° field of vision. The first series of Fw.190s, the A-1, entered service in July 1941. The A-2 and A-3 followed, different largely in engine performance and armament. The first A-4s appeared in 1942, joined by the A-5, A-6 and A-7 in 1943. The A-8, the last of the series, was notable for its improved engine. Each of the listed models had numerous corresponding sub-models, varying in role and armament. There were also other entire series: the fighter-bomber F series introduced in 1942, followed by the G series. The final variant was the Fw.190 D, which appeared in early 1944, of which 700 were built.

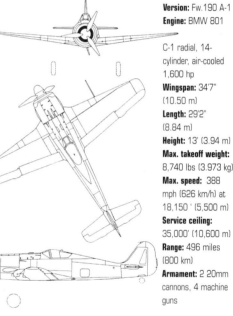

Version: Fw.190 A-1
Engine: BMW 801

C-1 radial, 14-cylinder, air-cooled 1,600 hp
Wingspan: 34'7" (10.50 m)
Length: 29'2" (8.84 m)
Height: 13' (3.94 m)
Max. takeoff weight: 8,740 lbs (3.973 kg)
Max. speed: 388 mph (626 km/h) at 18,150 ' (5,500 m)
Service ceiling: 35,000' (10,600 m)
Range: 496 miles (800 km)
Armament: 2 20mm cannons, 4 machine guns

■ FOKKER DR.I

The Fokker triplane was one of WW I's most famous fighters, with an exemplary performance sufficient to ensure notoriety. It was also the plane behind the exploits of the German ace, Manfred von Richthofen, and his Jagdgeschwader squadron – otherwise known as the 'Red Baron' and his 'Flying Circus' – which gave it legendary status. The Fokker Dr.I first saw the battlefront on August 28, 1917. By May 1918, 171 of them were flying for a number of different squadrons, all at the front lines. It is noteworthy that the circumstances surrounding von Richthofen's death on April 21, 1918, while flying a Fokker triplane, are still hotly argued.

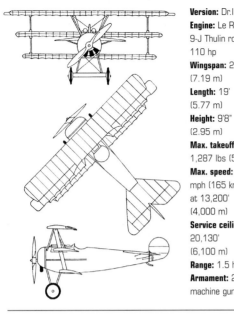

Version: Dr.I
Engine: Le Rhône 9-J Thulin rotary, 110 hp
Wingspan: 23'8" (7.19 m)
Length: 19' (5.77 m)
Height: 9'8" (2.95 m)
Max. takeoff weight: 1,287 lbs (585 kg)
Max. speed: 102 mph (165 km/h) at 13,200' (4,000 m)
Service ceiling: 20,130' (6,100 m)
Range: 1.5 hours
Armament: 2 machine guns

■ FOKKER E

The Fokker E.III's debut on the western front in August 1915 caused panic in the Allied high command. Specifically, the German fighter was the first plane outfitted with fixed forward-firing machine guns, synchronized to shoot through the spinning propeller, giving it an enormous advantage over its adversaries. Known as the 'Fokker Scourge,' the plane rendered British and French pilots virtually impotent in combat, and soon Germany was enjoying absolute air superiority. But the Allies were quick to respond: in early 1916 they introduced two formidable new fighters to the front, the de Havilland D.H.2 and the Farman F.E.2b and gradually regained parity in the skies.

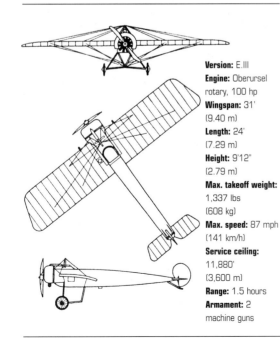

Version: E.III
Engine: Oberursel rotary, 100 hp
Wingspan: 31' (9.40 m)
Length: 24' (7.29 m)
Height: 9'12" (2.79 m)
Max. takeoff weight: 1,337 lbs (608 kg)
Max. speed: 87 mph (141 km/h)
Service ceiling: 11,880' (3,600 m)
Range: 1.5 hours
Armament: 2 machine guns

■ FRIEDRICHSHAFEN G.III

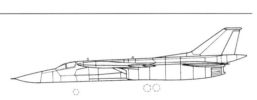

Engine: 2 Mercedes D.VIa, 6-cylinder inlines, liquid-cooled, 260 hp each – **Wingspan:** 78'4" (23.75 m) – **Length:** 42'3" (12.85 m) – **Height:** 12' (3.66 m) – **Max. takeoff weight:** 8,668 lbs (3,940 kg) – **Max. speed:** 87.42 mph (141 km/h at 3300' (1,000 m) – **Service ceiling:** 14,880' (4,510 m) – **Range:** 5 hours – **Armament:** 2-4 machine guns; 2,200 lbs(1,000 kg) bombs

Used in the deadly raids over France and Belgium during WW I, the Friedrichshafen was one of Germany's most effective heavy bombers. This big twin-engine biplane was designed in 1914 and reached its optimal configuration in 1917 with the G.III. The first of these began service in February 1917, flying alongside the Gotha G.V and the Zeppelin Staaken R, planes notorious for their incursions into British airspace, in particular for their raids over London. Three German squadrons were equipped with Friedrichshafen bombers, of which 338 units were built. The G.III remained in service to the very end of the war.

■ GENERAL DYNAMICS F-111

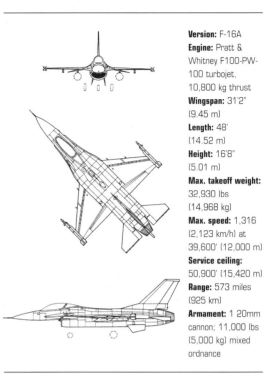

Version: F-111F – **Engine:** 2 Pratt & Whitney TF30-P-100 turbofans, 11,385 kg thrust each – **Wingspan:** (extended) 64'4" (19.20 m) – **Length:** 74' (22.40 m) – **Height:** 17'4" (5.22 m) – **Max. takeoff weight:** 99,790 lbs (45,359 kg) – **Max. speed:** 1,447 mph (2,335 km/h) at 35,210' (10,670 m) – **Service ceiling:** 59,400' (18,000 m) – **Range:** 1,327 miles (2,140 km) – **Armament:** 1 30mm multi-barrel cannon; 31,440 lbs (14,290 kg) mixed ordnance

The General Dynamics F-111 was the first airplane with foldable or 'swing wings' to be used in wartime operations. In fact, more than 30 years after its introduction, a version of this large, powerful twinjet bomber is still in use in electronic warfare missions. The F-111 program, jointly commissioned by the USAF and the US Navy, was launched in November 1962. The Navy, however, rejected the plane, leaving its development exclusively to the Air Force. A small batch of the F-111A, the first version, was delivered in 1967, and from there several other versions evolved, ending with the F-111F, a tactical fighter-bomber which flew as a prototype in May 1973. When the last 106 F-111Fs to be built left the factory in November 1976, the total of all the series came to 562 units. The original F-111s were retired from service in 1997 after a long and distinguished career, but the EF-111A Raven, the variant designed for electronic warfare, is still widely used.

■ GENERAL DYNAMICS F-16

Version: F-16A
Engine: Pratt & Whitney F100-PW-100 turbojet, 10,800 kg thrust
Wingspan: 31'2" (9.45 m)
Length: 48' (14.52 m)
Height: 16'8" (5.01 m)
Max. takeoff weight: 32,930 lbs (14,968 kg)
Max. speed: 1,316 (2,123 km/h) at 39,600' (12,000 m)
Service ceiling: 50,900' (15,420 m)
Range: 573 miles (925 km)
Armament: 1 20mm cannon; 11,000 lbs (5,000 kg) mixed ordnance

Among the finest interceptors ever built, the General Dynamics F-16 is recognized as the modern equivalent of the great fighters of the past, such as the Spitfire and the Zero. Fast, powerful and supremely agile, the F-16 is a true success story: nearly 4,300 units built for more than 25 client countries. The project began in the '70s with the USAF's announcement of its need for a new light fighter. This need had emerged during the Vietnam conflict, where American planes had a hard time matching the superior maneuverability of Soviet MiGs, especially in close combat. General Dynamics responded to the call with the F-16, which was also chosen by NATO. In June 1975 the plane was adopted by Belgium, Denmark, Norway, and the Netherlands to replace the Lockheed F-104 Starfighter. The F-16A prototype flew in December 1976, and the Air Force authorized production in January 1979. The second principal version was the F-16C. Delivered in July 1984, it was characterized by better avionics, heavier armament and a more powerful engine. Further modifications led to new versions, including the two-seater F-16D. Production continued throughout the '80s and '90s.

■ GLOSTER GLADIATOR

The British Gladiator served with honor during the first two years of WWII on the European, African and Mediterranean fronts, and enjoyed notable success with foreign buyers. Of the 527 units built by spring 1940, 216 were exported to various European countries, and even to China. The first planes of the Mk.I series entered service in January 1937. This model differed from the prototype in that it had a new 840-hp Mercury engine, a sliding canopy, and 4 Browning machine guns instead of the original pairs of Vickers and Lewis guns. The Mk.II followed soon thereafter, with an important propeller modification: the Mk.I had a two-blade wooden prop, the II had a three-blade fixed-pitch metal prop. The Mk.II led to the Sea Gladiator, adapted for ship deck takeoff and landing. When WW II broke out, Gladiators were serving in 13 of the Fighter Command's 35 squadrons. In November 1939 two squadrons were sent to France, where they fought until May 1940, when it became clear that the old biplane design was no match for the Luftwaffe's more modern planes.

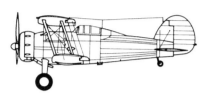

Version: Mk.I – **Engine:** Bristol Mercury IX radial, 9 cylinders, air-cooled, 840 hp – **Wingspan:** 32'4" (9.83 m) – **Length:** 27'6" (8.36 m) – **Height:** 10'5"(3.15 m) – **Max. takeoff weight:** 4,741 lbs (2,155 kg) – **Max. speed:** 252 mph (407 km/h) at 14,586' (4,420 m) – **Service ceiling:** 33,000' (10,000m) – **Range:** 428 miles (690 km) – **Armament:** 4 machine guns

■ GLOSTER METEOR MK.III

Engine: 2 Rolls-Royce Derwent 1s, 905 kg thrust each
Wingspan: 43'3" (13.11 m)
Length: 41'6" (12.58 m)
Height: 13' (3.96 m)
Max. takeoff weight: 13,772 lbs (6,260 kg)
Max. speed: 492 mph (793 km/h) at 30,195' (9,150 m)
Service ceiling: 44,220' (13,400 m)
Range: 1,337 miles (2,156 km)
Armament: 4 20mm cannons

The Gloster Meteor, the first British jet fighter, was also the first operative Allied jet in WW II. Design and testing began in August 1940 while the Battle of Britain was in full swing. Since the Germans were working on the same technology, its development became a veritable race against time. The Meteor's career began on July 27, 1944 with the Mk.1. In 1945 the Mk.III, with improved power and performance, joined the ranks. As fate would have it, the Meteor never had a chance to test itself in a dogfight against its Luftwaffe counterpart, the Messerschmitt Me.262.

■ GLOSTER METEOR NF.11

Just as the Meteor was being perfected in the form of the F series, WW II ended. Nonetheless, the F series went into mass production and a number of versions were developed. The assembly line remained active until 1954, having churned out 3,545 units distributed over 11 basic versions. The main variants were the F.4 and F.8 fighters, of 1948 and 1950 respectively. Other types included planes for training, photo-reconnaissance and night-fighting. The first of these, the NF.11, appeared in May 1950, to be followed by three more versions. In addition to service in the RAF, the Meteor also flew under the flags of at least eleven other nations, including Belgium, France, Argentina, Denmark, Brazil, Egypt, Israel and Sweden. In the Netherlands, Fokker built 330 units under a licensing agreement.

Engine: 3 Rolls-Royce Derwent 8 turbojets, 1,587 kg thrust each – **Wingspan:** 43'3" (13.10 m) – **Length:** 48'9" (14.78 m) – **Height:** 14' (4.24 m) – **Max. takeoff weight:** 19,993 lbs (9,088 kg) – **Max. speed:** 595 mph (960 km/h) at 9,900' (3,000 m) – **Service ceiling:** 40,234' (12,192 m) – **Range:** 9,176 miles (1,480 km) – **Armament:** 4 20mm cannons

■ GOTHA G

For the English, particularly for Londoners, the word Gotha was synonymous with panic, destruction and despair. From May 1917 and throughout 1918, these large bombers made a series of incursions – 27 in all – into London's airspace. Historically speaking, this was the first prolonged bombing campaign with a single objective. Even if physical damage was not very serious, the psychological effects on the population were devastating. Design of the Gotha began in early 1915 and, after three more or less successful versions, reached its ideal configuration in the G.IV, the first to be used in the raids on London. From summer 1917 the G.IV was flanked by the more powerful G.V.

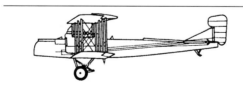

Version: G.V. – **Engine:** 2 Mercedes D.VIa inlines, 6-cylinder, liquid cooled, 260 hp each – **Wingspan:** 77'9" (23.70 m) – **Length:** 40'6" (12.36 m) – **Height:** 14'2" (4.30 m) – **Max. takeoff weight:** 8,765 lbs (3,967 kg) – **Max. speed:** 65 mph (140 km/h) at sea level – **Service ceiling:** 21,320' (6,500 m) – **Range:** 6 hours – **Armament:** 3-4 machine guns; 1,325 lbs (600 kg) bombs

■ GRUMMAN F-14 TOMCAT

The Grumman F-14 Tomcat is one of the finest naval fighters ever built. Thanks to its variable-sweep wings it is equally efficient in high-altitude interception, low-

altitude assault and air-to-air combat. Though designed back in the 1960s, improved avionics and more powerful engines make the Tomcat one of the US Navy's most trustworthy weapons even today.

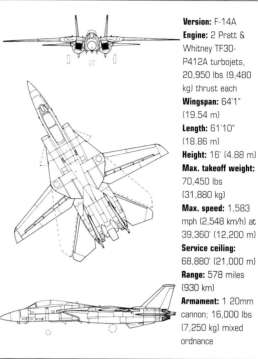

Version: F-14A
Engine: 2 Pratt & Whitney TF30-P412A turbojets, 20,950 lbs (9,480 kg) thrust each
Wingspan: 64'1" (19.54 m)
Length: 61'10" (18.86 m)
Height: 16' (4.88 m)
Max. takeoff weight: 70,450 lbs (31,880 kg)
Max. speed: 1,583 mph (2,548 km/h) at 39,360' (12,200 m)
Service ceiling: 68,880' (21,000 m)
Range: 578 miles (930 km)
Armament: 1 20mm cannon; 16,000 lbs (7,250 kg) mixed ordnance

The first prototype, the YF-14A, made its test flight on December 21, 1970. The Navy received its first operative F-14A in June 1972; by 1980 344 units out of the 557 ordered had been delivered. The Tomcat's exceptional versatility caused the Navy to rethink its original plans to use it exclusively as an interceptor. This versatility was further augmented in the late '70s with the addition of an advanced photo-recon system, installed in a ventral canoe. The plane continued to be upgraded throughout the 1980s, culminating in the F-14 Plus of 1987 (38 units built) and the final version, the F-14D Super Tomcat of 1989. This latter incorporated the more powerful engines of the F-14 Plus, along with new avionics, improved radar and better armament. Delivery of the 37 units built began in 1990. No new versions were developed after this point, though many older models were converted to the new standard.

■ GRUMMAN F4F-3 WILDCAT

Engine: Pratt & Whitney R-1830-76 Twin Wasp radial, 14-cylinder, air-cooled, 1,200 hp – **Wingspan:** 38' (11.58 m) – **Length:** 28'9" (8.76 m) – **Height:** 11'10" (3.60 m) – **Max. takeoff weight:** 7,020 lbs (3,176 kg) – **Max. speed:** 330 mph (531 km/h) at 21,320' (6,500 m) – **Service ceiling:** 37,500' (11,430 m) – **Range:** 845 miles (1,360 km) – **Armament:** 4 machine guns; 200 lbs (91 kg) bombs

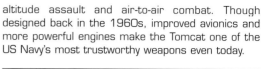

With the Grumman F4F Wildcat of 1940, the first in a long line of affectionately dubbed 'Cats, the United States Navy made a definitive shift from the biplane to the modern monoplane. A number of the 8,000 F4Fs that were built served in Britain's Fleet Air Arm under the name Martlet. The prototype flew on September 2, 1937, with unsatisfactory results. The diminutive fighter would undergo nine months of further testing and fine-tuning before being approved. The first production run was a mere 54 units.

■ GRUMMAN F4F-4 WILDCAT

Engine: Pratt & Whitney R-1830-86 Twin Wasp radial, 14-cylinder, air-cooled, 1,200 hp – **Wingspan:** 38' (11.58 m) – **Length:** 28'9" (8.76 m) – **Height:** 11'10" (3.60 m) – **Max. takeoff weight:** 7,425 lbs (3,360 kg) – **Max. speed:** 318 mph (512 km/h) at 19,350' (5,900 m) – **Service ceiling:** 34,900' (10,640 m) – **Range:** 770 miles (1,240 km) – **Armament:** 6 machine guns; 200 lbs (91 kg) bombs

The F4F-4, the second version of the Grumman Wildcat, appeared in 1941 and became the most extensively produced of all. Compared to its predecessor, the number of guns jumped from four to six, and the wings were foldable, which allowed aircraft carriers to host more planes. The F4F-4 took part in all Pacific theater the naval operations, and remained in production even after the appearance of the more modern Hellcat and Corsair.

■ GRUMMAN F6F HELLCAT

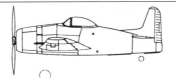

Version: F6F-3 – **Engine:** Pratt & Whitney R-2800-10 Double Wasp radial, 18-cylinder, air-cooled, 2,000 hp – **Wingspan:** 42'10" (13.06 m) – **Length:** 33'10" (10.24 m) – **Height:** 13' (3.99 m) – **Max. takeoff weight:** 11,400 lbs (5,162 kg) – **Max. speed:** 376 mph (605 km/h) at 17,300' (5,270 m) – **Service ceiling:** 538,400' (11,700 m)– **Range:** 11,088 miles (1,750 km) – **Armament:** 6 machine guns

The numbers confirm that the Hellcat was a worthy successor to the Wildcat: between August 1943 and the end of the war, 12,275 Hellcats were built. The first left the assembly line in early October 1942. On January 16, 1943 the aircraft carrier *Essex* was outfitted with a squadron of F6F-3s, and seven months later, this plane flew from the decks of the *Yorktown*, the *Independence* and *Essex* to attack the Marcus Islands. 4,403 F6F-3s were produced before the Navy moved on to the F6F-5 in April 1944. Of these, 223 were configured as night-fighters. Similarly, 1,434 of the 7,868 F6F-5s that were built fulfilled that same role (series code F6F-5N).

The last version derived from the 5 was the F6F-5P, specializing in photo-reconnaissance. From its first attack mission in August 1943 against the Japanese in the Marcus Islands, the Hellcat's career proceeded without interruption, and without limits on its role. It participated in every naval and amphibian operation in the Pacific as fighter, bomber, night-fighter and recon plane.

■ GRUMMAN F8F BEARCAT

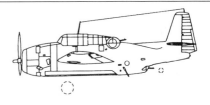

Version: F8F-1 – **Engine:** Pratt & Whitney R-2800-34W Double Wasp radial, 18-cylinder, air-cooled, 2,100 hp – **Wingspan:** 35'10" (10.92 m) – **Length:** 28'3" (8.61 m) – **Height:** 13'9" (4.21 m) – **Max. takeoff weight:** 12,975 lbs (5,872 kg) – **Max. speed:** 420 mph (677 km/h) at 19,700' (6,000 m) – **Service ceiling:** 38,700' (11,800 m) – **Range:** 1,100 miles (1,780 km) – **Armament:** 6 20mm cannons

The last of the famous piston-engine Grumman 'Cats,' the Bearcat would share the same destiny as the F7F Tigercat. Brought to term too late to serve in WWII, it was essentially a 'transition' plane that was rendered obsolete by the appearance of the first jets before it had even had a chance to demonstrate its excellent qualities. The Bearcat, still considered one of the best carrier-based fighters ever built, flew as a prototype in August 1944. Fast and heavily armed, it won over the Navy command, which immediately ordered 4,000 of them. The end of hostilities one year later drastically reduced the demand, though development of numerous variants pressed forward. For example, France used the F8F-2 of 1948 during its campaign in Indochina.

■ GRUMMAN F9F PANTHER

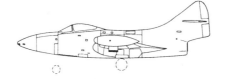

Version: F9F-2 – **Engine:** Pratt & Whitney J42-P-6 turbojet, 5,000 lbs (2,270 kg) thrust – **Wingspan:** 38' (11.58 m) – **Length:** 37'3" (11.35 m) – **Height:** 11'4" (3.45 m) – **Max. takeoff weight:** 19,540 lbs (8,842 kg) – **Max. speed:** 525 mph (846 km/h) at 22,000' (6,700 m) – **Service ceiling:** 44,600' (13,600 m) – **Range:** 1,350 miles (2,180 km) – **Armament:** 4 20mm cannons; 2,000 lbs (905 kg) mixed ordnance

Grumman's debut in the newborn field of jet-powered combat aircraft just after the end of WWII is represented by the F9F, a successful family of carrier-based fighters of which more than 3,000 were built, and which remained in service until the 1970s. The prototype flew on November 24, 1947, and the first series (F9F-2) became operative two years later. After a number of subsequent versions, the evolution of the plane reached its high point in 1951 with the

introduction of the XF9F-6, which featured a delta wing with a 35-degree sweep. The increase in performance was notable enough that the new plane, designated Cougar, 1,958 units were built in several versions. The Grumman F9F-2 has the distinction of being the first US Navy jet to see combat: Korea, in 1950.

■ GRUMMAN TBF AVENGER

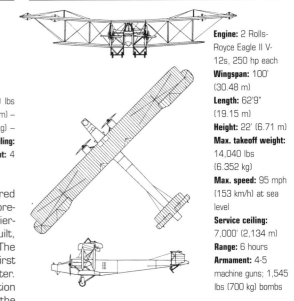

Version: TBF-1 – **Engine:** Wright R-2600-8 Cyclone radial, 14-cylinder, air-cooled, 1,700 hp – **Wingspan:** 54'2" (16.51 m) – **Length:** 40' (12.19 m) – **Height:** 16'5" (5.00 m) – **Max. takeoff weight:** 15,950 lbs (7,215 kg) – **Max. speed:** 271 mph (436 km/h) at 12,000' (3,660 m) – **Service ceiling:** 22,300' (6,800 m) – **Range:** 1,210 miles (1,950 km) – **Armament:** 3 machine guns; 1,600 lbs (725 kg) bombs

A total of 9,836 units were built during WWII. After distinguishing itself on both the European and Pacific fronts, the TBF Avenger remained in service until 1954. In the post-war period the Avenger could be found in the air forces of numerous nations: Canada, France, Uruguay, the Netherlands, Japan and New Zealand. It was in Japan, former enemy now ally, that the Avenger concluded its career twenty years after its introduction. It was a rather large monoplane, amply armed, with a hold capable of carrying a torpedo or the equivalent weight in bombs. From the two principal variants numerous sub-series were derived, variously used for photo-reconnaissance, infrared night recon, and even troop transport.

■ HANDLEY PAGE 0/100

Engine: 2 Rolls-Royce Eagle II V-12s, 250 hp each **Wingspan:** 100' (30.48 m) **Length:** 62'9" (19.15 m) **Height:** 22' (6.71 m) **Max. takeoff weight:** 14,040 lbs (6.352 kg) **Max. speed:** 95 mph (153 km/h) at sea level **Service ceiling:** 7,000' (2,134 m) **Range:** 6 hours **Armament:** 4-5 machine guns; 1,545 lbs (700 kg) bombs

The first heavy night bomber to see battle during WWI, the Handley Page 0/100 was designed with the aim of striking Germany itself. Of the original series, which went operative in November 1916, only 40 units were ordered. In 1917 the improved 0/400 had a better response, with 550 units ordered and built. Both versions were used extensively. During the last year of WWI, the Handley Page 0/400 regularly penetrated the heart of Germany, hitting the industrial areas of the Saar and Ruhr valleys. Many remained in service until 1920.

■ HANRIOT HD.1

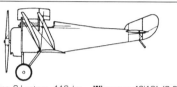

Engine: La Rhône 9J rotary, 110 hp – **Wingspan:** 42'10" (8.68 m) – **Length:** 33'10" (5.85 m) – **Height:** 13' (2.55 m) – **Max. takeoff weight:** 11,400 lbs (605 kg) – **Max. speed:** 376 mph (183 km/h) at sea level – **Service ceiling:** 38,400' (6,300 m) – **Range:** 2.5 hours – **Armament:** 1 machine gun

Designed in 1916 by Pierre Dupont, the Hanriot HD.1 had the misfortune of existing at the same time as other, more famous French fighters such as the Nieuport and the Spad. The French military, having already committed to these latter planes, chose to stick with them for understandable logistical reasons and never bought the Hanriot. The small and agile fighter nevertheless had the chance to show its worth in the Belgian and Italian air forces, where it was used on various battlefronts. In Italy the Hanriot was built under license by Macchi, which produced 831 units between 1917 and the end of the war.

■ HAWKER HURRICANE

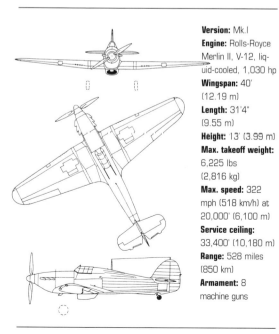

Version: Mk.I
Engine: Rolls-Royce Merlin II, V-12, liquid-cooled, 1,030 hp
Wingspan: 40' (12.19 m)
Length: 31'4" (9.55 m)
Height: 13' (3.99 m)
Max. takeoff weight: 6,225 lbs (2,816 kg)
Max. speed: 322 mph (518 km/h) at 20,000' (6,100 m)
Service ceiling: 33,400' (10,180 m)
Range: 528 miles (850 km)
Armament: 8 machine guns

The Hurricane will remain indelibly associated with the Battle of Britain. With limited numbers of Spitfires available, this fighter bore the brunt of the Luftwaffe's initial fury – indeed, more than half of all the German planes shot down in the first year of the war were the victims of Hurricanes. Production lasted from 1936 to the end of 1944, with 14,231 units built. It was used as a night-fighter, fighter-bomber and even as a ground attack plane. The first Mk.1's left the assembly line in October 1937 and were assigned to the first division of the Fighter Command two months later. When war broke out, 497 Hurricanes were distributed among 18 squadrons, 11 of which were sent to France. Just before the Battle of Britain began, the number of squadrons had jumped to 26, and by early August it was 32. The Hurricane was also widely used in naval contexts. The Sea Hurricane was adapted to be launched by catapult from the decks of merchant ships. Many were exported, including nearly 3,000 to the Soviet Union.

■ HAWKER SEA FURY

Version: FB.11 – **Engine:** Bristol Centaurus 18 radial, 18-cylinder, air-cooled, 2,550 hp – **Wingspan:** 38'5" (11.71 m) – **Length:** 34'8" (10.56 m) – **Height:** 15'9" (4.82 m) – **Max. takeoff weight:** 12,530 lbs (5,670 kg) – **Max. speed:** 460 mph (740 km/h) at 18,000' (5,482 m) – **Service ceiling:** 36,000' (10,976 m) – **Range:** 700 miles (1,128 km) – **Armament:** 4 20mm cannons; 2,000 lbs (905 kg) mixed ordnance

The last piston-engine fighter of Britain's Fleet Air Arm, the Sea Fury was also one of the best of its generation. Commissioned by the RAF during the thick of WWII, the swift little single-seater wasn't ready until war's end. It was then assigned an entirely different role from that for which it had been conceived: a carrier-based fighter. Despite having to compete against newer jet-powered fighters, the Sea Fury refused to be outdone and the Royal Navy kept it at battle readiness from 1947 to 1954, using more than 600 of the overall production of 860 units. In Korea the Sea Fury proved to be superior to the more modern enemy jets. The project, which had begun in 1943, culminated in the F.B.11 of 1947, the version produced in the largest numbers.

■ HAWKER SIDDELEY (BAE) HARRIER

The revolutionary Harrier was history's first fixed-wing airplane of the 'VTOL' type – or 'vertical takeoff and landing.' Conceived way back in 1957, versions of the famous 'Jump Jet,' perhaps the most iconic of which is the AV-8B II, are still being developed today. The prototype P.1127 began test flights in 1960 but production didn't begin until much later with the GR.Mk.I version – first flight December 1967, delivered to the Royal Air Force in April 1969, of which

78 units were built. The GR.Mk.3 of 1976 (36 units) followed. In the meantime, the United States had acquired 12 Harrier Mk.50s (designated AV-8A) for the Marines. Additional commissions between 1971 and 1977 brought the production total to 112. Great Britain developed a version for the Royal Navy as well, the Sea Harrier FRS.Mk.1, which first flew on August 20, 1978. Then McDonnell-Douglas was given license to build the Harrier in America, and everything changed. The AV-8B that went into production in January of 1984 is a total redesign of its predecessor. 295 were ordered and built, along with 28 TAV-8B training planes. Other clients of the Harrier include Spain, India and Italy, the latter of which uses it aboard the aircraft carrier *Garibaldi*. The most recent versions are the American AV-8D night-fighter and the RAF's GR.Mk.9, which made its first flight on May 30, 2003.

Version: GR.Mk.I
Engine: Rolls-Royce Bristol Pegasus Mk.101 turbojet, 19,000 lbs (8,598 kg) thrust
Wingspan: 25'3" (7.70 m)
Length: 45'6" (13.87 m)
Height: 11'3" (3.43 m)
Max. takeoff weight: 22,055 lbs (9,979 kg)
Max. speed: 737 mph (1,186 km/h)
Service ceiling: 50,000' (15,244 m)
Range: 2,300 miles (3.700 km)
Armament: 2 30mm cannons; 5,000 lbs (2,262 kg) mixed ordnance

■ HEINKEL HE.111

Version: He.111 H-2 – **Engine:** 2 Junkers Jumo 211 A-3, V-12s, liquid-cooled, 1,100 hp each – **Wingspan:** 74'2" (22.60 m) – **Length:** 53'9" (16.39 m) – **Height:** 13'2" (4.00 m) – **Max. takeoff weight:** 30,940 lbs (14,000 kg) – **Max. speed:** 252 mph (405 km/h) – **Service ceiling:** 27,880' (8,500 m) – **Range:** 1,280 miles (2,060 km) – **Armament:** 6 machine guns; 5,500 lbs (2,490 kg) bombs

The archetypal Luftwaffe bomber, the Heinkel He.111 was developed in 1934 to fill the double role of civilian transport and bomber. Produced throughout the entire war, some 7,000 units were built in several dozen versions. The first appeared in 1939, with replacement of the older Daimler

Benz engine by the more powerful Junkers Jumo. Other significant changes included a modified wing structure and complete redesign of the forward portion of the fuselage. The He.111 saw action from the outset of war, first in Poland and then in France, where it showed itself to be a formidable strategic weapon. Its phase-out began during the Battle of Britain: the Heinkel was too vulnerable to the superb British fighters and required too large an escort to reach its target.

■ HEINKEL HE-219

Version: He-219 A-2/R1 – **Engine:** 2 Daimler Benz DB 603A V-12s, liquid-cooled, 1,750 hp each – **Wingspan:** 60'9" (18.50 m) – **Length:** 51' (15.55 m) – **Height:** 13'6" (4.11 m) – **Max. takeoff weight:** 24,750 lbs (11,200 kg) – **Max. speed:** 416 mph (670 km/h) at 23,000' (7,000 m) – **Service ceiling:** 41,650' (12,700 m) – **Range:** 1,240 miles (2,000 km) – **Armament:** 6 20mm cannons

The He-219 was the Luftwaffe's best night-fighter. Introduced to the battlefront in 1943, this fast and powerful twin-engine would have significantly influenced the course of the war if had been available in greater numbers; however, luckily for the Allies, only 300 were ever built. Design began in the mid-1940 and the prototype flew on November 15, 1942. The first battle-ready version was the A-2/R1, while the one produced in the largest quantities was the more heavily armed A/7. Production was abandoned around mid-1944.

■ ILYUSHIN IL-10

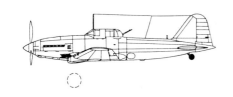

Engine: Mikulin AM.42, V-12, liquid-cooled, 2,000 hp – **Wingspan:** 38' (13.90 m) – **Length:** 28'9" (12.20 m) – **Height:** 11'10" (3.50 m) – **Max. takeoff weight:** 7,020 lbs (6,335 kg) – **Max. speed:** 330 mph (500 km/h) at 21,320' (2,800 m) – **Range:** 845 miles (650 km) – **Armament:** 3 20mm cannons

While basically derived from the Ilyushin Il-2, the Il-10 underwent substantial modifications to the engine, landing gear, armament and aerodynamics. The results of the first test flights were so encouraging that the Ilyushin Il-10 was chosen over the Sukhoi Su-6 and was immediately put in production. After serving nobly in the closing years of WWII, the Il-10 remained in service until the 1950s, participating extensively in the Korean War.

■ JUNKERS JU.87 STUKA

During the first year of WWII, the name Stuka was synonymous with destructiveness and invincibility. 'Stuka' is in fact a generic abbreviation of the German term for 'dive bomber' *(Sturzkampfflugzeug)*, but in the end came to be associated with a single plane, the Ju.87. Peerless in its role, the Stuka remained in production until 1944, with a total of 5,700 units built in about ten versions.

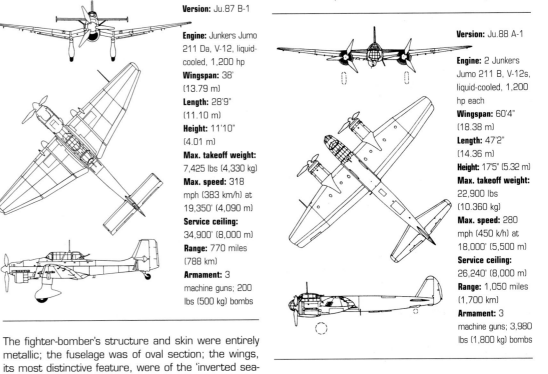

Version: Ju.87 B-1

Engine: Junkers Jumo 211 Da, V-12, liquid-cooled, 1,200 hp
Wingspan: 38' (13.79 m)
Length: 28'9" (11.10 m)
Height: 11'10" (4.01 m)
Max. takeoff weight: 7,425 lbs (4,330 kg)
Max. speed: 318 mph (383 km/h) at 19,350' (4,090 m)
Service ceiling: 34,900' (8,000 m)
Range: 770 miles (788 km)
Armament: 3 machine guns; 200 lbs (500 kg) bombs

The fighter-bomber's structure and skin were entirely metallic; the fuselage was of oval section; the wings, its most distinctive feature, were of the 'inverted seagull' type, and the fixed landing gear was sheathed in conspicuous fenders. The first version, dubbed the A-1, appeared in early 1937, followed by the first variant of the B series, the Ju.87 B-1 of 1938. Then came the next most widely produced series, the D, which featured a more powerful Jumo engine. From the Ju.87 D-1 came the most specialized of all the Stukas: the G-1, designed exclusively for anti-tank operations. The Stuka was a fixed presence in all the theaters of war. In fact, three Ju.87 B-1s executed the first aerial bombardment of WWII, striking Polish territory in a preliminary attack on September 1, 1939.

■ JUNKERS JU.88

Bomber, night-fighter, dive bomber, torpedo launcher, assault fighter, reconnaissance plane. Considered the backbone of the Luftwaffe, the Junkers Ju.88 was the most versatile plane in the German arsenal. From 1939 to 1945 more than 16,000 were built in dozens of versions. Yet unlike other aircraft produced in such large numbers over many years, the Ju.88's basic structure remained practically the same, proof of the original design's extraordinary quality. Like the Stuka, the low-winged monoplane was made entirely of metal. The first version, the Ju.88 A-1, was delivered in the summer of 1939 just before the invasion of Poland, and first saw

battle on September 26, just after. In the following months, however, particularly during the Battle of Britain, certain practical problems emerged and numerous modifications had to be made, resulting in the more dependable A-4. A total of 17 versions of the A series were eventually built. Meanwhile, the prototype of the B series flew in early 1940, and production began spreading to yet other versions, the most important of which were the C and G, designed explicitly for night-fighter missions. The last series, the S bomber, appeared in 1943 with a more efficient aerodynamic design, a restructured prow and the elimination of the gondola.

Version: Ju.88 A-1

Engine: 2 Junkers Jumo 211 B, V-12s, liquid-cooled, 1,200 hp each
Wingspan: 60'4" (18.38 m)
Length: 47'2" (14.36 m)
Height: 17'5" (5.32 m)
Max. takeoff weight: 22,900 lbs (10.360 kg)
Max. speed: 280 mph (450 k/h) at 18,000' (5,500 m)
Service ceiling: 26,240' (8,000 m)
Range: 1,050 miles (1,700 km)
Armament: 3 machine guns; 3,980 lbs (1,800 kg) bombs

■ LOCKHEED C-130 HERCULES

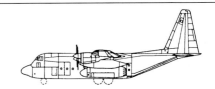

Version: C-130H – **Engine:** 4 Allison T56-A-7 turboprops, 4,050 hp each – **Wingspan:** 132'6" (40.41 m) – **Length:** 97'9" (29.79 m) – **Height:** 38'4" (11.68 m) – **Max. takeoff weight:** 155,380 lbs (70,308 kg) – **Max. speed:** 360 mph (579 km/h) at 20,000' (6,100 m) – **Service ceiling:** 33,000' (10,060 m) – **Range:** 3,820 miles (6,145 km) – **Load:** 92 passengers or 35,800 lbs (16,194 kg)

The Lockheed C-130 Hercules is essentially the evolution of the legendary Douglas C-47 military transport. Still in production after more than half a century, this tough, versatile and dependable giant is used by the air forces of some 60 nations, where it has been adapted to various roles in addition to heavy transport, including photo reconnaissance, mid-air refueling, combat rescue and target acquisition. The program was launched on February 2, 1951 and the prototype flew on August 23, 1954. The original A series was followed by numerous others: the most heavily produced were the E (first flight August 1961) and the H (December 1964), while the most recent is the J (April 1996), equipped with more powerful engines driving more efficient 6-blade propellers. As of 2003, overall production exceeded 2,200 units.

■ LOCKHEED GALAXY

Version: C-5A – **Engine:** 4 General Electric TF39-GE-1 turbojets, 41,100 lbs (18,600 kg) thrust each – **Wingspan:** 222'9" (67.88 m) – **Length:** 247'10" (75.54 m) – **Height:** 65'1" (19.85 m) – **Max. takeoff weight:** 770,870 lbs (348,810 kg) – **Max. speed:** 571 mph (919 km/h) at 25,000' (7,620 m) – **Service ceiling:** 33,980' (10,360 m) – **Range:** 5,940 miles (9,560 km) – **Load:** 345 passengers or 291,000 lbs (130,950 kg)

Designed for massive strategic airlifts, this behemoth of the skies is capable of transporting nearly 140 tons of equipment over distances approaching 6,000 miles and at speeds just shy of the sound barrier. Conceived in the early 1960s, the C-5A made its first flight on June 30, 1968 and entered into service in December 1969. The total production of 81 units ended with the last delivery in March 1973. A second version, the C-5B, appeared in 1985, vaunting improved avionics and a more robust structure. 50 units of the B were produced before the program was shut down.

■ LOCKHEED STARFIGHTER

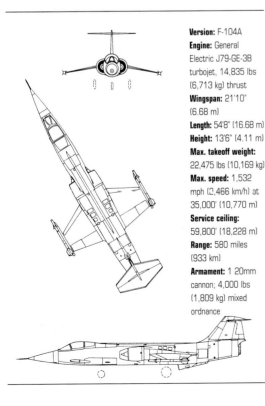

Version: F-104A
Engine: General Electric J79-GE-3B turbojet, 14,835 lbs (6,713 kg) thrust
Wingspan: 21'10" (6.68 m)
Length: 54'8" (16.68 m)
Height: 13'6" (4.11 m)
Max. takeoff weight: 22,475 lbs (10,169 kg)
Max. speed: 1,532 mph (2,466 km/h) at 35,000' (10,770 m)
Service ceiling: 59,800' (18,228 m)
Range: 580 miles (933 km)
Armament: 1 20mm cannon; 4,000 lbs (1,809 kg) mixed ordnance

Born of experience acquired during the Korean War, the Starfighter prototype earned enthusiastic applause when it first flew on March 4, 1954. The US Marine Corps ordered a substantial number, but were dissatisfied after receiving the first delivery in 1958 and drastically reduced its request. The F-104 had better luck in NATO circles. The modified F-104G (June 1960) was developed for the allied countries and was purchased in significant quantities by Germany, Canada, the Netherlands, Belgium, Japan and Italy – this last country having been responsible for developing the final version of the Lockheed fighter, the F-104S, which featured updated avionics and improved armament. The Italian version entered service in 1969, with an eventual total of 205 units produced for the Aeronautica Militare Italiana and 40 for the Turkish air forces. Still on the front lines 50 years after its first flight, the Starfighter stands as one of the great combat planes of the last century. A total of 2,578 F-104s have been built, the majority under license in Europe, Canada and Japan, the countries that used it most extensively. The F-104 was the US Air Force's first Mach 2 fighter.

■ LOCKHEED F-117A NIGHTHAWK

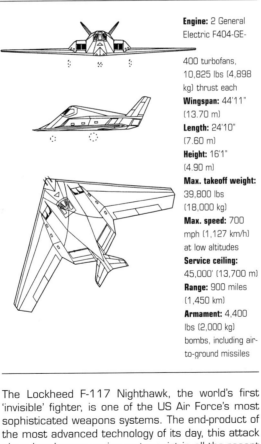

Engine: 2 General Electric F404-GE-400 turbofans, 10,825 lbs (4,898 kg) thrust each
Wingspan: 44'11" (13.70 m)
Length: 24'10" (7.60 m)
Height: 16'1" (4.90 m)
Max. takeoff weight: 39,800 lbs (18,000 kg)
Max. speed: 700 mph (1,127 km/h) at low altitudes
Service ceiling: 45,000' (13,700 m)
Range: 900 miles (1,450 km)
Armament: 4,400 lbs (2,000 kg) bombs, including air-to-ground missiles

The Lockheed F-117 Nighthawk, the world's first 'invisible' fighter, is one of the US Air Force's most sophisticated weapons systems. The end-product of the most advanced technology of its day, this attack plane has been a major protagonist in all the recent conflicts from the first Gulf War onward. The program was secret for more than twelve years: from January 1976 when Lockheed test flew a scale model in the Mojave Desert, to November 1988, when the US Department of Defense released a single black-and-white photograph of the completed plane. A year and a half later, on April 21, 1990,

the Nighthawk was officially presented at Nellis Air Force Base. At that point it had already been in active service, unknown to anyone, for seven years (October 1983), and had even flown combat missions in 1989 during the American intervention in Panama. The original plan was to build 100 units, but cost increases and funding cuts reduced the final production to 59 units.

■ LOCKHEED MARTIN-BOEING F-22 RAPTOR

Version: F-22A – **Engine:** 2 Pratt & Whitney F-119-PW-100 turbofans, lbs (14,175 kg) – **Wingspan:** 44'6" (13.56 m) – **Length:** 62' (18.90 m) – **Height:** 16'8" (5.08 m) – **Max. takeoff weight:** 60,150 lbs (27,216 kg) – **Max. speed:** 1,450 mph (2,336 km/h) at 40,000' (12,200 m) – **Service ceiling:** 65,000' (19,800 m) – **Range:** 920 miles (1,480 km) – **Armament:** 1 20mm cannon; 20,900 lbs (9,450 kg) mixed ordnance

The Raptor is the most advanced combat plane ever built, and is considered superior even to the superb European Typhoon multirole fighter. In addition to being an extraordinarily sophisticated and efficient weapons system, the F-22 is also the first air-superiority fighter with 'stealth' technology, which renders it invisible to enemy radar and electronic detection systems. The program, approved in April 1991, went through a long development and testing phase, thanks in part to delays caused by astronomical cost increases. It was only in 2001 that the US Department of Defense authorized the first production batch. The original order of 648 Raptors was first reduced to 339 and then to 295 units. The F-22 is scheduled to enter service in 2005.

■ LOCKHEED P-38 LIGHTNING

During WWII the Lightning held the record for shooting down Japanese planes – and in April 1943 shot down the one carrying Admiral Yamamoto, mastermind of the attack on Pearl Harbor. Known to the Germans as *Der Gabelschwanz Teufel* ('Forked-Tail Devil'), the P-38 was built in numerous versions – fighter-bomber, night-fighter, photo reconnaissance – for a total of 9,923 units. On June 23, 1937, a first prototype was ordered, and the XP-38 took to the air one and a half years later, on January 27, 1939. With the P-38D, the Lightning found its final operational configuration: in November 1941, the P-38E replaced the earlier version, adopting a 20mm gun and greater ammo capacity. The next model, the P-38F, went into production in early 1942. This version had more powerful engines and wing racks for bombs or supplementary fuel tanks. This was the first model to see large-scale combat, in Europe in mid-1942 and in North Africa in November 1942. The G and H versions followed, then came the J, among the best and most widely produced of the Lightning series (2,970 units), second only to the more powerful P-38L (3,923). The last Lightning was the P-38M, which was designed for night fighting. A second cockpit behind the pilot housed a radar operator.

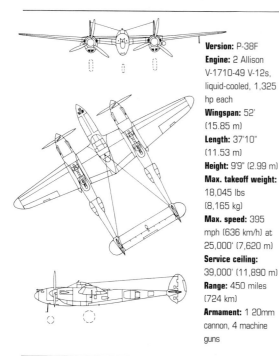

Version: P-38F
Engine: 2 Allison V-1710-49 V-12s, liquid-cooled, 1,325 hp each
Wingspan: 52' (15.85 m)
Length: 37'10" (11.53 m)
Height: 9'9" (2.99 m)
Max. takeoff weight: 18,045 lbs (8,165 kg)
Max. speed: 395 mph (636 km/h) at 25,000' (7,620 m)
Service ceiling: 39,000' (11,890 m)
Range: 450 miles (724 km)
Armament: 1 20mm cannon, 4 machine guns

■ LOCKHEED P-80 SHOOTING STAR

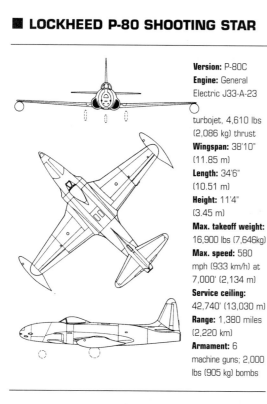

Version: P-80C
Engine: General Electric J33-A-23 turbojet, 4,610 lbs (2,086 kg) thrust
Wingspan: 38'10" (11.85 m)
Length: 34'6" (10.51 m)
Height: 11'4" (3.45 m)
Max. takeoff weight: 16,900 lbs (7,646kg)
Max. speed: 580 mph (933 km/h) at 7,000' (2,134 m)
Service ceiling: 42,740' (13,030 m)
Range: 1,380 miles (2,220 km)
Armament: 6 machine guns; 2,000 lbs (905 kg) bombs

The Lockheed F-80 was the American armed forces' first operational jet fighter. Though not completed in time to take part in WWII, the Shooting Star did see battle in Korea, where it was used extensively and to great effect. The three base versions of the fighter

(A, B and C) were produced until 1948 in 1,715 units, and remained in service until the arrival of the more modern F-84 and F-86. The version designed for training, the T-33, lasted a good deal longer: not only was it the USAF's standard trainer, it was also exported to some 40 other nations. A total of 5,691 were built through 1959, and another 866 were built under license in Canada and Japan.

■ MACCHI M.C.200 SAETTA

Engine: Fiat A.74 RC 38 radial, 14-cylinder, air-cooled, 840 hp – **Wingspan:** 35' (10.68 m) – **Length:** 26'10" (8.19 m) – **Height:** 11'6" (3.51 m) – **Max. takeoff weight:** 4,880 lbs (2,208 kg) – **Max. speed:** 318 mph (512 km/h) at 16,400' (5,000 m) – **Service ceiling:** 28,700' (8,750 m) – **Range:** 540 miles (870 km) – **Armament:** 2 machine guns

The Saetta was widely used by the Axis forces and proved to be a muscular and agile machine, more than capable of measuring up to the adversary. A total of 1,151 units were built between June 1939 and July 1942. The prototype flew on December 24, 1937. The first operational Saettas left the assembly lines in the summer of '39; when war broke out in September of that year 144 were already in service. However, the Macchi M.C.200 reached full combat readiness only in late 1940, after heavy modifications to the aerodynamically faulty wing profile and the elimination of the sliding cockpit canopy, which impeded the pilot from ejecting in case of emergency. The Saetta's first large-scale deployment was on the Greek and Albanian fronts, where it successfully challenged one of the era's great planes, the British Hurricane. It was then sent to the North African and Russian fronts, again showing itself to be as tough as it was dependable. With the appearance of the more modern M.C.202, the Saetta was gradually withdrawn from the front lines, but continued to serve as an assault fighter, escort and interceptor in its home territory.

■ MACCHI M.C.202 FOLGORE

All in all, the best Italian fighter of WWII, and among the most extensively used. More than 1,100 were built in a little over two years, and there wasn't a battlefront where it didn't make a contribution. The heir of the Saetta boasted exceptional flight performance characteristics: high maneuverability and climbing speed foremost among them. Much of the Folgore's excellence was owed to its engine, the brand new Daimler Benz DB 601, supplied by the Germans. The plane was designed by Mario Castoldi, creator of the Saetta, and in fact both planes have nearly identical wing and tail configurations. The newer plane's fuselage, however, was significantly more aerodynamic. The only weak point of the Folgore was its armament: it had only two 12.7mm machine guns, syn-

chronized to fire through the propellers. The problem was somewhat solved in later versions, which had two additional small-caliber guns in the wings. The M.C.202 was first used in Libya in November 1941. Soon thereafter it was assigned to the Balkan, Mediterranean, and Russian fronts.

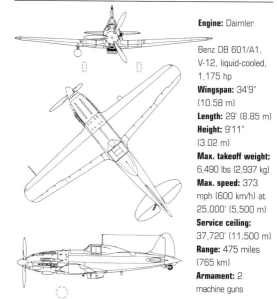

Engine: Daimler Benz DB 601/A1, V-12, liquid-cooled, 1,175 hp
Wingspan: 34'9" (10.58 m)
Length: 29' (8.85 m)
Height: 9'11" (3.02 m)
Max. takeoff weight: 6,490 lbs (2,937 kg)
Max. speed: 373 mph (600 km/h) at 25,000' (5,500 m)
Service ceiling: 37,720' (11,500 m)
Range: 475 miles (765 km)
Armament: 2 machine guns

■ MARTIN B-26 MARAUDER

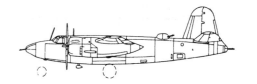

Engine: 2 Pratt & Whitney R-2800-41 Double Wasp radials, 18-cylinder, air-cooled, 2,000 hp each – **Wingspan:** 65' (19.81 m) – **Length:** 58'3" (17.75 m) – **Height:** 19'10" (6.05 m) – **Max. takeoff weight:** 34,080 lbs (15,422 kg) – **Max. speed:** 317 mph (510 km/h) at 14,500' (4,420 m) – **Service ceiling:** 23,600' (7,200 m) – **Range:** 1,150 miles (1,850 km) – **Armament:** 6 machine guns; 3,000 lbs (1,358 kg) bombs

Few planes have ever been both so hated and so loved by the men who flew them as the Marauder. The B-26 medium bomber was, quite simply, a difficult aircraft to fly: its characteristics allowed very little margin of error, especially in landing. Nonetheless, it proved to be a good plane, and in some ways even safer than others. The 5,157 Marauders built between February 1941 and March 1945 operated without interruption in both the European and Pacific theaters. The first planes of the A series (139 units built) were delivered in 1941, but assignment to the front lines was delayed due to the difficulty of training pilots to fly them, so it wasn't until April 1942 that the Marauder saw combat in the Pacific, later taking part in the Battle of Midway as an anti-submarine torpedo bomber. In the meantime production had been halted as a result of debate as to the aircraft's safety. After a few modifications in this regard, however, production resumed.

■ MAURICE FARMAN M.F.7

Engine: Renault V-8, air-cooled, 70 hp – **Wingspan:** 51' (15.54 m) – **Length:** 37'3" (11.35 m) – **Height:** 11'4" (3.45 m) – **Max. takeoff weight:** 1,890 lbs (855 kg) – **Max. speed:** 59 mph (95 km/h) at sea level – **Service ceiling:** 13,120' (4,000 m) – **Range:** 3.5 hours – **Armament:** none

The two most widely deployed reconnaissance planes of WWI were both French: the Maurice Farman M.F.7 of 1913 and the M.F.11 of 1914. These two biplanes served in practically every reconnaissance arm of the air forces of Britain, France, Belgium and Italy from the beginning of the war until 1915, at which time more modern aircraft replaced them. Of the two, the M.F.11 was more effective; it was structurally more robust, was armed with a machine gun, and was capable of carrying a cache of small bombs. In fact, it was a British M.F.11 that executed the first night bombardment of WWI, on December 21, 1914.

■ MCDONNELL F-4 PHANTOM II

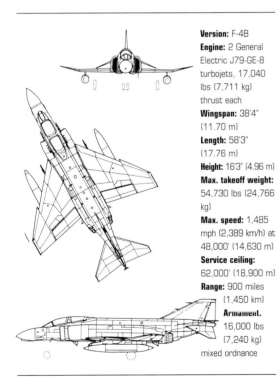

Version: F-4B
Engine: 2 General Electric J79-GE-8 turbojets, 17,040 lbs (7,711 kg) thrust each
Wingspan: 38'4" (11.70 m)
Length: 58'3" (17.76 m)
Height: 16'3" (4.96 m)
Max. takeoff weight: 54,730 lbs (24,766 kg)
Max. speed: 1,485 mph (2,389 km/h) at 48,000' (14,630 m)
Service ceiling: 62,000' (18,900 m)
Range: 900 miles (1,450 km)
Armament: 16,000 lbs (7,240 kg) mixed ordnance

The McDonnell F-4 Phantom II is unanimously recognized as one of the best fighter-bombers ever built. The plane earned its enviable reputation in all of the principal conflicts of the last fifty years, from Vietnam to the Middle East, with corroborating testimony from dozens of client countries. The project began in 1953 and the prototype flew on May 27, 1958. The base version, intended for Navy carrier operations and the Marines, was the F-4B of 1961, followed by the F-4J of 1966. The Phantom II was the first fighter designed explicitly for carrier operations, but was not limited to this role. In fact the USAF adopted the F-4C (first flight May 1963) and developed numerous other series, which remained active until 1981, with a total of 5,195 produced.

■ MCDONNELL-DOUGLAS F-15 EAGLE

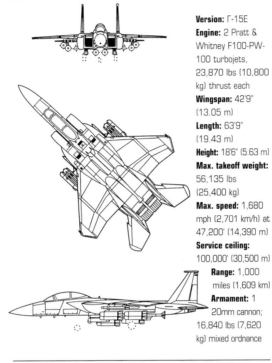

Version: F-15E
Engine: 2 Pratt & Whitney F100-PW-100 turbojets, 23,870 lbs (10,800 kg) thrust each
Wingspan: 42'9" (13.05 m)
Length: 63'9" (19.43 m)
Height: 18'6" (5.63 m)
Max. takeoff weight: 56,135 lbs (25,400 kg)
Max. speed: 1,680 mph (2,701 km/h) at 47,200' (14,390 m)
Service ceiling: 100,000' (30,500 m)
Range: 1,000 miles (1,609 km)
Armament: 1 20mm cannon; 16,840 lbs (7,620 kg) mixed ordnance

Today, after nearly 30 years of service, the F-15 Eagle is still the USAF's quintessential fighter and the best operational multirole combat plane in the world. The program was launched in 1965, in response to a request for a single-seat twin-engine jet capable of functioning as a pure fighter as well as executing offensive patrol and escort missions. The plane was to perform at Mach 1.2 at sea level, Mach 2.2 at operational altitude, with a top speed of Mach 2.5. The first F-15A prototype flew on June 27, 1972, entering into service in January 1976. A total of 365 F-15As were built, along with 59 two-seat F-15B trainers. In 1979 production shifted to two new versions (F-15C and the F-15D trainer, 409 and 61 units built, respectively), which featured state-of-the-art avionics and greater range. The version known as the Strike Eagle (F-15E two-seater) was designed to simultaneously fill two very different roles: long-range all-weather strike missions, and air-to-air combat. The first planes of the 392 Strike Eagles ordered were delivered in 1988. Only three other nations are permitted to operate the F-15: Israel, Japan, and Saudi Arabia. The F-15 continues to play an active role in USAF operations.

■ MCDONNELL-DOUGLAS F/A-18 HORNET

Designed in the early 1970s, the F/A-18 Hornet is still an important plane for both the US Navy and the Marines. The most recent version of this big multirole fighter, the F/A-18E/F, has raised the already brilliant performance features of the original to greater heights. Conceived with the aim of finding an effective replacement for the F-4 Phantom II in the air defense and attack roles, the Hornet entered service in 1983, with a total of 1,150 being built. Improvements to the F/A-18 have gone on uninterruptedly since. The first F/A-18C, equipped with better avionics and heavier armament, flew in September 1986 and was delivered the following year. The 18D, a two-seat night-fighter, appeared in 1988. The project for the F/A-18E/F, designated Super Hornet, was launched in 1991, with delivery of the larger and more powerful plane beginning in 1999 and still underway. Various versions of the Hornet occupy a privileged place in the air forces of Canada, Australia, Spain and Kuwait.

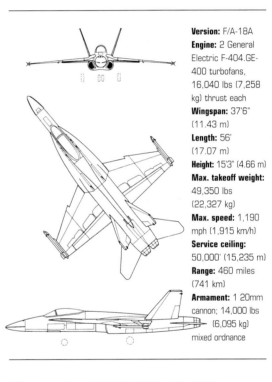

Version: F/A-18A
Engine: 2 General Electric F-404.GE-400 turbofans, 16,040 lbs (7,258 kg) thrust each
Wingspan: 37'6" (11.43 m)
Length: 56' (17.07 m)
Height: 15'3" (4.66 m)
Max. takeoff weight: 49,350 lbs (22,327 kg)
Max. speed: 1,190 mph (1,915 km/h)
Service ceiling: 50,000' (15,235 m)
Range: 460 miles (741 km)
Armament: 1 20mm cannon; 14,000 lbs (6,095 kg) mixed ordnance

■ MESSERSCHMITT BF.109

The Bf.109 was one of Germany's main fighter planes in WWII, the direct adversary of the Supermarine Spitfire. Nearly 35,000 Bf.109s were built. The project began in the summer of 1934, and the result was a slender monoplane with low-slung wings, entirely made of metal, with a closed cockpit and retractable landing gear. The first Bf.109 Bs were sent to Spain, which were followed then by the more heavily armed C, and the D, which was the first to use the Daimler Benz DB 600 engine. Very few of the latter version were produced, but it represented the passage to the first truly mass-produced model, the Bf.109 E of 1939. By the end of that year 1,540 units had been built, so that with the outbreak of war in September, the Luftwaffe's fighter squadrons were already well populated by the E. Lessons learned during the grueling Battle of Britain gave rise to the F series, which brought significant improvements to the preceding versions. The Bf.109 G appeared in 1942, and the final version, the K, was introduced in the last year of the war.

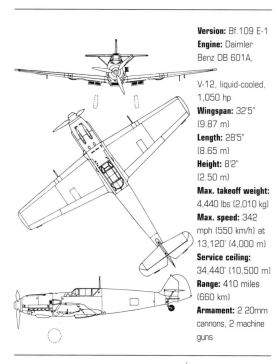

Version: Bf.109 E-1
Engine: Daimler Benz DB 601A,

V-12, liquid-cooled, 1,050 hp
Wingspan: 32'5" (9.87 m)
Length: 28'5" (8.65 m)
Height: 8'2" (2.50 m)
Max. takeoff weight: 4,440 lbs (2,010 kg)
Max. speed: 342 mph (550 km/h) at 13,120' (4,000 m)
Service ceiling: 34,440' (10,500 m)
Range: 410 miles (660 km)
Armament: 2 20mm cannons, 2 machine guns

■ MESSERSCHMITT BF.110 ZERSTÖRER

Version: Bf.110 C-1 – **Engine:** 2 Daimler Benz DB 601 A-1 V-12s, liquid-cooled, 1,050 hp each – **Wingspan:** 32'5" (16.25 m) – **Length:** 28'5" (12.07 m) – **Height:** 8'2" (4.12 m) – **Max. takeoff weight:** 4,440 lbs (6,028 kg) – **Max. speed:** 342 mph (540 km/h) at 13,120' (6,000 m) – **Service ceiling:** 34,440' (10,000 m) – **Range:** 410 miles (1,125 km) – **Armament:** 2 20mm cannons, 5 machine guns

The Bf.110 was designed in 1934, together with the 109. It was a sleek, all-metal twin-engine, with its offensive armament concentrated in the foremost part of the nose, and space in its long enclosed cockpit for a crew of three. The dive flaps were split to allow a wider firing cone for the single defensive gun in the tail. The prototype flew on May 12, 1936 and was judged unsatisfactory because of its limited maneuverability. The first Bf.110s of the C series appeared in 1939, with improvements incorporated, eventually evolving through several variants into the D. After suffering heavy losses in the Battle of Britain, the Germans responded with Bf.110 E and F. Accepting that the 110 would never be a great fighter, the E and F were assigned new roles as ground attack plane and fighter-bomber. In 1942 the Bf.110 G-4 night-fighter appeared, and the 110 final-

ly found its ideal role. Apart from certain sacrifices of performance due to the intricate system of antennae installed on the nose, it turned out to be one of the best night-fighters of its time. Production went ahead up until the final months of the war, slowing down only in the first three months of 1945, when only 45 units left the assembly lines. Total production of all the series ran to approximately 6,050 units.

■ MESSERSCHMITT ME.163 KOMET

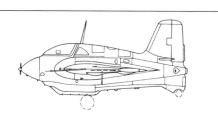

Version: Me.163 B-1A – **Engine:** Walter HWK 509 A-2 rocket, 3,315 lbs (1,500 kg) thrust – **Wingspan:** 30'6" (9.30 m) – **Length:** 18'8" (5.70 m) – **Height:** 8'3" (2.50 m) – **Max. takeoff weight:** 8,730 lbs (3,950 kg) – **Max. speed:** 560 mph (900 km/h) – **Service ceiling:** 39,360' (12,000 m) – **Range:** 7.5 minutes – **Armament:** 2 20mm cannons

Just over 300 Komets came off the assembly lines before production was interrupted, the vast majority of which were of the B-1A series (237 units in 1944, 42 in January of 1945). The Messerschmitt Me.163 was essentially a glider, which used its unique rocket-propulsion system in short bursts during key moments in its necessarily brief sorties: takeoff, ascent and combat pursuit/evasion. The project was initiated in late 1938 and proceeded rather slowly. The first prototype flew without an engine – towed and released by a Bf.110 – in early 1941. Then on August 13 it made its first powered flight. On October 2 it reached Mach 0.84, making it the fastest plane in the world at the time. The prototype of the B flew on February 21, 1943. The dilation of the time frame is understandable, since the form, propulsion system and function of the Komet were all revolutionary and required extensive testing and fine-tuning. No less important a factor was the difficulty of training of the pilots. The Me.163 was a tiny monoplane of the 'flying wing' type, without horizontal tail stabilizers or landing gear. The fuselage was basically a rocket with a cockpit; it was armed with two wing-mounted cannons. The Komet used a wheeled dolly for takeoff, which was then jettisoned. After a maximum of 7.5 minutes of engine time, the Komet landed like a glider on a skid fixed to its belly. The 163 would have achieved greater success if the war had not ended before its numerous defects could be resolved.

■ MESSERSCHMITT ME.262

The Me.262 could have changed the course of WWII if it had been used exclusively in the one role for which it was best suited, that of the pure fighter. Instead, production was spread out over a series of versions in a losing battle to adapt the plane to other roles, such as bomber and night-fighter. As a result,

of the 1,430 units produced in the closing months of the war, fewer than a quarter of the planes made it to operational status: they were therefore unable to make a significant contribution. The original model, the A-1a, was armed with four 30mm cannons. This was followed by the A-1a/U1, U2 and U3, the first with six guns, the second designed for all-weather fighting and the third for photographic reconnaissance. This imprudent dispersiveness continued into the next series: the Me.262 A-2a was a bomber with a 2,200-lb capacity, and the A-3a was a ground attack plane. In October 1944 the B series appeared, a night-fighter denominated Me.262 B-1a/U1, but it was still in the prototype stage by the time the war ended. Despite the indecision underlying its production, the Me.262 was undeniably a superb plane.

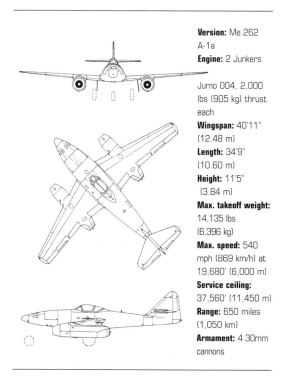

Version: Me.262 A-1a
Engine: 2 Junkers

Jumo 004, 2,000 lbs (905 kg) thrust each
Wingspan: 40'11" (12.48 m)
Length: 34'9" (10.60 m)
Height: 11'5" (3.84 m)
Max. takeoff weight: 14,135 lbs (6,396 kg)
Max. speed: 540 mph (869 km/h) at 19,680' (6,000 m)
Service ceiling: 37,560' (11,450 m)
Range: 650 miles (1,050 km)
Armament: 4 30mm cannons

■ MIKOYAN-GUREVICH MIG-15

The appearance of the Soviet MiG-15 in the skies over Korea toward the end of 1950 was a nasty surprise for the Americans. The deft and diminutive fighter immediately demonstrated itself to be superior to America's combat jets, and within weeks of its introduction the Soviets had decisively gained air supremacy. The MiG-15 was developed immediately after WWII, requiring only a few months to bring to completion. The project was made possible by a British engine: the Rolls-Royce Nene which, in one of those ironies so common in international politics, Britain had granted the Soviet Union a license to build. The prototype flew on December 30, 1947 and production steamed ahead for the next five years, totaling 8,000 units in the USSR alone, to which must then be added the MiGs built under license in Poland, Czechoslovakia, and the People's Republic of China. The fighter was adopted by some 20 Soviet allies. Its NATO codename was FAGOT.

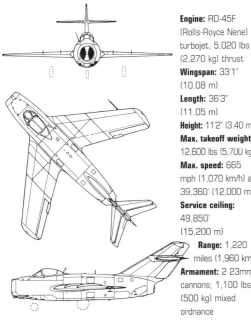

Engine: RD-45F
(Rolls-Royce Nene)
turbojet, 5,020 lbs
(2,270 kg) thrust
Wingspan: 33'1"
(10.08 m)
Length: 36'3"
(11.05 m)
Height: 11'2" (3.40 m)
Max. takeoff weight:
12,600 lbs (5,700 kg)
Max. speed: 665
mph (1,070 km/h) at
39,360' (12,000 m)
Service ceiling:
49,850'
(15,200 m)
Range: 1,220
miles (1,960 km)
Armament: 2 23mm
cannons; 1,100 lbs
(500 kg) mixed
ordnance

■ MIKOYAN-GUREVICH MIG-17

Exploiting the experience acquired with the MiG-15, engineers Mikoyan and Gurevich designed an even better combat jet, the MiG-17, free of its predecessor's admittedly few limitations. The prototype of the MiG-17, codenamed FRESCO by the NATO command, flew for the first time in January 1950 and was delivered to the Soviet armed forces two years later. Numerous versions were developed over the course of its massive production: 9,000 units in the USSR up until 1958, plus those built in Poland, Czechoslovakia and China. The MiG-17F, characterized by a Klimov engine with afterburner, structural modifications, and improvements to the aerodynamics, was the best of the MiGs.

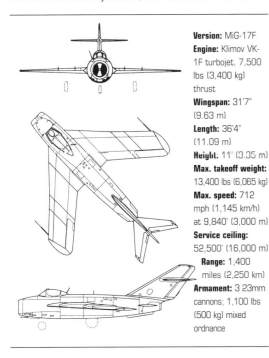

Version: MiG-17F
Engine: Klimov VK-
1F turbojet, 7,500
lbs (3,400 kg)
thrust
Wingspan: 31'7"
(9.63 m)
Length: 36'4"
(11.09 m)
Height: 11' (3.35 m)
Max. takeoff weight:
13,400 lbs (6,065 kg)
Max. speed: 712
mph (1,145 km/h)
at 9,840' (3,000 m)
Service ceiling:
52,500' (16,000 m)
Range: 1,400
miles (2,250 km)
Armament: 3 23mm
cannons; 1,100 lbs
(500 kg) mixed
ordnance

■ MIKOYAN-GUREVICH MIG-19

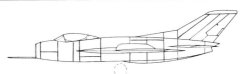

Engine: 2 Mikulin AM-5 turbojets, 6,720 lbs (3,040 kg) thrust each –
Wingspan: 29'6" (9.00 m) – **Length:** 42'10" (13.08 m) – **Height:** 13'2"
(4.02 m) – **Max. takeoff weight:** 19,225 lbs (8,700 kg) – **Max. speed:**
920 mph (1,480 km/h) at 20,000' (6,100 m) – **Service ceiling:** 58,700'
(17,900 m) – **Range:** 1,370 miles (2,200 km) – **Armament:** 1 37mm
cannon; 2,200 lbs (1,000 kg) mixed ordnance

If the MiG-15 was the Soviet equivalent of the American F-86 Sabre, then MiG-19 was its counterpart to the F-100 Super Sabre. The new Soviet fighter appeared in September 1953 and remained in production in the USSR from that year until the late 1960s, with more than 5,000 units built. From 1957 it was built under license in Czechoslovakia (designated S-105) and from 1961 in China (F-6). Like its predecessor, the MiG-19 equipped the air forces of the East European bloc along with those of several other Soviet allies. The NATO codename for the 19 was FARMER.

■ MIKOYAN-GUREVICH MIG-21

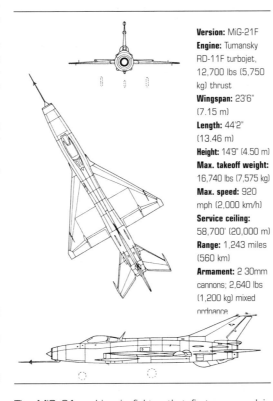

Version: MiG-21F
Engine: Tumansky
RD-11F turbojet,
12,700 lbs (5,750
kg) thrust
Wingspan: 23'6"
(7.15 m)
Length: 44'2"
(13.46 m)
Height: 14'9" (4.50 m)
Max. takeoff weight:
16,740 lbs (7,575 kg)
Max. speed: 920
mph (2,000 km/h)
Service ceiling:
58,700' (20,000 m)
Range: 1,243 miles
(560 km)
Armament: 2 30mm
cannons; 2,640 lbs
(1,200 kg) mixed
ordnance

The MiG 21, a bisonic fighter that first appeared in 1954 and went into mass production in 1956, was another outstanding member of the MiG family. The first definitive version was the MiG-21F, which first flew in 1957 and was delivered in early 1958. As with the earlier MiGs, the production numbers of the 21 (4,000 in the USSR) have to be calculated with Czech and Chinese production figures being unknown. Curiously, the MiG-21

was also built under license for the first time in a non-Eastern Bloc country: India. Dubbed FISHBED by NATO, the MiG-21 served in the air forces of 23 nations.

■ MIKOYAN-GUREVICH MIG-25

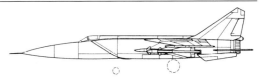

Engine: 2 Tumansky R-266 turbojets, 27,185 lbs (12,300 kg) thrust each
– **Wingspan:** 45'9" (13.95 m) – **Length:** 73'2" (22.30 m) – **Height:** 18'4"
(5.60 m) – **Max. takeoff weight:** 80,000 lbs (36,200 kg) – **Max. speed:**
2,100 mph (3,380 km/h) at 63,000' (19,200 m) – **Service ceiling:**
80,000' (24,400 m) – **Range:** 700 miles (1,130 km) – **Armament:** 2
23mm cannons; 4 air-to-air missiles

At the end of the 1960s the noble lineage of MiG combat aircraft gave birth to a new and powerful prince among planes, the MiG-25. This formidable air superiority interceptor, capable of operating at three times the speed of sound, was produced in several versions for a total of approximately 500 units. The project was begun in the late '50s at the height of the arms race against the United States. The existence of a prototype was officially announced in 1965, along with the alarming claim of a record having been set: the MiG-25 had flown a 620-mile circuit at an average speed of 1,442 miles per hour carrying a 4,400-lb payload. Two years later, four of the new planes were exhibited in the military parade at Domodedovo. NATO's codename for the 25 was FOXBAT.

■ MIKOYAN-GUREVICH MIG-29

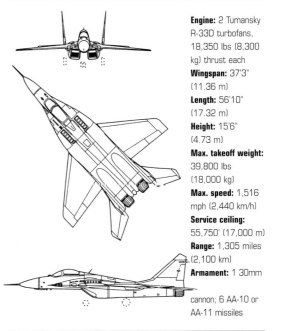

Engine: 2 Tumansky
R-33D turbofans,
18,350 lbs (8,300
kg) thrust each
Wingspan: 37'3"
(11.36 m)
Length: 56'10"
(17.32 m)
Height: 15'6"
(4.73 m)
Max. takeoff weight:
39,800 lbs
(18,000 kg)
Max. speed: 1,516
mph (2,440 km/h)
Service ceiling:
55,750' (17,000 m)
Range: 1,305 miles
(2,100 km)
Armament: 1 30mm
cannon; 6 AA-10 or
AA-11 missiles

The Soviet counterpart to the American F/A-18 Hornet, the MiG-29 (dubbed FULCRUM by the

M M

Western alliance) was one of the last great combat aircraft built by the USSR prior to the fall of the Berlin Wall, indeed, it was one of the great fighters of all time. The design project began in the 1960s, with the aim of developing a new multirole plane that would replace the MiG-21 and 23 in tactical and air defense roles. Official announcement of the project was made in 1972 and the first 14 prototypes were ready two years later, though they didn't actually fly until October 1977. The green light for mass production was given in 1982, and delivery of the new fighter began in August 1983. Of the 2,000 units built, the Soviets retained 800 and distributed the remaining 1,200 among 21 other nations, including Poland, Slovakia, Hungary, Bulagria, Croatia, Yugoslavia, Iraq, Iran, Kazakhstan, Malaysia, and Cuba. An interesting footnote: Germany inherited 24 MiG-29s from former East Germany, making it NATO's only Soviet plane.

■ MITSUBISHI A6M2 REISEN

Among the immortal fighter planes in the history of modern warfare, the superb Mitsubishi A6M Reisen – better known as the 'Zero' – stands as tall as any. This fast, tough and extremely agile monoplane, a major player in the war in the Pacific, earned its fame from day one: it took the Americans years to build anything that could match it. The project was launched in summer 1937, and the prototype flew on April 1, 1939 with such success that very little further testing was required. The A6M2 version was developed over the summer of 1940 and by September the plane was already on the front lines in Japan's war with China.

On December 7, 1941, Japan entrusted the attack on Pearl Harbor to the Zero, jewel in the crown of the Imperial Navy's carrier-based air forces. And from that day until the Battle of Midway in June 1942, the Zero, vastly superior to contemporary American fighters, maintained absolute dominion of the skies.

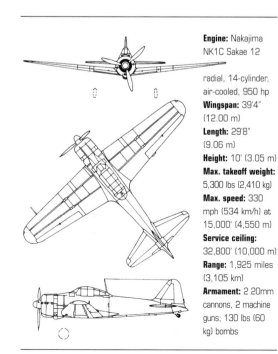

Engine: Nakajima NK1C Sakae 12 radial, 14-cylinder, air-cooled, 950 hp **Wingspan:** 39'4" (12.00 m) **Length:** 29'8" (9.06 m) **Height:** 10' (3.05 m) **Max. takeoff weight:** 5,300 lbs (2,410 kg) **Max. speed:** 330 mph (534 km/h) at 15,000' (4,550 m) **Service ceiling:** 32,800' (10,000 m) **Range:** 1,925 miles (3,105 km) **Armament:** 2 20mm cannons, 2 machine guns; 130 lbs (60 kg) bombs

■ MITSUBISHI A6M5 REISEN

The Mitsubishi Zero underwent constant evolution during WWII. In 1943 the Americans introduced Hellcat and the Corsair; aircraft finally able to find some weak points in the hitherto unbeatable Zero: insufficient armament, structural weakness, and limited protection of the cockpit and fuel tanks. In response Japan introduced the A6M5 that same year, and though it was objectively the best Zero of all, fewer than a thousand were produced, which simply wasn't enough. A final version with a more powerful engine, the A6M8, debuted in 1945. Again, Japanese industry was unable to build enough of them to make a difference. Total production for all versions of the plane was 10,449 units.

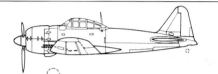

Engine: Nakajima NK1F Sakae 21 radial, 14-cylinder, air-cooled, 1,130 hp – **Wingspan:** 39'4" (11.00 m) – **Length:** 29'8" (9.12 m) – **Height:** 10' (3.50 m) – **Max. takeoff weight:** 5,300 lbs (2,733 kg) – **Max. speed:** 330 mph (564 km/h) at 15,000' (6,000 m) – **Service ceiling:** 32,800' (11,740 m) – **Range:** 1,925 miles (1,920 km) – **Armament:** 2 20mm cannons, 2 machine guns; 130 lbs (60 kg) bombs

■ MITSUBISHI G4M

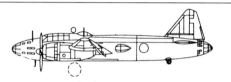

Version: G4M1 – **Engine:** 2 Mitsubishi MK4A Kasei 11 radials, 14-cylinder, 1,530 hp each – **Wingspan:** 82' (25.00 m) – **Length:** 65'7" (20.00 m) – **Height:** 19'7" (6.00 m) – **Max. takeoff weight:** 20,900 lbs (9,500 kg) – **Max. speed:** 265 mph (428 km/h) at 13,800' (4,200 m) – **Service ceiling:** 29,000' (8,840 m) – **Range:** 3,750 miles (6,030 km) – **Armament:** 1 20mm cannon, 4 machine guns; 1,760 lbs (800 kg) bombs or one torpedo

From September 1939 to August 1945, 2,446 G4M bombers in three principal versions rolled off the assembly lines. The airplane's career began in the final months of the war with China (May 1940) and ended when two G4M1s, painted white with green crosses in the place of the usual red discs symbolizing the Rising Sun, transported a Japanese delegation to Ie-Shima to negotiate the final terms of surrender (August 19, 1945). Nicknamed 'Betty' by the Allies, the G4M operated with devastating efficacy against American ships and ground forces, despite extreme vulnerability due to the large fuel tanks it contained in the wings. The project began in late 1937. In 1940 mass production was authorized, and the first battle-ready planes were delivered in April 1941 and immediately dispatched to China. When the Japanese attacked the US in December 1941, the G4M1 already had a good deal of combat experience. The more powerful G4M2 was introduced in 1942 (1,154 units total) and was followed in 1944 by the final version of the 'Betty', the G4M3, of which only 60 units were built.

■ MORANE-SAULNIER N

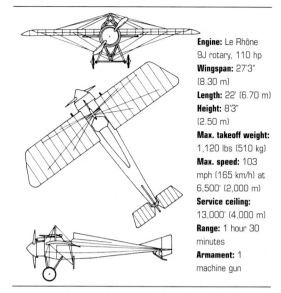

Engine: Le Rhône 9J rotary, 110 hp **Wingspan:** 27'3" (8.30 m) **Length:** 22' (6.70 m) **Height:** 8'3" (2.50 m) **Max. takeoff weight:** 1,120 lbs (510 kg) **Max. speed:** 103 mph (165 km/h) at 6,500' (2,000 m) **Service ceiling:** 13,000' (4,000 m) **Range:** 1 hour 30 minutes **Armament:** 1 machine gun

The Morane-Saulnier family of monoplane fighters was one of the most important of WWI up until 1916, thanks in large part to the fact that the L version of 1913 was the first fighter to introduce a fixed, forward-firing machine gun to the nose. The technology for synchronizing the gun with the propeller had not yet been developed, so the Morane used a much more rudimentary system: two steel plates were attached to the prop blade, simply deflecting the bullets that would otherwise have shattered the propeller. This solution proved to be as effective as it was simple, and so it was applied to subsequent versions as well, including the Morane-Saulnier N of 1914. The N, however, was the least fortunate of the series, penalized by its excessive landing speed and the extreme sensitivity of its controls, effectively making it a plane that only the most expert pilots could fly. Only 49 of them were ever built.

■ MRCA TORNADO

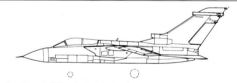

Version: Tornado IDS – **Engine:** 2 Turbo Union RB.199-34R-04 turbojets, 13,460 lbs (6,120 kg) thrust each – **Wingspan:** 45'7" (13.90 m) – **Length:** 54'9" (16.70 m) – **Height:** 18'8" (5.70 m) – **Max. takeoff weight:** 38,940 lbs (17,700 kg) – **Max. speed:** 1,320 mph (2,125 km/h) at 36,000' (11,000 m) – **Service ceiling:** 57,400' (17,500 m) – **Range:** 810 miles (1,300 km) – **Armament:** 2 27mm cannons; 12,100 lbs (5,500 kg) mixed ordnance

Before the advent of the Eurofighter Typhoon, the Tornado was Europe's most advanced multirole fighter. The project was initiated in 1969 with the foundation of the tri-national consortium, Panavia (Britain, Germany, Italy), the aim of which was to develop a combat plane for the three member nations, equal in quality to those of the two superpowers. The success of the twin-engine jet with 'swing wings' (or variable-geometry wings, to use the proper term) surpassed all expectations. The original production run was supposed to stop at 809 units, of which 138 were training planes. Distribution was: 100 for Italy, 324 for Germany, and 385 for Britain, whose allocation included 220 Tornado IDSs (the standard interdiction and attack version for all three partners) and 165 ADVs, an air defense version developed specifically for the RAF. But orders from other nations – predominantly from Saudi Arabia, Jordan and Oman – and requests for an electronics countermeasure version nudged production numbers up significantly. The Tornado first flew on August 14, 1974; it was operative by 1982 and entered combat for the first time in the Gulf War.

■ NIEUPORT 11 BÉBÉ

Originally designed as a competition plane, the Nieuport 11 became one of the most famous WWI fighters and the preferred plane of the some of the war's greatest aces. Hundreds were built, and were active on all fronts. Nicknamed Bébé, or 'baby,' for its small dimensions, it was designed by Gustave Delage for the Gordon Bennett Trophy race of 1914. The outbreak of war caused the competition to be cancelled, but not without both the British and French military having noticed the little biplane's excellent qualities. As such, it was put into production as a fighter. The Nieuport 11 joined the front lines in the summer of 1915 and proved to both fast and maneuverable, a worthy match for Germany's deadly Fokker monoplanes. Italy joined its allies in choosing the Bébé, which was built under license by Macchi (646 units) and remained that country's standard fighter until 1917.

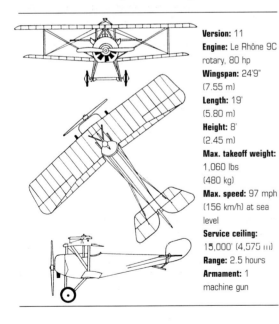

Version: 11
Engine: Le Rhône 9C rotary, 80 hp
Wingspan: 24'9" (7.55 m)
Length: 19' (5.80 m)
Height: 8' (2.45 m)
Max. takeoff weight: 1,060 lbs (480 kg)
Max. speed: 97 mph (156 km/h) at sea level
Service ceiling: 15,000' (4,575 m)
Range: 2.5 hours
Armament: 1 machine gun

■ NIEUPORT 17

The Nieuport 17 was the logical and natural evolution of the Bébé. Significantly larger, sturdier and better armed, it was considered one of the finest combat planes of its day, unquestionably one the best Allied fighters until the arrival of the peerless Spad S.VII. The Nieuport 17 reached the front in March 1916, gradually replacing the more outdated planes in the French arsenal. The 17 was also adopted by Great Britain, Holland, Belgium, Russia and Italy. Macchi built 150 under license; they were operative by October 1916.

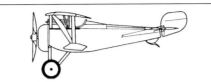

Engine: Le Rhône 9J rotary, 110 hp – **Wingspan:** 26'10" (8.17 m) – **Length:** 18'11" (5.77 m) – **Height:** 8' (2.44 m) – **Max. takeoff weight:** 1,240 lbs (565 kg) – **Max. speed:** 110 mph (177 km/h) at 6,560' (2,000 m) – **Service ceiling:** 17,400' (5,300 m) – **Range:** 2 hours – **Armament:** 2 machine guns

■ NORTH AMERICAN B-25 MITCHELL

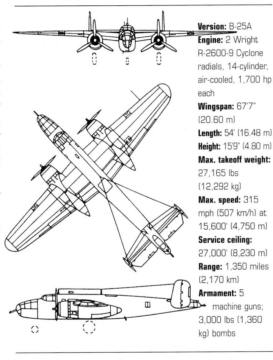

Version: B-25A
Engine: 2 Wright R-2600-9 Cyclone radials, 14-cylinder, air-cooled, 1,700 hp each
Wingspan: 67'7" (20.60 m)
Length: 54' (16.48 m)
Height: 15'9" (4.80 m)
Max. takeoff weight: 27,165 lbs (12,292 kg)
Max. speed: 315 mph (507 km/h) at 15,600' (4,750 m)
Service ceiling: 27,000' (8,230 m)
Range: 1,350 miles (2,170 km)
Armament: 5 machine guns; 3,000 lbs (1,360 kg) bombs

On April 18, 1942, 700 miles off the coast of Japan, 16 twin-engine bombers took off from the American carrier *Hornet* for one of the most spectacular and audacious missions of the entire war: the first aerial bombardment of Tokyo. Known to history as Doolittle's Raid, the mission was a success, thanks to the quality and ductility of the North American B-25 Mitchell, unanimously considered one of the best medium bombers of the war era. More than 10,500 B-25's were built in numerous versions between 1940 and 1945. The plane's unusual name, Mitchell, was given in honor of William 'Billy' Mitchell, the general who had theorized the doctrine of air superiority back in the 1920s and so wisely urged the United States to strengthen its air forces. The 40 B-25s of the A series were sent in 1941 to the 17th Bombardment Group, where they proved so effective that 120 more from the B series quickly followed. Serious production began with the C series (1,619) and the D (2,290), at which point the B-25 began being distributed among the Allies, Britain and the Soviet Union above all. The B-25H was the most heavily armed version, and was thus particularly suited to anti-ship missions. The final version, the J, was also the one built in the greatest quantities.

■ NORTH AMERICAN F-86 SABRE

'MiG Killer' was the name given to the North American F-86 Sabre, and an appropriate name it was. The first jet-powered fighter with backswept wings used by the US Air Force, the Sabre was the plane that allowed the Americans to achieve air parity in the Korean War after months of being crushed by the MiG-15. Total production of the Sabre was approximately 8,670 units, some of which were built under license in Canada, Australia, Japan and Italy. It was distributed to all of the NATO countries, as well as to others outside the alliance. The project was begun in 1944; the prototype flew in October 1947. Numerous versions were developed for different roles, including a radar-equipped all-weather fighter. The first was the F-86D of 1951; the most extensively produced was the K of 1954. This latter version, built under license in Italy, became an important plane for the Aeronautica Militare Italiana, which since 1956 had been flying the F-86E.

Version: F-86E
Engine: General Electric J47-GE-13 turbojet, 5,585 lbs (2,538 kg) thrust
Wingspan: 37'1" (11.30 m)
Length: 37'6" (11.43 m)
Height: 14'8" (4.47 m)
Max. takeoff weight: 16,400 lbs (7,419 kg)
Max. speed: 675 mph (1,086 km/h)
Service ceiling: 48,300' (14,720 m)
Range: 785 miles (1,260 km)
Armament: 6 machine guns; 2,000 lbs (905 kg) mixed ordnance

■ NORTH AMERICAN F-100 SUPER SABRE

The F-100 Super Sabre is inaugurated the era of the supersonic fighter jet in the Western world. Although derived from the F-86 Sabre, it was in reality a completely different plane. The project for the F-100 Super Sabre, of which 2,294 units in four main versions were built, was initiated in February 1949. The first prototype flew on May 5, 1953. The first variant, the F-100A, entered in service in 1954, but operational status was delayed by several grave accidents. The F-100B and C appeared in 1955, this latter optimized as a fighter-bomber, followed by the F-100D of 1956, which featured a better engine, improved avionics and heavier armament (1,274 units built). The last version was the F, a two-seater training plane, from 1957. The F-100 in all its incarnations remained in service until 1972, concluding its 18-year career in the closing months of the Vietnam War.

Version: F-100D
Engine: Pratt & Whitney J-57-P-21A turbojet, 17,000 lbs (7,692 kg) thrust
Wingspan: 38'9" (11.81 m)
Length: 47' (14.32 m)
Height: 15' (4.57 m)
Max. takeoff weight: 34,750 lbs (15,800 kg)
Max. speed: 865 mph (1,390 km/h) at 35,000' (10,670 m)
Service ceiling: 45,000' (13,720 m)
Range: 1,500 miles (2,415 km)
Armament: 4 20mm cannons; 7,500 lbs (3,395 kg) mixed ordnance

NORTH AMERICAN P-51 MUSTANG

The importance of the P-51 Mustang, America's best WWII fighter, and a plane good enough to have lasted well into the jet age, is most eloquently expressed in numbers: 15,686 planes produced; 4,950 enemy aircraft destroyed in combat and another 4,131 destroyed on the ground; 213,873 missions flown in the European theater alone; 20 nations eventually adopted the plane for their air forces.

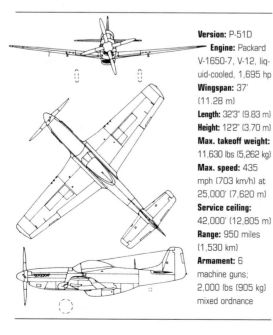

Version: P-51D
Engine: Packard V-1650-7, V-12, liquid-cooled, 1,695 hp
Wingspan: 37' (11.28 m)
Length: 32'3" (9.83 m)
Height: 12'2" (3.70 m)
Max. takeoff weight: 11,630 lbs (5,262 kg)
Max. speed: 435 mph (703 km/h) at 25,000' (7,620 m)
Service ceiling: 42,000' (12,805 m)
Range: 950 miles (1,530 km)
Armament: 6 machine guns; 2,000 lbs (905 kg) mixed ordnance

The first production prototype flew on May 1, 1941. A second was sent to the British for test flying in November, where it was designated the Mustang Mk.1. By April 1942 a number or Mk.1s were ready to enter service in the RAF as tactical recon fighters. September of that same year saw the first prototype of the P-51B, an entirely different plane equipped with a Packard-built Merlin engine. The B went into production in summer 1943 and Great Britain, which called it Mustang Mk.III, soon received about a thousand of them. The Mk.III first entered battle with the 8th Air Force in Britain on December 1. In spring 1944 the most successful version of the Mustang appeared, the P-51D (more than 8,000 units built). Rearward visibility was improved by replacing the original birdcage cockpit canopy with a Plexiglas bubble, a flap was added to the vertical stabilizer to compensate for a reduction of the lateral surface area, and four machine guns became six. The fastest Mustang was the last, the H, which was rated at 487 mph at 25,000 feet. The H made it off the assembly lines in time to participate in the last operations against the Japanese; only 555 units were built.

NORTHROP B-2 SPIRIT

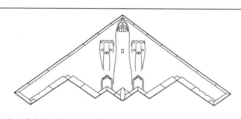

Version: B-2A – **Engine:** 4 General Electric F118-GE-110 turbofans, 19,000 lbs (8,620 kg) thrust each – **Wingspan:** 172' (52.40 m) – **Length:** 69' (21.03 m) – **Height:** 17' (5.18 m) – **Wing surface:** 5,000 sq ft (464.50 sq m) – **Max. takeoff weight:** 376,000 lbs (170,550 kg) – **Max. speed:** 630 mph (1,010 km/h) at 40,000' (12,190 m) – **Service ceiling:** 50,000' (15,240 m) – **Range:** 6,600 miles (12,200 km) – **Armament:** 50,000 lbs (22,680 kg) ordnance, in variable combinations of guided missiles, nuclear bombs, gravity bombs, sea mines, etc.

The Northrop B-2 Spirit is the first 'invisible' strategic bomber. Popularly known as the 'Stealth Bomber,' the B-2 was developed in response to the US Air Force's request for a plane that could penetrate deep into enemy airspace without detection by even the most sophisticated electronic countermeasure and air defense systems. The program was initiated in the late 1970s and the prototype flew on July 17, 1989. Cost overruns have drastically reduced expected production levels: of the 132 B-2s originally planned, only 21 have been built, at nearly $2 billion each.

PIAGGIO P.108

The Italian 'flying fortress,' although developed in 1939, didn't fly its first mission until June 1942. Built in limited numbers, the P.108 had neither the opportunity nor the time to demonstrate its noteworthy potential, given Italy's collapse the following year. The 108 was a low-wing four-engine bomber, made entirely of metal, with retractable landing gear and a payload capacity of nearly 4 tons of bombs, impressive for the time. The plane immediately caught the interest of technicians and mil-

itary officials alike, and it was assigned to the 274th Squadron of the Regia Aeronautica – the Italian air force – where it was without peer. Its only real deployment was in Gibraltar and Algeria, this latter around the time of the Allied landing in North Africa. In September 1943 most of the surviving P.108s fell into the hands of the Germans, who failed, however, to take advantage of the plane's excellent qualities.

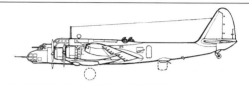

Version: P.108 B – **Engine:** 4 Piaggio PXII RC 35 radials, 18-cylinder, air cooled, 1,350 hp each – **Wingspan:** 105' (32.00 m) – **Length:** 75'2" (22.92 m) – **Height:** 25'3" (7.70 m) – **Max. takeoff weight:** 66,000 lbs (29,885 kg) – **Max. speed:** 260 mph (420 km/h) at 12,800' (3,900 m) – **Service ceiling:** 26,400' (8,050 m) – **Range:** 2,200 miles (3,514 km) – **Armament:** 7 machine guns; 7,750 lbs (3,500 kg) bombs

REGGIANE RE.2005 SAGITTARIO

Many described the Re.2005 as the most aesthetically beautiful airplane of WWII. Work on the prototype began in 1941, and the first Sagittario flew on May 9, 1942. In truth, the Reggiane fighter had attempted a first flight a week earlier, but a faulty strut in the landing gear had caused an accident. The Ministry of War ordered 16 of the prototypes, called the 'zero series,' then another 18 pre-production models, and finally gave the go-ahead for a production run of 750 units in February 1943. Only 29 made it off the assembly lines however, the rest remaining on paper. The Sagittario was assigned to the 362nd Squadron of the 22nd group, based in Naples-Capodichino, and went operational in May of 1943. The group was sent to Sicily at the time of the Allied invasion, where the Reggiane operated from the base in Capua until August. After the armistice, the remaining Re.2005's were destroyed to avoid their falling into German hands.

Engine: Daimler Benz DB 605/A, V-12s, liquid-cooled, 1,475 hp – **Wingspan:** 36'1" (11.00 m) – **Length:** 28'8" (8.73 m) – **Height:** 10'4" (3.15 m) – **Max. takeoff weight:** 7,980 lbs (3,610 kg) – **Max. speed:** 400 mph (644 km/h) at 23,600' (7,200 m) – **Service ceiling:** 39,400' (12,000 m) – **Range:** 775 miles (1,250 km) – **Armament:** 3 20mm cannons

REPUBLIC F-105 THUNDERCHIEF

A major participant in the Vietnam War, the powerful and sophisticated Thunderchief was a veritable flying arsenal, capable of supersonic low-altitude delivery of 7 tons of mixed ordnance. The prototype flew on October 22, 1955; the first operational version was the F-105B (May 1958). The definitive configuration was achieved in the second version, the D of 1959. The final version was the F-105F, an advanced two-seat training plane, completed in 1963. It first saw battle in Vietnam on March 1, 1965; the planes that survived the war were used by the Air National Guard until 1984. In all, 824 Thunderchiefs were built.

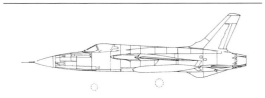

Version: F-105D – **Engine:** Pratt & Whitney J75-P-19 turbojet, 26,500 lbs (11,910 kg) thrust – **Wingspan:** 34'10" (10.64 m) – **Length:** 64'3" (19.58 m) – **Height:** 19'8" (5.99 m) – **Max. takeoff weight:** 48,500 lbs (21,948 kg) – **Max. speed:** 1,420 mph (2,280 km/h) at 38,000' (11,590 m) – **Service ceiling:** 52,000' (15,844 m) – **Range:** 2,000 miles (3,220 km) – **Armament:** 1 20mm cannon; 14,000 lbs (6,335 kg) mixed ordnance

■ REPUBLIC F-84 THUNDERJET

Conceived as the successor to the P-47 Thunderbolt, the F-84 played an important role in the Korean War. The prototype flew on February 28, 1946 and a year later the first operational version appeared, the F-84B. After the G series of 1950 the design of the Thunderjet underwent a radical transformation, replacing the base model's conventional wing with a backswept wing more appropriate to a jet, and as such became the P-84F of 1952. The new design added longevity to the plane's career, bringing it well into the 1970s. In all, 7,886 F-84s were built.

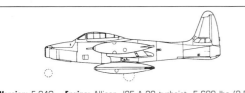

Version: F-84G – **Engine:** Allison J35-A-29 turbojet, 5,600 lbs (2,540 kg) thrust – **Wingspan:** 36'5" (11.10 m) – **Length:** 38' (11.61 m) – **Height:** 12'6" (3.83 m) – **Max. takeoff weight:** 23,500 lbs (10,670 kg) – **Max. speed:** 622 mph (1,000 km/h) at sea level – **Service ceiling:** 40,500' (12,340 m) – **Range:** 2,000 miles (3,220 km) – **Armament:** 6 machine guns; 4,000 lbs (1,814 kg) mixed ordnance

■ REPUBLIC P-47 THUNDERBOLT

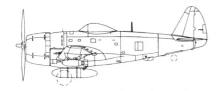

Version: P-47D – **Engine:** Pratt & Whitney R-2800-59 Double Wasp radial, 18-cylinder, air-cooled, 2,000 hp – **Wingspan:** 47'4" (14.42 m) – **Length:** 36' (11.00 m) – **Height:** 14'2" (4.31 m) – **Max. takeoff weight:** 19,500 lbs (8,800kg) – **Max. speed:** 428 mph (689 km/h) at 30,000' (9,150 m) – **Service ceiling:** 42,000' (12,800 m) – **Range:** 475 miles (765 km) – **Armament:** 8 machine guns; 2,000 lbs (905 kg) bombs

The Thunderbolt was built in numerous versions for a total of 15,683 units, and was omnipresent in Europe and the Pacific from early 1943 onward. The prototype, designated XP-47B, flew for the first time on May 6, 1941. In January 1944 the 56th Fighter Group of the Britain-based 8th Air Force was the first unit to operate the new fighter in battle. Soon thereafter the P-47D went into mass production. Equipped with a more powerful engine, the D was built in numerous production lots with various designations, each with minor improvements. The P-47D-25, for example, adopted a rib-less bubble canopy that ensured a 360-degree field of vision for the pilot. The final variant was the P-47N. Designed specifically for the exigencies of the Pacific theater, some 1,800 were built. The last them were delivered in late 1945.

■ SAAB 37 VIGGEN

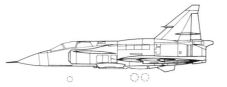

Version: AJ37 – **Engine:** Volvo Flygmotor RM8A turbojet, 38,700 lbs (11,800 kg) thrust – **Wingspan:** 34'9" (10.60 m) – **Length:** 53'6" (16.30 m) – **Height:** 18'4" (5.60 m) – **Max. takeoff weight:** 35,360 lbs (16,000 kg) – **Max. speed:** 1,327 mph (2,135 km/h) – **Service ceiling:** 60,000' (18,300 m) – **Range:** 621 miles (1,000 km) – **Armament:** 13,250 lbs (6,000 kg) mixed ordnance

In the long series of superb combat planes built by Saab beginning in the late 1940s, a place of honor is reserved for the Viggen, a rugged and sophisticated multirole designed to be ductile enough for integration into the complex Swedish national defense system. The program was launched in mid-1960s; the prototype flew on February 8, 1967. The first production model was the AJ37 of 1971, primarily an attack plane but also equipped to function as an interceptor. These roles were inverted in the second version, the AJ37 of 1977, whose primary function became interception. The Viggen entered service in June 1971; total production was 329 units.

■ SAAB JAS-39 GRIPEN

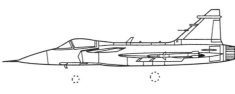

Engine: General Electric/Volvo Flygmotor RM12 (F404J) turbofan, 18,100 lbs (8,190 kg) thrust – **Wingspan:** 26'3" (8.00 m) – **Length:** 46'3" (14.10 m) – **Height:** 15'5" (4.70 m) – **Max. takeoff weight:** 17,700 lbs (8,000 kg) – **Max. speed:** 1,625 mph (2,135 km/h) – **Service ceiling:** 65,600' (20,000 m) – **Range:** 497 miles (800 km) – **Armament:** 1 27mm Mauser cannon; 14,400 lbs (6,500 kg) mixed ordnance

The Saab JAS-39 Gripen (or 'Gryphon'), a light multirole fighter, is considered the world's best in its category. The program was initiated in the late 1970s with the aim of developing a plane capable of replacing the 37 Viggen. The first prototype flew on December 9, 1988. Then, after a long design and testing phase, the first of 204 Gripens were delivered to the Swedish air forces in 1997. Development of the Gripen project is scheduled to continue through the first two decades of the new millennium.

■ SIAI MARCHETTI S.M.79 SPARVIERO

It began its military career as a traditional bomber, but the S.M.79 found its true identity in another role: that of torpedo bomber, where it proved to be without rival. From October 1936 to June 1943, 1,217 Sparvieros left the assembly line. The low-winged, three-engine monoplane had a wood-and-metal structure and a skin of mixed materials. It was originally conceived as an 8-seat civilian transport, and quickly established a reputation for speed and excellent handling. This of course attracted the attention of the Italian military authorities, who asked for a bomber version. The resulting plane did not differ structurally from the original. The only significant variations were the addition of a gondola beneath the fuselage and a raised cockpit, this latter being responsible for earning the S.M.79 the nickname of 'Hunchback.' The Marchetti bomber's first military use was in February 1937 in the Spanish Civil War, during which the civilian version of the S.M.79 continued its activities as a competition and commercial plane. When WWII broke out, the Regia Aeronautica had 594 militarized Sparvieros.

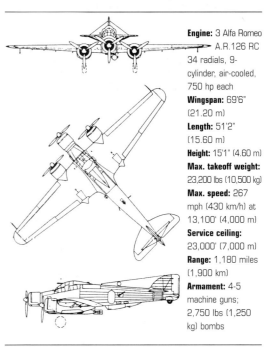

Engine: 3 Alfa Romeo A.R.126 RC 34 radials, 9-cylinder, air-cooled, 750 hp each – **Wingspan:** 69'6" (21.20 m) – **Length:** 51'2" (15.60 m) – **Height:** 15'1" (4.60 m) – **Max. takeoff weight:** 23,200 lbs (10,500 kg) – **Max. speed:** 267 mph (430 km/h) at 13,100' (4,000 m) – **Service ceiling:** 23,000' (7,000 m) – **Range:** 1,180 miles (1,900 km) – **Armament:** 4-5 machine guns; 2,750 lbs (1,250 kg) bombs

■ SIKORSKY ILYA MOUROMETZ V

The first true giants of the sky were born in the Russian Czarist era's closing years, fathered by the brilliant young engineer, Igor Ivanovich Sikorsky, future inventor of the helicopter. Sikorsky began designing large, multi-engine transport planes in 1912; when war broke out, his huge machines were developed for military use. The name Ilya Mourometz, a Russian hero, was given to the five resulting versions. The first to be used as a bomber was the V of 1915, of which 32 units were built. Over the next two years these planes made more than 400 raids over German and Lithuanian airspace.

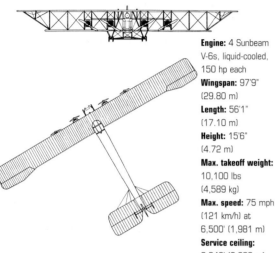

Engine: 4 Sunbeam V-6s, liquid-cooled, 150 hp each
Wingspan: 97'9" (29.80 m)
Length: 56'1" (17.10 m)
Height: 15'6" (4.72 m)
Max. takeoff weight: 10,100 lbs (4,589 kg)
Max. speed: 75 mph (121 km/h) at 6,500' (1,981 m)
Service ceiling: 9,840' (3,000 m)
Range: 5 hours
Armament: 3-7 machine guns; 1,150 lbs (523 kg) bombs

■ SOPWITH CAMEL

The curriculum vitae of the Sopwith Camel, one of the Allies' best WWI fighters, need contain only one line: 1,294 enemy planes shot down in less than two years of operation. The project began in late 1916 and delivery of the first Camels started in May 1917. The little biplane's chief virtue was its extreme maneuverability, due in part to the gyroscopic effect of its rotary engine, making it the ideal plane for close combat. In the hands of an expert pilot, the Camel was a lethal weapon, capable of outclassing any plane the enemy sent up against it, with the occasional exception of the Fokker triplane.

Version: F.1 – **Engine:** Clerget 9B rotary, 130 hp – **Wingspan:** 28' (8.53 m) – **Length:** 18'9" (5.72 m) – **Height:** 8'6" (2.59 m) – **Max. takeoff weight:** 1,450 lbs (659 kg) – **Max. speed:** 115 mph (185 km/h) at 6,500' (1,981 m) – **Service ceiling:** 19,000' (5,792 m) – **Range:** 2.5 hours – **Armament:** 2 machine guns

■ SOPWITH TRIPLANE

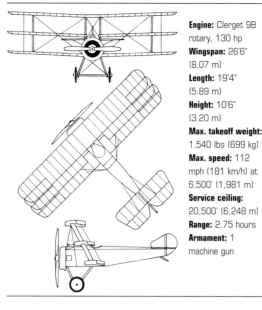

Engine: Clerget 9B rotary, 130 hp
Wingspan: 26'6" (8.07 m)
Length: 19'4" (5.89 m)
Height: 10'6" (3.20 m)
Max. takeoff weight: 1,540 lbs (699 kg)
Max. speed: 112 mph (181 km/h) at 6,500' (1,981 m)
Service ceiling: 20,500' (6,248 m)
Range: 2.75 hours
Armament: 1 machine gun

In February 1917, the Sopwith triplane appeared on the western front. Incontestably superior to any and every German fighter, it wreaked havoc in the enemy ranks. In response, 14 German manufacturers scrambled to develop planes of the same type, hoping at least to match the quality of the British fighter, the best features of which were its exceptional maneuverability and climbing speed. However, the triplane's career was brief, shadowed by that of its more illustrious successor, the immortal Camel. Production shut down after just 144 units, and starting in July 1917, the triplane was gradually withdrawn from the front, but not before it had made an important contribution to the Allied effort, if only for a few months.

■ SPAD S.VII

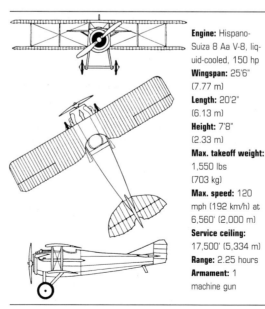

Engine: Hispano-Suiza 8 Aa V-8, liquid-cooled, 150 hp
Wingspan: 25'6" (7.77 m)
Length: 20'2" (6.13 m)
Height: 7'8" (2.33 m)
Max. takeoff weight: 1,550 lbs (703 kg)
Max. speed: 120 mph (192 km/h) at 6,560' (2,000 m)
Service ceiling: 17,500' (5,334 m)
Range: 2.25 hours
Armament: 1 machine gun

The Spad family of combat planes represented the culmination of aeronautical technology of the last

three years of WWI; they are generally considered the best fighters of the period. The key to the Spad's success was its superb aerodynamic design matched with an innovative engine, the Hispano-Suiza 'V-8', a significant step forward with respect to the rotary engines of the time. The result was a fast and powerful family of planes, built by the thousands and quickly adopted by the Allied air forces. The first Spad was the S.VII of 1916, favorite of the great Italian ace Francesco Baracca, who continued to fly it even after the introduction of the S.XIII.

■ SPAD S.XIII

The appearance of more powerful versions of the Hispano-Suiza engine led Spad designer Louis Béchéreau to develop a new project intended to improve upon the success of the S.VII. The felicitous outcome was the Spad S.XIII biplane, which was larger, faster, more agile, and more heavily armed than its predecessor. The prototype flew on April 4, 1917 and was immediately approved as a worthy replacement for the S.VII's and Nieuports which then equipped the French fighter squadrons. The S.XIII was a key factor in the Allied conquest of air supremacy. A total of 8,472 of them were built.

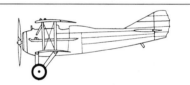

Engine: Hispano-Suiza 8 Bec V-8, liquid-cooled, 235 hp – **Wingspan:** 26'10" (8.20 m) – **Length:** 20'8" (6.30 m) – **Height:** 7'11" (2.42 m) – **Max. takeoff weight:** 1,800 lbs (820 kg) – **Max. speed:** 138 mph (222 km/h) at 6,560' (2,000 m) – **Service ceiling:** 21,800' (6,650 m) – **Range:** 2 hours – **Armament:** 1 machine gun

■ SUKHOI SU-17

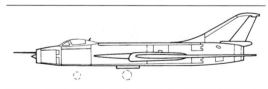

Engine: Lyulka AL-21F-3 turbojet, 25,000 lbs (11,340 kg) thrust – **Wingspan:** 45'11" (14.00 m) – **Length:** 61'6" (18.75 m) – **Height:** 15'7" (4.75 m) – **Max. takeoff weight:** 41,800 lbs (19,000 kg) – **Max. speed:** 1,430 mph (2,305 km/h) – **Service ceiling:** 59,000' (18,000 m) – **Range:** 390 miles (630 km) – **Armament:** 2 20mm cannons; 11,000 lbs (5,000 kg) mixed ordnance

Characterized by a variable geometry wing designed to optimize performance at radically differing altitudes, the Su-17 was exhibited for the first time in the Domodedovo military parade of 1967. It was produced in significant quantities and in several versions, varying in avionics, armament and engine. After resolving some grave initial shortcomings – a very poor turn radius in particular – the Su-17 became operational in 1972, assigned to the tactical wings of the Soviet air force and navy. In the early

1980s more than 600 of them, in various versions, were in active service. Designated FITTER by NATO, the Su-17 was exported to many countries, including Czechoslovakia, Poland, Algeria, Iraq, and Peru.

■ SUKHOI SU-27

Developed at the height of the Cold War as a reponse to the American F-15 and F-16 fighters, the Sukhoi Su-27 (codename FLANKER) remains one of the Russian Federation's most advanced combat aircraft. This is because, in addition to the original model's already exceptional performance ratings and formidable bombload capacity, constant and numerous improvements have been made to the plane over the years. At least 400 Su-27's currently serve the Russian air force, while the other 400 or so of the total production of circa 800 are in service in several former Soviet republics (Byelorussia, Ukraine, Georgia, Armenia, Azerbaijan, Kazakhstan) as well as in China, India, Vietnam, Syria, Ethiopia and Yemen.

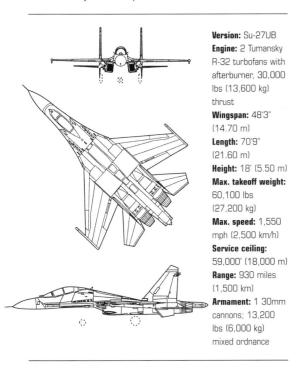

Version: Su-27UB
Engine: 2 Tumansky R-32 turbofans with afterburner, 30,000 lbs (13,600 kg) thrust
Wingspan: 48'3" (14.70 m)
Length: 70'9" (21.60 m)
Height: 18' (5.50 m)
Max. takeoff weight: 60,100 lbs (27,200 kg)
Max. speed: 1,550 mph (2,500 km/h)
Service ceiling: 59,000' (18,000 m)
Range: 930 miles (1,500 km)
Armament: 1 30mm cannons; 13,200 lbs (6,000 kg) mixed ordnance

■ SUPERMARINE SPITFIRE

20,351 planes, 40 versions: those numbers alone indicate the significance of this great British WWII fighter. Compared to its principal Luftwaffe opponent, the Messerschmitt Bf.109, the Spitfire was slightly faster and infinitely more maneuverable. Production of the Mk.1 began in 1937. When war was declared in 1939, only 9 squadrons were flying Spitfires. This figure jumped to 19 just prior to the Battle of Britain. The M.II appeared toward the end of 1940, followed by the first version, the Mk.IV, designed for photo reconnaissance, and then by the Mk.V in March 1941. The Mk.VC was used as a fighter-bomber, outfitted with a bay capable of carrying 500 lbs of bombs. The first planes of the

Mk.IX series were introduced in July 1942, more or less contemporaneously with the Mk.VI, VII, VIII and XI. The following year saw the arrival of the Mk.XII and XIV, the latter of which was designed as a pure interceptor. The Spitfire continued to evolve throughout the war and even afterwards. The post-war Mk.XIX photo recon version, with a Griffon engine now replacing the original Merlin, set the Spitfire speed record at 460 miles per hour. The last Spitfire was built in 1947.

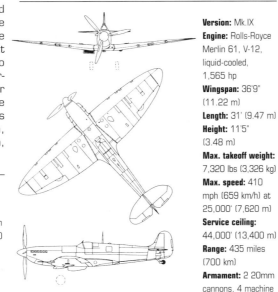

Version: Mk.IX
Engine: Rolls-Royce Merlin 61, V-12, liquid-cooled, 1,565 hp
Wingspan: 36'9" (11.22 m)
Length: 31' (9.47 m)
Height: 11'5" (3.48 m)
Max. takeoff weight: 7,320 lbs (3,326 kg)
Max. speed: 410 mph (659 km/h) at 25,000' (7,620 m)
Service ceiling: 44,000' (13,400 m)
Range: 435 miles (700 km)
Armament: 2 20mm cannons, 4 machine guns

■ TUPOLEV TU-16

The Tupolev Tu-16 was one of the most widely circulated combat planes of the early years of the Cold War. The prototype was officially presented in 1954, and the first Tu-16's were delivered before year's end. Production moved ahead at a brisk pace, generating several different versions. The first was the Tu-16A, followed by an anti-ship version, the 16B. Subsequent variants had notably improved avionics and upgraded armaments. All in all, more than 2,000 Tu-16s were built, with production under license in China proceeding throughout the 1970s. The Tu-16 was active in the air forces of nations outside the Eastern Bloc as well, such as Egypt and Syria, which used the plane in the Six-Day War with Israel.

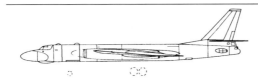

Version: Tu-16A – **Engine:** 2 Mikulin AM-3M turbojets, 20,900 lbs (9,500 kg) thrust each – **Wingspan:** 108' (32.93 m) – **Length:** 114'2" (34.80 m) – **Height:** 35'5" (10.80 m) – **Max. takeoff weight:** 149,600 lbs (68,000 kg) – **Max. speed:** 587 mph (945 km/h) – **Service ceiling:** 42,640' (13,000 m) – **Range:** 3,580 miles (5,760 km) – **Armament:** 6 23mm cannons; 19,800 lbs (9,000 kg) mixed ordnance

■ TUPOLEV TU-20

This impressively mighty four-engine bomber first appeared in 1954. Clearly derived from the commercial transport Tu-144, it was driven by four extremely powerful turboprops, each of which drove in turn a pair of enormous counter-rotating propellers with a diameter of nearly 19 feet. Though such a design might have been seen as anachronistic at the height of the jet age, the Tu-20 proved to be an excellent combat plane. In fact, subsequent versions were still in service in the 1990s performing strategic reconnaissance, anti-ship and radar functions. The final version was the Tu-142 of 1970, which was successful enough that production of numerous sub-series was resumed in 1980. The NATO codename for this burly giant was, appropriately, BEAR.

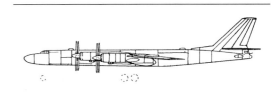

Engine: 4 Kuznetsov NK-12MV turboprops, 15,000 hp each – **Wingspan:** 159' (48.50 m) – **Length:** 155'9" (47.50 m) – **Height:** 38'8" (11.78 m) – **Max. takeoff weight:** 338,800 lbs (154,000 kg) – **Max. speed:** 500 mph (805 km/h) at 41,000' (12,500 m) – **Service ceiling:** 44,000' (13,400 m) – **Range:** 780 miles (12,550 km) – **Armament:** 6 23mm cannons; 37,200 lbs (11,340 kg) mixed ordnance

■ VICKERS VIMY

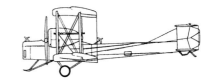

Engine: 2 Rolls-Royce Eagle VIII V-12s, liquid-cooled, 360 hp each – **Wingspan:** 72'5" (20.73 m) – **Length:** 43'6" (13.27 m) – **Height:** 15' (4.57 m) – **Max. takeoff weight:** 12,540 lbs (5,670 kg) – **Max. speed:** 103 mph (165 km/h) at sea level – **Service ceiling:** 7,000' (2,134 m) – **Range:** 8 hours – **Armament:** 4 machine guns; 4,800 lbs (2,180 kg) bombs

A contemporary of the Handley Page V/1500, the Vickers Vimy represents the final generation of British heavy bombers of the WWI period. Designed to have a range that would allow it to reach Berlin, the imposing twin-engine biplane was not completed in time to participate in the conflict in any substantial way: only three planes were operational before the armistice was signed. However, the Vimy had been a good investment. It not only served the Royal Air Force until 1924, but also made several record long-distance flights, including the first easterly crossing of the Atlantic, piloted by Alcock and Brown, in June of 1919. The Vimy's longest flight was the England-Australia raid in November of that same year: 11,130 miles in just under 130 hours of flight time.

■ VOISIN 5

The first Allied air combat kill of WWI occurred on October 5, 1914, almost above Reims. The victim was a German Aviatik, the victor a French Voisin 3. This plane, designed by Gabriel Voisin in the years just before the war, was built in increasingly more powerful versions until 1915. It became the standard light bomber of the war's opening years. The first version, the Voisin 3 of 1914, had the largest production volume and was adopted by nearly all the Allied nations' air forces. In 1915, versions 4 and 5 appeared, differing from their predecessor in two noteworthy ways: they had a more powerful engine, and a heavy 37mm or 47mm cannon could be mounted on the nose.

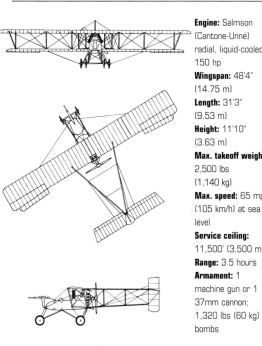

Engine: Salmson (Cantone-Unné) radial, liquid-cooled, 150 hp
Wingspan: 48'4" (14.75 m)
Length: 31'3" (9.53 m)
Height: 11'10" (3.63 m)
Max. takeoff weight: 2,500 lbs (1,140 kg)
Max. speed: 65 mph (105 km/h) at sea level
Service ceiling: 11,500' (3,500 m)
Range: 3.5 hours
Armament: 1 machine gun or 1 37mm cannon; 1,320 lbs (60 kg) bombs

■ VOUGHT F4U CORSAIR

In production for more than a decade, in service until 1965, the Vought F4U Corsair was the bane of the Japanese, who nicknamed it 'Whispering Death.' The project was initiated in early 1938 at the behest of the US Navy. The tremendous power of the Double Wasp engine required a large propeller to absorb it. But the 13-foot prop had to be kept from touching the ground somehow, so the designers came up with an ingenious solution which became the Corsair's distinguishing feature: the inverted gull wing. This eliminated the necessity of excessively long landing-gear struts, which never would have survived the violence of a carrier-deck landing. The development process was long and fraught with problems; in fact, the Corsair wasn't delivered to the Marines on Guadalcanal until February 1943, and the Navy didn't take it into battle until September. A total of 12,571 Corsairs of various types were built, the F4U-1 being the most numerous.

Version: F4U-1D
Engine: Pratt & Whitney R-2800-8W Double Wasp radial, 18-cylinder, air-cooled, 2,000 hp
Wingspan: 40'10" (12.47 m)
Length: 33'4" (10.16 m)
Height: 15'1" (4.60 m)
Max. takeoff weight: 13,100 lbs (5,950 kg)
Max. speed: 425 mph (684 km/h) at 20,000' (6,100 m)
Service ceiling: 37,000' (11,280 m)
Range: 1,000 miles (1,609 km)
Armament: 6 machine guns; 2,000 lbs (905 kg) bombs

■ YAKOVLEV YAK-9

Version: Yak-9D
Engine: Klimov M.105PF, V-12, liquid-cooled, 1,260 hp
Wingspan: 32'9" (10.00 m)
Length: 28' (8.55 m)
Height: 8' (2.44 m)
Max. takeoff weight: 6,885 lbs (3,115 kg)
Max. speed: 373 mph (600 km/h) at 11,500' (3,500 m)
Service ceiling: 32,800' (10,000 m)
Range: 807 miles (1,300 km)
Armament: 1 20mm cannon, one machine gun

The Yakovlev fighter was one of the most important combat planes the Soviet Union produced during WWII. More than 30,000 of them were built, 16,769 of which were of the Yak-9 series, one of the last great piston-engine fighter planes. The Yak-9P, last of the series, was still being used in the Korean War, well into the jet age. The first Yak-9, derived from the Yak-7B, appeared in 1942; the main improvements were greater speed and range. It reached the front in August and proved to be relatively effective against the more advanced German fighters. Further improvements were made as production proceeded, resulting in the 9D of 1943, the version built in the greatest quantities. The Yak-9 was a favorite among foreign air forces that were supporting the Soviets on their home ground, including Poland's 1st Fighter Regiment and France's famous Groupe de Chasse Normandie-Niemen.

■ ZEPPELIN STAAKEN R

On September 17, 1917, Londoners saw their nightmare attacker, the Gotha bomber, joined by another, even more fearsome enemy. On that day the British capital suffered the first in a long series of raids by a new German strategic bomber, the Zeppelin Staaken R.VI, the largest and most lethal of its kind. This cruelly efficient war machine, heavily defended by as many as 7 machine guns and capable of carrying more than 2 tons of bombs, flew 52 sorties into English airspace, throwing the population into panic each time. On one of these raids, on February 16, 1918, a Staaken dropped the history's first one-ton bomb, striking the Chelsea Royal Hospital in the heart of London, killing dozens and wounding more. The R program (R for *Riesenflugzeug*, or 'giant plane') was begun in late 1914. The R.VI was the first production plane; 18 of them were built.

Version: R.VI – **Engine:** 4 Mercedes D.IVa, 6-cylinder inlines, liquid-cooled, 260 hp each – **Wingspan:** 138'5" (42.20 m) – **Length:** 72'6" (22.10 m) – **Height:** 20'8" (6.30 m) – **Max. takeoff weight:** 26,000 lbs (11,764 kg) – **Max. speed:** 84 mph (135 km/h) at sea level – **Service ceiling:** 14,000' (4,268 m) – **Range:** 7-10 hours – **Armament:** 4-7 machine guns; 4,400 lbs (2,000 kg) bombs

CIVIL AIRCRAFT

■ A.E.G. J.II

The J.II was essentially a ground attack plane modified for commercial use after the First World War. Military fittings were stripped, and a cabin replaced the rear cockpit. From 1919 onward, these planes delivered mail and commercial cargo for Deutsche Luft Reederei. Four of them survived until 1926, the year they were turned over to Deutsche Lufthansa.

Engine: Benz Bz.IV, 6-cylinder inline, liquid-cooled, 200 hp – **Wingspan:** 44'2" (13.46 m) – **Length:** 25'11" (7.90 m) – **Max. takeoff weight:** 3,564 lbs (1,620 kg) – **Max. speed:** 93 mph (150 km/h) – **Service ceiling:** 14,850' (4,500 m) – **Range:** 350 miles (565 km)

■ AEROCURVO PONZELLI-MILLER

The Sicilian engineer Franz Miller founded Italy's first aeronautical workshop and placed it at the disposal of anyone who wanted to build a flying machine. One of the first fruits of this initiative was the Aerocurvo, an unusual contraption with curved dihedral wings. Though the project was a failure, it captured the interest of airplane aficionados and laid the foundation for other, more successful ventures.

Engine: Miller 4-cylinder inline, air-cooled, 50 hp – **Wingspan:** 23' (7 m) – **Length:** 23' (7 m) – **Wing surface:** 237 sq ft (22 sq m) – **Max. takeoff weight:** 550 lbs (250 kg)

■ AIRBUS A-320

Designed in the early 1980s, the A-320 was an instant success. By the time it was ready to enter into service for Air France (April 18, 1988), the little 180-seat twin-jet had accumulated nearly 500 orders and options from 20 airlines. There are several reasons for this success, the first of which was good timing: the A-320 responded perfectly to the category most in demand in the world market at the time, that of the short- to medium-range 150-seat liner. Secondly, the A-320 was completely new from inside out, with innovative technologies and features that established it as the spearhead of a new generation of commercial aircraft.

Version: A-320-100 – **Engine:** 2 General Electric CFM56-A1 turbofans, 25,000 lbs (11,340 kg) thrust each – **Wingspan:** 111'3" (33.91 m) – **Length:** 123'3" (37.57 m) – **Height:** 38'9" (11.80 m) – **Empty weight:** 88,815 lbs (40,370 kg) – **Max. takeoff weight:** 149,600 lbs (68,000 kg) – **Cruising speed:** 560 mph (903 km/h) at 28,000' (8,530 m) – **Service ceiling:** 39,000' (11,887 m) – **Range:** 2,015 miles (3,243 km)

■ AIRBUS A-380

The Airbus A-380, the European consortium's most ambitious project, is a direct challenge to American industry in the prestigious wide-body passenger liner sector. Defined as the successor of the Boeing B-747 Jumbo, the A-380 is a 555-840-seat behemoth, scheduled to go operational in the first three months of 2006. The program, inaugurated in 1994, examined numerous configurations before settling on the double-decker (two levels running the entire length of the aircraft). In addition to this base version, there are at least two other variants underway: the super-long-range A-380-800R, and the cargo carrier A-380-800F. The prototype will fly in 2005. As of June 2003, the number of orders stood at 129 units from 11 different airlines.

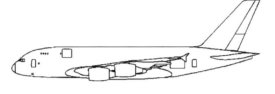

Version: A-380 – **Engine:** 4 Rolls-Royce Trent RB-967s or Engine Alliance GP-7267s – **Wingspan:** 261'9" (79.80 m) – **Length:** 239'6" (73.00 m) – **Height:** 79' (24.10 m) – **Wing surface:** 9,095 sq ft (845 sq m) – **Empty weight:** 613,360 lbs (276,800 kg) – **Max. takeoff weight:** 1,232,200 lbs (560,000 kg) – **Cruising speed:** 894 mph (1,440 km/h) at 35,000' (10,675 m) – **Service ceiling:** 43,000' (13,120 m) – **Range:** 9,200 miles (14,800 km)

■ AIRCO (DE HAVILLAND) D.H.4

The first commercial flights in Great Britain were made with modified warplanes. Among the first to be adapted for passenger flights was the D.H.4A. Built by Airco, a de Havilland subsidiary. Starting in 1919, Aircraft Transport and Travel and Handley Page Transport began to use the D.H.4.A regularly. In August two routes were established: to Amsterdam and then from Hounslow to Le Bourget. Nine more routes to France and the Netherlands were opened soon thereafter, all served by the D.H.4. On December 4, 1920, the hardy little plane set a record for the London-Paris route of 1 hour 48 minutes.

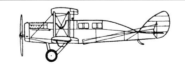

Version: D.H.4A – **Engine:** Napier Lion II, 12-cylinder W-block, liquid-cooled, 450 hp – **Wingspan:** 42'5" (12.93 m) – **Length:** 123'3" (8.56 m) – **Height:** 28'1" (3.55 m) – **Max takeoff weight:** 3,200 lbs (1,447 kg) – **Max. speed:** 150 mph (241 km/h)

■ ANTOINETTE IV

Technically speaking, the Antoinette IV debuted at Issy on October 9, 1908, but in fact its designer, Léon Levavasseur, did not give it the definitive configuration for which it became known until early 1909. The modification consisted in the near doubling of the wing

surface, which went from 322 square feet in the prototype to nearly 550. The plane thus found the elegance of proportion and line that characterize its every aspect, from the delicately attenuated fuselage to the trapezoidal plan and dihedral section of the wing, to its sculptural cruciform rudder.

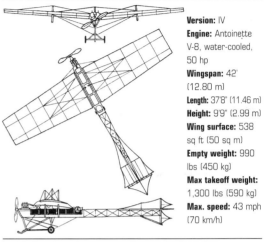

Version: IV
Engine: Antoinette V-8, water-cooled, 50 hp
Wingspan: 42' (12.80 m)
Length: 37'8" (11.46 m)
Height: 9'9" (2.99 m)
Wing surface: 538 sq ft (50 sq m)
Empty weight: 990 lbs (450 kg)
Max takeoff weight: 1,300 lbs (590 kg)
Max. speed: 43 mph (70 km/h)

■ ANTONOV AN-225 MRIYA

The Antonov An-225 Mriya (Russian for 'dream') is the largest airplane ever built, in keeping with the time-honored tradition of aeronautical gigantism so dear to the Russians. It was conceived in mid-1985 with the intention of developing an even larger and more powerful plane than the already colossal An-124 Ruslan, another heavy transport from the 1980s, in order to execute special missions linked to the space program. The design and testing phase lasted a little less than four years, and the prototype flew on December 28, 1988. On May 13, 1989 the An-225 was used for the first time to piggyback the Russian space shuttle Buran. Only one Mriya has been built to date.

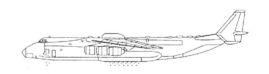

Engine: 6 Lotarev D18T turbofans, 25,000 lbs (23,401 kg) thrust each – **Wingspan:** 290' (88.40 m) – **Length:** 275'6" (84 m) – **Height:** 59'4" (18.10 m) – **Empty weight:** 770,000 lbs (350,000 kg) – **Max takeoff weight:** 1,320,600 lbs (600,000 kg) – **Cruising speed:** 528 mph (850 km/h) at 39,000' (12,340 m) – **Service ceiling:** 40,500' (12,340 m) – **Range:** 2,800 miles (4,500 km)

■ ARMSTRONG WHITWORTH A.W.155 ARGOSY I

The Argosy was developed on the explicit request of Imperial Airways for a plane that would ensure comfortable and dependable passenger service as well as efficient postal and cargo transport. The first requirement was amply satisfied: in 1926 Imperial used its three Argosy Is to inaugurated three routes from London to Paris, Brussels and Cologne. On May 1, 1927 a luxury service to the French capital was introduced, and in 1929 the fleet was augmented by four new planes from the second series, the Argosy II.

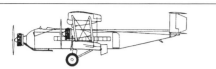

Version: Argosy I – **Engine:** 3 Armstrong Siddeley Jaguar III radials, 14-cylinder, air-cooled, 385 hp each – **Wingspan:** 90' (27.43 m) – **Length:** 64'6" (19.66 m) – **Height:** 19' (5.79 m) – **Max. takeoff weight:** 1,800 lbs (8,154 kg) – **Cruising speed:** 90 mph (145 km/h) – **Range:** 400 miles (650 km)

■ BAC-AÉROSPATIALE CONCORDE

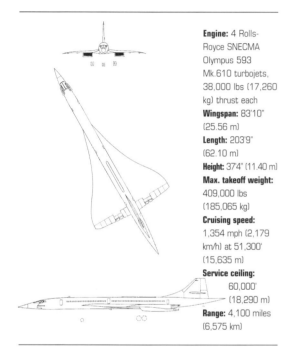

Engine: 4 Rolls-Royce SNECMA Olympus 593 Mk.610 turbojets, 38,000 lbs (17,260 kg) thrust each **Wingspan:** 83'10" (25.56 m) **Length:** 203'9" (62.10 m) **Height:** 37'4" (11.40 m) **Max. takeoff weight:** 409,000 lbs (185,065 kg) **Cruising speed:** 1,354 mph (2,179 km/h) at 51,300' (15,635 m) **Service ceiling:** 60,000' (18,290 m) **Range:** 4,100 miles (6,575 km)

The Concorde program was launched on November 29, 1962 with the signing of a cooperation agreement by the French and British governments, their respective national airlines, and by the manufacturers contracted to build the plane: BAC and Aérospatiale for the body, Rolls-Royce and SNECMA for the engines. The first prototype flew on March 2, 1969, but regular service didn't begin until January 21, 1976. Air France's inaugural route was Paris-Dakar-Rio de Janeiro, while British Airways opted to open the age of supersonic air travel with service from London to Bahrain. Soon both airlines were covering the historic North Atlantic route to New York and Washington, D.C. After almost 25 years of activity on the most prestigious international routes, a tragic accident that killed more than 100 people led the two airlines to announce the retirement of the world's first and only supersonic passenger liner.

■ BELL X-1

The advent of the jet engine rekindled the passion for speed records that had characterized the first half of the century, posing altogether new challenges. The

first of them, the sound barrier, was broken on October 14, 1947 by the legendary test pilot Chuck Yeager in a Bell X-1, the first rocket-powered American aircraft and grandfather of all the planes of the Experimental Research Aircraft program. In the quest for ever more ambitious goals, three dramatically improved versions were developed during the late 1950s, the X-1A, 1B and 1D. With the first of these Yeager flew at 1,650 mph, more than twice the speed of sound, in December 1953, while Murray reached 90,000 feet of altitude in June 1954. The last verion was the X-1E of 1955, designed to test a new type of wing. The X-1s made a total of 156 flights, the last in 1958.

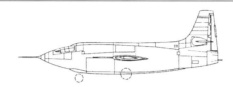

Engine: Reaction Motor XLR-11-RM-1 rocket engine, 6,000 lbs (2,721 kg) thrust – **Wingspan:** 28' (8.53 m) – **Length:** 31' (9.45 m) – **Height:** 10'9" (3.30 m) – **Max. takeoff weight:** 12,000 lbs (5,443 kg) – **Max. speed:** 960 mph (1,545 km/h) – **Service ceiling:** 70,000' (21,340 m)

■ BELL X-2

Engine: Curtiss Wright XLR25-CW-3-rocket engine, 15,000 lbs (6,804 kg) thrust **Wingspan:** 34'9" (10.59 m) **Length:** 45'4" (13.84 m) **Height:** 11'9" (3.58 m) **Max. takeoff weight:** 24,900 lbs (11,300 kg) **Max. speed:** 2,090 mph (3,369 km/h) **Service ceiling:** 126,165' (38,465 m)

Bell's second experimental aircraft (aptly named X-2) was ordered in 1946 in anticipation of the inevitable need for a plane that could fly even higher and faster than the X-1. More specifically, the new plane was designed to study the behavior of the backswept wing, the ideal form for supersonic flight. Only two were built, one of which crashed on May 12, 1953, during the prototyping phase, leaving only a single aircraft to bear the weight of the ambitious program. Test flights began in November 1955. The principal records claimed by the X-2 were for altitude (126,200', September 7, 1956, pilot Iven Kincheloe) and speed (2,094 mph, September 27, pilot Milburn Apt). This latter, however, came at no small cost: immediately after clocking this historic record, the plane went out

of control and crashed, killing the pilot and putting an end to the X-2 program.

■ BELLANCA W.B.2 COLUMBIA

Engine: Wright J-5 Whirlwind radial, 9-cylinder, air-cooled, 200 hp – **Wingspan:** 46'4" (14.12 m) – **Length:** 27' (8.23 m) – **Height:** 8'5" (2.57 m) – **Max. takeoff weight:** 5,400 lbs (2,450 kg) – **Cruising speed:** 105 mph (170 km/h) – **Service ceiling:** 13,000' (3,960 m)

The Bellanca W.B.2 monoplane, baptized Columbia, was one of many planes that attempted the transatlantic crossing. Piloted by C.D. Chamberlain and C.A. Levine, the W.B.2 took off from New York on June 4, 1927 for Berlin, non-stop. The goal was achieved, though not to the letter: the pilots overshot the German capital due to a navigational miscalculation and landed in Eisleben.

■ BLÉRIOT 110

Engine: Hispano-Suiza V-12, liquid-cooled, 600 hp – **Wingspan:** 87' (26.50 m) – **Length:** 47'10" (14.57 m) – **Height:** 16'1" (4.90 m) – **Empty weight:** 6,570 lbs (2,980 kg) – **Max. takeoff weight:** 16,000 lbs (7,250 kg) – **Max. speed:** 1,30 mph (210 km/h) – **Range:** 6,600 miles (10,600 km)

Designed by the engineer Filippo Zappata, the Blériot 110 was a plane built to break records, and this is precisely what it did for the better part of the early 1930s. In February 1931, pilots Lucien Bossoutrot and Maurice Rossi remained uninterruptedly aloft for 75 hours and 22 minutes, covering 5,482 miles on a closed course, establishing the world record for distance and endurance. A year later they smashed their own record by flying 6,588 miles in 76 hours and 34 minutes, again on a closed course. On August 5, 1933, Rossi and Paul Codos claimed the straight-line distance record as well, covering the 5,656 miles from New York to Rayaq, Syria in 55 hours and 30 minutes.

■ BLÉRIOT 5190 SANTOS-DUMONT

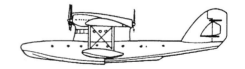

Engine: 4 Hispano-Suiza 12 Nbrs, V-12, liquid-cooled, 650 hp each – **Wingspan:** 141' (43 m) – **Length:** 85'3" (26 m) – **Max. takeoff weight:** 48,500 lbs (22,000 kg) – **Cruising speed:** 120 mph (190 km/h) – **Range:** 1,990 miles (3,200 km)

Designed in 1928 but not prototyped until 1933, this long-range hydroplane was intended to make mail runs between Europe, Africa, and South America. Service between Dakar (W. Africa) and Natal (Brazil) began on November 27, 1934. Flying the colors of Air France, the Santos-Dumont – of which only one was built – made 22 crossings, significantly reducing the flight time between Toulouse and Buenos Aires.

■ BLÉRIOT XI

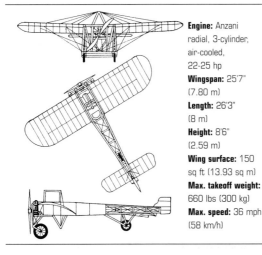

Engine: Anzani radial, 3-cylinder, air-cooled, 22-25 hp
Wingspan: 25'7" (7.80 m)
Length: 26'3" (8 m)
Height: 8'6" (2.59 m)
Wing surface: 150 sq ft (13.93 sq m)
Max. takeoff weight: 660 lbs (300 kg)
Max. speed: 36 mph (58 km/h)

Two 'firsts' highlight the Blériot XI's career. In addition to its sporting achievements, it was the first plane to be purchased by the French armed forces, and more spectacularly, the first plane in history to fly a military mission: on October 23, 1911 during the Italian-Turkish War, Commander Carlo Piazza flew a Blériot XI on a reconnaissance sortie over enemy lines – making the Blériot XI the world's first warplane.

■ BOEING 247

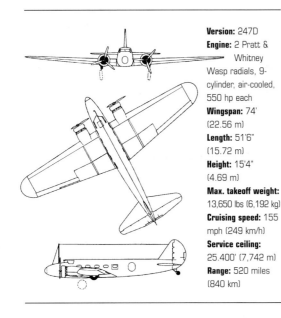

Version: 247D
Engine: 2 Pratt & Whitney Wasp radials, 9-cylinder, air-cooled, 550 hp each
Wingspan: 74' (22.56 m)
Length: 51'6" (15.72 m)
Height: 15'4" (4.69 m)
Max. takeoff weight: 13,650 lbs (6,192 kg)
Cruising speed: 155 mph (249 km/h)
Service ceiling: 25.400' (7,742 m)
Range: 520 miles (840 km)

It would be difficult to overestimate the importance of the 247 for the evolution of civil transport in America.

The first of the 75 planes built made its maiden flight on February 8, 1933 and on March 30 entered into service for United Air Lines, which was so impressed with the 247 that by the end of June the airline already had 30 of them flying its most prestigious domestic routes. Structurally based on a military design, the 247 was a low-wing monoplane built entirely of metal, with retractable landing gear, an innovative feature at the time. The 247 so reduced standard flying times that the entire American aeronautical industry was forced to develop new planes to compete with it. Most important among them were the Douglas DC-1 and DC-2.

■ BOEING 314 YANKEE CLIPPER

In mid-1939 this huge four-engine 'flying boat' initiated a regular New York- Newfoundland (Canada)-Southampton (Britain) passenger service, often doubling as a postal courier. The outbreak of WWII forced the cancellation of these services, but all 12 of the Yankee Clippers that Boeing had built remained in service elsewhere.

Version: 314A – **Engine:** 4 Wright GR-2600 Cyclone radials, 14-cylinder, air-cooled, 1,600 hp each – **Wingspan:** 152' (46.33 m) – **Length:** 106' (32.31 m) – **Height:** 27'7" (8.41 m) – **Max. takeoff weight:** 82,500 lbs (37,422 kg) – **Cruising speed:** 183 mph (294 km/h) – **Service ceiling:** 13,400' (4,085 m) – **Range:** 3,500 miles (5,630 km)

■ BOEING 707

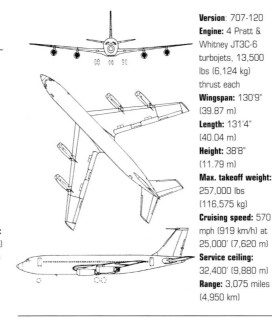

Version: 707-120
Engine: 4 Pratt & Whitney JT3C-6 turbojets, 13,500 lbs (6,124 kg) thrust each
Wingspan: 130'9" (39.87 m)
Length: 131'4" (40.04 m)
Height: 38'8" (11.79 m)
Max. takeoff weight: 257,000 lbs (116,575 kg)
Cruising speed: 570 mph (919 km/h) at 25,000' (7,620 m)
Service ceiling: 32,400' (9,880 m)
Range: 3,075 miles (4,950 km)

The Boeing 707 was the first American jet-powered commercial airplane. Though America had lost the race to build the first jet liner to the British, it had the merit of having developed the first economically

viable one, as amply demonstrated by the 707's starring role in the world air-travel market for more than two decades. The project was initiated in 1952 when Boeing authorized the construction of a prototype, which flew on July 15, 1954. Nicknamed 'Dash Eighty,' the plane destined to become the immortal 707 underwent an arduous process of testing and tweaking. Its first success was in the military sector: on September 1, 1954 Boeing received an order for 29 planes to be used as mid-air refuelers, designated KC-135 Stratotanker. This paved the way for civilian production. In Pan Am 1955 ordered large numbers of the original version (707-120), and soon all the world's major airlines followed suit. The other main variant was the 707-320 of 1959, modified for intercontinental flights.

■ BOEING 727

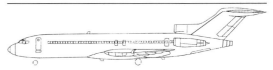

Version: 727-200 – **Engine:** 3 Pratt & Whitney JT8D-9A turbojets, 14,500 lbs (6,580 kg) thrust each – **Wingspan:** 108' (32.92 m) – **Length:** 153'2" (46.69 m) – **Height:** 34' (10.36 m) – **Max. takeoff weight:** 184,800 lbs (83,820 kg) – **Cruising speed:** 592 mph (953 km/h) – **Service ceiling:** 33,000' (10,060m) – **Range:** 2,650 miles (4,260 km)

In the great race to conquer the international market, Boeing won hands down with the 727 trijet, the world's best selling passenger plane during the jet age's first three decades. To give an idea: the forecast was for 250 planes; in the end 1,831 were built. The design phase was begun in December 1960, the 100 series went into service in 1964, the 200 in 1967. As of 2001, approximately 1,300 727s were still in active service, a testament to the plane's unparalleled reliability and versatility.

■ BOEING 737

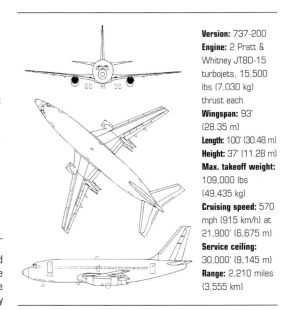

Version: 737-200
Engine: 2 Pratt & Whitney JT8D-15 turbojets, 15,500 lbs (7,030 kg) thrust each
Wingspan: 93' (28.35 m)
Length: 100' (30.48 m)
Height: 37' (11.28 m)
Max. takeoff weight: 109,000 lbs (49,435 kg)
Cruising speed: 570 mph (915 km/h) at 21,900' (6,675 m)
Service ceiling: 30,000' (9,145 m)
Range: 2,210 miles (3,555 km)

The smallest of Boeing's jet aircraft was the 737, a twinjet, high-capacity liner for short- to medium-range flights. The project was launched in 1964, and within a year Lufthansa ordered 21 planes on the basis of the idea alone. The prototype flew in April 1967 and delivery began in December. There were two base versions: the 200 and the 200C/QC, this latter outfitted to convert to either passenger or cargo service. A sub-variant, the 200 Long Range, was designed for lower fuel consumption, hence its name.

■ BOEING 747

The Boeing 747 of 1969 launched the 'wide-body' jet era. The idea was to design and mass-produce the world's largest commercial airplane, one capable of carrying more than 400 passengers, thereby revolutionizing the global air travel market's basic economics. The aim was fully met on February 9, 1969, when the first B-747 made its maiden flight. Immediately dubbed 'Jumbo Jet,' this 'father' of all the wide-bodies established new operational standards: all major airlines had to acknowledge and embrace them. Pan American was again first to adopt the 747; it began flying the prestigious New York-London route on January 22, 1970. Several versions followed the original 100 series, from the 200 (first flight October 1970, first delivery January 1971) to the final variant, the 747-400 of 1985, which featured improved aerodynamics, avionics and fuel consumption.

Version: 747-200
Engine: 4 Pratt & Whitney JT9D-7/3a turbojets, lbs (21,319 kg) thrust each
Wingspan: 83'10" (59.64 m)
Length: 203'9" (70.66 m)
Height: 37'4" (19.33 m)
Max. takeoff weight: 409,000 lbs (332,900 kg)
Cruising speed: 1,354 mph (910 km/h) at (9,500 m)
Service ceiling: 60,000' (13,715 m)
Range: 4,960 miles (8,000 km)

■ BOEING 777

The hi-tech 777 resulted from Boeing's wish to take the enormous advances in engine design and flight systems and incorporate them into a twinjet passenger plane that maximized payload capacity and range. The 200 version of 1995 was followed by others, each aimed at increasing load and range. Though the 777's wingspan is larger than the 747's, the 777 is only two-thirds the weight of the 747.

Version: 777-200
Engine: 2 Pratt & Whitney 4073A turbofans, 47,000 lbs (33,340 kg) thrust each
Wingspan: 197'8" (60.25 m)
Length: 209' (63.72 m)
Height: 60'6" (18.44 m)
Max. takeoff weight: 500,000 lbs (226,245 kg)
Cruising speed: 553 mph (890 km/h)
Service ceiling: 37,900' (11,555 m)
Range: 4,660 miles (7,500 km)

■ BOEING SA-307 STRATOLINER

Among the most outstanding aircraft of the WWII era, the four-engine SA-307 Stratoliner was the first commercial plane outfitted with a pressurized cabin, and therefore the first to be capable of high-altitude passenger service. Design of this innovative aircraft began in late 1934, which created enough interest that Pan Am and TWA had already ordered a number of Stratoliners before the prototype had even been built. The first SA-307 flew on December 31, 1938, and delivery to the two airlines began in 1940. Pan Am withdrew its Stratoliner fleet from service in 1948, TWA in 1951.

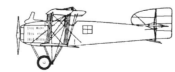

Version: SA-307B – **Engine:** 4 Wright GR-1820 Cyclone radials, 9-cylinder, air-cooled, 900 hp each – **Wingspan:** 107'3" (32.69 m) – **Length:** 74'4" (22.66 m) – **Height:** 20'9" (6.33 m) – **Max. takeoff weight:** 42,000 lbs (19,050 kg) – **Cruising speed:** 222 mph (357 km/h) – **Service ceiling:** 26,200' (7,985 m) – **Range:** 2,300 miles (3,700 km)

■ BREGUET 14

Version: 14T – **Engine:** Renault 12FCX, V-12, liquid-cooled, 300 hp – **Wingspan:** 47'2" (14.36 m) – **Length:** 29'6" (8.99 m) – **Height:** 10'9" (3.30 m) – **Max. takeoff weight:** 4,375 lbs (1,984 kg) – **Max. speed:** 78 mph (125 km/h) at 6,560' (2,000 m) – **Service ceiling:** 14,750' (4,500 m) – **Range:** 2,860 miles (460 km)

The earliest commercial routes were opened and serviced by planes designed for military use. The Breguet 14T, which enjoyed the same success after WWI as it had during it, did just this: the plane opened the first commercial route between Toulouse and Barcelona on Christmas Day, 1918, and subsequently pioneered several African routes.

■ BREGUET XIX SUPER TR

On September 1, 1930 the bright red Breguet XIX Point d'Interrogation ('Question Mark') took off from Le Bourget airfield bound for New York. The goal was to cross the Atlantic in the opposite direction of Lindbergh's historic flight made three years earlier. And the tough little biplane succeeded. Piloted by Dieudonné Costes and Maurice Bellonte, the XIX covered the 3,700 miles in 37 hours 18 minutes, at an average speed of 104 mph.

Engine: Hispano-Suiza 12 Nb, V-12, liquid-cooled, 650 hp – **Wingspan:** 60' (18.30 m) – **Length:** 35'2" (10.72 m) – **Height:** 13'4" (4.06 m) – **Max. takeoff weight:** 14,800 lbs (6,700 kg) – **Max. speed:** 152 mph (245 km/h) at 3,000' (900 m) – **Service ceiling:** 22,000' (6,700 m) – **Range:** 5,900 miles (9,500 km)

■ CALDERARA HYDRO-RACER

Italian interest in the hydroplane was piqued in 1910 when Mario Calderara designed and built one at the La Spezia shipyards. Calderara, an army officer, was in fact the first Italian pilot, trained in 1909 by Orville Wright himself. The plane was not developed further, and in 1912 the Italian naval command requested Short Bros. to supply a number of S.41 hydroplanes.

Engine: Gnome rotary, 100 hp – **Wingspan:** 60'8" (18.50 m) – **Length:** 54'2" (16.50 m) – **Wing surface:** 753 sq ft (70 sq m) – **Max. takeoff weight:** 2,650 lbs (1,200 kg) – **Max. speed:** 62 mph (100 km/h) – **Range:** 6.5 hours

■ CURTISS–COX CACTUS KITTEN

Engine: Curtiss C-12, V-12, liquid-cooled, 435 hp – **Wingspan:** 20' (6.10 m) – **Length:** 19'6" (5.87 m) – **Height:** 8'6" (2.59 m) – **Empty weight:** 1,940 lbs (878 kg) – **Max. takeoff weight:** 2,410 lbs (1,090 kg) – **Max. speed:** 190 mph (306 km/h)

The Cactus Kitten, the only triplane ever to participate in sporting competitions, was the third in a series of racing planes built by Curtiss for the oil magnate S.E.J. Cox. The first two were a monoplane and biplane, respectively, designed for the Gordon Bennett Cup of 1920. The triplane, tested in October by Bert Acosta, demonstrated exceptional speed, but it still couldn't beat the Curtiss CR-1, which made up in turning speed what it lacked in open-throttle straight flight.

■ CURTISS CR-1

Engine: Curtiss CD-12, V-12, liquid-cooled, 405 hp – **Wingspan:** 22'8" (6.91 m) – **Length:** 21' (6.40 m) – **Height:** 8' (2.44 m) – **Empty weight:** 1,740 lbs (787 kg) – **Max. takeoff weight:** 2,170 lbs (982 kg) – **Max. speed:** 200 mph (322 km/h) – **Service ceiling:** 24,000' (7,315 m) – **Range:** 235 miles (378 km)

Considered the most aerodynamic plane of its time, the CR-1 was designed explicitly and exclusively for speed racing. On November 3, 1921 it took part in the annual Pulitzer Trophy Race, where pilot Bert Acosta crushed the hopes of his adversaries with an average speed of 177 miles per hour, taking home the prize.

■ CURTISS CR-3

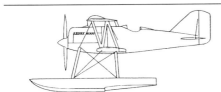

Engine: Curtiss D-12, V-12, liquid-cooled, 450 hp – **Wingspan:** 22'8" (6.91 m) – **Length:** 25' (7.63 m) – **Height:** 10'4" (3.15 m) – **Empty weight:** 2,124 lbs (961 kg) – **Max. takeoff weight:** 2,750 lbs (1,246 kg) **Max. speed:** 195 mph (314 km/h) – **Service ceiling:** 12,900' (5,852 m) **Range:** 520 miles (840 km)

The Curtiss CR-3 hydro-racer, a 'navalized' and improved version of the already superb CR-1, was one of the highest expressions of a generation of competition planes that prospered in the America of the 1920s. The main modifications with regard to the CR-1, apart from the conspicuous addition of pontoons, consisted in amplifying the tail elements' surface areas and installing flow radiators on the wings. Two CR-3's finished first and second in the 1923 Schneider Cup (the 7th competition).

■ CURTISS GOLDEN FLYER

Derived from the Golden Bug and modified for greater speed, the Golden Flyer took part in the

Grande Semaine d'Aviation de la Champagne (more commonly known as the Reims Air Meet) in August 1909. The plane proved itself to be one of the finest of its era, winning the Gordon Bennett Trophy on August 28 and the Prix de la Vitesse the following day. In an further distinction, a Golden Flyer made the first-ever takeoff and landing on the deck of a warship.

Engine: Curtiss V-8, water-cooled, 50 hp **Wingspan:** 28'9" (8.76 m) **Length:** 28'5" (8.66 m) **Height:** 9' (2.74 m) **Wing surface:** 256 sq ft (23.79 sq m) **Empty weight:** 550 lbs (249 kg) **Max. takeoff weight:** 830 lbs (376 kg) **Max. speed:** 45 mph (72 km/h)

■ CURTISS HYDRO

After the success of his Golden Flyer of 1909, Glenn Hammond Curtiss began developing a long series of hydroplanes that would qualify him as the best designer, builder, and pilot of this type of aircraft. On January 11, 1911 a modified Golden Flyer made the world's first water takeoff, and six months later the US Navy ordered an optimized version from Curtiss, designated A.1. When Theodore G. Ellyson climbed aboard the A.1, he not only became the first Navy pilot, but effectively gave birth to naval aviation.

Version: A-1 – **Engine:** Curtiss V-8, water-cooled, 75 hp – **Wingspan:** 37' (11.28 m) – **Length:** 27'8" (8.43 m) – **Height:** 9'4" (2.84 m) – **Wing surface:** 330 sq ft (30.75 sq m) – **Max. takeoff weight:** 1,580 lbs (715 kg) – **Max. speed:** 78 mph (105 km/h)

■ CURTISS R3C

The R3C hydroplane was similar in most ways to the R2C, which the Navy had developed to compete in the 1923 Pulitzer Trophy competition. The notable exception was its new 610-hp engine, which powered it to victory in both the Schneider Cup and the Pulitzer Trophy of 1925, eliminating any possible doubts as to the paramount quality of Curtiss hydroplanes.

Version: R3C-2 **Engine:** Curtiss V-1400, V-12, liquid-cooled, 610 hp **Wingspan:** 22' (6.71 m) **Length:** 20'2" (6.15 m) **Height:** 10'4" (3.15 m) **Empty weight:** 2,140 lbs (968 kg) **Max. takeoff weight:** 2,750 lbs (1,245 kg) **Max. speed:** 265 mph (426 km/h) **Service ceiling:** 26,400' (8,050 m) **Range:** 250 miles (402 km)

■ CURTISS T.32 CONDOR

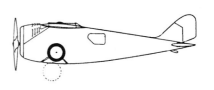

Engine: 2 Wright Cyclones, 9-cylinder radials, air-cooled, 760 hp each – **Wingspan:** 82' (25 m) – **Length:** 48'7" (14.81 m) – **Height:** 16'4" (4.98 m) – **Max. takeoff weight:** 17,520 lbs (7,927 kg) – **Cruising speed:** 145 mph (233 km/h) – **Service ceiling:** 23,000' (7,011 m) – **Range:** 650 miles (1,045 km)

The T.32 Condor was the last civil transport biplane built in America. The 45 planes produced by Curtiss went into service for Eastern Air Transport and American Airways in 1933. But despite its considerable safety and comfort – it was the first plane to be outfitted with sleeping berths for night flights – the Condor soon had to give way to the more modern Boeing 247.

■ DAYTON-WRIGHT R.B.

Engine: Hall-Scott, 6-cylinder inline, liquid-cooled, 250 hp – **Wingspan:** 21'2" (6.45 m) – **Length:** 22'8" (6.91 m) – **Height:** 8' (2.44 m) – **Empty weight:** 1,400 lbs (635 kg) – **Max. takeoff weight:** 1,850 lbs (839 kg) – **Max. speed:** 200 mph (322 km/h)

For the last of the illustrious Gordon Bennett races, the USA developed the Dayton-Wright R.B, a small but fast monoplane with a sleek aerodynamic line. Designed with the help of Orville Wright, it was distinctive for its plywood and balsa structure, manually retractable landing gear, and its completely enclosed cockpit. Though it didn't win the race, its several design innovations exerted a lasting influence.

■ DE HAVILLAND D.H.66 HERCULES

Built to transport mail, cargo and up to seven passengers throughout the British Empire, the Hercules worked so well for Imperial Airways that West Australian Airways adopted it as well. This hefty trimotor biplane had a wood-and-metal structure, with a skin made entirely of canvas. The planes in service with the Australian airline were modified to accommodate twice the number of passengers by covering the cockpit and reorganizing the interior.

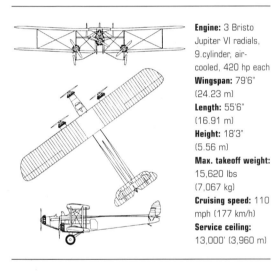

Engine: 3 Bristo Jupiter VI radials, 9.cylinder, air-cooled, 420 hp each
Wingspan: 79'6" (24.23 m)
Length: 55'6" (16.91 m)
Height: 18'3" (5.56 m)
Max. takeoff weight: 15,620 lbs (7,067 kg)
Cruising speed: 110 mph (177 km/h)
Service ceiling: 13,000' (3,960 m)

■ DE HAVILLAND D.H.88 COMET

Spectacular distance and endurance flights were the specialty of this streamlined British twin-engine, originally built to participate in the great Britain-Australia raid of 1933, held to celebrate the centennial of Queen Victoria's birth. The Comet won the race with a flight time of 70 hours 54 minutes, and later went on to claim an impressive series of records that earned it a well-deserved place of honor in the history of aviation.

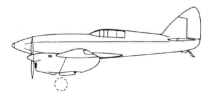

Engine: 2 de Havilland Gypsy Six Rs, 6-cylinder inline air-cooled, 230 hp each – **Wingspan:** 44' (13.41 m) – **Length:** 29' (8.83 m) – **Height:** 10' (3.05 m) – **Empty weight:** 2,850 lbs (1,288 kg) – **Max. takeoff weight:** 5,325 lbs (2,410 kg) – **Max. speed:** 237 mph (381 km/h) – **Service ceiling:** 19,000' (5,790 m) – **Range:** 2,900 miles (4,700 km)

■ DE HAVILLAND D.H.106 COMET

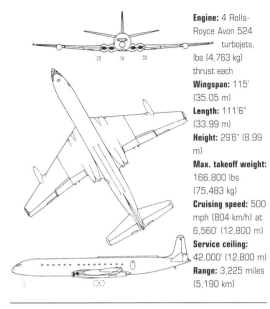

Engine: 4 Rolls-Royce Avon 524 turbojets, lbs (4,763 kg) thrust each
Wingspan: 115' (35.05 m)
Length: 111'6" (33.99 m)
Height: 29'6" (8.99 m)
Max. takeoff weight: 166,800 lbs (75,483 kg)
Cruising speed: 500 mph (804 km/h) at 6,560' (12,800 m)
Service ceiling: 42,000' (12,800 m)
Range: 3,225 miles (5,190 km)

The Comet story began in 1944. De Havilland dusted off its D.H.88 project to create a jet-powered commercial liner for the world premium North Atlantic route. The going was tough: five years before the prototype flew in July 1949; two more before BOAC began taking delivery of the Comet, and not until 1952 could BOAC launch the first regular London-to-Johannesburg passenger service. It was worth the wait; the Comet was an immediate success worldwide. Then disaster struck: on three separate occasions, Comets exploded in flight due to a structural flaw which created a deadly decompression. It was back to the drawing board. The result was the Comet 4, which appeared in 1958, but by then the market had been all but monopolized Boeing and Douglas jets. Production went ahead nevertheless, de Havilland having found a steady demand from South American and African airlines.

■ DEMOISELLE 20

Designed by Santos-Dumont, this elegant monoplane was built in a dozen or so units, some of which were sold to amateur aviation enthusiasts looking for an affordable way to participate in the newborn phenomenon. The last Demoiselle was built in 1910.

Engine: Dutheil-Chalmers (Darracq), 2-cylinder, water-cooled, 35 hp – **Wingspan:** 16'9" (5.10 m) – **Length:** 26'3" (8.00 m) – **Height:** 7'10" (2.40 m) – **Wing surface:** 110 sq ft (10.20 sq m) – **Max. takeoff weight:** 316 lbs (143 kg) – **Max. speed:** 56 mph (90 km/h)

■ DEPERDUSSIN HYDRO-RACER

In its wheeled version, the Deperdussin hydroplane won the 1912 Gordon Bennett Trophy; in 1913 it won the first Schneider Cup competition. This monoplane, with its plywood fuselage and clean, aerodynamic line, was the first aircraft to break the 200km/h (124 mph) barrier.

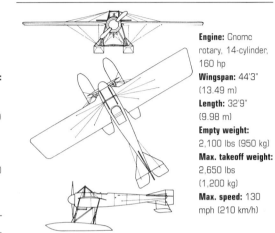

Engine: Gnome rotary, 14-cylinder, 160 hp
Wingspan: 44'3" (13.49 m)
Length: 32'9" (9.98 m)
Empty weight: 2,100 lbs (950 kg)
Max. takeoff weight: 2,650 lbs (1,200 kg)
Max. speed: 130 mph (210 km/h)

■ DEWOITINE D.338

The last and the best transport plane built in France prior to WWII was the Dewoitine D.338, an elegant and modern trimotor. The plane first flew in 1935, and Air France put it into service the following year to cover the most prestigious routes to Europe, South America, Africa and the Far East. After the war, 8 of the surviving 9 D.338s were used to serve the Paris-Nice route. A total of 31 were produced.

Engine: 3 Hispano-Suiza 9V 16/17 radials, 9-cylinder, air cooled, 650 hp each – **Wingspan:** 96'3" (29.35 m) – **Length:** 72'7" (22.13 m) – **Max. takeoff weight:** 24,650 lbs (11,150 kg) – **Cruising speed:** 162 mph (260 km/h) – **Service ceiling:** 16,000' (4,900 m) – **Range:** 1,200 miles (1,950 km)

■ DORNIER DO.J WAL

For fifteen years these big odd-looking hydroplanes were among the most widespread of their category. The prototype was completed in Germany in 1922, but as the WWI treaty prohibited German production, CMASA in Italy built 150 of the total 300 units. Italy was also the Do.J's main user for a while. In 1933 improved German-built versions appeared, mainly used forpostal runs between Germany and South America. As a transatlantic mail truck, the trusty Dornier made 328 successful crossings.

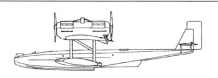

Engine: 2 Rolls-Royce Eagle IXs, V-12s, liquid-cooled, 360 hp each – **Wingspan:** 73'10" (22.50 m) – **Length:** 56'8" (17.25 m) – **Height:** 17' (5.20 m) – **Max. takeoff weight:** 12,600 lbs (5,700 kg) – **Cruising speed:** 87 mph (140 km/h) – **Service ceiling:** 11,500' (3,500 m) – **Range:** 1.370 miles (2,200 km)

■ DOUGLAS DC-3

Douglas' DC-1 and DC-2 transport planes burst into aviation's aristocracy, but the legendary DC-3 was a king. Over time the DC-3 underwent innumerable modifications, above all to the engines and interior configuration. After debuting with American Airlines on the nonstop New York-Chicago route in June 1936, every American and most European airlines adopted the DC-3, also used extensively as a military transport. The DC-3 made Douglas a ruling force in world aviation for almost a half-century.

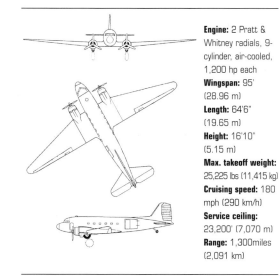

Engine: 2 Pratt & Whitney radials, 9-cylinder, air-cooled, 1,200 hp each
Wingspan: 95' (28.96 m)
Length: 64'6" (19.65 m)
Height: 16'10" (5.15 m)
Max. takeoff weight: 25,225 lbs (11,415 kg)
Cruising speed: 180 mph (290 km/h)
Service ceiling: 23,200' (7,070 m)
Range: 1,300 miles (2,091 km)

■ DOUGLAS DC-4

Engine: 2 Pratt & Whitney R-2000 Twin Wasp radials, 14-cylinder, air-cooled, 1,450 hp each – **Wingspan:** 117'6" (35.81 m) – **Length:** 93'10" (28.62 m) – **Height:** 27'6" (8.38 m) – **Max. takeoff weight:** 74,000 lbs (33,475 kg) – **Cruising speed:** 227 mph (365 km/h) at 10,000' (3,050 m) – **Service ceiling:** 22,300' (6,800 m) – **Range:** 2,140 miles (3,444 km)

The DC-4 was intended to repeat the DC-3's commercial sector success, but in 1942, before the first passenger version was built, the military monopolized production. The 1,162 DC-4 military transports made 79,642 wartime transoceanic crossings. At war's end Douglas revived the commercial program, but built only 79 planes, one of which, the 'Sacred Cow,' became the first official presidential transport.

■ DOUGLAS DC-6

Version: DC-6B
Engine: 4 Pratt & Whitney R-2800-CB16 Double Wasp radials, 18-cylinder, air-cooled, 2,400 hp each
Wingspan: 117'6" (35.81 m)
Length: 105'8" (32.20 m)
Height: 28'5" (8.66 m)
Max. takeoff weight: 100,300 lbs (45,400 kg)
Cruising speed: 307 mph (494 km/h) at 22,400' (6,830 m)
Service ceiling: 25,000' (7,620 m)
Range: 3,900 miles (6,270 km)

The Douglas DC-6 predictably followed the DC-4. Larger, more powerful, with a pressurized passenger cabin, it achieved the commercial success denied its predecessor. Ironically, the project was initiated by the military. The prototype flew on February 15, 1946 and, with military orders filled, commercial production began. The airlines responded immediately and enthusiastically. The DC-6's career lasted until the 1970s.

■ DOUGLAS DC-7

Version: DC-7C – **Engine:** 2 Wright R-3350-18EA1 Turbo Compound radials, 18-cylinder, air-cooled, 3,400 hp each – **Wingspan:** 127'3" (38.80 m) – **Length:** 112'3" (34.23 m) – **Height:** 30'9" (9.37 m) – **Max. takeoff weight:** 139,150 lbs (63,106 kg) – **Cruising speed:** 300 mph (486 km/h) at 23,300' (7,106 m) – **Service ceiling:** 28,400' (8,656 m) – **Range:** 5,975 miles (9,616 km)

The DC-7 was the response to an American Airlines' request for a plane able to compete with Lockheed's Super Constellation, ordered by rival TWA. Douglas designed a larger, sturdier and faster plane, the prototype of which flew on May 18, 1953. The final and best version of the DC-7 was the C (first flight December 1955), in which the problems of the preceding series – excessive noise and inadequate fuel capacity – were fully resolved.

■ DOUGLAS DC-8

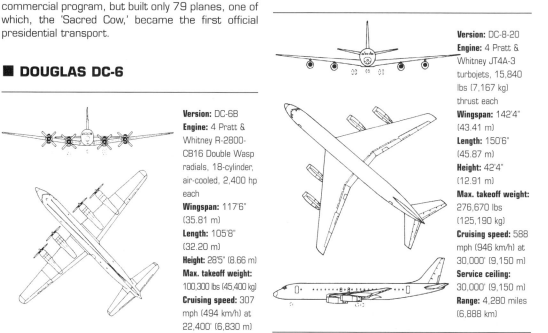

Version: DC-8-20
Engine: 4 Pratt & Whitney JT4A-3 turbojets, 15,840 lbs (7,167 kg) thrust each
Wingspan: 142'4" (43.41 m)
Length: 150'6" (45.87 m)
Height: 42'4" (12.91 m)
Max. takeoff weight: 276,670 lbs (125,190 kg)
Cruising speed: 588 mph (946 km/h) at 30,000' (9,150 m)
Service ceiling: 30,000' (9,150 m)
Range: 4,280 miles (6,888 km)

The DC-8 was the Boeing 707's direct competitor, and every bit as good a plane. The project was launched on June 7, 1955. Pan American was the first airline to order the new jetliner. The commercial success of the various versions of the DC-8 was such that by 1979 the worldwide fleet approached 500 planes.

■ DOUGLAS DWC/0-5 WORLD CRUISER

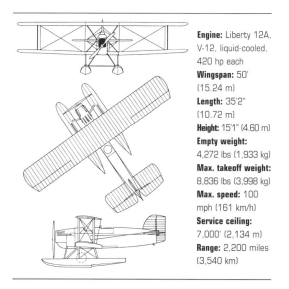

Engine: Liberty 12A, V-12, liquid-cooled, 420 hp each
Wingspan: 50' (15.24 m)
Length: 35'2" (10.72 m)
Height: 15'1" (4.60 m)
Empty weight: 4,272 lbs (1,933 kg)
Max. takeoff weight: 8,836 lbs (3,998 kg)
Max. speed: 100 mph (161 km/h)
Service ceiling: 7,000' (2,134 m)
Range: 2,200 miles (3,540 km)

Born as a military plane, it was modified and renamed World Cruiser for an historic undertaking of 1924: a round-the-world distance and endurance raid, leaving Seattle on April 6. Of the four DWCs (named Seattle, Boston, Chicago and New Orleans) that started, only two returned; the others were lost in flight. Flight time was 371 hours, average speed 75 mph.

■ DOUGLAS X-3

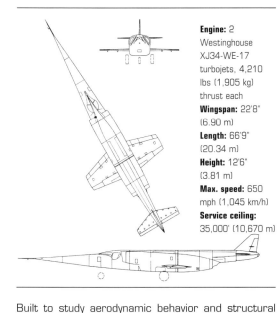

Engine: 2 Westinghouse XJ34-WE-17 turbojets, 4,210 lbs (1,905 kg) thrust each
Wingspan: 22'8" (6.90 m)
Length: 66'9" (20.34 m)
Height: 12'6" (3.81 m)
Max. speed: 650 mph (1,045 km/h)
Service ceiling: 35,000' (10,670 m)

Built to study aerodynamic behavior and structural thresholds in prolonged supersonic flight, the sole X-3 ever built first flew on October 20, 1952. It remained active for three years, but underpowered engines prevented it from achieving the established goals. The X-3's short-winged, knife-like configuration earned it the nickname 'Stiletto.'

■ EMBRAER 170

Version: 170 LR – **Engine:** 2 General Electric CF34-8E turbofans, 14,150 lbs (6,400 kg) thrust each – **Wingspan:** 85'3" (26.00 m) – **Length:** 98'1" (29.90 m) – **Height:** 31'9" (9.67 m) – **Empty weight:** 45,750 lbs (20,700 kg) – **Max. takeoff weight:** 79,550 lbs (35,990 kg) – **Cruising speed:** 540 mph (870 km/h) – **Service ceiling:** 41,000' (12,500 m) – **Range:** 2,417miles (3,889 km)

In the crowded regional air transport marketplace, the family of twinjets built by the Brazilian company Embraer emerged one of the most interesting phenomena of the 1990s. The small 50-seat commuter ERJ-145 (first flight August 1995) and its cousin ERJ-135 were ordered by the hundreds by numerous American and European airlines. Hoping to repeat their success with a more capacious and efficient plane, in February 1999, Embraer announced the new 70-seat ERJ-170 and three sub-series (ERJ-175, 190 and 195), with passenger capacities of 78, 98 and 108, respectively. The new short- to medium-range jets had been completely redesigned and updated with respect to their already highly advanced predecessors, especially in terms of range.

Alitalia was among the many airlines that had placed orders, and it received its first six 170s in

November 2003 and holds an option on six more. Alitalia uses the Brazilian twinjets to connect its own minor airports with the major European hubs. The 170 LR fleet currently serves the Rome-Vienna route, and flies out of Milan's Linate airport to Vienna, Frankfurt, Brussels, Naples and Catania.

■ ETRICH TAUBE

Designed in Austria by Igo Etrich, the bird-like Taube (meaning 'dove') was one of the best early monoplanes. The prototype was presented in 1910, then contracted out to a dozen manufacturers, who produced it in different configurations and dimensions, using a variety of different engines. It served in WWI, mostly as a reconnaissance scout.

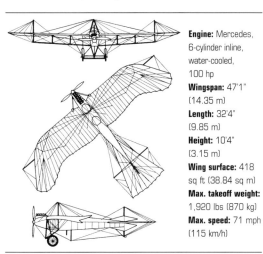

Engine: Mercedes, 6-cylinder inline, water-cooled, 100 hp
Wingspan: 47'1" (14.35 m)
Length: 32'4" (9.85 m)
Height: 10'4" (3.15 m)
Wing surface: 418 sq ft (38.84 sq m)
Max. takeoff weight: 1,920 lbs (870 kg)
Max. speed: 71 mph (115 km/h)

■ FARMAN F.60 GOLIATH

Introduced in 1918 as a bomber, this large biplane was successfully transformed for civilian use and became the most import transport plane of the immediate post-war period. Practically every major European airline purchased the Farman, which also served in less aeronautically developed countries like Czechoslovakia, Romania and South America. It also had a career as a competition plane, breaking several world records.

Engine: 2 Salmson C.M.9 radials, 9-cylinder, liquid cooled, 260 hp each
Wingspan: 80'3" (24.46 m)
Length: 47' (14.33 m)
Max. takeoff weight: 10,540 lbs (4,770 kg)
Cruising speed: 75 mph (120 km/h) at 6,560' (2,000 m)
Service ceiling: 13,120' (4,000 m)
Range: 250 miles (400 km)

■ FIAT G.18V

Introduced in 1935, the G.18V was Italy's most modern civil transport aircraft of the period. Overall configuration and many specific characteristics were quite similar to those of the first Douglas DCs, in some cases even superior. Avio Linee Italiane bought the twin-engine Fiat and initially used it on domestic routes. In 1938 service was open to London and other European capitals. With the outbreak of WWII, the plane was adapted for troop transport duties.

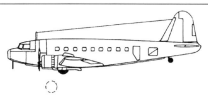

Engine: 2 Fiat A.80 RC 41 radials, 18-cylinder, air-cooled, 1,000 hp each – **Wingspan:** 82' (25.00 m) – **Length:** 61'9" (18.81 m) – **Height:** 16'5" (5.01 m) – **Max. takeoff weight:** 23,900 lbs (10,800 kg) – **Cruising speed:** 250 mph (340 km/h) – **Service ceiling:** 28,500' (8,700 m) – **Range:** 1,000 miles (1,610 km)

■ FOCKE WULF FW.200 CONDOR

In 1936, in an effort to compete with the Douglas DC-3, Deutsche Lufthansa commissioned Focke Wulf to design a world-class four-engine passenger plane. Of the 12 Condors built, Lufthansa bought 10 and the other two were acquired by the Sindacato Condor Limitada of Brazil. Over the course of the war all but two of Lufthansa's Condor fleet were militarized. The last flight under the company flag took place on April 14, 1945, from Barcelona to Berlin.

Version: Fw.200A
Engine: 4 BMW 132 G radials, 9-cylinder, air-cooled, 720 hp each
Wingspan: 108'3" (33.00 m)
Length: 78'3" (23.85 m)
Height: 20'8" (6.30 m)
Max. takeoff weight: 32,250 lbs (14,600 kg)
Cruising speed: 200 mph (322 km/h) at 9,850' (3,000 m)
Service ceiling: 22,000' (6,700 m)
Range: 777 miles (1,250 km)

■ FOKKER C-2 AMERICA

As fine a plane as it was, the trimotor Fokker C-2 America is perhaps best known for what it failed to do. On June 29, 1927 four men – Richard Byrd,

Bert Acosta, Bert Balchen and George Noville – took off from New York with the intention of reaching Paris, but weather conditions at Le Bourget forced a sea landing just off the coast of Vers-sur-Mer.

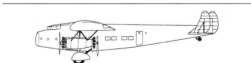

Engine: 3 Wright R-730 Whirlwind radials, 9-cylinder, air-cooled, 220 hp each – **Wingspan:** 108'3" (21.70 m) – **Length:** 78'3" (14.80 m) – **Height:** 20'8" (3.69 m) – **Max. takeoff weight:** 32,250 lbs (3,360 kg) – **Cruising speed:** 200 mph (177 km/h) – **Service ceiling:** 22,000' (5,000 m)

■ FOKKER F.32

The F.32 was the largest Fokker plane built in America, and also the last civil transport designed by the great Dutch engineer for manufacture overseas. With its 99-foot wingspan and 32-seat capacity, the F.32 was the perfect swansong for the 'Flying Dutchman,' as Anton Fokker was known, before General Motors absorbed his American subsidiary in 1929. The plane was developed that same year, making its first flight in September. Two airlines, Universal and Western Air Express, pre-ordered the F.32, but after an accident that destroyed the prototype only Western went through with the acquisition of five planes. The F.32 served the San Francisco-Los Angeles route, distinguishing itself as much for dependability as for excellent performance characteristics. The US Army evaluated the plane for use as a military transport, but never followed through on the initiative.

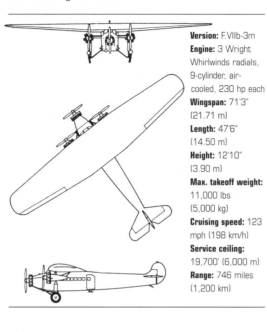

Engine: 4 Pratt & Whitney Hornet radials, 9-cylinder, air-cooled, 575 hp each – **Wingspan:** 99' (30.18 m) – **Length:** 69'9" (21.28 m) – **Height:** 16'6" (5.03 m) – **Max. takeoff weight:** 24,275 lbs (10,985 kg) – **Cruising speed:** 123 mph (198 km/h) – **Service ceiling:** 13,500' (4,115 m) – **Range:** 740 miles (1,191 km)

■ FOKKER F.VII

The most popular of the series of commercial transports that Fokker built was the F.VII, a robust and versatile high-wing trimotor. The F.VIIb-3m version (designed in 1928 at the request of the Australian polar explorer Hubert Wilkins, who wanted an airplane suited to arduous long-distance flying) vaunts a number of extraordinary achievements. Among them was the Pacific crossing from San Francisco to Brisbane of 1928, when Charles Kingsford Smith flew a model named 'The Southern Cross' 7,800 miles in just under 84 hours. In that same year, Amelia Earhart flew the only F.VIIb-3m seaplane ever built to become the first woman to cross the Atlantic. Then in 1928, the

plane opened the first route to New Zealand, while about the same time KLM was operating the plane on what was the world's longest regular passenger route, from Amsterdam to Jakarta. And in the summer of 1930 Kingsford Smith made his epic 50,000-mile circumnavigation in 'The Southern Cross.' In the commercial sector the Fokker was equally successful. The parent company built 70 planes and licensed out the construction of approximately 70 more to satisfy the demand from the world's great airlines.

Version: F.VIIb-3m **Engine:** 3 Wright Whirlwinds radials, 9-cylinder, air-cooled, 230 hp each **Wingspan:** 71'3" (21.71 m) **Length:** 47'6" (14.50 m) **Height:** 12'10" (3.90 m) **Max. takeoff weight:** 11,000 lbs (5,000 kg) **Cruising speed:** 123 mph (198 km/h) **Service ceiling:** 19,700' (6,000 m) **Range:** 746 miles (1,200 km)

■ FOKKER T.2

The success enjoyed by Anton Fokker's first two commercial transports, the F.II and F.III, was not shared by the third, the F.IV of 1921. Derived from its predecessors, with greater dimensions and capacity (10 passengers), the plane failed to find buyers among the airlines of the period. The only two planes ever built were sold to the US Army, which operated them for a while as military transports under the designation T.2. One of the two planes had an occasion to dress up in civilian garb for a sporting feat: in May 1923 pilots McReady and Kelly made a nonstop coast-to-coast crossing of the American continent in world record time. The other plane, redesignated A.2, was transformed into an air ambulance.

Engine: Liberty 12-A, V-12, liquid-cooled, 420 hp – **Wingspan:** 99' (24.79 m) – **Length:** 69'9" (14.79 m) – **Height:** 16'6" (3.60 m) – **Max. takeoff weight:** 24,275 lbs (4,880 kg) – **Max. speed:** 123 mph (155 km/h)

■ FORD 4.AT TRIMOTOR

With more than 200 of them built, the Ford Trimotor was used on domestic routes by virtually every American airline. As such, this hardworking

aircraft, nicknamed 'Tin Goose,' played a determining role in pioneering the now vast American air traffic network. The Trimotor remained in service with the majors until 1934, when the Douglas DC-2 displaced it. After that, they were sold off for use as personal or corporate planes. The Trimotor's greatest claim to fame, however, is linked to that of Admiral Richard Byrd, who used the plane, named 'Floyd Bennett' to commemorate the pilot of this name, to become, on November 29, 1929, the first man to reach the South Pole.

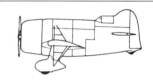

Engine: 3 Wright J-6 Whirlwind radials, 9-cylinder, air-cooled, 300 hp each – **Wingspan:** 74' (22.56 m) – **Length:** 49'10" (15.19 m) – **Height:** 11' (3.58 m) – **Max. takeoff weight:** 10,160 lbs (4,598 kg) – **Cruising speed:** 107 mph (172 km/h) – **Service ceiling:** 16,500' (5,030 m) – **Range:** 570 miles (917 km)

■ GEE BEE R-1

Engine: Pratt & Whitney Wasp Jr. radial, 9-cylinder, air-cooled, 800 hp – **Wingspan:** 25' (7.62 m) – **Length:** 17'9" (5.41 m) – **Height:** 8'1" (2.47 m) – **Empty weight:** 1,845 lbs (835 kg) – **Max. takeoff weight:** 3,080 lbs (1,395 kg) – **Max. speed:** 296 mph (476 km/h)

The Gee Bee family was designed for one task alone: speed racing. From the first version to the last, every Gee Bee adhered to the same structural concept: the entire plane was built around a disproportionately huge radial engine, with body dimensions kept to a minimum. To compensate for the forward weight of the motor, the cockpit was incorporated into the tail. The R-1 took the Thompson Trophy of 1932.

■ GEE BEE Z

Engine: Pratt & Whitney Wasp Jr. radial, 9-cylinder, air-cooled, 535 hp – **Wingspan:** 23'6" (7.16 m) – **Length:** 15'1" (4.60 m) – **Max. takeoff weight:** 2,285 lbs (1,034 kg) – **Max. speed:** 286 mph (460 km/h) – **Range:** 1,000 miles (1,610 km)

Tiny and stout like a flying cork, the Gee Bee Z was the most famous American competition plane of its day. Designed by Robert Hall, production of this model was discontinued just as a Z was busy winning the 1931 Thompson Trophy with an unbeatable median speed of 193 miles per hour.

■ HANDLEY PAGE H.P.42

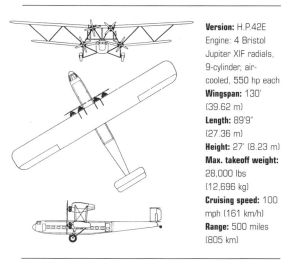

Version: H.P.42E
Engine: 4 Bristol Jupiter XIF radials, 9-cylinder, air-cooled, 550 hp each
Wingspan: 130' (39.62 m)
Length: 89'9" (27.36 m)
Height: 27' (8.23 m)
Max. takeoff weight: 28,000 lbs (12,696 kg)
Cruising speed: 100 mph (161 km/h)
Range: 500 miles (805 km)

From 1931 to 1939, the Handley Page H.P.42E was the image of Imperial Airways, Britain's premier airline. Slow, majestic and supremely safe, these enormous biplanes continued to operate even when Britain's airports were filling up with rather more modern aircraft. The H.P.42E proudly stood for air travel that placed passenger safety and comfort above all else. The prototype, baptized 'Hannibal,' first flew on November 17, 1930; a test run for a London-Paris link was made in June 1931. A total of eight H.P.42's were built for Imperial, subdivided into the airline's European and Asian divisions (42W and 42E, respectively). After a decade of service and more than 10 million miles of flight, the H.P.42 could make the enviable claim of never having had a single accident. It was the first four-engine aircraft ever built, and ranked as the world's largest plane for a number of years.

■ HOWARD DGA-6 MR. MULLIGAN

Engine: Pratt & Whitney Wasp radial, 9-cylinder, air-cooled, 830 hp – **Wingspan:** 31'8" (9.65 m) – **Length:** 25' (7.64 m) – **Height:** 11' (3.35 m) – **Empty weight:** 2,600 lbs (1,176 kg) – **Max. takeoff weight:** 4,220 lbs (1,909 kg) – **Max. speed:** 292 mph (470 km/h) at 11,000 (3,350 m) – **Range:** 1,750 miles (2,815 km)

The last few Thompson Trophy races showcased this elegant high-wing monoplane, seemingly more a leisure plane than a racer. But on September 2, 1935, 'Mr. Mulligan' took the trophy with an average speed of 220 mph – just two days after having won the equally prestigious Bendix Trophy. The DGA ('Darn Good Aircraft') was no empty boast.

■ HUGHES H-1

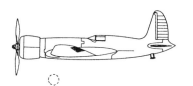

Engine: Pratt & Whitney Twin Wasp radial, 14-cylinder, air-cooled, 1,000 hp – **Wingspan:** 32' (9.75 m) – **Length:** 28'2" (8.58 m) – **Max. takeoff weight:** 5,525 lbs (2,500 kg) – **Max. speed:** 365 mph (587 km/h) – **Service ceiling:** 20,000' (6,100 m) – **Range:** 2,500 miles (4,023 km)

One of the last American racers, the Hughes H-1 was the pet project of the 'Flying Billionaire,' Howard Hughes, who built the plane in 1935 with the express aim of winning the Thompson and Bendix trophies. The H-1 was unable to participate in either race, but on September 13, 1935 it did set the world speed record at 352 mph.

■ HYDRAVION FABRE

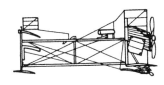

Engine: Gnome rotary, 7-cylinder, 50 hp each – **Wingspan:** 45'11" (14.00 m) – **Length:** 27'10" (8.50 m) – **Height:** 12' (3.66 m) – **Wing surface:** 183 sq ft (17 sq m) – **Max. takeoff weight:** 1,050 lbs (475 kg) – **Max. speed:** 55 mph (89 km/h)

The father of the hydroplane was the French engineer, Henri Fabre. While in Europe and America everyone clamored to build machines that would take off and land on the ground, Fabre had been working since 1909 to build one that would do so on water. His first attempt was unsuccessful, but the second went down in history: on March 28, 1910, in the harbor of La Mède, Fabre took off from the water's surface, flew 500 yards at about six feet of altitude, and landed safely on the water, thereby anticipating the American hydroplane king, Glenn Curtiss, by a full year.

■ ILYUSHIN IL-18

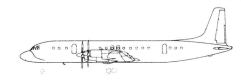

Engine: 4 Ivchenko AI-20K turboprops, 4,000 hp each – **Wingspan:** 122'8" (37.40 m) – **Length:** 117'9" (35.90 m) – **Height:** 33'4" (10.16 m) – **Max. takeoff weight:** 135,250 lbs (61,200 kg) – **Cruising speed:** 400 mph (644 km/h) at 26,250' (8,000 m) – **Service ceiling:** 35,250' (10,750 m) – **Range:** 3,000 miles (4,827 km)

An element of Aeroflot's early 1950s program to improve its fleet, the Ilyushin Il-18 immediately claimed a place as one of the best commercial turboprops in the world. Of the 500 or so planes constructed, 80 went into service for airlines of the Soviet alliance nations. The project was begun toward the end of 1954 and the prototype flew on June 4, 1957. After extensive testing and fine-tuning the Il-18 went into production, and on April 20, 1959 it made its first regular passenger flight under the Aeroflot flag. The original version of the 18 had a capacity of 80 passengers, which was quickly upped to 110 in the modified Il-18V. The last two production models were the D of 1962 and the E of 1965, each of them improving the avionics, cabin configuration and range of its predecessor.

■ ILYUSHIN IL-62

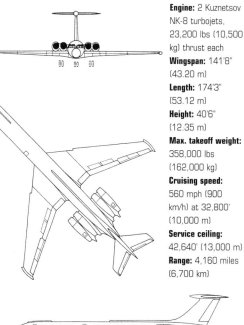

Engine: 2 Kuznetsov NK-8 turbojets, 23,200 lbs (10,500 kg) thrust each
Wingspan: 141'8" (43.20 m)
Length: 174'3" (53.12 m)
Height: 40'6" (12.35 m)
Max. takeoff weight: 358,000 lbs (162,000 kg)
Cruising speed: 560 mph (900 km/h) at 32,800' (10,000 m)
Service ceiling: 42,640' (13,000 m)
Range: 4,160 miles (6,700 km)

The first long-range quadrimotor commercial jet built in the Soviet Union was Ilyushin Il-62. It was a contemporary of the similar British BAC VC-10, characterized by the unusual coupling of the engines on either side of the tail. The project was officially announced on September 24, 1962. The plane was to have a 180-passenger capacity and a range capable of covering the distance between Moscow and New York, about 4,800 miles. The prototype flew in January 1963, and after a lengthy testing cycle Aeroflot assigned its new jetliner to the Moscow-Montreal route, which it first flew on September 15, 1967. A little less than a year later the Il-62s were reassigned, this time to New York. The principal variants were the M of 1971 and the MK of 1978, the main improvements in both being fuel economy and range, which approached 6,000 miles in the MK.

■ ILYUSHIN IL-86

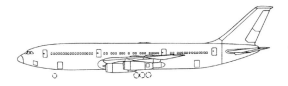

Engine: 4 Kuznetsov NK-86 turbojets, 28,750 lbs (13,000 kg) thrust each – **Wingspan:** 151'2" (46.08 m) – **Length:** 197'6" (60.21 m) – **Height:** 51'5" (15.68 m) – **Max. takeoff weight:** 455,250 lbs (206,000 kg) – **Cruising speed:** 590 mph (950 km/h) at 26,250' (11,000 m) – **Service ceiling:** 36,000' (11,000 m) – **Range:** 2,240 miles (3,600 km)

The Soviet Union's entry into the wide-body era was signaled by the Ilyushin Il-86, a 350-seat giant which was unable, however, to compete with its direct rival, the Boeing 747. The project was initiated in 1971 and the prototype flew for the first time on December 22, 1976. The Il-86 program's main objective was to activate regular 'jumbo jet' service to and from Moscow in time for the 1980 Olympic Games, which were to be held in the Soviet capital. But the development and testing phase went on much longer than planned, due in large part to problems with the Kuznetsov engines; these put out less power while consuming more fuel than its builders had anticipated. Passenger service didn't get underway until December 27, 1980, when the Il-86 flew the then domestic route between Moscow and Tashkent, Uzbekistan. International connections were inaugurated in July 1981 on the Moscow-East Berlin route.

■ JUNE BUG

Engine: Curtiss V-8, air-cooled, 40 hp – **Wingspan:** 45'11" (14.00 m) – **Max. takeoff weight:** 650 lbs (295 kg)

The June Bug, the American Experimental Association's third project, was also Glenn Curtiss's first. During the month of July 1908 this early biplane completed more than 30 successful takeoffs and landings. On July 4 of that year, Curtiss and the June Bug claimed the prize sponsored by *Scientific American* magazine for the first official flight of more than one kilometer: the Bug stayed in the air for 42.5 seconds, covering 1.551 kilometers, easily making the minimum distance. On August 29 Curtiss outdid himself by flying nearly four kilometers, or a little over two miles.

■ JUNKERS F.13

Despite vigilant Allied controls after the end of the WWI, the Germans managed to build, distribute and operate significant numbers of a superlative transport plane, the Junkers F.13. The career of the small monoplane, one of the first to be made entirely of metal, testifies to its contribution to commercial aviation: the 322 planes produced worked tirelessly

for practically the entire period between the two world wars, spread among 30 airlines in a dozen countries. Incredibly, the maiden flight of the F.13 prototype set a world load/altitude record, reaching 22,100 feet with eight passengers aboard. The first regular passenger flight of the F.13 was in 1921 with Junkers-Luftverkehr, transport division of the manufacturing giant. It finished its career with Lufthansa in 1938.

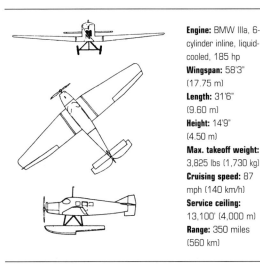

Engine: BMW IIIa, 6-cylinder inline, liquid-cooled, 185 hp

Wingspan: 58'3" (17.75 m)

Length: 31'6" (9.60 m)

Height: 14'9" (4.50 m)

Max. takeoff weight: 3,825 lbs (1,730 kg)

Cruising speed: 87 mph (140 km/h)

Service ceiling: 13,100' (4,000 m)

Range: 350 miles (560 km)

■ JUNKERS JU.52/3M

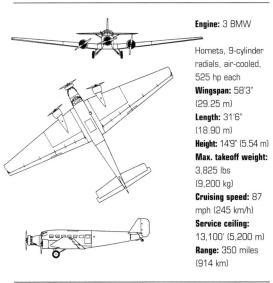

Engine: 3 BMW Hornets, 9-cylinder radials, air-cooled, 525 hp each

Wingspan: 58'3" (29.25 m)

Length: 31'6" (18.90 m)

Height: 14'9" (5.54 m)

Max. takeoff weight: 3,825 lbs (9,200 kg)

Cruising speed: 87 mph (245 km/h)

Service ceiling: 13,100' (5,200 m)

Range: 350 miles (914 km)

Surely the most renowned of all German transport planes, the Junkers Ju.52/3m made its prototype flight on April 30, 1931. Before establishing itself as an indispensable military cargo transport – the Luftwaffe had nearly 5,000 of them built during the course of WWII – the Junkers trimotor played an important commercial role. Between 1932 and 1939 no fewer than 200 Ju.52s were produced for approximately 30 airlines from all over the world. At the end of 1940 Lufthansa was operating a fleet of 78, deploying them on its European and Asian routes. The career of the Ju.52/3m extended well beyond the war, particularly in Spain and France.

■ LAIRD LC-DW-300 SOLUTION

Engine: Pratt & Whitney Wasp Jr. radial, 9-cylinder, air-cooled, 470 hp – **Wingspan:** 21' (6.40 m) – **Length:** 19'6" (5.94 m) – **Empty weight:** 1,380 lbs (625 kg) – **Max. takeoff weight:** 1,900 lbs (860 kg) – **Max. speed:** 202 mph (325 km/h)

With the exception of its radial engine and fendered landing gear, the Solution follows the line of Glenn Curtiss's racers. The biplane, designed and built by Matt Laird in just under a month, won the first Thompson Trophy at the 1930 National Air Races with an average speed of 202 mph.

■ LATÉCOÈRE 300

Engine: 4 Hispano-Suiza 12 Nbrs, V-12, liquid-cooled, 650 hp each – **Wingspan:** 145' (44.19 m) – **Length:** 85'10" (26.18 m) – **Max. takeoff weight:** 50,800 lbs (23,000 kg) – **Cruising speed:** 100 mph (161 km/h) – **Service ceiling:** 15,000' (4,600 m) – **Range:** 3,000 miles (4,825 km)

One of the best hydroplanes of the 1930s, the Latécoère 300 was a typical product of the era of the great transoceanic crossings. This big quadrimotor with a central fuselage ski was designed in 1931 at the request of the French government, which needed a postal transport capable of hauling a 1-ton payload on the South Atlantic route. The first plane entered into service on New Year's Eve, 1933 and immediately broke a record, flying the 2,286 miles from Marseilles to St. Louis, Senegal in just 24 hours. Baptized 'Croix du Sud,' or 'Southern Cross,' the plane completed some 15 crossings from Dakar to Natal, Brazil before disappearing at sea on December 7, 1936. Another 6 planes were built – 3 for Air France, delivered in 1936, and 3 for the navy.

■ LATÉCOÈRE 521

In 1933 the growing competition for the transatlantic routes compelled Latécoère to design a gigantic six-engine flying boat, the 521, able to carry 30 passengers on the North Atlantic route and 70 within the Mediterranean network. The first five planes began flying in 1934. The 521 demonstrated its full potential in a successful experimental Paris-Lisbon-Azores-New York flight, but access to the lucrative US market was impeded by the outbreak of war in Europe. Four of the five hydroplanes were taken over by the French naval command.

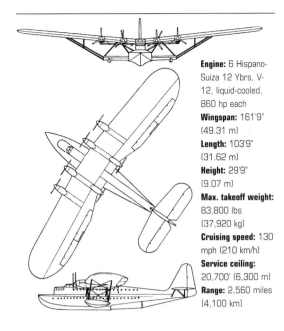

Engine: 6 Hispano-Suiza 12 Ybrs, V-12, liquid-cooled, 860 hp each
Wingspan: 161'9" (49.31 m)
Length: 103'9" (31.62 m)
Height: 29'9" (9.07 m)
Max. takeoff weight: 83,800 lbs (37,920 kg)
Cruising speed: 130 mph (210 km/h)
Service ceiling: 20,700' (6,300 m)
Range: 2,560 miles (4,100 km)

■ LEVASSEUR PL-8 OISEAU BLANC

Engine: Lorraine-Dietrich V-12, liquid-cooled, 450 hp each – **Wingspan:** 48' (14.63 m) – **Length:** 32' (9.75 m) – **Height:** 13' (3.96 m) – **Max. takeoff weight:** 10,950 lbs (4,954 kg) – **Cruising speed:** 120 mph (193 km/h) – **Range:** 3,725 miles (6,000 km)

On May 8, 1927, an ungainly but ambitious biplane piloted by Charles Nungesser and François Coli took off from Le Bourget airport with the intention of flying nonstop to the North American continent. It was the first time anyone had tried to cross the Atlantic in an easterly direction. The plane had been modified to give it a range of 30 hours. But as it approached Newfoundland a blizzard struck, and the plane and its pilots were lost without a trace.

■ LIORÉ ET OLIVIER LEO H-47

Engine: 4 Hispano-Suiza 12 Ydrs, V-12, liquid-cooled, 880 hp each – **Wingspan:** 104'6" (31.80 m) – **Length:** 69'6" (21.18 m) – **Height:** 23'8" (7.20 m) – **Max. takeoff weight:** 39,560 lbs (17,900 kg) – **Cruising speed:** 180 mph (290 km/h) at 8,200' (2,500 m) – **Service ceiling:** 23,000' (7,000 m) – **Range:** 2,485 miles (4,000 km)

WWII blocked the development of yet another promising hydroplane, the Lioré et Olivier LeO H-47.

Like the Latécoère 300, designed at government request in 1931, the similar H-47 was commissioned three years later by the same patron. The prototype flew on July 25, 1936, but final testing was hindered by a major accident and production didn't get started until 1938. The first of five planes ordered for Air France was completed that same year, but a world war was knocking at the door, and the program was soon abandoned.

■ LIORÉ ET OLIVIER LEO-213

Engine: 2 Renault 12Jas, V-12, liquid-cooled, 450 hp each – **Wingspan:** 76'10" (23.43 m) – **Length:** 52'4" (15.95 m) – **Height:** 14'1" (4.30 m) – **Max. takeoff weight:** 12,580 lbs (5,692 kg) – **Cruising speed:** 108 mph (175 km/h) at 3,280' (1,000 m) – **Service ceiling:** 14,760' (4,500 m) – **Range:** 350 miles (560 km)

Like the contemporary Handley Page H.P.42, the LeO-213 stood above all for passenger comfort and safety, so much so that it was referred to as a 'luxury liner.' The prototype appeared in 1928, and the 11 aircraft produced between then and 1931 were operated by Air Union on its two most important routes, Paris-London and Paris-Lyon-Marseilles. In 1933 Air France acquired the planes, and used them intensively. The stately twin-engine 12-passenger biplane offered gracious service and elevated safety standards until phased out in 1934.

■ LOCKHEED 10/A ELECTRA

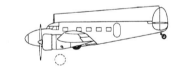

Engine: 2 Pratt & Whitney Wasp Jr. radials, 9-cylinder, air-cooled, 420 hp each – **Wingspan:** 55' (16.76 m) – **Length:** 38'6" (11.75 m) – **Height:** 10' (3.05 m) – **Max. takeoff weight:** 10,500 lbs (4,763 kg) – **Cruising speed:** 203 mph (327 km/h) – **Service ceiling:** 20,000' (6,100 m) – **Range:** 750 miles (1,207 km)

The 10/A Electra marks Lockheed's joining of Boeing vs Douglas battle for commercial market supremacy. The project was developed in 1933 and the prototype flew on February 1934. Compared to the Boeing 247, the Electra performed better in flight, was faster and cost much less to build. Commercial success was understandably immediate: starting with Northwest Airlines in 1934, transport companies lined up to buy the new Lockheed commuter. Total production was 148 planes in several versions. The hardy twin-engine had a competition career as well. In fact, Amelia Earhart was flying an Electra in her attempt to cross the Pacific Ocean: she disappeared on July 3, 1937.

■ LOCKHEED CONSTELLATION

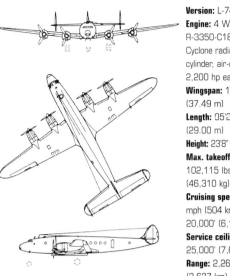

Version: L-749
Engine: 4 Wright R-3350-C18-BA3 Cyclone radials, 28-cylinder, air-cooled, 2,200 hp each
Wingspan: 123' (37.49 m)
Length: 95'2" (29.00 m)
Height: 23'8" (7.21 m)
Max. takeoff weight: 102,115 lbs (46,310 kg)
Cruising speed: 313 mph (504 km/h) at 20,000' (6,100 m)
Service ceiling: 25,000' (7,620 m)
Range: 2,260 miles (3,637 km)

One of the last great piston-driven four-engine transports, the Lockheed Constellation was a major star until the advent of the jet. Derived from the C-49 military cargo plane, it entered the commercial market right after the war, finding an immediate buyer in Pan American, which first flew the Constellation in its new role on February 3, 1946. All the other major airlines followed suit. The most successful early variant was the L-749 of 1947, used mostly for transatlantic travel. The plane gained international fame in 1950 with the introduction the radically redesigned L-1049 Super Constellation. Other, always better versions, followed; the last was the L-1649 Starlifter of 1956. In total, 529 Constellations were built.

■ LOCKHEED L-188 ELECTRA

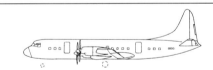

Version: L-188A – **Engine:** 4 Allison 501-D13A turboprops, 3,750 hp each – **Wingspan:** 99' (30.18 m) – **Length:** 104'6" (31.85 m) – **Height:** 32'1" (9.78 m) – **Max. takeoff weight:** 116,000 lbs (52,608 kg) – **Cruising speed:** 404 mph (652 km/h) at 22,000' (6,700 m) – **Service ceiling:** 27,000' (8,230 m) – **Range:** 2,760 miles (4,458 km)

The elegant Lockheed L-188 was America's first non-military turboprop. Designed in 1955, it was produced in A and C versions differing in capacity and range. The prototype first flew on December 6, 1957 and the first of the 170 planes produced appeared in 1958. Two major accidents interrupted commercial use until 1961, when Lockheed implemented a modification program for planes in service or under construction. Despite the ambitious name evoking the famous 1930s twin-engine, the Electra did not have an exceedingly brilliant career, remaining in the shadow of the competition's new jetliners.

■ LOCKHEED VEGA

Engine: Wright Whirlwind J-5 radial, 9-cylinder, air-cooled, 220 hp – **Wingspan:** 41' (12.50 m) – **Length:** 27'6" (8.38 m) – **Height:** 8'6" (2.59 m) – **Max. takeoff weight:** 3,470 lbs (1,574 kg) – **Cruising speed:** 118 mph (190 km/h) – **Service ceiling:** 15,000' (4,570 m) – **Range:** 900 miles (1,450 km)

The Lockheed Vega, veritable icon of the late 1920s, was a high-wing single-engine transport, built in five base versions for a total of 131 planes. This compact yet refined monoplane gained fame not only for its commercial validity, but also for its sporting accomplishments, foremost among which were Wiley Post's round-the-world raids of 1931 and 1933. The first (June 23) saw Post and Harold Gatty climb aboard a Vega 5 christened 'Winnie Mae' and then fly it for a distance of circa 15,500 miles in 107 hours and 2 minutes. For the second (July 13), Post chose to go it alone, once again in a Vega. His record time of 7 days 18 hours 49 minutes (effective flight time 115 hours 36 minutes) remained untouched for 14 years.

■ MACCHI CASTOLDI M.C.72

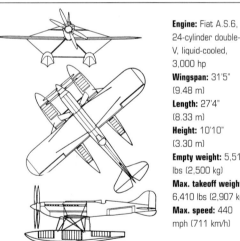

Engine: Fiat A.S.6, 24-cylinder double-V, liquid-cooled, 3,000 hp
Wingspan: 31'5" (9.48 m)
Length: 27'4" (8.33 m)
Height: 10'10" (3.30 m)
Empty weight: 5,510 lbs (2,500 kg)
Max. takeoff weight: 6,410 lbs (2,907 kg)
Max. speed: 440 mph (711 km/h)

The Macchi-Castoldi M.C.72 stands among the immortals of aviation for the world speed record it set on October 23, 1934, a record which to this day remains unbeaten for the category of piston-engine float planes. This brawny hydro-racer was developed to compete in the 1931 Schneider Cup competition, but was unable to participate due to problems with its enormous engine, the mighty 3,000-horsepower Fiat A.S.6. But this was only a temporary setback, and the M.C.72 more than made up for it in the years to follow. In April 1933 Francesco Agello broke the existing record with a speed of 422.5 mph. Then, again at the controls, he pushed it to the still unbroken world record of 440.7 mph. A total of five M.C.72s were built.

■ MACCHI M.39

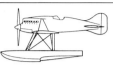

Engine: Fiat A.S.2, V-12, liquid-cooled, 800 hp – **Wingspan:** 30'4" (9.26 m) – **Length:** 22'1" (6.73 m) – **Height:** 10' (3.06 m) – **Max. takeoff weight:** 3,475 lbs (1,575 kg) – **Max. speed:** 260 mph (416 km/h)

The Macchi M.39 was the winner of the ninth Schneider Cup competition. Held on November 12-13, 1926 at Hampton Roads, Virginia, the race was essentially a grudge match between the Italians and the Americans, the two great hydro-racing powers. The Americans had won the two previous competitions, so the stakes were high. Three M.39s were entered, piloted by Mario De Bernardi, Arturo Ferrarin, and Adriano Bacula. Only two finished the race, but did so well: De Bernardi took first place at 246 mph, while Bacula was third at 217 (second place went to Christian Frank Schilt in a Curtiss R3C-2, 231 mph). The Macchi M.39s' extraordinary performance quashed all rivalry with the Americans: citing economic reasons, the US government announced its withdrawal from future Schneider Cup competitions.

■ MACCHI M.C.94

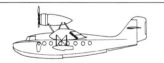

Engine: 2 Wright SGR.1820 Cyclone radials, 9-cylinder, air-cooled, 770 hp each – **Wingspan:** 74'9" (22.79 m) – **Length:** 50'11" (15.52 m) – **Height:** 17'10" (5.45 m) – **Max. takeoff weight:** 17,200 lbs (7,800 kg) – **Cruising speed:** 155 mph (250 km/h) at 3,280' (1,000 m) – **Service ceiling:** 19,000' (5,800 m) – **Range:** 860 miles (1,375 km)

Italian hydroplane production enjoyed great success and prestige during the 1930s in both the sporting and commercial sectors. The Macchi M.C.94, designed by Mario Castoldi and introduced in 1933, was a 12-passenger twin-engine aircraft of the flying boat class. The Ala Littoria national airline ordered twelve 94s and had them in service by 1936. In 1939 three of these were sold to the Corporacion Sud-Americana de Transportes Aereos, an affiliate of Ala Littoria, which operated the hydroplanes between Buenos Aires, Montevideo and Rosario. The others remained active for the duration of WWII in Ala Littoria's communications division.

■ MACCHI M.C.100

In 1938, wishing to repeat the Macchi M.C.94's success, Mario Castoldi began planning a new, larger flying boat with three engines instead of two, and with passenger capacity increased to 26. The M.C.100 prototype flew on January 7, 1939, when a number of hydrodynamic problems showed up that seriously

compromised the M.C.100's performance on water. Try as he did, Castoldi was never able to resolve them. The plane never made it to the marketplace: the only three that were produced were militarized and used as transports during the war.

Engine: 3 Alfa Romeo A.R. 126 RC10 radials, 10-cylinder, air-cooled, 800 hp each – **Wingspan:** 87'7" (26.71 m) – **Length:** 58' (17.69 m) – **Height:** 20'1" (6.12 m) – **Max. takeoff weight:** 29,100 lbs (13,200 kg) – **Cruising speed:** 164 mph (263 km/h) – **Service ceiling:** 21,300' (6,500 m) – **Range:** 875 miles (1,400 km)

■ MARTIN M.130 CHINA CLIPPER

Toward the end of 1935, Martin decided to create an airliner capable of the grueling trans-Pacific flight while providing maximum passenger luxury. The result was the M.130, a regally immense flying boat that Pan Am introduced into service on October 21, 1936, opening an ambitious new route: San Francisco to Manila via Honolulu, Midway, Wake Island and Guam. The distance per leg varied between 1,260 and 2,410 miles, and the M.130 showed itself capable of handling them easily. In all, the journey took five days, with 60 hours of effective flight time. The three planes built were christened China Clipper, Philippine Clipper and Hawaii Clipper. Their illustrious commercial career lasted until 1942; the US Navy then requisitioned them.

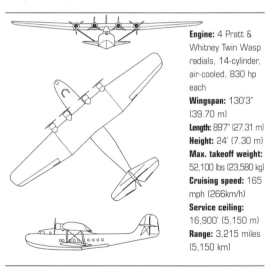

Engine: 4 Pratt & Whitney Twin Wasp radials, 14-cylinder, air-cooled, 830 hp each
Wingspan: 130'3" (39.70 m)
Length: 897' (27.31 m)
Height: 24' (7.30 m)
Max. takeoff weight: 52,100 lbs (23,580 kg)
Cruising speed: 165 mph (266km/h)
Service ceiling: 16,900' (5,150 m)
Range: 3,215 miles (5,150 km)

■ MARTIN MARIETTA X-24

During the 1970s NASA developed the first 'lifting bodies,' or flying machines without wings, the lift for which is provided by the form of the fuselage itself. After a rocket engine took such a craft to altitude, it glided back to earth without power. The earliest attempts – the Northrop HL-10 and the M2-F2 – led to the hypothesis that the technology might be transferred to the nascent Space Shuttle project, effectively making it a wing-less glider that would be nonetheless maneuverable in atmospheric flight. Although the idea was eventually discarded in favor of a delta wing, the program forged ahead until December 1972 with the Martin Marietta X-24A, whose improbable shape earned it the nickname of 'Flying Potato.'

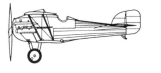

Engine: Thiokol XLR-11 rocket engine, 16,900 lbs (3,625 kg) thrust – **Wingspan:** 13'9" (4.16 m) – **Length:** 24'6" (7.47 m) – **Height:** 10'4" (3.15 m) – **Max. takeoff weight:** 11,000 lbs (4,990 kg) – **Max. speed:** 1,050 mph (1,686 km/h) – **Service ceiling:** 74,640' (22,756 m) – **Range:** 15 minutes

■ MARTINSYDE SEMIQUAVER

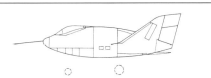

Engine: Hispano-Suiza 8Fb, V-8, liquid-cooled, 320 hp – **Wingspan:** 20'2" (6.15 m) – **Length:** 19'3" (5.86 m) – **Height:** 7'1" (2.17 m) – **Empty weight:** 1,525 lbs (692 kg) – **Max. takeoff weight:** 2,000 lbs (905 kg) – **Max. speed:** 162 mph (260 km/h)

The Aerial Derby, the great British aviation event instituted in 1912 then abruptly interrupted by WWI, was resumed in 1919, signaling the beginning of a new phase of the world's love affair with the airplane. Such events attracted thousands of aviation enthusiasts, and stimulated designers and manufacturers to build ever faster and more efficient machines. The Martinsyde Semiquaver was among the show planes of the 1920 Derby. Expressly built for the event, the little plane with the funny name took the speed prize. Piloted by Francis Courtney, it breezed past the competition at 156 mph.

■ MCDONNELL-DOUGLAS DC-9

Version: DC-9-10 – **Engine:** 2 Pratt & Whitney JTD-5 turbojets, 12,250 lbs (5,560 kg) thrust each – **Wingspan:** 89'4" (27.25 m) – **Length:** 104'4" (31.82 m) – **Height:** 27'6" (8.38 m) – **Max. takeoff weight:** 77,700 lbs (35,245 kg) – **Cruising speed:** 564 mph (903 km/h) at 25,000' (7,620 m) – **Service ceiling:** 35,000' (10,675 m) – **Range:** 1,000 miles (1,601 km)

The McDonnell-Douglas DC-9, still very active in the new millennium nearly forty years after it first flew as a prototype in February 1965, has had few peers in the short- to medium-range passenger liner category. Developed from the prolific Douglas DC family, the venerable twinjet went into production in 1965. Stimulated by heavy demand, an ample range of versions followed whose progress was reflected in an ever greater seating capacity: from 90 in the first series (DC-9-10, 1965) to 139 in the DC-9-50 of 1974. A major redesign program was launched in 1977, giving rise to a new base version, the 172-seat Super 80. Numerous sub-series followed, varying in dimension and capacity, always improving in performance and flexibility.

■ MCDONNELL-DOUGLAS DC-10

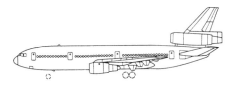

version: DC-10-30 – **Engine:** 3 General Electric CF6-50A turbojets, 49,250 lbs (22,330 kg) thrust each – **Wingspan:** 165'4" (50.41 m) – **Length:** 182' (55.50 m) – **Height:** 58'1" (17.70 m) – **Max. takeoff weight:** 565,000 lbs (256,225 kg) – **Cruising speed:** 567 mph (908 km/h) at 30,000' (9,145 m) – **Service ceiling:** 33,400' (10,180 m) – **Range:** 7,230 miles (11,580 km)

The first response to the Boeing 747 challenge in the high-capacity category came from McDonnell-Douglas with its DC-10 trijet. In 1966 American Airlines asked not merely for a competitive wide-body, but one that could take off and land on relatively short runways. The first DC-10-10 flew on August 29, 1970, and service began on August 5 of the following year on the Los Angeles-Chicago route. The first version built explicitly for intercontinental routes was the DC-10-30 of 1972, a plane that enjoyed notable success with the major European airlines, KLM and Swissair being first among them to place orders. The last version was the DC-10-40, also from 1972.

■ MCDONNELL-DOUGLAS MD-11

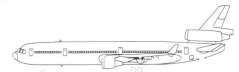

Engine: 3 General Electric CF6-80C2 turbofans, 61,500 lbs (27,896 kg) thrust each – **Wingspan:** 169'5" (51.66 m) – **Length:** 200'9" (61.21 m) – **Height:** 57'9" (17.60 m) – **Max. takeoff weight:** 602,625 lbs (273,300 kg) – **Cruising speed:** 582 mph (932 km/h) at 30,000' (9,150 m) – **Service ceiling:** 32,600' (9,935 m) – **Range:** 8,000 miles (12,840 km)

The great market advantage Boeing gained during the 1980s in the long-range high-capacity sector rekindled the old flame of competition among the major manufacturers. McDonnell-Douglas recognized that its DC-10 was no longer a viable alternative to the B-747 and decided to develop a successor that would be. The program that resulted in the MD-11 was launched on December 30, 1986. The first prototype flew on January 10, 1990 and on December 20 the plane entered into service with Finnair. The market received the new wide-body well: in the first year alone McDonnell-Douglas secured 172 firm orders and 182 options from 32 airlines.

■ NASA/ROCKWELL INTERNATIONAL SPACE SHUTTLE ORBITER

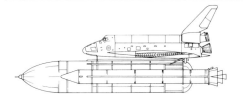

Engine: 3 Rocketdyne SSME rocket engines, 470,000 lbs (213,192 kg) thrust each – **Wingspan:** 78' (23.79 m) – **Length:** 122'3" (37.26 m) – **Height:** 56'7" (17.25 m) – **Max. takeoff weight:** 156,000 lbs (70,600 kg) – **Orbit speed:** 17,500 mph (28,160 km/h)

The first Shuttle, the Enterprise OV-101, rolled out of its hangar on September 17, 1976. This aircraft, which never went into space, underwent an intense series of tests between 1977 and 1979 designed to study its aerodynamic characteristics in general and its behavior during approach and landing in particular. Enterprise performed these tests essentially as a glider, flown to altitude on the back of a Boeing B-747. The first space mission was flown by the second Shuttle, Columbia (OV-102), on April 12, 1981, piloted by Robert Crippen under the command of John Young. A third Shuttle was created by upgrading the original test craft (Challenger, OV-099, first flight April 4, 1983). This was followed by Discovery and Atlantis (OV-103 and 104). Discovery was first launched on August 30, 1984, Atlantis on October 3, 1985. A sixth vehicle, Endeavor (OV-105) built to replace Challenger, which had exploded in flight on January 28, 1986. Endeavor made its space debut on May 7, 1992. On February 1, 2003, another accident destroyed Columbia. Since then the program has been at a standstill, after having flown a total of 112 missions.

■ NAVY CURTISS NC-4

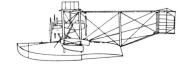

Engine: 4 Liberty 12s, V-12, liquid-cooled, 400 hp each – **Wingspan:** 126 (38.40 m) – **Length:** 68'3" (20.80 m) – **Height:** 24'6" (7.46 m) – **Max. takeoff weight:** 27,400 lbs (12,422 kg) – **Max. speed:** 91 mph (146 km/h) – **Service ceiling:** 4,500' (1,372 m) – **Range:** 1,478 miles (2,366 km)

The NC-4 was the first plane to fly from North America to Europe, covering the 1,400 miles between Newfoundland and the Azores. This seaplane was part of a series built in 1918 to counter the threat German submarines posed to Allied convoys. The war ended before they could be used, but in order to exploit this powerful and innovative plane, a transatlantic crossing was organized. The NC-1 and NC-3 had to withdraw, but the NC-4 reached the Azores, hopped to Lisbon and eventually to Plymouth, England, arriving on May 31, 1919. The historic plane is now exhibited at the Smithsonian Institute, Washington D.C.

■ NIEUPORT 29V

One of the premier competition planes of the early '20s, the Nieuport 29V won many trophies, including the prestigious Gordon Bennett and Deutsche de la Meurthe award, in the air meets that captivated Europe after WWI. On September 28, 1920, Sadi Lecointe flew his Nieuport 29V to win the Bennett clocking an average speed of 165.5 mph, after having already won the other prize – with its appetizing 20,000-franc purse – in January of that same year. Two years later, on September 30, Fernand Lasne pushed the 29V to 182 mph, claiming both the trophy and the speed record for a 300-km closed course.

Engine: Hispano-Suiza 8Fb, V-8, liquid-cooled, 300 hp – **Wingspan:** 17'11" (5.46 m) – **Length:** 20'4" (6.20 m) – **Height:** 8'3" (2.50 m) – **Max. takeoff weight:** 1,520 lbs (690 kg) – **Max. speed:** 190 mph (302 km/h)

■ NIEUPORT-DELAGE 42

Another thoroughbred designed by Gustave Delage, the 42 was the winner of the two Beaumont Cup races, with its proncely 100,000 francs to the pilot who could average better than 290 km/h on a 300-km circuit. Sadi Lecointe won the 1924 race with a speed of 317.4 km/h (198 mph), winning again in 1925 at 312.4 km/h (195 mph).

Engine: Hispano-Suiza 51, V-12, liquid-cooled, 545 hp – **Wingspan:** 31'2" (9.50 m) – **Length:** 24' (7.30 m) – **Height:** 8'3" (2.50 m) – **Max. takeoff weight:** 2,580 lbs (1,170 kg) – **Max. speed:** 198 mph (317 km/h)

■ NIEUPORT-DELAGE 1921

The famous French airplane designer Gustave Delage cleverly adapted all his experience in building military planes to his racers. He developed the Nieuport-Delage 1921 to win the Deutsche de la Meurthe race of the plane's name-year. Pilot Georges Kirsch did just that, crushing six adversaries with a speed of 177 miles per hour.

Engine: Hispano-Suiza 8Fb, V-8, liquid-cooled, 320 hp – **Wingspan:** 26'3" (8.00 m) – **Length:** 20' (6.10 m) – **Height:** 6'8" (2.02 m) – **Empty weight:** 1,700 lbs (769 kg) – **Max. takeoff weight:** 2,235 lbs (1,014 kg) – **Max. speed:** 210 mph (336 km/h)

■ NORTH AMERICAN X-15

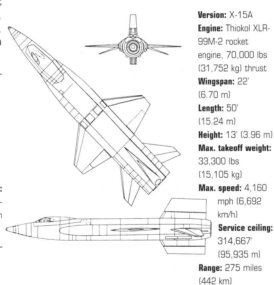

Version: X-15A
Engine: Thiokol XLR-99M-2 rocket engine, 70,000 lbs (31,752 kg) thrust
Wingspan: 22' (6.70 m)
Length: 50' (15.24 m)
Height: 13' (3.96 m)
Max. takeoff weight: 33,300 lbs (15,105 kg)
Max. speed: 4,160 mph (6,692 km/h)
Service ceiling: 314,667' (95,935 m)
Range: 275 miles (442 km)

The first of North American's three X-15s left the factory on October 15, 1958 and hit the air on March 10, 1959, when a B-52 bomber adapted for the purpose made a test ferry run. In May 1960, its XLR-99 rocket engine ready, the X-15 began a series of test flights. Then, from November 1960 to October 24, 1968 – date of the last of the 199 experimental missions flown by the three planes – the X-15 began shattering every speed and altitude record, e.g.: 4,520 mph (Bob White, November 9, 1961), 265,476 feet (Joe Walker, April 30, 1962), 354,200 feet (Walker, August 22, 1963). The research was dangerous and a forced landing nearly destroyed the second X-15, leading to the creation of the sole X-15 A-2. The damaged craft was sent to North American for repair, but ended up with modified in the fuselage, fuel tanks and heat sheathing, making it the fastest X-15 of all: on October 3, 1967, William Knight set the all-time speed record for a winged aircraft at 4,520 mph. The momentous flight damaged the plane again, irreparably this time. The third X-15 was destroyed in November 1967.

■ POTEZ 62

Among the French 1930s commercial transport aircraft, the Potez 62 occupies a place of honor. This rugged and dependable high-wing twin-prop was Air France's workhorse, serving its European routes and later its internal South American routes as well. The project, derived from the Potez 54 bomber, was launched in 1934, the prototype making its first flight on January 28, 1935 and service commencing in April. A total of 21 planes were built for Air France.

Engine: 2 Gnome-Rhône 14 Krs Mistral Major radials, 14-cylinder, air-cooled, 300 hp each – **Wingspan:** 73'7" (22.44 m) – **Length:** 56'9" (17.32 m) – **Max. takeoff weight:** 16,540 lbs (7,500 kg) – **Cruising speed:** 175 mph (280 km/h) at 6,560' (2,000 m) – **Service ceiling:** 24,600' (7,500 m) – **Range:** 620 miles (1,000 km)

■ ROE TRIPLANE I

The first flight in England by a plane built in England and powered by an English engine was made on July 23, 1909 by Alliott Verdon Roe, an Englishman. The vehicle was a triplane, the first of a series built by Roe. The 9-horsepower engine was barely strong enough to get the plane off the ground: it stayed aloft for just 270 meters. The second version, this one equipped with a 20-hp motor, might have worked better but its performance at the Blackpool meet in October 1909 was compromised by heavy rain. After these experiments with triplanes, Roe dedicated himself with greater success to the biplane formula.

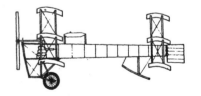

Engine: J.A.P. V-4, air-cooled, 20 hp each – **Wingspan:** 20' (6.10 m) – **Length:** 23' (7.01) – **Height:** 11' (3.35 m) – **Wing surface:** 217 sq ft (20.21 sq m) – **Empty weight:** 300 lbs (136 kg) – **Max. takeoff weight:** 450 lbs (204 kg) – **Max. speed:** 25 mph (40 km/h)

■ RYAN NYP SPIRIT OF ST. LOUIS

On May 20, 1927 the 'Spirit of St. Louis,' a small high-wing monoplane piloted by Charles Lindbergh took off from Roosevelt Field, New York. When he touched down at Paris' Le Bourget airport 33 hours, 30 minutes, 28 seconds, and 3,540 miles later, he became the first man to make a non-stop solo flight across the Atlantic Ocean. The planes was built in two months by a small factory in San Diego, where Lindbergh had found a designer whose enthusiasm matched his own.

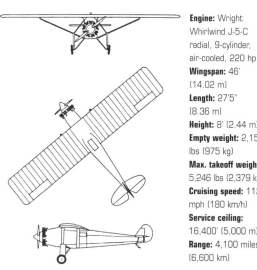

Engine: Wright Whirlwind J-5-C radial, 9-cylinder, air-cooled, 220 hp **Wingspan:** 46' (14.02 m) **Length:** 27'5" (8.36 m) **Height:** 8' (2.44 m) **Empty weight:** 2,150 lbs (975 kg) **Max. takeoff weight:** 5,246 lbs (2,379 kg) **Cruising speed:** 112 mph (180 km/h) **Service ceiling:** 16,400' (5,000 m) **Range:** 4,100 miles (6,600 km)

■ SANTOS DUMONT 14 BIS

Europe came late to powered flight – nearly three years after that historic morning at Kill Devil Hill, a year after the record 38-minute flight of Orville and Wilbur's Flyer III. The exact date was September 13, 1906; the site, Bagatelle, just outside Paris. It was there that the Santos-Dumont 14 bis, namesake of the Brazilian engineer who designed and built it, made its historic 'flight' of 23 feet. On October 23 the distance was increased to 197 feet. The best result came on November 12, when the plane stayed aloft for 12 seconds, covering 720 feet of distance while ascending to an altitude of 20 feet. It was still a long way from the Flyer, but the first step had been taken.

Engine: Antoinette V-8, water-cooled, 50 hp – **Wingspan:** 36'9" (11.20 m) – **Length:** 31'10" (9.70 m) – **Height:** 11'2" (3.40 m) – **Wing surface:** 560 sq ft (52 sq m) – **Max. takeoff weight:** 660 lbs (300 kg) – **Max. speed:** 25 mph (40 km/h)

■ SAVOIA S.12 BIS

After the 1913 and 1914 Schneider Cup competitions, the world's most prestigious hydroplane race was next held on September 10, 1919 in Bournemouth, England. The brilliant performance of the Savoia S.13 piloted by Guido Jannello was in vain; heavy fog had led to a series of errors and his run was annulled. But in Venice, on

September 21, 1920), the Italians regained their pride: another Savoia, the S.12 bis, piloted by Luigi Bologna, won the Cup with a speed of 107 mph.

Engine: Ansaldo V-12, liquid-cooled, 500 hp – **Wingspan:** 38'5" (11.72 m) – **Length:** 32'8" (9.95 m) – **Height:** 12'6" (3.81 m) – **Empty weight:** 2,625 lbs (1,191 kg) – **Max. takeoff weight:** 3,840 lbs (1,740 kg) – **Max. speed:** 140 mph (222 km/h)

■ SAVOIA MARCHETTI S.16 TER

The S.16 was a fine competition seaplane with a central ski. In 1920 it set the record for the longest raid by a plane of its category, and in 1924 it set the hydroplane altitude record. But its greatest feat came the following year. In an S.16 baptized 'Gennariello,' Francesco De Pinedo took off from Lake Maggiore on April 20, 1925 and then made what was at the time the longest flight in history: 34,200 miles, 360 hours of flight time, spanning three continents. After De Pinedo's exploit, several commercial airlines adopted the plane.

Engine: Lorraine (Isotta-Fraschini), V-12, liquid-cooled, 400 hp – **Wingspan:** 50'10" (15.50 m) – **Length:** 44'3" (13.50 m) – **Height:** 12' (3.66 m) – **Max. takeoff weight:** 5,850 lbs (2,652 kg) – **Cruising speed:** 110 mph (175 km/h) – **Service ceiling:** 9,850' (3,000 m) – **Range:** 620 miles (1,000 km)

■ SHORT S.8 CALCUTTA

Engine: 3 Bristol Jupiter XIF radials, 9-cylinder, air-cooled, 450 hp each – **Wingspan:** 93' (28.34 m) – **Length:** 66'9" (20.34 m) – **Height:** 23'9" (7.24 m) – **Max. takeoff weight:** 22,500 lbs (10.190 kg) – **Cruising speed:** 97 mph (156 km/h) – **Service ceiling:** 13,500' (4,100 m) – **Range:** 650 miles (1,050 km)

This plane enabled Imperial Airways to complete a very important international route: the 'Spice Road' of the skies, the passage to India. The trimotor hydroplane was used to cover the Mediterranean leg of the journey from London to Karachi. The first of the five Calcuttas built flew on February 21, 1928 and service was inaugurated on April 16, 1929. The plane remained active well into the next decade.

■ SHORT S.26

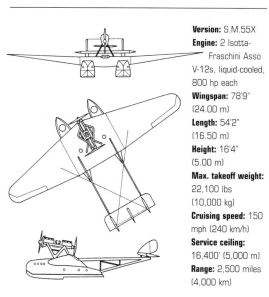

Engine: 4 Bristol Hercules IV radials, 14-cylinder, air-cooled, 1,380 hp each – **Wingspan:** 134'4" (40.95 m) – **Length:** 101'4" (30.89 m) – **Height:** 37'7" (11.46 m) – **Max. takeoff weight:** 73,500 lbs (33,340 kg) – **Cruising speed:** 180 mph (290 km/h) at 7,500' (2,290 m) – **Service ceiling:** 20,000' (6,100 m) – **Range:** 3,200 miles (5,150 km)

As with many commercial aircraft developed in the late 1930s, WWII prevented the Short S.26 from having a chance to demonstrate its potential. This gigantic four-engine hydroliner was designed in 1938 for Imperial Airways, which needed a plane capable of providing fast, nonstop passenger and cargo service across the Atlantic. Three planes were built in 1939, the year war was declared. One survived the conflict and flew the BOAC flag from September 1946 to September 1947, on the Britain-Egypt route.

■ SIAI MARCHETTI S.M.55

Version: S.M.55X **Engine:** 2 Isotta-Fraschini Asso V-12s, liquid-cooled, 800 hp each **Wingspan:** 78'9" (24.00 m) **Length:** 54'2" (16.50 m) **Height:** 16'4" (5.00 m) **Max. takeoff weight:** 22,100 lbs (10,000 kg) **Cruising speed:** 150 mph (240 km/h) **Service ceiling:** 16,400' (5,000 m) **Range:** 2,500 miles (4,000 km)

The SIAI Marchetti S.M.55 twin-fuselage flying boat was built in five base versions: the A, M and X for the military; the C and P for civilian use, with space for 9 to 12 passengers. The first long-distance flight was made in 1927 by Francesco De Pinedo and Carlo Del Prete aboard a plane of the first series, christened 'Santa Maria.' In subsequent years the S.M.55 would make a southern crossing of the Atlantic, fly to the North Pole in search of Nobile's lost dirigible, and complete a raid from Orbetello, Italy to Rio de Janeiro. In 1933 Italo Balbo organized an unprecedented spectacle starring the S.M.55X: departing from Orbetello, 25 planes crossed the Atlantic in formation, touching down in New York and returning to Rome for a 12,300-mile roundtrip.

■ SIAI MARCHETTI S.M.64

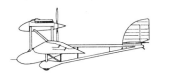

Engine: Fiat 22T, V-12, liquid-cooled, 590 hp – **Wingspan:** 70'6" (21.49 m) – **Length:** 29'6" (8.99 m) – **Height:** 12'1" (3.68 m) – **Empty weight:** 5,300 lbs (2,400 kg) – **Max. takeoff weight:** 15,500 lbs (7,000 kg) – **Max. speed:** 145 mph (235 km/h) – **Range:** 7,150 miles (11,505 km)

One of history's great long-distance competition planes, the SIAI Marchetti S.M.64 was the product of the boundless enthusiasm and ingenuity of its designers, Alessandro Marchetti and Arturo Ferrarin. The 64 undertook its first adventure between May 31 and June 2 1928, breaking three records in a single flight. With Ferrarin, Carlo Del Prete and the mechanic Capannini on board, the plane flew 4,762 miles in 58 hours 53 minutes 53 seconds of flight time, setting the world records for duration, for distance on a closed course, and for average speed over 5,000 kilometers (139 km/h; 86 mph). On July 5 the plane broke the straight-line record, flying 4,467 miles from Montecelio, Italy to Natal, Brazil. Lastly, on May 31, 1930, the 64 bested its own record for distance on a closed course, covering 5,087 miles in 67 hours and 13 minutes.

■ SIAI MARCHETTI S.M.66

Engine: 3 Fiat A24.R, V-12s, liquid-cooled, 750 hp each – **Wingspan:** 108'3" (33.00 m) – **Length:** 54'6" (16.63 m) – **Height:** 16' (4.89 m) – **Max. takeoff weight:** 25,600 lbs (11,600 kg) – **Cruising speed:** 138 mph (222 km/h) – **Service ceiling:** 18,000' (5,500 m) – **Range:** 800 miles (1,290 km)

Direct descendent of the S.M.55, the SIAI Marchetti S.M.66 was the final version of the twin-fuselage flying boat formula. This plane served the Mediterranean network from 1932 to the outbreak of WWII. Aero Espresso, SANA, SAM adopted it (3, 4, and 7 planes, respectively), then Ala Littoria, which had no fewer than 27 S.M.66's flying the Rome-Tripoli-Tunis route, eventually adding Brindisi-Athens-Rhodes-Alexandria. During WWII, planes were used for sea rescue missions.

■ SIAI MARCHETTI S.M.73

After its successful seaplanes, SIAI Marchetti developed a long series of conventional transport aircraft that dominated Italian commercial aviation in the 1930s. First came the S.M.73, with the prototype appearing in June 1934. The tri-prop, low-wing configuration of this first model became the distinguishing feature of SIAI's production for the next decade. The first five S.M.73s went to the Belgian

airline Sabena, which bought another 7 built under license for use on the long and arduous African routes. Ala Littoria bought around 20, Avio Linee Italiane 6, and the Czech airline CSA 5.

Engine: 3 Alfa Romeo 126 RC 34 radials, 9-cylinder, air-cooled, 750 hp each – **Wingspan:** 78'9" (24.00 m) – **Length:** 60'3" (18.37 m) – **Height:** 14'7" (4.45 m) – **Max. takeoff weight:** 23,800 lbs (10,800 kg) – **Cruising speed:** 175 mph (280 km/h) – **Service ceiling:** 23,000' (7,000 m) – **Range:** 620 miles (1,000 km)

■ SIAI MARCHETTI S.M.74

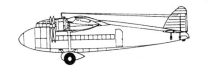

Engine: 4 Piaggio Stella X.RC radials, 9-cylinder, air-cooled, 700 hp each – **Wingspan:** 97'4" (29.68 m) – **Length:** 70'1" (21.36 m) – **Height:** 18' (5.50 m) – **Max. takeoff weight:** 30,100 lbs (14,000 kg) – **Cruising speed:** 185 mph (300 km/h) – **Service ceiling:** 23,000' (7,000 m) – **Range:** 1,250 miles (2,000 km)

The only exception to the SIAI trimotor formula was the S.M.74, a large four-engine transport of which only three were built. The prototype flew on November 6, 1934 and Ala Littoria began service on July 18, 1935 on the Rome-Marseilles-Lyon-Paris route. In summer 1936 the three planes were assigned to the Rome-Brindisi route, and later to Libya. When WWII broke out the planes were expropriated by the Regia Aeronautica and used as troop and cargo transports. None survived the war.

■ SIAI MARCHETTI S.M.83

Engine: 3 Alfa Romeo 126 RC 34 radials, 9-cylinder, air-cooled, 750 hp each – **Wingspan:** 69'6" (21.20 m) – **Length:** 53'2" (16.20 m) – **Height:** 15'1" (4.60 m) – **Max. takeoff weight:** 23,950 lbs (10,400 kg) – **Cruising speed:** 250 mph (400 km/h) at 16,400' (5,000 m) – **Service ceiling:** 23,000' (7,000 m) – **Range:** 1,420 miles (2,280 km)

The last commercial trimotor SIAI Marchetti built before WWII was the S.M.83, derived from the S.M.79 bomber. It was introduced in October 1937, and the total of 23 planes built included three versions: the base version for short- to medium-range passenger runs; the A for transatlantic duties; and the T for postal transport. The LATI airline put the S.M.83 into service in December 1939, followed

by Sabena and the Romanian airline Lares. However, WWII ended this promising airplane's career, one among other casualties.

■ SIAI MARCHETTI S.M.87

Engine: 3 Fiat A.80 RC 41 radials, 18-cylinder, air-cooled, 1,000 hp each – **Wingspan:** 97'5" (29.70 m) – **Length:** 73'2" (22.30 m) – **Height:** 19'10" (6.06 m) – **Max. takeoff weight:** 38,400 lbs (17,400 kg) – **Cruising speed:** 225 mph (365 km/h) at 13,500' (4,100 m) – **Service ceiling:** 20,500' (6,250 m) – **Range:** 1,365 miles (2,200 km)

After the S.M.74 diversion, SIAI Marchetti returned to its trusty trimotor formula with the S.M.75 of 1937. A highly successful plane (90 units sold), notably superior in performance to its predecessor, the S.M.73, provided the basis for a seaplane version sent to South America in 1939 to serve the internal routes of the Argentine airline Corporacion Sud-Americana de Transportes Aereos, an affiliate of Ala Littoria. Four such planes, designated S.M.87, were produced overall. Not surprisingly, WWII put an end to the program.

■ SOPWITH TABLOID

Engine: Gnome Monosoupape, single-valve rotary, 100 hp – **Wingspan:** 25'6" (7.77 m) – **Length:** 24' (7.32 m) – **Height:** 8'5" (2.57 m) – **Wing surface:** 240 sq ft (22.30 sq m) – **Empty weight:** 990 lbs (450 kg) – **Max. takeoff weight:** 1,435 lbs (650 kg) – **Max. speed:** 92 mph (148 km/h)

Britain's first real claim to aeronautical credibility came when its Sopwith Tabloid won the second Schneider Cup competition, held at Monaco in April 1914. The competition version was in fact a conventional biplane, modified by addition of pontoons for the race. Piloted by Howard Pixton, the Tabloid registered an average speed of 87 miles per hour, then flew two additional laps to hit a threshold of 92, establishing a new speed record for the category.

■ SPAD S.20 BIS

In France the immediate postwar years saw the formidable military planes built by Spad enter sporting competitions. The S.20 bis was probably the most successful. Among its many victories, it was an unlucky second place finish that best demonstrates the plane's mettle. On September 28, 1920, the last Gordon Bennett race was held at Étampes, outside Paris. The Spad S.20 bis flown by Bernard de Romanet ran into lubrication problems during the race and had to land for repairs. Despite being on the ground for a full half-hour, the little Spad managed to place second, behind Sadi Lecointe's Nieuport 29V.

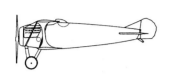

Engine: Hispano-Suiza 8Fb, V-8, liquid-cooled, 320 hp – **Wingspan:** 21'3" (6.47 m) – **Length:** 23'6" (7.18 m) – **Height:** 8'3" (2.50 m) – **Empty weight:** 1,960 lbs (890 kg) – **Max. takeoff weight:** 2,315 lbs (1,050 kg) – **Max. speed:** 192 mph (309 km/h)

■ SUD AVIATION SE.210 CARAVELLE

An effective, versatile twinjet, the Caravelle anticipated a structural configuration that became a paradigm in subsequent generations of short- to medium-range civil transport planes. The Se.210's commercial success was facilitated by an enlightened government policy that provided incentives to the industry. The first production planes were delivered to Air France, which assigned them to Paris-Rome-Istanbul route in May 1959. Other European airlines lined up and soon production was at full capacity. The Caravelle III entered into service on May 23, 1960 with Alitalia. There followed other variants, equipped with new Pratt & Whitney engines. Production shut down with the completion of the 280th plane.

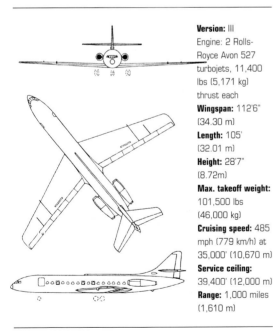

Version: III
Engine: 2 Rolls-Royce Avon 527 turbojets, 11,400 lbs (5,171 kg) thrust each
Wingspan: 112'6" (34.30 m)
Length: 105' (32.01 m)
Height: 28'7" (8.72m)
Max. takeoff weight: 101,500 lbs (46,000 kg)
Cruising speed: 485 mph (779 km/h) at 35,000' (10,670 m)
Service ceiling: 39,400' (12,000 m)
Range: 1,000 miles (1,610 m)

■ SUPERMARINE S.6B

The last Schneider Cup competition – still aviation's most captivating competition – was something of a farce: only one plane competed. On September 13, 1931, at Lee-on- Solent, the English hydro-racer

Supermarine S.6B flew against the clock as its French and Italian adversaries, unable to ready their planes on time, watched from the ground. Piloted by John Boothman, the plane registered an average speed of 340 mph, a new world record for the category. Britain had won by default before the race began, given the absence of competition, but the new record suggested that it would have won anyway.

Engine: Rolls-Royce R, V-12, liquid-cooled, 2,350 hp – **Wingspan:** 30' (9.14 m) – **Length:** 28'9" (8.78 m) – **Height:** 12'3" (3.73m) – **Empty weight:** 4,590 lbs (2,082 kg) – **Max. takeoff weight:** 6,088 lbs (2,761 kg) – **Max. speed:** 408 mph (656 km/h)

■ SUPERMARINE SEA LION

Britain won the 1914 Schneider Cup with a Sopwith Tabloid; it won again in 1922 with the superlative Supermarine Sea Lion, powered by the 450-hp Napier Lion, one of the best British engines of the time. The competition, held on August 12 at Naples, was especially important to the Italians, who had won the two previous Cups. They entered three planes: a Macchi M.17, a Savoia S.51 and a Macchi M.7. But the Sea Lion, piloted by Henry C. Baird, was untouchable at 146 mph.

Engine: Napier Lion, 12-cylinder W-block, liquid-cooled, 450 hp – **Wingspan:** 32' (9.75 m) – **Length:** 28'9" (7.54 m) – **Empty weight:** 2,110 lbs (958 kg) – **Max. takeoff weight:** 2,850 lbs (1,291 kg) – **Max. speed:** 160 mph (257 km/h) – **Range:** 3 hours

■ TRAVEL AIR MYSTERY SHIP

The undisputed star of the 1929 National Air Races was a stylish little civilian monoplane with an intriguing name that enjoyed near mythic status among aviation enthusiasts. The Travel Air Mystery Ship was built in great secrecy during summer 1928 by Herbert Rawdon and Walter Burhan. An interesting feature was its interchangeable wings of different lengths and profiles for different kinds of racing. In the so-called 'unlimited free-for-all' race, pilot Doug Davis zipped past his adversaries, the majority of them military entries flying the most advanced fighters of the period, with an average speed of 199 miles per hour and a fastest lap of 209 mph. This was the first time a radial engine-powered aircraft had broken the 200-mph barrier.

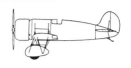

Engine: Wright Whirlwind R-975 J-6, 9-cylinder, air-cooled, 420 hp – **Wingspan:** 29'2" (8.89 m) – **Length:** 20'2" (6.15 m) – **Height:** 8'9" (2.67 m) – **Empty weight:** 1,473 lbs (668 kg) – **Max. takeoff weight:** 1,938 lbs (879 kg) – **Max. speed:** 209 mph (336 km/h) – **Range:** 525 miles (845 km)

■ TUPOLEV TU-104

The Tupolev Tu-104 was the first Soviet jet-powered commercial airplane, and when the British Comet was grounded after the two accidents of 1954, it was the only operative commercial jet in the world. The project began in 1953 and the prototype was ready to fly by June 1955. On September 15, 1956 it flew its maiden voyage with Aeroflot on the Moscow-Omsk-Irkutsk route. The original series was followed in 1957 by a second version, the Tu-104A, which had a bigger engine and greater seating capacity. Two years later came the final version, the B, which carried nearly twice as many passengers as its predecessor. A total of approximately 200 Tu-104's were built.

Engine: 2 Mikulin AM-3M turbojets, 19,200 lbs (8,700 kg) thrust each
Wingspan: 113'4" (34.54 m)
Length: 127'5" (38.85 m)
Height: 39' (11.90 m)
Max. takeoff weight: 167,600 lbs (76,000 kg)
Cruising speed: 497 mph (800 km/h) at 32,800' (10,000 m)
Service ceiling: 37,700' (11,500 m)
Range: 1,925 miles (3,100 km)

■ VERVILLE VCP-R

The final Gordon Bennett race was followed just two months later by the first Pulitzer Trophy race, a new competition designed to test pure speed. It was sponsored by the famous American publishers Ralph, Joseph Jr. and Herbert Pulitzer. The race was held at Mitchell Field, Long Island on November 25, 1920 before an enthusiastic crowd of 25,000. Victory went to the Verville VCP-R, the official US Army entry. Piloted by Corliss C. Mosely, the plane averaged 157 mph. Second place was taken by another modified military plane, the Thomas-Morse MB-3, flown by Harold E. Hartley.

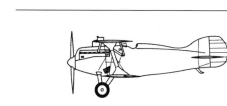

Engine: Packard 1A-2025, V-12, liquid-cooled, 638 hp – **Wingspan:** 27'6" (8.38 m) – **Length:** 24'2" (7.36 m) – **Height:** 8'8" (2.64 m) – **Empty weight:** 2,450 lbs (1,111 kg) – **Max. takeoff weight:** 3,200 lbs (1,451 kg) – **Max. speed:** 186 mph (299 km/h) – **Range:** 186 miles (300 km)

■ VERVILLE-SPERRY R-3

The tireless Glenn H. Curtiss, pioneer in virtually every area of aviation, developed a formidable family of racing thoroughbreds which won four Pulitzer Trophies: 1921 (in a CR-1, average speed 177 mph), 1922 (R-6, 206 mph), 1923 (R2-C1, 244 mph) and 1925 (R3C-1, 249 mph). The only race that Curtiss failed to totally dominate was that of 1924, held at Cleveland: the innovative Verville-Sperry R-3 monoplane won this with a speed of 216.5 mph. In a supreme twist of irony, the R-3's winning engine was designed and built by none other than a certain Mr. Glenn Curtiss.

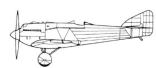

Engine: Curtiss D-12A, V-12, liquid-cooled, 520 hp – **Wingspan:** 30'1" (9.19 m) – **Length:** 23'6" (7.16 m) – **Height:** 7'1" (2.16 m) – **Empty weight:** 2,000 lbs (905 kg) – **Max. takeoff weight:** 2,475 lbs (1,123 kg) – **Max. speed:** 235 mph (378 km/h) – **Service ceiling:** 22,900' (6,980 m)

■ VICKERS F.B.28 VIMY COMMERCIAL

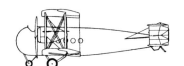

Engine: 2 Rolls-Royce Eagle VIIIs, V-12, liquid-cooled, 360 hp each – **Wingspan:** 27'6" (20.47 m) – **Length:** 24'2" (13.00 m) – **Height:** 8'8" (4.65 m) – **Max. takeoff weight:** 3,200 lbs (5,663 kg) – **Cruising speed:** 186 mph (135 km/h) – **Service ceiling:** (3,200 m) – **Range:** 186 miles (724 km)

One of Britain's first commercial airplanes derived from the Vickers Vimy bomber of WWI fame. Following Alcock's and Brown's successful transatlantic flight which demonstrated the Vimy's great potential, three of the bombers were modified to accommodate 10 passengers. The prototype of the civil version assumed its definitive form in 1920.

Renamed the Vickers F.B.28 Vimy Commercial, it made its inaugural flight from Croydon to Brussels on May 9th of that year. The three planes branched out to serve other European routes, remaining busy throughout the first half of the 1920s.

■ VICKERS VISCOUNT

The world' first commercial turboprop plane was Britain's Vickers Viscount. On July 29, 1950, BEA conducted a test run on the London-Paris route with the first Viscount, marking an important milestone in civil aviation. The new four-engine turboprop's regular use began in April 1953, and major European and American airlines clamored to get their hands on the 444 Viscounts built through 1959. The prototype flew in July 1948 and the first production plane of the 700 series was test-flown in April 1950. The second principal version was the 800 of 1952 – larger, sturdier and faster than it predecessor. The Viscount had as many sub-series as it did clients, for Vickers took great pains to customize its planes according to each buyer's needs The Viscount remained in service for nearly 30 years, unflappable in the face of competition from the new jetliners.

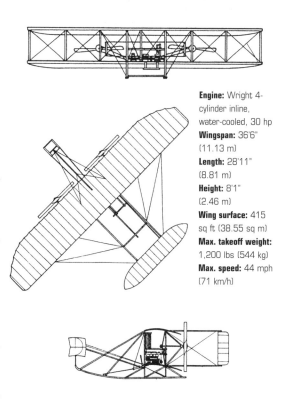

Version: 700
Engine: 4 Rolls-Royce Dart R Da.3 505 turboprops, 1,540 hp each
Wingspan: 81'9" (28.55 m)
Length: 24'2" (24.94 m)
Height: 27'9" (8.46 m)
Max. takeoff weight: 50,000 lbs (22,680 kg)
Cruising speed: 315 mph (508 km/h) at 20,000' (6,100 m)
Service ceiling: 27,500' (8,380 m)
Range: 950 miles (1,530 km)

■ VOISIN FARMAN BIPLANE

Gabriel and Charles Voisin, the first Europeans to build motorized aircraft on a commercial scale, achieved their success with a plane built in collaboration with another great French pioneer, Henri Farman. From its first flight at Issy on September 30, 1907, the biplane continued to command respect from early aviation insiders. On October 26 it flew 771 meters (2,529 feet) in 52 seconds, and on November 9 it broke the 1,000-meter and 1-minute marks. The three men continued to improve their biplane, winning the Deutsch-Archdeacon prize in January 1908, and making the first cross-country flight in the history of

European aviation when, on October 30, 1908, Farman flew from Bouy to Reims, a total of 17 miles.

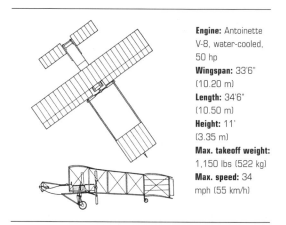

Engine: Antoinette V-8, water-cooled, 50 hp
Wingspan: 33'6" (10.20 m)
Length: 34'6" (10.50 m)
Height: 11' (3.35 m)
Max. takeoff weight: 1,150 lbs (522 kg)
Max. speed: 34 mph (55 km/h)

■ WRIGHT A

The official indifference with met the Flyer III in 1905 prompted the Wright brothers to a drastic decision: improve the machine in secret and wait for skepticism to dissipate. When they emerged from their retreat in 1908, they presented a rather more powerful and efficient plane, capable, moreover, of carrying a passenger in addition to the pilot. The plane was the Wright A, which made its first flight on May 8, 1908. The A did more than merely impress onlookers, it enjoyed a noteworthy commercial success as well: the US Department of War ordered one, and Britain, France and Germany made requests to build it under license.

Engine: Wright 4-cylinder inline, water-cooled, 30 hp
Wingspan: 36'6" (11.13 m)
Length: 28'11" (8.81 m)
Height: 8'1" (2.46 m)
Wing surface: 415 sq ft (38.55 sq m)
Max. takeoff weight: 1,200 lbs (544 kg)
Max. speed: 44 mph (71 km/h)

INDEX OF ILLUSTRATIONS

■ WRIGHT FLYER I

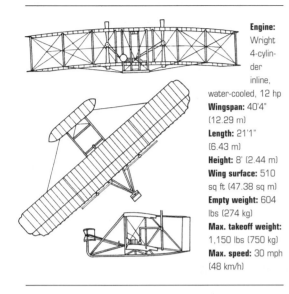

Engine: Wright 4-cylinder inline, water-cooled, 12 hp
Wingspan: 40'4" (12.29 m)
Length: 21'1" (6.43 m)
Height: 8' (2.44 m)
Wing surface: 510 sq ft (47.38 sq m)
Empty weight: 604 lbs (274 kg)
Max. takeoff weight: 1,150 lbs (750 kg)
Max. speed: 30 mph (48 km/h)

With the Flyer I, Orville and Wilbur Wright inaugurated the age of powered flight on December 17, 1903. This machine, awe-inspiring for its incalculable historical import, was built during the summer of that year, and represented the culmination of years of study and testing conducted by the pioneering brothers with various types of gliders. After the success of that momentous day, the first Flyer was replaced with a slightly modified and more powerful version. Test flights were made from May 23 to December 9, but the airplane was still imperfect. The problems weren't resolved until 1905 with the Flyer III. In one of the many flights it made between June and October of that year, it set the record for duration by remaining aloft for 38 minutes and 3 seconds (October 5). The Wrights offered the Flyer III to the War Department which, in one of history's great acts of bureaucratic blindness, refused it.

■ WRIGHT FLYER R

In 1910 the Wright brothers radically modified their original design, building a number of experimental versions aimed for the most part at increasing speed. With the B model, the configuration became more conventional; the elevators were moved to the tail and the landing sled was supplemented by four flanking wheels. The US Army immediately placed an order for the plane. Meanwhile the Wrights were developing versions upon versions, from the single-seat EX to the competition R, nicknamed 'Baby Wright,' to the 60-horsepower 'Baby Grand,' In 1910 Orville participated in an air meet with this latter plane at Belmont Park, taking it to a speed of between 71 and 75 mph.

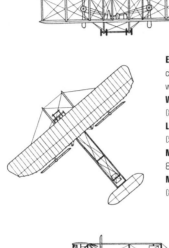

Engine: Wright 4-cylinder inline, water-cooled, 30 hp
Wingspan: 26'6" (8.07 m)
Length: 19'6" (5.94 m)
Max. takeoff weight: 860 lbs (390 kg)
Max. speed: 50 mph (80 km/h)

INDEX OF ILLUSTRATIONS